Following in Father's Footsteps

FOLLOWING IN
Father's Footsteps

Social Mobility in Ireland

Michael Hout

Harvard University Press
Cambridge, Massachusetts
London, England
1989

"Digging" from *Poems, 1965–1975,* by Seamus Heaney. Copyright © 1966, 1969, 1972, 1975, 1980 by Seamus Heaney. Reprinted by permission of Farrar, Straus and Giroux, Inc., and Faber & Faber, Ltd.

This book is printed on acid-free paper, and its binding materials
have been chosen for strength and durability.

Library of Congress Cataloging-in-Publication Data

Hout, Michael.
    Following in father's footsteps : social mobility in Ireland / Michael Hout.
       p.   cm.
    Bibliography: p.
    Includes index.
    ISBN 0-674-30728-3 (alk. paper)
    1. Social mobility—Ireland.   2. Social mobility—Northern Ireland.   I. Title.
    HN400.3.Z9S654 1989   89-32790
    305.5 ' 13 ' 09415—dc20   CIP

To my father and mother—
Sidney F. Hout
Martha Jane Hout

Acknowledgments

The research reported in this book has received financial support from the John Simon Guggenheim Memorial Foundation, the Ireland Fund, the University of Arizona, the Survey Research Center and the Committee on Research at the University of California at Berkeley, the National Science Foundation (SES 8607038), and Andrew M. Greeley Enterprises. The Social Science Research Council of the United Kingdom funded the collection and initial coding of the data through grants to Professor John A. Jackson (HR 1430/1). Over and beyond financial backing, I have enjoyed the intellectual support and stimulation provided by friends on the three campuses where I have worked on this project.

In Tucson, Albert Bergesen, Otis Dudley Duncan, Roberto Fernandez, Neil Fligstein, Debra Friedman, Doug McAdam, William H. Sewell, Jr., Michael Sobel, and the late Beverly Duncan listened to my hunches, commented on my papers, and inspired me by their good examples. From the beginning, Father Andrew M. Greeley has helped shape the project with his enormous energy. When the University of Arizona granted me tenure, I gave a party. Andy helped us celebrate that night, and at one point he said, "Now that tenure is out of the way, what are you doing about a sabbatical?" My wife, Flowe, and I responded vaguely; we said something about maybe going to France. Andy asked, "Why not Ireland?" Why not, indeed? We were on our way. Since then, Andy has been an active benefactor, sharing his sociological imagination in dozens of phone conversations and too few face-to-face conversations.

When we got to Dublin my family and I were more than a little dislocated. We received the special assistance we needed from Father Conor Ward and his family. He made room for me in the department he chairs, arranged for us to rent his nephew's house, and turned us over to the care of his sister and brother-in-law, Evelyn and Malachy O'Gallagher. I learned what I know about Ireland from my associates at University College, Trinity

College, and the Economic and Social Research Institute—all in Dublin. In particular, I benefited enormously from lunches and teas with Teresa Brannock, Pat Clancy, Jeffery Cook, Mary Kelly, Des McCluskey, Kieran McKeown, Billy Roache, David Rottman, Brendan Whelan, Chris Whelan, and fellow visitor John Hannigan.

Two colleagues merit special mention. This project was born the day I met John Jackson. I had a small agenda in mind; he encouraged me to take full advantage of the abundant data he had gathered. Throughout my involvement in this project he has answered with care every question about technical details, concepts, and definitions. On the same day that John urged me to begin work, he said, "You must get together with Raftery." Adrian Raftery and I hit it off immediately, and we have been collaborating ever since.

In Berkeley, I have been aided by Rumi Price, Yu-teh Chang, Elaine Mosakowski, Michele Dillon, Melanie Archer, and Rebecca Gradolph. And Glenn Carroll, Leo Goodman, Jerome Karabel, Nancy Scheper-Hughes, Kim Voss, and Erik Wright have been wonderful to work with. Very special thanks go to Paul Sniderman, one of the grandest colleagues anyone ever had. In Oakland, the Oakland School of Sociology—Michael Burawoy, Tom Gold, David Matza, Richard Ofshe, and Dr. Stan Lieberson, chairman of the school board—helped me through some difficult days.

Several friends have kept me from embarrassing myself in print by reading all or part of this manuscript. Robert Erikson, Harry Ganzeboom, David Grusky, Bob Hauser, Pat Roos, Don Treiman, Raymond Wong, and Yu Xie have taken time away from their own writing to help me with mine. My wife, in addition to drawing the "Turfcutter," read preliminary versions of several chapters and suggested revisions. My son Ben contributed the graph in Chapter 1 and helped me with the index.

Some of the material in this book has been presented elsewhere. Portions of Raftery and Hout (1985), Hout (1986), and Hout and Jackson (1986) have found their way into these pages. Chapter 3 was presented at the annual meeting of the International Sociological Association (ISA) Research Committee on Stratification and Mobility, Budapest, September 1984; Chapter 6, at the CASMIN Conference, Günzberg, West Germany, March 1988; Chapter 7, at the annual meetings of the Population Association of America, New Orleans, April 1988; and Chapter 10, at the annual meeting of the ISA Research Committee on Stratification and Mobility, Madison, August 1988.

Contents

Turfcutter

Digging

Seamus Heaney

Between my finger and my thumb
The squat pen rests, like a gun.

Under my window, a clean rasping sound
When the spade sinks into gravelly ground:
My father, digging. I look down

Till his straining rump among the flowerbeds
Bends low, comes up twenty years away
Stooping in rhythm through potato drills
Where he was digging.

The coarse boot nestled on the lug, the shaft
Against the inside knee was levered firmly.
He rooted out tall tops, buried the bright edge deep
To scatter new potatoes that we picked
Loving their cool hardness in our hands.

By God, the old man could handle a spade.
Just like his old man.

My grandfather cut more turf in a day
Than any other man on Toner's bog.
Once I carried him milk in a bottle
Corked sloppily with paper. He straightened up
To drink it, then fell to right away

Nicking and slicing neatly, heaving sods
Over his shoulder, going down and down
For the good turf. Digging.

The cold smell of potato mould, the squelch and slap
Of soggy peat, the curt cuts of an edge
Through living roots awaken in my head.
But I've no spade to follow men like them.

Between my finger and my thumb
The squat pen rests.
I'll dig with it.

Introduction

Earning a living in Ireland changed dramatically during the lifetime of most workers employed in the 1970s. The white-collar worker, pen in hand, replaced Heaney's digger and his spade. Between 1959 and 1973 living standards improved at a rate of over 3 percent per year. A government-sponsored influx of new industry fueled progress. After a century of dependence on agriculture, Irish manufacturing came into bloom. By 1983 the Republic of Ireland exported more manufactured goods than agricultural products. In that year computers produced by American firms in Irish factories headed the list of manufacturing exports. Some of the policies designed to aid new industry eventually spilled over to help established business. Investment—domestic and foreign, North and South—transformed Ireland in the course of a generation. In short, Ireland underwent the kind of economic miracle now associated with Southeast Asia.

Demographic change, particularly a reversal of the flow of emigration, accompanied the economic miracle. It used to be said that Ireland's leading export was her people. Rural unemployment drove young people from the land. Their migration to the United States, Canada, England, and Australia led to a sustained population decline. While the rest of the world's population exploded, emigration halved the population of Ireland in little over a century. During the 1950s an outflow of 40,000 people a year was a social problem of great concern. By 1970 emigration had slowed sufficiently that, for the first time since record keeping began, the number of immigrants balanced the number of emigrants.

Most of the economic and demographic growth came between 1959 and 1973. The growth of that period affected the job prospects and living standards of individual Irish workers in a variety of ways. The changes swept broadly, altering the face of Ireland in the course of little more than a decade. Since 1974 Ireland has reversed course again, plummeting to such depths that the *Economist* (16–22 January 1988) called Ireland "the poorest of the rich." Since this book is about mobility and industrialization, the emphasis is on 1959–1973.

Sociologists and historians have often investigated the link between the Industrial Revolution and social mobility, motivated by the hopeful thesis that industrialization brings with it not only a rural-to-urban mobility occasioned by growth in manufacturing and commercial agriculture but also a new openness in the processes that match workers to jobs. The Industrial Revolution altered forever the conditions of work. Society after society shifted the focus of economic activity from countryside to factory, from handmade to machine-made goods (and on to services), from proprietorship to wage and salary labor. The class structure, too, was recast. The landed aristocracy withered away or went into business. A middle class of owners, managers, and professionals sprang up alongside a new industrial working class. An army of salesmen, clerical workers, and technicians, who had both middle-class and working-class characteristics, was recruited.

New positions mean opportunity. The sociologist asks, "Opportunity for whom?" One possibility is that the new positions are rationed according to the old rules. If the old system apportioned *one* good job to a person of working-class background for every *four* jobs apportioned to people from middle-class backgrounds, then the new system might maintain the same four-to-one ratio. Another possibility is that the old rules are rewritten during the course of industrialization. The emergence of modern labor markets under industrial capitalism may undercut the inequities of the old order. Competition cannot sustain the waste inherent in inequality of opportunity. Thus, industrial expansion and economic development supposedly generate market pressures that eradicate (or at least mitigate) class barriers to opportunity. Geographical mobility, political organization of the working class, and expansion of the state (especially through public education) are other factors that might weaken class barriers over time (Treiman 1970). The main theoretical task at hand in this book is to evaluate these conjectures in light of the Irish experience with economic growth during the 1959–1973 period.

The Irish Mobility Study

This book is part of an ongoing tradition of national mobility studies. But it is more than an Irish replication of well-rehearsed findings from other studies. Research on other countries focuses on workers' social origins and destinations, whereas the Irish Mobility Study maps out the entire life course. Every job held by every worker is enumerated. This unique feature of the Irish study makes for a richer picture of social mobility than is available in other national studies. The completeness of these work histories is particularly important given the timing of the survey at the height of the Irish economic upswing.

Complete work histories for Irish workers who lived through the period of rapid industrialization make possible the most thorough test to date of the thesis that industrialization increases social mobility. Myriad other studies have looked at this important question, yet it remains unresolved because of flaws in the design or execution of those studies. A test of the thesis of industrialization requires high-quality data, repeated observations of the same workers (or at least the same society) throughout the course of economic development, and a cultural context that is comparable to that in the countries for which contemporary data are available. At a minimum, this implies a market economy and a nuclear family system (Featherman, Jones, and Hauser 1975). Some of the other studies measure occupational standing crudely or inaccurately. Others use fine data but are limited to cross-national comparisons. Still others contain data on selected cohorts so that they do not allow aggregation to the entire labor force.

The Irish Mobility Study satisfies each prerequisite for a test of the thesis of industrialization. The data are high quality, they cover the entire period of industrial renewal in Ireland, the context is European, and the respondents represent the whole labor market. In the winter of 1973–74, over 4,500 workers representing the male labor forces in each part of Ireland were interviewed. Workers described, among other things, their complete employment histories. Their experiences span the dramatic economic changes in Ireland during the 1960s. The economic gains that show up on the ledgers of the Republic of Ireland and of Northern Ireland are realized in the job shifts and geographical mobility of the workers in this sample. In this sense the study lives up to the challenge laid down by C. Wright Mills (1961) to do fundamental sociology, by which he meant an analysis of social structure as revealed through the intersection of biography and history.

The workers in this study are nearly equally divided between the Republic of Ireland and the province of Northern Ireland in the United Kingdom. In Northern Ireland both religious traditions are represented proportionately in a roughly two-to-one ratio of Protestants to Catholics.

One-fifth of all the workers have lived outside Ireland (mostly in England) during their work lives, so these workers, like their societies, are touched by emigration. Roughly three-fourths of the workers were in the labor force before 1959 (the beginning of rapid economic development in the Republic), and the other quarter had not yet begun working, so it is possible to examine career beginnings before and after the changes of the early 1960s.

Macroeconomic studies describe the aggregate shifts that constitute industrial change (Kennedy 1971; FitzGerald 1972; Kennedy and Dowling 1975; Lee 1979). Behind the macrostatistics lie the thousands of separate moves from schoolhouse to work force, from farm to factory, from shop to office, from English firm to Irish firm, that constitute industrial change in Ireland. This study focuses on the microdynamics of industrialization—the job shifts of individual Irish workers. The pattern of worker movements through the rapidly changing labor market yields information about the effect of development on mobility that is not available in either macroeconomic studies or other kinds of mobility studies.

My goal here is to address the long-standing question of how industrial development influences social mobility. Crucial to the answer is the unique Irish data set that capitalizes on methodological advances and the timing of economic development in Ireland. Along the way a number of related issues will be raised: the controversy within sociology over the definition of structural and exchange mobility, the concern in Irish Studies with the role of education and religion in Irish mobility, and the concern of "new urban historians" (Thernstrom 1969, 1973; Sewell 1985) with the process and sequence of mobility.

Above all, this is a study of social mobility. The following pages will be preoccupied with the relative social levels of new and traditional occupations in Irish social structure and with whether movement among these levels constitutes upward, downward, or lateral mobility. Has the growth of employment in manufacturing and new services reversed traditional patterns of inequality in Irish society, or have the modern occupations been integrated into a consistent social structure? The answer to this question cannot be found in the distribution of current occupations, no matter how detailed. The number, strength, and persistence of social class boundaries that limit opportunity appear in the relationships among the social positions that workers occupy throughout their lifetimes. If we know that employment in the service sector of some country increased from, say, 25 to 35 percent of a country's labor force while employment in agriculture decreased from 35 to 25 percent, we can make a number of inferences about that society; but we cannot infer whether individuals who used to work in agriculture now work in services. Nor can we tell from macrochange whether the social distance between agriculture and services is increasing or decreasing. These are questions about micro-dynamics and about the social structure that emerges from micro-dynamics. The answers can be found in mobility tables constructed from the employment histories of workers who lived through the changes.

Interest in the link between industrialization and social mobility has a long history in sociology. But the present study offers more than simply the Irish variant on the national mobility study. Whereas previous work has had to struggle with data collected too long after industrialization, or data recovered from incomplete archives compiled at the time of industrialization, the Irish Mobility Study on which this book is based has gathered high-quality data on individuals who lived through the Irish industrial revolution. Given that advantage, this research constitutes the most compelling test to date of the thesis that industrialization promotes social mobility.

Did the economic changes of the 1960s make it easier for sons to follow in their fathers' footsteps? Well, in Irish fashion, they did and they did not. To follow in his father's footsteps, a son had to stay at home. Emigration spurred Irish leaders to action in the 1950s. The economic development plan in the Republic garnered public support from its prospects as a cure for depopulation. On the one hand, in a broad sense, by curbing the tide of emigration—and even bringing some sons back to Ireland—the changes made it more likely that a son would literally tread on his father's soil. On the other hand, by contributing to the continued concentration of farm-lands, by creating new jobs on a scale never before seen in Ireland, and by attracting ever more people to Dublin and Belfast, the changes made following in their fathers' footsteps no less hard for sons North and South who wished to do so. Nevertheless, real progress was evident to the average Irish citizen. The choice was no longer between staying at home or leaving Ireland. One could, in the late 1960s and early 1970s, leave home while staying in Ireland. Occupational choice had become a reality.

The changing demographic and economic contexts altered the Irish class structure. Sociologists differ on whether the changing class structure was the cause or the effect of mobility (Parkin 1971; Mayer and Carroll 1987). The view taken here that changes in class structure cause changes in mobility is termed *structuralist,* while the view that changes in the class structure result from changes in mobility is called *interactionalist.* The structuralist view ties the class structure to specific occupational positions. The appearance of new occupations and the expansion and contraction of old ones produce, for structuralists, changes in class structure. These changes stimulate mobility directly because the redistribution of the available positions creates contemporary employment opportunities that do not appear in the distribution of social origins among contemporary workers.[1] This disparity between origins and potential destinations makes some mobility inevitable as an unambiguous consequence of change in class structure. The interactionalist view distinguishes between class structure and the functional division of labor in society.[2] Change in the division of labor stimulates mobility which may or may not affect class structure.

Neither structuralists nor interactionalists would doubt that there was a redistribution of social positions in Ireland between the late 1950s and the early 1970s. The array of jobs represented in the Irish economy, North and South, was far more diverse in the 1970s than it had been in the 1950s. The question is, Who benefited? Was the restructuring of the Irish economy a revolution that swept away all advantages that came before?[3] Probably not. What then was the social consequence of the changing contexts? One possibility is that greater diversity translates into more inequality of opportunity. Those workers in the positions of advantage at the beginning of the 1960s might very well have capitalized on the new opportunities, leaving behind those who began the period of change in less advantageous circumstances. That happened to the black population of the United States when the burdens of discrimination were lessened (Wilson 1978; Hout 1984a, 1986). Another theory is that the younger generation was favored. Perhaps the workers who were unfettered by the past were best able to take advantage of the emerging opportunities.

Research on occupational mobility and industrialization suggests some hypotheses. First, it is useful to decompose overall social mobility into the constituent flows between pairs of social categories. An example of this type of flow is the movement from farm origins to an upper-middle-class destination. Such a flow would include the son of a farmer who is currently employed as a solicitor. It might be contrasted with a flow from lower-middle-class origins to a lower-working-class destination, as when the son of an office clerk works as a janitor. Some flows may be increased by the changing context, and others, presumably, are decreased. For example, it is reasonable to assume that flows from farm origins to upper-middle-class destinations will increase if the changing context decreases the number of farmers and increases the number of upper-middle-class positions. Conversely, the flow from upper-middle-class origins to farm destinations probably declines under such circumstances. This kind of change in mobility is known as structural mobility. The changes in Northern Ireland and the Republic redistributed the labor force in ways that probably fostered structural mobility into professions, management, technical fields, and crafts. The same redistribution in all likelihood fostered structural mobility out of farming, small enterprise, and unskilled labor.

Equality of opportunity is also important for mobility. The amount of mobility between, say, upper-middle-class and lower-working-class positions will be greater if occupational opportunity is equally distributed to all than if the middle-class origins of some give them advantages over the working-class origins of others. If some positions have advantages over others, then some flows will be more common than expected under equal opportunity while other flows will be less common than expected. Societies with a high degree of equality in occupational opportunity are said to be more open than those that exhibit many barriers to opportunity for workers with low-status origins. The objective of mobility research is to quantify those barriers so that the degree of openness in one society can be compared with the degree of openness in another and so that openness in a given society can be examined over time.

Depending on the research into occupational mobility used, one might hypothesize that the openness of Irish society increases, holds steady, or even decreases. Or one might refuse to hypothesize. In the first systematic treatment of the topic, Sorokin (1927) eschewed all generalizations. He noted a pattern of "trendless fluctuations" in mobility in modern societies and cautioned sociologists to expect few regularities. Instead, every case study had to be investigated in full. Duncan (1966a, p. 53) echoed Sorokin by concluding that "the connection, if any, between economic growth and social mobility falls into the domain of *contingent* rather than *necessary* relationships . . . the generalizations reached concerning interrelations of mobility and economic development must be in large part empirical generalizations, supported or rationalized as well as they may be by some not very specific deductions from apparently applicable postulates."

Good advice notwithstanding, there is a large literature postulating the general effects of macrochanges on microdynamics (Treiman 1970). The thesis of industrialization is the most widely tested and least widely supported among the theories in this literature. Through the course of industrialization, it is supposed, overall rates of mobility increase, occupational inheritance declines, the origins of contemporary workers come to differ substantially from the distribution of available positions, education becomes more important for the sorting of individuals into occupational roles, and cross-national differences in mobility disappear. Proponents of this hypothesis find support in the patterns of cross-national differences in occupational mobility (Lipset and Bendix 1959; Cutright 1968; Hazelrigg 1974; Erikson, Goldthorpe, and Portocarero 1978, 1982; Tyree et al. 1979; Raftery 1983; Grusky and Hauser 1984; Simkus 1985) and in the repeated cross-sections for some countries (e.g., Rogoff 1953a; Featherman and Hauser 1978, pp. 135–138, 199–216; Hout 1984a, b). Yet all such findings are the subject of debate. Contrary evidence has been found in the same data and in other data—sometimes by the same researchers. Though few students of stratification continue to press the claims of Lipset and Zetterberg (1956) that mobility rates are "universally high," many claim that the underlying structures of occupational opportunity, such as openness or fluidity, indexed by mobility rates that are purged (more or less adequately) of the difference between the distributions of origins and destinations, are constant or resistant to change (Rogoff 1953b; Duncan 1966a; Hauser et al. 1975a, b; Goldthorpe and Llewellyn 1978; Goldthorpe 1980, p. 81); that cross-national variations in mobility rates are attributable to cross-national variations in the dissimilarities between origin and destination distributions (Featherman et al. 1975; Hazelrigg and Garnier 1976; Hardy and Hazelrigg 1978; Erikson et al. 1982, 1983; McClendon 1980; Grusky and Hauser 1984); that the correlation between industrialization and patterns of net mobility is weak or nonexistent (Hazelrigg and Garnier 1976; Hardy and Hazelrigg 1978; Grusky and Hauser 1984); or that factors other than industrialization are crucial for temporal or cross-national variation in mobility (Heath 1981, pp. 206–210; Erikson et al. 1983; Grusky and Hauser 1984; Hauser 1984; Simkus 1984, 1985; Whelan and Whelan 1984, pp. 127–129).

Presumably the debate could be resolved in part with some combination of better data and more powerful data-analytic techniques. But cross-national comparisons and repeated cross-national replications are inherently limited. Even if the questions about cross-national variations in mobility rates and changes over time in aggregate rates for particular societies could be resolved, a disjuncture remains between theory and research in this area because these studies address the questions indirectly. Research has shown how mobility rates may differ at different levels of industrialization and how they may change over time for aggregate labor markets. Lacking are continuous time studies that track individuals as industrialization alters the array of occupational opportunities and barriers placed before them. Research has provided repeated snapshots of societies at different stages of economic development. But in order to understand the effect of industrialization on occupational mobility, it is necessary to observe directly the job changes that constitute industrialization.

Continuous time studies are rare, in large part, because the continuous time data are lacking. The critical decades of rapid industrial change have passed for the home nations of most investigators. While historians' studies of cities and counties have reconstructed some of what went before, their studies are not definitive (e.g., Thernstrom 1964, 1973; Thernstrom and Sennett 1969; Knights 1971; Sewell 1976, 1985; Sharlin 1979; Aminzade 1981; Zunz 1983). Among the problems of historical studies are a sample selection bias that favors the immobile, a high sample attrition over time, and a lack of consistent methodology for determining which changes are due to industrialization and which changes are attributable to other factors. The goal here is to provide some of the direct observation that is missing on the changes that constitute industrialization by dealing with one case study.

1 The Context of Social Change in Ireland

If we remain the last Catholic country in Western Europe, that is because we have been remote, rural, and poor. All these things are passing.
  —Cardinal Tomas O'Fiaich, 1986

No earthly power has the right to take away from us our God-given heritage.
  —Motto of the Ulster Resistance

Social mobility reflects the openness and fairness of society by documenting the persistence of social and economic advantages from one generation to another. The volume of social mobility is directly and indirectly related to a number of other indicators of social structure. Economic, demographic, and political conditions among others can influence the degree and character of social mobility. This case study views the mobility of Irish workers during a period of intense social change with an eye toward understanding the context of mobility in a changing society.

The economic context is of special importance. Manufacturing and services emerged late by European standards. Until the end of the 1960s, agriculture dominated the Irish economy. But when changes finally did come, they transformed Irish society very rapidly. Because of the timing and pace of development, Ireland provides an interesting test of the thesis that industrialization affects social mobility.

The elements of the Irish context are best understood in terms of a number of reversals of historical precedent that occurred in the last forty years (the most dramatic change coming early in the period). A century of economic stagnation was reversed to produce economic growth, a century of emigration was reversed to produce population growth, and half a century of staunch isolationism was reversed to stimulate foreign investment and European partnership.

There is also the failure to reverse the partition of Ireland that occurred in 1921. Ironically, it might be possible to report the results of this study without many references to partition. Taking the political realities of two

Irelands for granted is the prudent course for anyone whose principal interest lies in socioeconomic matters. The economic links between the Republic and the North are so meager, and their positions in the larger world trade context are so nearly isomorphic, that ignoring the politics that divides them advances the narrative without doing undue damage to the explanation. Indeed, this is one of the many ironies in the partition of Ireland: an issue that stirs the hearts and minds of Irishmen and women so much has very little to do with bread and butter. To be sure, the British domination of the Irish economy retarded industry and agriculture alike. British colonialism in Ireland displaced the development of industry through the dumping of British manufactured goods. It retarded agriculture at the same time by protecting rural privilege and suppressing indigenous farmers who were more likely to invest in land and other agricultural capital (e.g., Cullen 1972; Lyons 1973; Hechter 1975; Brown 1984).

The fact of partition nonetheless sets the Irish Mobility Study apart from others. The leading works in the field describe social stratification in large, postindustrial societies like Britain and the United States—nations with secure borders and strong national cultures. Ireland is small. It is following a distinctive path of development. And it is divided. Sharp cultural distinctions divide Ireland from other countries, to be sure. One has a distinct sense of place in Ireland. But that sense of place is sectarian, not national. Culture divides Irishmen within the borders as well as setting them off from other Europeans. Assessing just how important the Irish case can be for understanding mobility processes is probably not possible without a retelling of the events that led up to partition. The interplay of social forces that split Ireland politically damaged the economies of both parts but left their economic structures unaltered. Part of understanding Ireland is coming to grips with the fact that one of the bloodiest civil revolutions of this century produced no social revolution. Without a social revolution, the social structure of inequality in the independent Republic of Ireland differs little from the social structure of inequality in Northern Ireland. And the changes in mobility that have taken place since 1959 have come about without a substantial change in the underlying opportunity structure.

Detailed consideration of emigration and economic growth requires less justification. Both more directly affect mobility. Economic growth creates employment opportunities. In that way growth leads to both less emigration and more mobility. The prevalence of emigration and the absence of economic growth in both parts of Ireland explain the crises they faced in the 1950s. The reversal of Ireland's fortunes in the 1960s was inextricably tied to the reversal of emigration and underdevelopment.

The Economic Context in the Republic of Ireland

The Republic of Ireland and the province of Northern Ireland achieved what was for them an unprecedented degree of economic growth in the 1960s. The route to prosperity differed in the North and in the South. The Republic of Ireland undertook rational economic planning and redirected state intervention in the economy. In a fundamental change of course, the new policies reversed decades of ideological commitment to self-sufficiency, encouraged foreign investment, and stimulated consumption. The economy responded with sustained growth. In Northern Ireland, the picture brightened largely because of the spread of the English economic boom of the times. English firms set up shop in Belfast and elsewhere in Northern Ireland; established Northern Irish firms won contracts to supply industry in London and the Midlands. Some pump-priming measures were undertaken by the Ulster government, but diffusion was the prime source of prosperity (Buckland 1983).

These economic improvements slowed (and nearly stopped) emigration. Many expatriates returned home. The staggering economies began to walk and, eventually, broke into something of a trot.

In the early 1950s the Republic of Ireland had the appearance of a Jeffersonian democracy. Small, independent farmers dominated politics, demography, and the economy. In the cities, independently owned shops outnumbered factories. Yet an ideal forged in the eighteenth century proved to be difficult to live out in the middle of the twentieth century. The Republic achieved a democracy of small-scale enterprise by way of an ideology of self-sufficiency, which permeated economic policy from the earliest days of Saorstat Eireann until a dramatic shift in policy took place in 1958. The Second World War drew Ireland out of its shell. The very act of declaring neutrality committed Ireland to participation in the great debates of the age. It spawned a national sense of purpose and a feeling that Ireland (in union with other small nations) could promote the cause of peace in the face of a superpower stand-off. This new awareness stretched beyond geopolitics into microeconomics. In the postwar era small farms and small shops were no longer acceptable; the disparity between the standard of living in Ireland and life in the two places that offered themselves as a basis for comparison—England and the United States—

tempted many Irish to leave and convinced others that improvements had to be made at home (Brown 1985, p. 143). The realities of partition, meager industrialization, and emigration left the Irish feeling immobile, cut off, left behind in the 1950s. The response to this stagnation brought Ireland out of the crisis of confidence that marked the 1950s into the well-earned spirit of accomplishment that marked the 1960s.

Three passages capture the changes in how the Irish thought about economic matters, showing the reorientation of public purpose in the Republic: First, ideological self-sufficiency:

> The Ireland which we dreamed of would be the home of a people who valued material wealth only as a basis of right living, of a people who were satisfied with frugal comfort and devoted their leisure to the things of the spirit; a land whose countryside would be bright with cozy homesteads, whose fields and villages would be joyous with the sounds of industry, the romping of sturdy children, the contests of athletic youths, the laughter of comely maidens; whose firesides would be forums for the wisdom of old age. It would, in a word, be the home of a people living the life that God desires men should live. (Eamon de Valera, 1943)[1]

Then, despair in the face of economic stagnation and rampant emigration:

> After thirty-five years of native government people are asking whether we can achieve an acceptable degree of economic progress. The common talk among parents in the towns, as well as in rural Ireland, is of their children having to emigrate as soon as their education is completed in order to secure a reasonable standard of living. (T. K. Whitaker, 1958)[2]

And, finally, a sense of national accomplishment:

> No longer is this the rural island of the emigrants, but a fast-growing industrializing frontier on the edge of industrial Europe. (*Irish Times,* 11 September 1979)

The eloquence of Whitaker's statement is remarkable for a government position paper. Perhaps even more remarkable is the fact that the document proposed specific measures to reverse the course of economic stagnation in the Republic. Most remarkable of all, the measures worked, producing real improvements in employment and income that gave rise to the air of national accomplishment reflected in the statement in the *Irish Times* some twenty years later.

The economic problems faced by the Republic in the 1950s were bred of a failed policy of economic nationalism. The government policies of favoring domestic manufactured goods over imports through stiff tariffs and of maintaining a positive balance of payments may have been well suited to the earliest years of independence, but they worked to Ireland's disadvantage during the period of worldwide economic expansion that followed the Second World War.[3]

These policies had less to do with academic economics than with the politics of nationalism; they were ingrained in the ideology that fueled Irish independence. From the inception of the Sinn Fein organization in 1907–1908, the ideal of a self-sufficient Ireland formed the core of that party's program of economic independence for Ireland.[4] Fianna Fail, constitutional successor to Sinn Fein, from its formation adopted and implemented the platform of self-sufficient economic nationalism. As soon as Fianna Fail came to power under the leadership of Eamon de Valera in 1932, it began the process of extricating Saorstat Eireann from the unfavorable terms of trade with Britain that characterized the period of union and the early days of independence. Fianna Fail under de Valera pursued the complementary policy of expanding the existing system of tariffs by an order of magnitude. These policies guided the Irish economy throughout de Valera's terms in office, which spanned most of the period from 1932 to 1958.[5] The coalition governments that filled the gaps in de Valera's terms did little to change the economic structure that had been molded to Fianna Fail's specifications (there was little they *could* do in their brief interregna).

The policy of substituting goods produced in Ireland for the most common imports might have succeeded if domestic capital could have rallied to meet the demand for imported goods. Capital in Ireland was just too weak to respond. Part of the legacy of internal colonialism was a severe capital shortage (Hechter 1975). The British in Ireland were hated because they owned everything in sight. And when the Irish threw them out, the British took their money with them. Few Irishmen had the money to start producing on a scale sufficient to replace the volume of imports. If facilities were to be built without domestic sources of capital, the money would have to be borrowed—a process that is seldom the preferred way to start an industrial revolution, even in the best of times. The Depression was the worst of times. And if these economic barriers were not high enough, de Valera and his followers in Fianna Fail had a phobia about borrowing. They claimed (justifiably) that foreign debt could threaten Irish independence.[6]

During a depression, caution and prudence make economic sense. So the policies that protected foreign reserves in the 1930s were probably a good idea. But the worldwide expansion of the 1950s left cautious Ireland behind, in part because Irish policy makers let employment and investment go slack while they guarded their nest egg (external reserves). Thus, when exports failed to grow in 1953, the government took steps to keep down imports, including imports of capital goods that might have led to a long-run increase in production and a solution to the export problem. "Had there been greater concern with employment, these export difficulties (in 1953 and 1954) would, in fact, have represented an argument for greater expansion of home demand to maintain the growth of overall demand" (Kennedy and Dowling 1975, p. 218). The culture of caution in Irish public administration at this time was so entrenched that when the government imposed budget cuts on departments in 1953 and 1954, the bureaucrats actually spent less than they were allocated! The budgets of 1953 and 1954 authorized the spending of £78.8 million on capital improvement (mainly for job-intensive construction of roads, housing, and schools), but actual expenditures in these categories were £11.3 million less than that allocation (an expenditure shortfall of 17 percent). The harm in fiscal short-sheeting of this sort was compounded by the scarcity of sources of private investment in job-producing activity in Ireland at this time, so that the shortfall in government spending translated immediately into a shortfall in employment, which contributed directly to the demoralizing emigration that marked this era. The bottom line was sluggish growth in national income (7.6 percent) for the period from 1949–1954 compared with Britain (14.6 percent) and the rest of Western Europe (29.3 percent; Whitaker 1956, p. 50). Industrial employment actually fell by 8.6 percent in five years, from 228,403 in 1953 to 210,324 in 1958. In a context of ideological commitment to economic nationalism, the about-face of 1958 was remarkable.

Economic nationalism and its deleterious consequences were discredited in 1958. De Valera, the champion of nationalism, moved from Taoiseach, or Prime Minister, to the ceremonial post of President. The new Fianna Fail administration, headed by Sean Lemass, adopted a cure for the ills of economic nationalism. The cure consisted of a cut in social spending, an increase in Central Bank control over the investment policies of member banks, and—the most fundamental change of all—a series of incentives *favoring* foreign investment in Irish businesses. The revolutionary shift from inhibiting foreign investment to encouraging it included the relaxation (and eventual repeal) of laws dictating a majority domestic interest in all firms doing business in Ireland, investment of government funds in industrial parks that were leased to foreign-owned companies (at rates that were probably below the market value of the facilities), tax credits for firms that provided jobs for Irish workers, and expansion of the Shannon duty-free zone.[7]

From a fiscal standpoint, these measures were a huge success in bringing capital and earnings into Ireland. During the 1960s, 350 new foreign-owned companies set up shop in the Republic (Walsh 1979, p. 32). These firms had an export orientation favored by the official government policy. Over 80 percent of the output of these 350 firms was exported. Exports and imports increased; even external reserves, long regarded as Ireland's nest egg, grew. The net capital flow averaged +£25 million a year during the 1960s (Kennedy and Dowling 1975, table 15).[8] The legacy of these changes persists in the trade statistics of the 1980s; in 1983 the ratio of exports to Gross Domestic Product (GDP) for Ireland was 0.48, third in the European Economic Community (EEC) behind Belgium and the Netherlands (Eurostat 1985, p. 269).

Most of the incentives that were offered to foreign firms and investors were available to domestic firms and investors as well. Unfortunately, few existing Irish firms and fewer Irish investors were in a position to take advantage of the incentives. Existing domestic firms had grown up with an orientation toward sheltered domestic markets. Only brewing (Guinness), distilling (Jameson), and biscuits (Jacob's) were strong exporters (they always had been, for all of these firms predated independence). Domestic capital was lacking and Irish technology lagged behind the rest of the world, putting domestic firms that wished to challenge the export markets at a decided disadvantage.

Despite the lackluster performance of domestic capital, overall production and personal income in the Republic boomed in the 1960s. Between 1955 and 1968, GDP (at 1958 factor prices) grew from £501 million to £732 million. Over half of the total increase of £231 million was industrial growth; £23 million (10 percent) was in agriculture, £86 million (37 percent) was in services, and £122 million (53 percent) was in manufacturing. Employment over the same period (1955–1968) declined by 81,000 jobs. The loss of jobs was concentrated in agriculture, where employment declined by 129,000.[9] Employment grew in services (+17,000 jobs) and in manufacturing (+31,000 jobs) but not enough to offset the drop in farm employment.

Perhaps most important among the changes was the new outlook of the citizens of the Republic. "A sense of a new age had entered the Irish collective mind" (Brown 1985, p. 186). The new age was modern and outward looking. The consumer society displaced frugal comfort. Although no single statistic can tell the whole of a complicated story, the one that most clearly shows the shift in Ireland is the rate of increase in car registrations in the early 1960s—an astounding 29.5 percent between 1958 and 1961 (Brown 1985, p. 186). But the change went beyond the four-wheeled trappings of modern life. Traffic jams and four-lane motorways were but the culmination of a process that began in World War II. Neutrality during the war forged a national identity for the citizens of the Republic-as-it-was rather than of a Republic-that-ought-to-be. Prior to World War II, the unit of Irish national identity was the whole island. Neutrality created a national cause that forged an identity that could be seated in the 26 counties. Concern with partition did not disappear, but the experience of standing alone as a nation against the pressures exerted by Winston Churchill (and eventually Franklin Roosevelt) dampened feelings of incompleteness.

What was being transformed is clarified by the typology of national identities devised by Clifford Geertz (1973, pp. 243–244). He casts some regimes and nationalist movements as "essentialist" movements. They find meaning and policy inspiration in national distinctiveness—in the unique elements of culture, history, religion, or language that set the emerging nation off from the oppressor who is trying to swallow up its indigenous culture. Other regimes and movements are "epochal." They are the stuff of domino theories—movements that take inspiration from the success of others. Sandinistas modeling themselves after the Cubans, Catholics in Northern Ireland adopting the tactics of black Americans, and Michael Collins appealing to Woodrow Wilson's principles of self-determination as grounds for Irish independence in 1921 are all examples of epochalism. Geertz takes pains to point out that both tendencies exist in emerging nations and in national movements. He regards as unlikely the prospect that one type of idea will achieve dominance over the other. He describes essentialism and epochalism as competing tendencies within movements. Yet in Ireland essentialism dominated for over 30 years, yielding to epochalism in a very dramatic way in the late 1950s.

Neutrality sowed the seeds of the shift from essentialism to epochalism as a way of defining national purpose (Share 1978; Brown 1985, pp. 139–152). Essentialism in Ireland emphasized the Gaelic heritage: the Irish language, economic nationalism, Catholicism, and the Gaelic games. "A principal effect of the efforts to define Irish identity in terms of local attributes such as religion, language, and culture in the first two decades of independence had tended to present the Irish manifestations of those things as in some way isolated and distinct from their expressions elsewhere, particularly in England and on the continent of Europe" (Brown 1985, p. 157). In one sense, then, neutrality was the highest expression of essentialism. Ireland was exempt from world war because it had no stake in the disputes of others. But in another sense, even adopting a stand for neutrality was taking a role in the affairs of the epoch. To be courted by Churchill and Roosevelt was to be included in the events of the epoch, to achieve an importance due only to members of the community of nations. Neutrality was not cowardice; it was a moral stand in favor of peace. It was a course that established foreign-policy priorities for successive Irish governments: sending troops to keep the peace in the Congo, then in Lebanon, and treating the United States and the Soviet Union alike through the Cold War, détente, the renewed tensions following Afghanistan, and, most recently, glasnost.[10]

The budding epochalism influenced the course of economic development in the Republic by shifting the basis of comparison from the bucolic ideal proclaimed by de Valera in his "frugal comfort" speech to the material comfort that could be found in the housing estates and suburbs of England and the United States. Before World War II, Ireland could be proud of its modest GNP per capita because the nation was not dragging itself down with the heavy costs of industrialization and urbanization—crowding, pollution, and depersonalization. After the war, though, Ireland could no longer ignore the advantages of industrializing—lowered mortality, higher education, and more leisure—because the basis of comparison was becoming broader. In time a more acute awareness of what others had accomplished sowed disaffection with frugal comfort.

The shift to an epochal outlook was bolstered by an increase in tourism in the 1950s. Many of the tourists were expatriate Irish men and women and the children of emigrants. Contact with these affluent visitors changed the meaning of emigration for the people who greeted them. Before the war, emigration was a form of exile. Emigrants left the pristine countryside that could not support them for the grime of American and English industrial cities. After the war, those cities changed for the better while the countryside stagnated. Emigrants who came home to visit in the 1950s brought with them the accouterments of the modern world. That they had money in their wallets was expected; more significantly, those wallets also contained pictures of detached houses and healthy children. More than crass money, the returning visitors had what we might now call a lifestyle and an attitude. Unseen thousands of emigrants were not so well off, of course, but the tourists held out to their siblings and cousins (and more consequentially, to their young nieces and nephews) the promise of a good life elsewhere. The doctrine of frugal comfort required the Irish to choose between living the clean, healthy life of the countryside and living the commercial life of the city. These tourists had both health and money. The emigrants who were doing well enough to come back to Ireland on tour had in their suburbs back home the clean air and leisure that the Irish country people had. They also had the big families, employment security, and toilets that the Irish lacked. The mass-communication media reinforced the evidence brought in by the tourists. From the Famine until the Depression, emigrants left because the Irish countryside could not support them. In short, they were pushed. In the 1950s, emigrants were lured by the siren call of a modern urban life that promised them more than the countryside had to offer. The expatriates who visited Ireland in the 1950s viewed themselves—and were viewed by their hosts—as successes. Among those left behind in Ireland there grew up a hope and a yearning that life at home could be just as good as life in England and America. To the political leaders of the 1950s it seemed that the only way to keep Ireland from depopulating itself altogether was to change the course of economic development. The implementation of Lemass's cure for Ireland's economic ills was the (desperate) political response to that hope and that yearning.

The Economic Context in Northern Ireland

Conditions in the North contrasted sharply with conditions in the Republic. Among the many contrasts that can be made, none is more telling than the difference in the expressed goals of the Free State leadership and those of the Unionist Party leadership of Northern Ireland. The philosophy of separatism guided the policies of independent Ireland. The overarching goal of each successive administration was to show how Ireland belonged in its own category among modern states, distinct in its culture, language, religion, and economy. Every governmental effort increased the chasm between Ireland and Britain.

By way of total contrast, the unionist leadership in Northern Ireland pursued a course calculated to minimize differences with England. In that regard, keeping living standards on a par with those in the rest of the United Kingdom proved to be the most difficult task. For although Northern Ireland achieved a greater degree of industrialization than the rest of Ireland, it was not up to the rest of the UK. Furthermore, the core of the Ulster economy was highly specialized. Two industries predominated: shipbuilding and linen manufacture, both of which declined for nearly all of the period of partition.[11] Therefore, the quest for parity in living standards ended up as a constant struggle between successive Northern Irish cabinets and their English counterparts over social spending in Ulster. Without enough jobs in Northern Ireland to keep living standards at the same level as those prevailing in the rest of the UK, the cabinets of Northern Ireland lobbied for development projects, housing, and welfare benefits sufficient to maintain parity.

The position taken by the Conservative and Labour governments who had to deal with these demands reflected a different interest. Their stated position was that social spending in Northern Ireland should not exceed social spending elsewhere in the UK (on a per capita basis) and that taxpayers in the rest of the UK should not have to shoulder an unfair burden in order to maintain Northern Ireland. Since economic conditions in Northern Ireland were generally worse than conditions in England or Scotland, regional balance in this form meant that each welfare recipient in Northern Ireland was likely to receive less than people on the dole in England. The Governments of Ireland Act of 1920 (the same one that established the home rule government of Northern Ireland) stipulated a formula that accomplished London's objective. The British and Northern Irish cabinets renegotiated the formula many times between 1923 and the conclusion of a final agreement in 1951. In the end, the system guaranteed to Northern Ireland a level of social services identical to the level available in England, Scotland, and Wales. In exchange, the citizenry of Northern Ireland paid the same amount in taxes as did people of the same income level living elsewhere in the UK.[12] The upshot of all this negotiation was a net flow of money earmarked for social spending from London to Belfast. In 1970 that commitment cost England £130 million (Lyons 1973, p. 742).

The cradle-to-grave welfare system that benefited Northern Ireland was far more extensive than the combination of social insurance, health care, and child support available in the Republic. Therefore, by maintaining parity with England, the unionists drove a wedge between Northern Ireland and the Republic. Social services north of the border were superior to those available in the South and West, as shown by two typical years (Lyons 1973, pp. 741–742):

Education (1964):
  95,000 secondary students in the North
  85,000 secondary students in the Republic (despite the fact that the population aged 14–18 in the Republic was twice the population of that age in Northern Ireland)
Insurance (1969):
  Unemployment benefit for a single man:
    £4.50/wk in Northern Ireland
    £3.25/wk in the Republic
  Unemployment benefit for a married man, two children:
    £9.20/wk in Northern Ireland
    £7.425/wk in the Republic
  Widow's pension:
    £4.50/wk in Northern Ireland
    £3.25/wk in the Republic

This welfare disparity held a strategic place in the politics of partition. Catholics depended more on social services than did Protestants in Northern Ireland. Few of the thousands of welfare-dependent Catholics in Northern Ireland could fail to notice the gap between the level of service that they were receiving and the level that they could hope to receive should similar circumstances befall them "after liberation." Nor did politicians in the Republic fail to notice. To achieve parity with Northern Ireland in the 1969–70 budget, the Republic would have had to increase social spending from £143 million to £293 million (105 percent), according to Garret Fitzgerald, who at the time was financial spokesman for the opposition (Lyons 1973, p. 142). Had Dublin magically won sovereignty over the North that year, the government would have faced a choice between cutting benefits to nationalist supporters in the six counties and replacing the £130 million contribution to Northern Irish social spending that came from London. The Republic could not absorb responsibility for social services and security in Northern Ireland without financial assistance from England or the United States (New Ireland Forum 1984).

Of course, the strength of the safety net built of welfare spending becomes irrelevant if economic growth reduces dependence on welfare. No one is going to ask about welfare if there are enough jobs to go around. Northern Ireland had some advantages over the Republic in that regard, too. The six counties of Northern Ireland were a privileged zone prior to 1921. Industrialization developed early in Ulster. That advantage disappeared when Britain was used as the basis of comparison. Unemployment in Northern Ireland fluctuated during the Depression of the 1930s but remained at least 20 percent higher than the unemployment level in England (Hechter 1975, p. 294). The position of Northern Ireland deteriorated during the war, and postwar recovery did not arrive on schedule. By the 1950s unemployment in Ulster was three times the average for Britain (e.g., 6.3 percent versus 2.2 percent in 1957; 6.8 percent versus 2.2 percent in 1969). The Westminster Parliament encouraged British firms to invest in Northern Ireland through a series of annual grants to industrialists, who in turn would invest in Northern Ireland. The first of these grants were the Industries Development Acts (1945–1953). They were followed in turn by the Capital Grants to Industry Acts (1954–1962), the Aid to Industry Acts (1961–1964), and the Industrial Advice and Enterprise Acts (1964 and 1967). Over 160 companies took advantage of these incentives, creating an estimated 50,000 jobs (Coogan 1966, pp. 294–295; Lyons 1973, p. 747).

The development concentrated in the Belfast area. Little occurred west of the Bann River, a traditional dividing line between Protestant Ulster and Catholic Ulster.[13] Only eight factories opened west of the Bann between 1961 and 1968. The consequences of this disparity in development can be seen in the unemployment rates of the Catholic cities of Derry (13.9 percent) and Strabane (18.2 percent) in 1968, when unemployment in all of Northern Ireland was 7.2 percent (O'Leary 1979, p. 161).

The majority of Catholics made some headway in the 1960s. Protestants certainly prospered. Farm income in Ulster reached a record level in 1964–1965 (Lyons 1973, p. 745). The overall growth of the UK economy spilled over into Northern Ireland. GNP figures are not available on a regional basis, but survey data indicate that incomes grew at 3.2 percent per annum between 1961 and 1968. This level is below that in the Republic but ahead of the 2.2 percent income growth in the UK as a whole (Kennedy and Dowling 1975, table 8).

Ireland in the European Context

The economic growth of the 1960s brought unprecedented growth to a hitherto backward region. In 1973 Ireland and the UK joined the EEC— the Common Market. But the civil parity of full partnership in the EEC is not to be mistaken for the economic parity of a standard of living comparable to that available on the continent. In 1979, GDP per capita in the Republic of Ireland was 64 percent of the EEC average, ninth of the ten members (Eurostat 1985, p. 40). Comparable figures for 1982 show the Republic at 67 percent of the EEC average and Northern Ireland at 69 percent, lowest among the regions of the UK (p. 57). These are not wealthy countries.

The Demographic Context

In the nineteenth century millions of Irish moved across the Irish Sea to England and farther away to the new cities of Canada, the United States, and Australia. Population on the island fell from 8.3 million in 1841 to a low of 4.2 million in 1961 (Jackson 1963, p. 25). During that time births exceeded deaths by a wide margin—even during the famine of the 1840s— but emigration outstripped natural increase. The magnitude of emigration is unknown for the time prior to the registration of births and deaths beginning in 1864, but 60,000 emigrants to America and an additional 40,000 to England are the best estimates for each year during the disastrous Famine years of the 1840s (Goldstrom 1981). For the next 120 years, emigration fluctuated around a very high average (see Figure 1.1). Peaks of emigration were reached in the 1880s and again in the 1950s (Kennedy 1973, p. 213). This emigration led to declines in the total population of Ireland between each of the censuses from 1841 to 1966, except between the censuses of 1946 and 1951 (when population in the Republic increased by 6,000). The decline of population has been greater in the Republic than in Northern Ireland. The population of the six counties that form Northern Ireland has increased gradually since 1901 (Jackson 1963, p. 25). Meanwhile, emigration from the Republic ebbed in the 1930s and then accelerated rapidly in the 1950s. Net emigration averaged 15,000 persons a year in the 1950s (Kennedy 1973, p. 213). In view of the fact that the combined adult population of all of Ireland was just under 3 million in 1951, almost 200,000 emigrants for the decade is staggering.[14]

The immediate causes of population decline in Ireland from 1841 to 1961 were high emigration, high average age at marriage, high proportion never marrying (especially among men), large sibships that resulted from relatively high marital fertility for a European country, and no significant increase in illegitimate births as late marriage and celibacy increased (Glass 1953; Jackson 1963; Kennedy 1973). As Jackson (1963, p. 25) points out, none of these features was unique to Ireland, but the combination

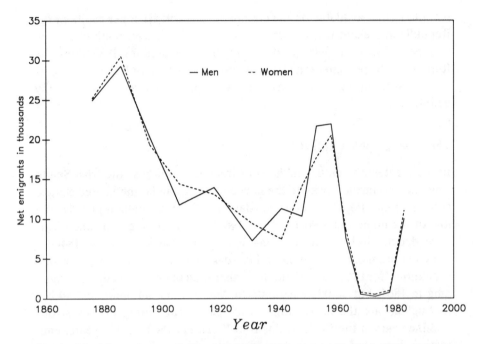

Figure 1.1   Net emigrants (in thousands), by sex and year: Ireland, 1871–1986.

was. Together they produced unprecedented population decline. The negative effect of emigration on population is direct; the effects of marriage
patterns and sibship sizes are less so. Late marriage and high celibacy
depress natural increase only if a society has low illegitimacy. Individuals
who are sexually inactive as they wait to marry shorten their reproductive
cycle. They also develop commitments to roles that may be incompatible
with having a large family when (and if) they eventually marry. Large sibships mean competition in the next generation as many brothers and sisters compete over typically small, impartible inheritances.

The key to all of these factors in Ireland was rampant emigration. The
outflow of young persons, especially of young women, produced the other
elements of population decline: the low sex ratio, high age at marriage,
high celibacy, and low illegitimacy rates. Prior to 1950, males had a better
chance than females of surviving to age 20 (Kennedy 1973, table 12). With
more women than men leaving Ireland, the sex ratio among those left
behind was imbalanced. In urban areas the imbalance was reversed by a
greater flow of women from the countryside to the city. The double debit

of high female emigration and rural-to-urban migration left the male bachelor in the countryside in dire straits. Urban women were not much better off. Kennedy (1973, table 19) shows how serious the situation was for the marriage prospects of rural men and urban women. Even if every eligible rural female and urban male had married, celibacy would have been high. The fact that many eligible persons did not marry—a demographic problem that might be called mismatch—exacerbated the problem. Kennedy (1973, table 57) demonstrates the prevalence of female celibacy in rural areas and male celibacy in urban areas. Overall, male celibacy was 35–90 percent higher in rural areas than in urban areas, whereas female celibacy was 20–35 percent higher in urban areas than in rural areas. Perhaps more important, rates of female celibacy were about 30 percent higher than male celibacy in urban areas, while rates of male celibacy were up to twice the rates of female celibacy in rural areas.

The root causes of emigration were economic. In the 1950s the economies of the Republic and Northern Ireland could not provide niches for everyone with an Irish birthright. Pushed by limited opportunities at home, many Irish sons and daughters must have found the prospects for a comfortable life in England appealing. Postwar reconstruction in England and its fruits created a demand for workers that could not be matched in the Irish cities, towns, or countryside. Even workers without skills could find work in England—or so it was hoped. These hopes were spurred by the advertisements that English employers placed in the Dublin, Cork, and Belfast dailies and by the experience of three generations of Irish immigrants living in England.

These immediate economic conditions favorable to migration from both parts of Ireland to England were bolstered by a social structure that had been forced to accommodate a century of outflow. In Jackson's (1963, p. 30) words: "Cause and effect cannot be readily separated in the case of a large-scale and long continued migration. Not only has the example of those who have already emigrated induced others to follow, but the structure of family and social life has become conditioned to a continual reorganization as members move away. Emigration is thus a normal and expected process in the community and not an exceptional experience." Indeed, as Scheper-Hughes (1979) details, child rearing and adolescent socialization in Kerry (a county of very high emigration) fostered and reinforced presumptions of emigration for some of the siblings even as there were attempts to ensure family continuity by selecting one of the brood to be left behind.

Crucial to this process is the pattern of inheritance of agricultural property in rural Ireland. Inheritance is taken up in detail in Chapter 6, which focuses on the farmers' sons in this study. Of importance here is the vaunted "stem family" system of rural Ireland. As Hannan (1982, pp. 142–143) notes, "Its main features are: (i) a familial economy, where farms are owned or securely rented and are large enough to support a family but not large enough to employ labor; (ii) a subsistence economy, where production for the market is not the dominating purpose of production: use values rather than exchange values are predominant; (iii) where impartible inheritance was the norm, as in Ireland, . . . characteristic inheritance, marriage, and property settlement arrangements guarantee the succession and marriage of heirs, the retirement of the old couple, and the settlement and usual emigration arrangements for the non-inheriting sons, and so on."

The Irish Mobility Study data allow identification of those men in the 1973 labor force who grew up on farms that employed only family labor: 27 percent of men living in the Republic and 16 percent of men living in Northern Ireland in 1973 grew up under such conditions.[15] But the system had changed. Commercialization of farming meant that more land was required for survival. Men were tied to the land by family obligations; women were not. The resulting imbalance of emigration decreased the number of prospective mates for bachelor farmers in the West of Ireland from two single women for every single farmer in 1951 to one single woman for every two single farmers in 1971 (Hannan 1982).

To follow in father's footsteps, a young man or woman must be able to live and work near home. In the Ireland of the 1950s, these rural changes and the lack of accommodating urban changes meant that an increasing proportion of the island's youth found it impossible or undesirable to stay. The roots of the problems of the 1950s go beyond economics, of course. The complexities of conflict, union, partition, and trade on terms disadvantageous to the Irish that underlie the history of Anglo-Irish relations provide an essential backdrop to understanding the microeconomic rationality of emigration in the 1950s (Beckett 1969; Lyons 1973; Hechter 1975).

The Political Context

The overriding political fact in Ireland today is the partition of the island into the independent Republic of Ireland in the South and West and the province of Northern Ireland, which is part of the United Kingdom, in the Northeast. Partition came in 1921. The social forces that led to partition derived from the collision of British expansionism and Irish nationalism. In every age claims of an indigenous Irish nationality separate from Britain have competed with counterclaims of a united nation throughout the British Isles. Centuries of conflict between Irish nationalists and an alliance of Irish unionists and British imperialists preceded the imposition of a union on the Irish by an act of the British Parliament in 1801. Union intensified the conflict. Both parliamentary initiatives in favor of home rule for Ireland and armed insurrection in the cause of an independent Ireland marked much of the period of union. The Irish War of Independence brought a bloody demise to the union in 1921. Even today, the question of union with Britain or the creation of a republic encompassing all of Ireland dominates the conflict in Northern Ireland. Irish nationalists, Irish unionists, British liberals, and British conservatives fought to a compromise that nobody wanted—the partition of Ireland. Each of these factions had internal divisions, the most important being the split within the ranks of Irish nationalism between those who favored dissolution of the union by an act of the British Parliament to reinstate Irish home rule and those who favored armed insurrection against the British.

Ireland had sought the return of self-government almost from the beginning of Union in 1801.[16] The high-water marks in that quest were Catholic emancipation in 1829 and the near-victory of Charles Stewart Parnell's revival of the home rule movement in 1885–1886. Parnell's campaign began with the parliamentary election of 1885, which was a turning point in many ways. On the eve of the election, few political observers in Ireland or England would have given Parnell's Irish nationalists favorable odds on winning the approval of the Westminster Parliament for home rule. Up to that time, Irish parliamentary politics reflected the political party alignments of Britain. Loosely organized nationalists appeared from time to time, but the dominant parties swallowed them up almost as quickly as they appeared. In 1885, bolstered by new party organization and electoral reforms, the nationalists won 85 of 105 seats in Ireland, including 17 of the 33 Ulster seats.[17] The most important consequence of this stunning electoral success was that it strengthened the case for parliamentary action and quelled popular support for the forces of armed revolution. When an armed uprising did occur in 1916, popular support was slow to develop, in part because of the promise of a parliamentary solution. The election of 1885 was also notable because it joined the fate of parliamentary nationalism to the Liberal Party in England. Forging this tie appeared to be a great victory at the time, but when the defeat of home rule brought down the Liberal Party government in 1886, the Irish nationalists were not free to trade political favors with the Conservative Party.[18] As a consequence, Conservative domination of the British Parliament over the next 20 years kept the issue in the background.[19]

A final consequence of the election of 1885 was to spawn the Unionist Party. When the Irish nationalists found a large constituency for an independent political party, unionists looked past their differences on social issues and formed their own party to counter the presence of a nationalist party. A process of electoral polarization set in, wiping out liberals and conservatives in Ireland, leaving only nationalists and unionists.

When the Liberal Party returned to power in England in December 1905, the major obstacle to home rule for Ireland was the House of Lords. At that point the Irish parliamentary nationalists, then under the leadership of John Redmond, had the support of the majority party in Commons. Because all legislation had to pass both houses, however, the presence of a large majority of the Lords that could be counted on to oppose all threats to the union diminished the Irish nationalists' chances. The liberal majority in Commons struggled with the Lords for several years. When the Lords vetoed the budget of 1909, a constitutional crisis ensued. An election was called, to gather a mandate for reducing the role of the House of Lords. The liberals formed a new government, with crucial help from the Irish nationalists. Eighteen months of negotiation between British liberals and conservatives produced the Parliament Act of 1911, eliminating the Lords' veto power.[20] The stage appeared to be set for an Irish nationalist victory on home rule.

The liberals and the Irish nationalists had the votes needed to pass the Home Rule Bill in Commons, and with the veto taken from the Lords, winning legislative approval of some form of home rule seemed to be just a matter of time. But the particulars of home rule were still open to negotiation. The Irish unionists held the key to the negotiations because any home rule scheme, no matter how popular it might be in Parliament, needed the acquiescence of the unionists in order to be an administrative success. Since by definition the unionists opposed the principle of home rule, the topic of negotiation was what they would accept in practice. The word forthcoming from Ulster was ominous. Unionist leaders—Sir Edward Carson, a Dubliner who led the unionist forces in parliament, and Sir James Craig of Belfast—made clear to all concerned that their followers were prepared to take up arms against any home rule government in Dublin.[21]

In a vain attempt to placate unionists, the Liberal prime minister Henry

Herbert Asquith in 1912 proposed a very weak Home Rule Bill. Many important powers, including taxation and police, remained under British control. Nonetheless, the Irish nationalists accepted the bill, viewing it as a first step toward independence. They reasoned that further steps could be taken once home rule was established in principle.[22] The Home Rule Bill progressed slowly through Commons, hampered by unionist and conservative opposition. A portentous moment came when in the course of debate T.G. Agar-Robartes, a liberal MP, proposed that part of Ulster (the counties of Antrim, Armagh, Down, and Londonderry) be excluded from home rule. The government rejected the amendment. Carson countered with an amendment excluding all of Ulster from home rule.[23] This amendment was defeated, and the bill passed in January of 1913; but from then on, partition of Ireland was never far from the surface of the home rule debate. Neither Irish nationalists nor Unionist Party favored partition, but it could not disappear as long as many English politicians saw it as the compromise they needed in order to settle the Irish question. The course of partition was advanced by an amendment to the Home Rule Bill of 1912, introduced by Asquith in 1914 (reluctantly accepted by the Irish nationalists), that gave any Ulster county the right to delay home rule by up to six years on the vote of a majority of its parliamentary electors. Carson rejected the amendment on behalf of the unionists, affirming that they opposed Irish home rule in principle, whether or not they were included in its practice. The amendment passed.

World War I intervened at this point. The Home Rule Bill of 1912 passed into law during the war, but it was not implemented until 1920 because all sides agreed that the administrative details could not be worked out while a war was on. Events in Ireland during the war swept this agreement among the parliamentary parties into the background.

The events that led to the establishment of Saorstat Eireann—the Irish Free State—began with the Easter Rising of 24 April 1916. An armed band under the leadership of Patrick Pearse occupied the General Post Office and other key buildings in and around Dublin on Easter Monday. Massive retaliation by the British—including heavy artillery that destroyed or damaged many public buildings in Georgian Dublin—put down the rebellion in less than a week. Orders of unconditional surrender were signed by Pearse and James Connolly on 30 April. Even sniping ceased by 1 May 1916.

Following the surrender, British troops swept the city and eventually the countryside, arresting a total of 3,430 men and 79 women for violations of martial law (Lyons 1973, p. 375). Nearly 2,000 of these were deported to

England and held for periods ranging from one to seven months. Brutal executions of many of the men who took part in the uprising created sympathy for the movement. Nationalist feeling had heretofore favored parliamentary measures over armed insurrection. At the time of the rising, there was some disappointment over the particulars of the Home Rule Bill of 1912, but support for parliamentary nationalism exceeded support for Sinn Fein and other revolutionary parties by a wide margin. The British reaction to the Easter Rising changed the balance of Irish nationalism. The deportations and executions, perhaps even more than the Rising itself, pushed the populace toward a more radical course. When on 10 April 1918 a bill to approve the drafting of Irishmen into the British army was introduced into the English House of Commons, the Irish nationalist MPs left Westminster and joined the opposition in Dublin. On 23 April 1918, a general strike crippled economic activity everywhere in Ireland except Belfast.

The country was polarized. Before the Easter Rising the parliamentary nationalists had the support of the majority of Irish men and women. By 1918 Sinn Fein and the Unionist Party had taken over. In the November 1918 general election, the parliamentary party won only six seats; other moderate parties were completely wiped out. Nearly all of the seats were split between the two extremist groups: the Unionist Party (23 seats) and Sinn Fein (73).

Sinn Fein won on a four-point platform of withdrawal from the Westminster Parliament, opposition to the draft (a moot point, given the armistice, but a popular principle), establishment of an Irish national assembly, and an appeal to the Paris Peace Conference for recognition of the Republic of Ireland as an independent nation under Wilson's doctrine of self-determination. In January 1919, even though many elected officials were in English jails, the victors sought to implement their platform. They refused to take their seats in Westminster, instead establishing Dail Eireann as the Irish national assembly in Dublin.[24]

England fought this rebellion, reinforcing the Royal Irish Constabulary with regular troops and special forces (Black and Tans). Guerrilla warfare with the Irish Republican army ensued. Civilian riots between Protestants and Catholics, especially in the cities of Londonderry and Belfast, also took many lives.[25] A truce was called for 11 July 1921, and negotiations began.

In the midst of the hostilities, the British implemented the Home Rule Bill of 1912, as amended at the time of suspension due to World War I in

1914. The device of implementation was the Government of Ireland Act of 1920. This act created two entities, "Northern Ireland" and "Southern Ireland," made up of 6 and 26 counties, respectively. Two separate home rule parliaments were established. Each was subject to review by the Westminster Parliament, and both North and South were to continue electing MPs to Westminster. Elections were called for May 1921. The Unionist Party won 40 of 52 seats in the North; Sir James Craig became prime minister. In the South the idea of partition was scorned, but Sinn Fein stood candidates for election to the home rule parliament as a means of securing its failure. When Sinn Fein won all but four seats, that goal was accomplished.[26]

In this context home rule got little attention in the peace talks of the summer and autumn of 1921. The key notion in the talks was the offer of dominion status for the 26 counties. The British goal was to keep Ireland in the Empire. To that end the British pressed for application of the concept of self-determination at the county level. Finally the leaders of the Irish delegation to the peace talks, Arthur Griffith and Michael Collins, decided that they were not going to win either a Republic of Ireland or jurisdiction over Ulster. So they signed the best deal that they thought would be forthcoming.

A civil war ensued in Ireland, splitting the Irish Republican army (IRA) into forces who favored the Treaty of 1921 and forces who opposed it. The protreaty forces won the war and governed Saorstat Eireann until 1932, when the antitreaty forces, reconstituted as Fianna Fail, won power in the general election. Under the leadership of Eamon de Valera, Fianna Fail governed Ireland until 1948. During this period the ties to Britain were diminished further. First, in a constitutional amendment in 1932, the Crown and the Governor-General were banished from internal affairs. Then, in 1937, a new constitution abolished Saorstat Eireann, creating Eire, "a sovereign, independent, democratic state"—a Republic of Ireland in every way except unity. The framers of the constitution of 1937 refrained from using the name "Republic of Ireland" because they could not secure jurisdiction over Northern Ireland. So complete was the separation that Eire remained neutral during World War II. The Republic of Ireland was declared by de Valera's successor, John A. Costello, in 1949. In April of that year the Westminster Parliament passed the Ireland Act, recognizing the Republic of Ireland as the 26 counties and stipulating that Northern Ireland would never be separated from the United Kingdom without the consent of the legislature of Northern Ireland.

In Northern Ireland the unionists set about establishing a home rule government they had never sought. James Craig wrote to Lloyd George in 1921, "As a final settlement and supreme sacrifice in the interests of peace, the Government of Ireland Act was accepted by Northern Ireland, although not asked for by her representatives" (Lyons 1973, p. 696). Home rule lasted 50 years until Westminster assumed direct rule again in 1972. The unionists, though split into two parties, governed throughout the period of home rule. The nationalist opposition also split into two constitutional parties and a revolutionary faction. Periods of calm accompanied the ascendancy of the constitutional faction; periods of turmoil followed the gains by the IRA and Sinn Fein. The turmoil is not all one-sided. Sectarian extremists abound on both sides, and the intensity of the turmoil is attributable to the action-reaction character of sectarian violence. As it was in 1912, the resolve among extreme unionists is to translate itself into armed defense of the union with Britain, just as the nationalist extremists express their commitment to the republican cause in armed opposition.

The religious differences between unionists and nationalists in Ireland are a shorthand for much deeper differences. The causes of the violence are not religious doctrines. True, nearly all nationalists are Catholic and nearly all unionists are Protestant—but the source of this correlation, like the source of the division itself, is historical, not doctrinal.

For the nationalists, the intensity of their commitment to an independent Irish nation comes from an ideology of occupation. They see themselves as the direct descendants of the original peoples of the island. In asserting this vision of their heritage, they deny the legitimacy of Protestant residence in Ulster. The nationalist credo asserts that Protestants were imposed on them by the British. According to this point of view, the unionist position comes from the historical migration of Calvinist Protestants from Scotland to Ireland; the unionists favor union with Britain because they are not really Irish. Even though most of the unionists were born in Ireland and hold a numerical majority, they seem to be outsiders—worse yet, many view them as an occupying presence that has no legitimate claim to power in Ulster or anywhere else in Ireland.

The civil and social wrongs imposed or simply tolerated over the years by the unionist-controlled Stormont parliament reinforce the nationalists' view. By suppressing the indigenous Irish, namely the Catholics, the Protestant establishment does the work that only an occupying force would accept. No fellow countryman could behave in such a way, according to the view of many nationalists, North and South.

The unionist extremists have a complementary view of the situation that informs their interpretation of specific issues. In their eyes Protestants have built all of the valuable and productive institutions in Ulster. They have earned their place in Ireland through three centuries of hard work and Protestant industry. The unionist extremists have no sympathy for the nationalist claims of precedence.

On top of this argument sits a substantial material interest. Most industrialists and large landowners in Ulster are Protestant. This fact often leads to the conclusion that all—or at least a majority—of the working class of Northern Ireland is Catholic. That is not true. The material roots of sectarian conflict in Ulster lie not in the supposedly perfect correlation between class and religion but in the reality of a very imperfect correlation. In fact, most working-class occupations in Northern Ireland divide pretty evenly between Catholics and Protestants. Given the overall religious composition of the province, this means that Catholics are overrepresented and Protestants underrepresented in working-class pursuits, but there are nonetheless thousands of working-class Protestants in a population of about one million Protestants. Indeed, if we take into account the Catholic predominance in farming, Protestants may well have been a majority of the working class in Ulster at the turn of the century. Referring to the 1880s, Lyons (1973, p. 289) says, "It followed that in lean times competition for jobs and land frequently became competition between Catholics and Protestants, overflowing often enough into violence and bloodshed."

Even among the Protestant ruling class, the material interest in unionism has less to do with the subjugation of the working class—which probably could be carried off under any nonsocialist regime—than with connections to export markets within the British free trade area. Protection designed to foster domestic Irish industry forms an important plank in the nationalist platform, as it has since the time of Parnell in the 1880s. Industry in Northern Ireland has grown up without protection. Those firms that survive are well adapted to free trade. Ulster industrialists of the last century feared that their trade would suffer if other countries retaliated against Irish protectionism by imposing duties on Ulster goods. Contemporary Northern industrialists perpetuate those interests and those concerns. The poverty and unrealized consumerism of the Irish population offer little hope of replacing lost foreign markets with domestic consumption, no matter how stimulated.

2   The Irish Mobility Study

During 1973 and 1974 John A. Jackson directed a large-scale survey of the male working-age population of the entire island. Separate surveys were carried out in Northern Ireland and in the Republic, but the goal in each region was the same: to interview a sample of 2,500 men aged 18–65 years about their work histories and related topics. Identical basic interview schedules were employed in the North and the Republic. The project, designed to study the determinants of occupational mobility in Northern Ireland and the Irish Republic, is here called the Irish Mobility Study.[1]

Data

The Electoral Registers of Northern Ireland's parliamentary constituencies and of the Republic's Dail constituencies were used as sampling frames from which to draw equal probability samples of the target population. The samples were stratified by size of place, giving the metropolitan centers of Dublin and Belfast special treatment that resulted in proper proportional representation for the two capital cities. In Belfast, five independent, systematically selected samples were drawn; in Dublin, four such samples were drawn. District election divisions were used as the primary sampling units (psu's) in Northern Ireland. There were 59 psu's in Northern Ireland, with a maximum of 73 respondents in any psu. Dail election districts for nonmetropolitan areas in the Republic were too small to be used as psu's, so special psu's were constructed (see O'Muircheartaigh and Wiggins 1977). Three psu's per constituency were the maximum, and there were less than 75 respondents per psu.

Once psu's were selected, a list of contacts was systematically selected from the election registers. The sample was corrected to give a probability of selection to those whose names did not appear on the electoral register that was equal to the probability of selection for men whose names appeared in the register. An amended "Kish technique" (Kish 1965, pp. 398–401) was implemented. All males on the register were selected with an equal probability. If they fell within the target age group of 18–65 years old and were still living at the selected address at the time of contact, they were interviewed. For households that contained males who were either not registered or had moved in since 15 September 1973 (a date chosen to signify the first day of interviewing even though fieldwork began about ten days earlier), then all males in the household were listed in descending order of age, and a selection table was used to choose one male to be interviewed. This ensured that males who had moved had a probability of selection at their new place of residence.

Sampling and interviewing in the Republic were under the control of the Economic and Social Research Institute (ESRI), a large center for social science research in Dublin. ESRI used its pool of experienced interviewers to make the 3,843 contacts in the original sample. Fieldwork commenced on 5 September 1973. The election registers do not reveal the age of electors, so many of the contacts were not part of the target population. Initial contacts identified 2,876 men aged 18–65, of whom 2,269 were interviewed. Response was significantly better in outlying areas than in Dublin. Response in some parts of Dublin was so bad that additional cases were added to the sample. In other parts of the country the sample was adjusted downward because the initial estimate of the ratio of eligible males to contacts proved to be lower than the achieved ratio. Even so, Dublin was somewhat underrepresented in the completed sample. A corrective weighting scheme was devised (O'Muircheartaigh and Wiggins 1977). The adjustments to the initial sample delayed completion of the fieldwork until 30 July 1974.

In Northern Ireland sampling and interviewing were supervised by Jackson. A team of interviewers was recruited from around the province, 35 percent of whom had prior interviewing experience. Because of the political instability in Northern Ireland, delays and interruptions were expected. Although some delays occurred, there were no serious incidents, and the interviewing was completed in Northern Ireland in a timely manner, three months before the fieldwork was completed in the Republic. The overall response rate for Northern Ireland was 73 percent; much closer to the response rate in the Republic than was originally anticipated.

Table 2.1
Contacts, identified population, and response rate
by region and metropolitan situs: men aged 18–65, Ireland, 1973

Place	Contacts set (1)	Men aged 18–64 identified (2)	Contact rate[a] (3)	Interviews (4)	Response rate[b] (5)
Republic	3843	2876	74.6%	2291	79.7%
Metro Dublin	1046	827	78.9	587	71.0
Elsewhere	2797	2049	73.2	1704	83.2
Northern Ireland	4436	3293	74.2	2416	73.4
Metro Belfast	1245	899	72.2	630	70.0
Elsewhere	3191	2394	75.0	1786	74.6

a. $100 \times (2) \div (1)$.
b. $100 \times (4) \div (2)$.

Table 2.2
Interviews by year, month, and region: men aged 18–65, Ireland, 1973

Year	Month	Republic N	Republic %	Northern Ireland N	Northern Ireland %
1973	August	1	<1%	84	3%
	September	319	14	738	31
	October	685	30	756	31
	November	642	28	429	18
	December	159	7	154	6
1974	January	8	<1	190	8
	February	202	9	32	1
	March	94	4	32	1
	April	75	3	—	—
	May	50	2	—	—
	June	52	2	—	—
	July	4	<1	—	—
Total		2291	100	2415	100

The results of the sampling are shown in Table 2.1. The achieved sample sizes are 2,291 in the Republic and 2,416 in Northern Ireland. The difference between metropolitan and nonmetropolitan areas is more pronounced in the Republic than in Northern Ireland. The main source of variation in response rate is the high rate of response in areas of the Republic outside of Dublin. Response rates in Dublin and all of Northern Ireland are about the same. Table 2.2 tabulates the interviews by month and region. It shows that the long duration of the fieldwork was due to the collection of a relatively small proportion of all cases. Only 20 percent of the interviewing carried over into 1974.

The Variables

This study makes use of only a small portion of the data collected. A wealth of attitudinal data is barely skimmed here. Complete family and residence histories are used only in an auxiliary way.

The primary goal of this study is to analyze the data on occupation at a variety of points in the respondents' life cycles. Complete work histories were gathered, beginning with current occupation and working back in time to the first occupation. These data are treated in three ways. First, occupations at crucial points in the respondent's life cycle are analyzed. These points are first occupation, first full-time occupation after leaving school, and "current" occupation. Since most of the men interviewed were employed at the time, for them current occupation was unambiguous. For those who were out of work at the time of the survey, their last occupation was substituted.[2] Second, occupations at specific ages are analyzed. Mobility tables from father's occupation to son's occupation at each specific age (for men employed at that age) are constructed, regardless of the year in which the given respondent achieved the specified age. These ages are spaced at ten-year intervals beginning at age 15 and continuing until age 45, which is often considered to be the peak of the socioeconomic life cycle. As desirable as it might be to look at mobility after the peak (and to test the notion that age 45 is the peak for all groups in Ireland), there are too few men over age 45 in the sample. Third, occupations in specific years are analyzed. Mobility tables from father's occupation to son's occupation in each year from 1959 to 1973 are constructed. The 1973 mobility table is the one that is most comparable to the British mobility table, because it excludes those members of the experienced civilian labor force in Ireland who were not employed at the time of the survey. Mobility tables for single-year turnover, such as occupation in 1963 by occupation in 1964, are also analyzed.

Attention is also given to socioeconomic origins, as indexed by the occupation held by the respondent's father while the respondent was growing up. The focus here is on the association between where in the class structure workers begin their lives and where they are when the survey encounters them. The practice of viewing the occupational mobility table as a matrix of population dynamics in which sons replace their fathers (Kahl 1964) is inappropriate for many reasons. Likewise, attempts to interpret the distribution of the father's occupations as an image of past occupational structure are bound to fail (Duncan 1966). The only conception of the mobility table that is logically consistent is the origin-destination view espoused here.

The father's occupation was determined at crucial points in the respondent's life: birth, age 14, age 16, when the respondent took his first job, when the respondent married, and the time of the interview. With the exception of father's occupation at respondent's birth, each of these versions of father's occupation appears in other research. The most common referents in other research to which the results in this study are compared are respondents at age 14 and respondents at age 16. The principal investigators in other studies chose to peg father's occupation in son's adolescence in the belief that it was best to measure father's occupation as close as possible to the time of school leaving, considering the importance of educational attainment for occupational destination. This timing of the measurement of father's occupation accords well with the perspective on the mobility table as a measure of the dependence of social destinations on social origins (Duncan 1966). Therefore, to maximize comparability with other studies (and in agreement with their theoretical justification of the timing decision), these two indicators of father's occupation are used here. To maximize the available data, the two indicators were combined. The age 14 indicator was given priority. If a valid occupational code was present for this variable, it was used. If no valid code was available for age 14, then the age 16 code was used. In most cases if the age 14 code was invalid, the age 16 code was also; but some cases were recovered by this procedure.

Other variables from the Irish Mobility Study that are used include geographical information, religion, marital status, family size, education, migration, and subjective indicators of mobility and social class placement. The geographical information is obtained from the interviewers' cover sheets. Included in the analysis is a dichotomy, "Republic" or "Northern Ireland," that is referred to as "region." Separate analyses of mobility in the three largest Irish cities—Dublin, Belfast, and Cork—are also presented.

Religion was obtained from respondents by asking, "Are you a Protestant or a Catholic?" Perhaps a more open-ended question such as, "What is your religious preference?" might be preferred, but the item must be used as given, with the recognition that it might somewhat suppress the incidence of reporting minority religions and, especially, the lack of affiliation with any religion. The problem is not as serious in Ireland as it might be in countries where religious affiliation and religious practice are less prevalent. By way of comparison, the UK Census of 1971 asked, "What is your religious preference?" No precisely comparable figures are available, but a tabulation of economically active males aged 15 and over shows 28.7 percent Catholic (the only category comparable to one from the Irish Mobility Study); the Irish study shows 30.1 percent Catholic among economically active men 18 to 65 years old. These figures show a very small difference, considering the different populations to which they refer. This finding supports the conclusion that the wording used in the Irish Mobility Study is not as serious an impediment to the measurement of religious preferences as a similar wording might be in other societies.

Marital status and family size data were collected by asking respondents to enumerate their engagements, marriages, and divorces, and the deaths of spouses. For each union respondents were asked to tell how many live births had occurred and to list all named children. Respondents were also asked to list their siblings. For wives, children, and siblings, information was collected on birth date, death date (if deceased), whether or not they lived in the respondent's household, religion, education, and current (or last) occupation. For siblings and children, current marital status was also obtained.

Complete educational histories were obtained by asking respondents to list the schools they attended, including the dates of attendance, the degree or certificate sought, whether or not it was completed, and whether or not a fee was required. The measures of educational attainment that form the basis for most other measures are a combination of level of education completed and type of school attended; they are coded as follows:

0   Incomplete primary education (respondents who left school before age 11 or who did not complete six years of school even if they stayed in school past their eleventh birthday)
1   Complete primary education (respondents who left school after completing their sixth year)
2   Incomplete nonacademic secondary education (respondents who enrolled in a trade school or a vocational school after primary school and who left school before they were 17 years old or without taking an O-level, A-level, or leaving certificate exam)
3   Incomplete academic secondary education (respondents who after primary school enrolled in an academic program, either "secondary school" in the

Republic or "grammar school" in Northern Ireland, and who left school before they were 17 years old or without taking an O-level, A-level, or leaving certificate exam)

4   Complete academic secondary education (respondents who after primary school enrolled in an academic program and who left school after taking an O-level, A-level, or leaving certificate exam)

5   Nonacademic third-level education (respondents who enrolled in a third-level technical, community, or polytechnic institution after completing second-level education)

6   Incomplete academic third-level education (respondents who enrolled in a training college or university after completing second-level education who did not receive a degree)

7   Complete third-level education (respondents who received a degree from a training college or university)

8   Postgraduate education (respondents who enrolled in an advanced-degree program after completing a degree program at a college or university)

These categories are combined in various ways in the analysis of educational attainment and of the consequences of education for occupational success. Among other treatments, these levels are transformed into a sequence of dummy variables for important educational transitions:

Entered second level (E2)
    1 if attainment score greater than one
    0 if attainment score equals one
Completed second level (C2)
    1 if attainment score greater than three
    0 if attainment score equals two or three[3]
Entered third level (E3)
    1 if attainment score greater than four
    0 if attainment score equals four[4]
Completed third level (C3)
    1 if attainment score greater than six
    0 if attainment score equals five or six[5]

A fifth dichotomous variable is used in some analyses. It codes respondents according to whether or not they attended an academic second-level institution.

The data from the Irish Mobility Study are supplemented with data from the Drumcondra study conducted by Vincent Greaney and Thomas Kellaghan (1984). The study began in 1967. A stratified sample of primary schools from the Republic was drawn for the purpose of norming responses to the items of the Drumcondra Verbal Reasoning Test (DVRT). The test was administered to students from these schools who were born in 1956. A total of 2,164 students of both sexes and all social classes took the test. From this sample of students, a random sample of 500 students was selected for follow-up. Students in this subsample were followed until they took their first paying jobs. Six students died or emigrated before leaving school, reducing the number of cases to 494.

Of the dozens of measures available for each student, this analysis limits attention to five:

Educational attainment
1   Primary school only
2   Incomplete junior cycle (first two years of secondary school)
3   Complete junior cycle
4   Incomplete senior cycle (last two years of secondary school)
5   Complete senior cycle
6   At least some third-level education
Father's or guardian's occupation in 1967 (hereafter social origins)
1   Agricultural laborer
2   Farmer
3   Lower manual
4   Upper manual
5   Lower nonmanual
6   Upper nonmanual
Mental ability
0–200   Score on the DVRT
Type of second-level school attended
1   Academic
0   Nonacademic
Gender
0   Female
1   Male

The educational categories were transformed into transition variables comparable to those in the Irish Mobility Study. The social origins data were also coded to prestige scores on the Hope-Goldthorpe scale.

Coding of Occupations

Goldthorpe and Hope (1974) describe a useful system of occupational coding. The first step is to convert the verbal descriptions of jobs transcribed on the questionnaires into the 224 unit group codes and 8 employment status codes of the British Census (OPCS 1970). The unit group–employment status combinations are then assigned reference numbers. The reference numbers can be recoded to the detailed and collapsed versions of the Hope-Goldthorpe scale. The occupational classification schemes of Erikson, Goldthorpe, and Portacarero (EGP 1979) and Goldthorpe (1980) are further reductions of the occupational data based on the collapsed version of the Hope-Goldthorpe scale.

The occupational classification scheme in this study is based on these procedures. The Irish context requires a few modifications. The large number of unpaid family members assisting on farms and in shops must be accommodated in the coding scheme.[6] Treating unpaid workers as separate from paid workers adds 2 categories to the 36 categories in the collapsed version of the Hope-Goldthorpe scale. Another 4 categories are added because of the distinction between proprietors and own-account workers with and without employees. This distinction, introduced by Erikson et al. (1979), is retained here. So the 36-category, collapsed version of Hope-Goldthorpe is extended to 42 categories for this study.

In addition, some unit group–employment status combinations occur in Ireland but not in England. Table 2.3 lists these "illegal" combinations, which must be assigned a reference group number or discarded. The largest number of allocations is for current occupation: 121 current occupations have allocated reference numbers (out of 4,250 current occupations coded); 97 father's occupations have allocated reference numbers; and 34 first occupations are allocated. This at first seems like a rather large number of allocations. These combinations, however, arise for a very small number of respondents.

Table 2.4 cross-classifies the men in the Irish Mobility Study according to their current or most recent occupations using the 42-category classification and region. Some data reduction is called for at this point. A few of the categories are too small for analysis. Even if they were not, a 42×42 mobility table is too big to work with. The categories are reduced in such a way as to preserve comparability between the results obtained here and those in Erikson et al. (1979), Goldthorpe (1980), Whelan and Whelan (1984), and Erikson and Goldthorpe (1987a,b). Accordingly, a hierarchy of classification schemes is strictly maintained. If two cases are in the same category of the 42-category classification, they both must be classified into the same category of some reduced classification. Furthermore, all classifications of between 9 and 42 categories must be intermediate between the detailed classification scheme and the EGP scheme; that

Table 2.3
Reference numbers allocated to combinations of unit group
and employment status not covered by Hope–Goldthorpe scheme

					Employment status			
Unit group #	Missing	Self-employed 25 +	Self-employed < 25	Self-employed 0	Manager 25 +	Manager < 25	Foreman or supervisor	Other
2	4001	—	—	—	—	—	4101	4201
3	4201	—	—	—	—	—	—	—
13	—	—	—	—	1407	—	—	—
25	—	—	—	—	1407	—	—	—
31	—	—	—	—	—	—	—	3004
42	—	—	—	—	1407	—	—	—
72	—	—	—	—	606	—	—	—
77	—	—	—	—	606	—	—	—
87	—	—	—	—	1407	—	—	—
96	—	—	—	—	606	—	3008	—
98	—	—	—	—	1601	—	—	—
108	3302	—	—	—	—	—	—	—
113	3302	—	—	—	—	—	—	—
115	604	—	—	—	—	604	604	604
117	—	—	—	—	—	1906	—	—
122	3112	—	—	—	—	—	—	—
123	—	—	—	—	—	—	—	1905
138	—	—	903	—	—	—	1406	1406
139	—	—	—	—	607	1406	—	—
142	—	—	—	—	1904	1904	—	1904
143	—	—	—	—	—	—	2203	1406
144	—	—	902	3403	2203	2203	—	—
145	—	—	—	3703	—	—	—	—
149	—	—	—	—	—	—	—	1903
155	—	—	101	—	—	1405	—	—
156	—	—	—	—	—	—	1403	1403
171	—	—	—	—	—	—	—	1405
172	—	—	—	—	—	2203	—	—
173	—	—	—	—	—	604	—	601
174	—	—	—	—	—	603	—	603
175	—	1703	1703	—	—	—	—	1404
176	—	—	—	—	—	—	1404	1404
177	—	—	—	—	—	—	—	1404
178	—	—	—	—	—	—	1404	1404
179	—	—	—	—	—	—	—	1406
180	—	201	902	3403	—	—	1404	1404
195	—	—	—	—	606	—	—	—
197	—	—	—	—	1802	—	—	—
200	—	—	—	—	—	—	1802	—
204	—	—	—	—	—	1802	1802	—
209	—	—	—	—	606	1801	1801	—
217	—	—	—	—	—	1802	—	—
221	4501	—	—	—	—	4301	—	—

Table 2.4
Distribution of current occupations by region:
men aged 18–65 in the experienced labor force, Ireland, 1973

Occupation	PREF+ code	Republic	Northern Ireland
Self–employed professionals I	Ia	.7%	.9%
Proprietors with 25+ employees		.3	.3
Salaried professionals I	Ib	2.3	2.9
Administrators & officials I		1.7	1.9
Industrial managers I		.5	.8
Administrators & officials II	II	1.1	.9
Technicians I		.9	1.5
Industrial managers II		1.6	1.5
Self–employed professionals II		.1	.0
Salaried professionals II		2.2	3.6
Supervisors of nonmanual employees I		.6	.1
Managers in services & small businesses		1.3	2.0
Supervisors of nonmanual employees II		.1	.3
Clerical & sales workers	IIIa	4.8	5.6
Proprietors with 1–24 employees	IVa	3.9	5.4
Self–employed workers I with employees		.0	.0
Self–employed workers II with employees		.0	.0
Self–employed workers III with employees		.0	.0
Proprietors with no employees	IVb	.1	.1
Self–employed workers I without employees		2.8	2.9
Self–employed workers II without employees		.8	.9
Self–employed workers III without employees		.1	.1
Service workers I	IIIb	.3	.3
Service workers II		1.5	1.3
Service workers III		1.9	2.3
Unpaid workers, nonfarm	VIIInf	.9	.4
Technicians II	V	3.2	3.3
Supervisors of manual employees I		1.7	2.4
Supervisors of manual employees II		1.5	2.0
Skilled manual workers, manufacturing I	VI	2.1	4.5
Skilled manual workers, manufacturing II		2.2	2.3
Skilled manual workers, manufacturing III		2.9	4.5
Skilled manual workers, construction		4.2	4.4
Skilled manual workers, other industries		1.5	2.2
Semiskilled manual workers, manufacturing	VIIss	2.7	5.5
Semiskilled manual workers, constr. & mining		.8	1.1
Semiskilled manual workers, other industries		9.4	11.4
Unskilled manual workers	VIIus	9.5	8.1
Farmers with employees & farm managers	IVc	3.9	2.6
Farmers without employees	IVd	15.2	6.1
Agricultural workers	VIIf	4.4	2.1
Unpaid workers, farm	VIIIf	3.7	1.4
Total		100.0	100.0
(N)		(2240)	(2345)

is, a scheme with, say, 14 categories must be constructed by combining categories from the 42-category scheme, and the EGP scheme must be obtainable by the combination of some of the 14 categories. This practice has the advantage of maximizing comparability between the results reported here and the results of other mobility studies that use the Hope-Goldthorpe or the EGP classifications.

Techniques described by Goodman (1981a) are used to reduce the number of categories to a number greater than 9 but less than 40. The criteria for combining categories allow the aggregation of pairs of occupational categories if the distinction between them does not contribute to the association between origins and destinations in a mobility table constructed from the categories under consideration. A distinction between a pair of occupational categories can be said to contribute to the association between origins and destinations if the odds of having a destination in occupation 1 in the pair relative to having a destination in occupation 2 in the pair is statistically independent of the occupation of origin, if the distribution of occupational origins for workers with destinations in occupation 1 is not significantly different from the distribution of origins among workers with destinations in occupation 2, or if the aggregation of occupations 1 and 2 does not significantly alter estimates of parameters of interest in some model of association for the mobility table (Hout 1983, pp. 72–76).

Table 2.5 shows the 16-category scheme that is preferred for this analysis, based on the Goodman criteria. This is referred to as the PREF scheme. The codes are the category numbers from the detailed classification in Table 2.4 that go into each category of the PREF scheme. Some of these categories can be aggregated according to the independence criteria; that is, the distribution of origins for some pairs of destinations are not significantly different, or the distribution of destinations is not significantly different for some pairs of origins. But these pairs are unique or nearly so in some way, such as involving a form of low-status self-employment or involving paid and unpaid work. Thus, the distinction is maintained in order to estimate the effects of considerations such as prestige, autonomy, and recruitment patterns on the pattern of mobility (Hout 1984a; Hout and Jackson 1986). Restricting attention to the Republic or to Northern Ireland may have produced a somewhat different outcome. The opportunity to compare the two societies in this study constrained the choices to that subset of occupational classifications that was acceptable (according to the Goodman criteria) in both regions. Table 2.5 also shows which combinations of occupations aggregate to form the EGP scheme, and it tabulates

Table 2.5

Percentage distribution of origins and destinations by region and classification scheme: men aged 18-65, Ireland, 1973

		Origins				Destinations			
		Republic		Northern Ireland		Republic		Northern Ireland	
Occupation	Code	PREF %	EGP %	PREF %	EGP %	PREF %	EGP %	PREF %	EGP %
Professionals & proprietors I*	Ia	.9 ⌐>	2.1	.9 ⌐>	3.1	1.1 ⌐>	5.8	1.2 ⌐>	6.9
Professionals & managers I	Ib	1.2 ⌐		2.2		4.7		5.7	
Professionals & managers II	II	4.4 —>	4.4	5.3 —>	5.3	8.2 —>	8.2	10.1 —>	10.1
Clerical & sales workers	IIIa	3.3 ⌐>	4.9	3.6 ⌐>	6.2	5.0 ⌐>	8.9	5.7 ⌐>	9.6
Service workers	IIIb	1.6 ⌐		2.6		3.9		3.9	
Proprietors with employees*	IVa	5.2 —>	5.2	5.8 —>	5.8	4.1 —>	4.1	5.5 —>	5.5
Proprietors without employees*	IVb	5.0 —>	5.0	4.0 —>	4.0	4.0 —>	4.0	4.3 —>	4.3
Unpaid workers, nonfarm	VIIInf	—	—	—	—	—	—	—	—
Technicians & foremen	V	3.6 ⌐>	14.7	4.9 ⌐>	21.2	6.7 ⌐>	20.7	7.9 ⌐>	25.6
Skilled manual workers	VI	11.1 ⌐		16.3		14.0		18.2	
Semiskilled manual workers	VIIss	10.3 —>	21.6	17.5 —>	27.9	13.6 —>	23.6	18.4 —>	26.6
Unskilled manual workers	VIIus	11.3 ⌐		10.4		10.0		8.2	
Farmers with employees*	IVc	8.2 ⌐>	34.3	7.3 ⌐>	21.3	4.1 ⌐>	20.0	2.6 ⌐>	8.8
Farmers without employees*	IVd	26.1 ⌐		14.0		15.9		6.2	
Agricultural workers	VIIf	7.8 —>	7.8	5.2 —>	5.2	4.6 —>	4.6	2.1 —>	2.1
Unpaid workers, farm	VIIIf	—	—	—	—	—	—	—	—
Total		100.0	100.0	100.0	100.0	100.0	100.0	100.0	100.0
(Cases)		(2130)	(2130)	(2292)	(2292)	(2130)	(2130)	(2292)	(2292)

*Self-employed workers.

the distributions of paid workers by origin, destination, region, and coding scheme.

The recorded volume of gross mobility, namely the percentage of workers whose current occupation differs from that of their father, depends on the level of occupational detail used in the calculation. A fine-grained occupational classification scheme can detect more mobility than a crude one can. The best occupational classification scheme is the one that records all of the sociologically meaningful moves while ignoring other (meaningless) moves. The finest-grained classification that is available in the Irish Mobility Study data is the combination of unit group and employment status. Including all economically experienced respondents—paid or unpaid, currently active or formerly active—produces maximum estimates of gross mobility of 78 percent for the Republic and 88 percent for Northern Ireland. Some of the mobility recorded in this way is substantively interesting; some of it is not. After all, the Irish data include observations on 938 combinations of unit group and employment status. In the calculation of overall gross mobility, a man who works as a crane and hoist operator whose father was an operator of earth-moving machinery looks just as mobile as a man who works as a chief executive officer of a firm employing more than 25 persons whose father was an agricultural laborer.

Some information will be lost in a data reduction endeavor such as the one undertaken here. The task is to minimize the loss and to assess accurately its consequences for the ensuing analysis. Table 2.6 presents estimates of mobility according to classification schemes of varying detail. Depending on the number and type of categories used, estimates of mobility in the Republic of Ireland range from 78 percent to 54 percent.[7] The range of estimates for Northern Ireland is from 88 percent to 62 percent.[8]

Two issues—one methodological, one substantive—arise from these calculations. The methodological issue is to measure the amount of information that is lost as one moves from a detailed classification to a less detailed one. A corollary of this undertaking is to point out what is hidden in other analyses of mobility data that use only the cruder classification schemes.

More important, it is necessary to determine why mobility in Northern Ireland is greater than mobility in the Republic. Mobility is the product of composition, structural mobility, and association. Differences in overall mobility between the Republic and Northern Ireland could reflect differences in any or all of these components.

Table 2.6
Gross mobility rates and tests of independence by classification
scheme and region: men aged 18–65, Ireland, 1973

Item (Class of workers)	Classification scheme[a]					
	UG/ES+ (All)	UG/ES (Paid)	PREF+ (All)	PREF (Paid)	EGP (Paid)	G7 (Paid)
Republic of Ireland						
Cases	2240	2130	2240	2130	2130	2130
Categories	938	938	16	14	9	7
Percentage mobile	78%	76%	71%	70%	60%	54%
Dissimilarity	—	—	24%	21%	20%	18%
Independence						
L^2	—	—	1827	1624	1347	912
df	—	—	225	169	64	36
Percentage of baseline L^2	—	—	—	100%	74%	50%
Quasi–independence						
L^2	—	—	894	669	282	176
df	—	—	209	155	55	29
Percentage of baseline L^2	—	—	—	100%	75%	32%
Northern Ireland						
Cases	2349	2292	2349	2292	2292	2292
Categories	938	938	16	14	9	7
Percentage mobile	88%	87%	76%	76%	65%	62%
Dissimilarity	—	—	19%	18%	17%	17%
Independence						
L^2	—	—	1398	1270	1065	732
df	—	—	225	169	64	36
Percentage of baseline L^2	—	—	—	100%	84%	58%
Quasi–independence						
L^2	—	—	723	586	256	145
df	—	—	209	155	55	29
Percentage of baseline L^2	—	—	—	100%	44%	25%

a.   UG/ES+ = unit group and employment status for economically active men; UG/ES = unit group and employment status for paid workers; PREF+ = preferred classification scheme for economically active men; PREF = preferred classification scheme for paid workers; EGP = classification scheme of Erikson, Goldthorpe, and Portocarero (1979); G7 = classification scheme of Goldthorpe (1980).

The bases of comparison among classification schemes are the models of perfect and quasi-perfect mobility (Goodman 1965, 1969).[9] If collapsing across some subset of occupational categories loses no information about the association between origins and destinations, then the likelihood ratio chi-square (L_0^2) values for perfect mobility before and after collapsing will be the same. If the only information lost is contained in the diagonal cell of the smaller table, then the L_{qi}^2 values for quasi-perfect mobility before and after collapsing will be the same. The changes in L_0^2 and L_{qi}^2 gauge the loss of information (Goodman 1981).

Values of L_0^2 and L_{qi}^2 are shown for a variety of more and less detailed classification schemes in Table 2.6. The size of L_0^2 in each column shows that the model of perfect mobility is a poor representation of occupational mobility in Ireland. This is no great surprise. The model of perfect mobility seldom fits data for national populations. The differences among the L_0^2 values, as measures of the amount of information lost when using the less detailed classification schemes instead of the PREF scheme, show clearly why PREF is preferred.

Comparing L_0^2 for the PREF and EGP schemes shows that EGP captures roughly five-sixths ($[1,347.10/1,624.11] \times 100 = 83$ percent) of the total association between origins and destinations; the remaining one-sixth of the association is hidden by combining categories of the PREF scheme to form the EGP scheme. The comparison between PREF and EGP in Northern Ireland is similar: about one-sixth ($100 - 84 = 16$ percent) of the association is due to differential mobility chances *within* EGP categories but *between* PREF categories. Using the G7 classification scheme devised by Goldthorpe (1980; Whelan and Whelan 1984) would reveal only a little over half of the association in both the Republic and Northern Ireland.

A large portion of the association between origins and destinations in Ireland, as elsewhere, is due to immobility. The model of quasi-perfect mobility (quasi-independence) takes strong association due to immobility for granted but proposes perfect mobility among categories on the condition that a move has occurred. The eighth line of each panel in Table 2.6 shows the likelihood ratio tests for this model (L_{qi}^2). Using L_{qi}^2 for comparisons among the occupational classification schemes confirms the earlier conclusion that collapsing categories loses significant information. Off-diagonal association in the 9×9 tables that use the EGP classification scheme is only slightly more than two-fifths (42 percent in the Republic and 44 percent in the North) of the off-diagonal association in the 14×14 tables that use the PREF classification scheme. Off-diagonal association in the 7×7 tables that use the G7 scheme contains a surprisingly small portion of the original off-diagnonal association.

The weakness of G7 is noteworthy because the single most reliable study of mobility in the Republic of Ireland relies on this scheme almost exclusively. Whelan and Whelan (1984) describe what they see as severe limitations on the mobility chances of working-class youth. Critics have accused them of overstating the case. Comparison between their classification scheme (G7) and the PREF scheme shows how their scheme masks a significant amount of the association between origins and destinations in Ireland. Thus, the inferences that Whelan and Whelan draw about lack of opportunity in Dublin's working class are, their critics notwithstanding, actually based on data that understate the strength of differential mobility. Part of the problem with G7 stems from its inability to distinguish farmers from other self-employed workers. Therefore, the relative lack of farmers in Dublin means that the difference among coding schemes is probably less in the data analyzed by Whelan and Whelan than in the data analyzed here. The Whelans' critics cannot put too much store in this conjecture, however, as comparisons that exclude men of farm origin also show that G7 misses important aspects of the association between origins and destination (see Table 3.4 in the next chapter).

Previous analyses of mobility in Northern Ireland are also called into question by these results. Miller's (1984) sanguine conclusions about equal access to employment opportunities for Catholics and Protestants in Northern Ireland (based on analysis of these Northern Irish data using G7) cannot be accepted at face value. More occupational detail is needed to extend Miller's limited comparison of Protestants and Catholics.

Statistical Inference

Most of these variables are categorical; that is, they are discrete characteristics that may or may not be ordered. Among the variables with an intrinsic order, only two variables have a natural metric of measurement: years of schooling and school leaving age. Even with education, some distinctions that cannot be ordered are introduced, such as distinctions between fee-paying and public education, between academic and vocational education, and between religious and secular schools. For that reason the methods appropriate to categorical data are used. These include simple percentages as well as a variety of log-linear and multiplicative models for cross-classifications (Goodman 1968, 1970, 1972a, 1978, 1984; Haberman 1974, 1979; Bishop, Fienberg, and Holland 1975; Fienberg 1980).

Sampling design affects how principles of statistical inference are applied. Test statistics assume a simple random sample from an infinite population. The Irish Mobility Study used a stratified sampling frame that was not a simple random sample. That kind of design is operationally indistinguishable from simple random sampling if the strata of the sampling frame are independent of the variables used in the analysis. In the Irish Mobility Study the key variables are occupational origins and destinations, and the strata used in the sampling design are clearly correlated with occupation because Belfast and Dublin were oversampled. These two large metropolitan areas will have more of some occupations, such as administrative and white-collar jobs in general, and less of others, most significantly agricultural jobs, than will the smaller cities and rural areas of Ireland. By oversampling the most distinct locations, the Irish Mobility Study is a better estimator of the occupational distribution than is a simple random sample of the same size. Thus, for most tabulations here, the sampling design is more efficient than simple random sampling.

The greater efficiency of the Irish Mobility Study suggests that a design effect should be estimated, so that significance tests based on the assumption of simple random sampling can be corrected. Without correction, standard formulas will return test statistics that are biased toward zero, making it possible that some null hypotheses that would be rejected if the design effect were known will not be rejected without the correction.

No attempt has been made to estimate the design effect, however, because two other factors are likely to bias tests in the other direction. First, many of the tables to appear here have a large number of empty cells and cells with few cases in them. Test statistics for such sparse tables tend to overstate significance (Haberman 1977). Furthermore, when a large number of tests are calculated, some true null hypotheses may be rejected by chance (Goodman 1969a), a problem known as simultaneous inference bias. The expected proportion of true null hypotheses to be rejected will be the same as the significance level employed in the tests (for example, 5 percent of true null hypotheses can be expected to be rejected if the .05 level is used). With these two influences favoring rejection of a null hypothesis, it was deemed imprudent to increase further the probability of rejection by introducing a sampling design effect. No claim is made that the absence of a design effect cancels the effects of sparse tables and simultaneous inference. The design effect is left off simply to avoid compounding these biases.

An important issue in any application of statistical models to data is how to judge the fit between model and data. Two theories of inference are current in modern statistics. The first is classical probability theory; the second is Bayesian theory. Both perspectives are useful in choosing among models. The classical procedure is to specify the probability distribution of the test statistic, compare the test statistic with a prespecified percentile of that probability distribution, and decide on the basis of the percentile whether or not the model fits the data. That is the approach employed in the usual kinds of chi-square tests. It is applied here, using both the Pearson chi-square (X^2):

$$X^2 = \Sigma_i \Sigma_j (f_{ij} - F_{ij})^2 / F_{ij} \tag{2.1a}$$

and the likelihood ratio chi-square (L^2):

$$L^2 = 2 \Sigma_i \Sigma_j f_{ij} \log (f_{ij} / F_{ij}) \tag{2.1b}$$

for $i = 1, \ldots, R$ [the number of rows in the table] and $j = 1, \ldots, R$; where f_{ij} is the observed count in cell (i,j) and F_{ij} is the count expected in cell (i,j) according to some statistical model, such as the model of independence. These statistics are compared with percentiles of the chi-square distribution following common procedures (e.g., Goodman 1970).

Bayesian methods introduced by Raftery (1986a,b) are also useful, especially in the context of comparing a specific null hypothesis that some particular model m is true (given the observed data) with a vague alternative hypothesis that some unspecified other model m' is true (given the same data). In the analysis of mobility tables, this is the usual comparison. Raftery proposes that when such vague comparisons are made, the preferred model is the specific one that has the highest probability of being true, given the observed counts $\{f_{ij}\}$. Of course, for any specific model m, the probability that m is true given $\{f_{ij}\}$ is unknown, but Raftery shows that the problem is tractable if m' is taken to be the saturated model, that is, a model in which the observed and expected frequencies are equal. Let B stand for the ratio of the conditional probability that m is the true model given the data to the conditional probability that the saturated model (namely, any model that reproduces the observed counts exactly) is true given the data, that is,

$$B = \frac{\text{prob (model } m \text{ is true given observed counts)}}{\text{prob (saturated model is true given counts)}} \tag{2.2}$$

then the large sample estimate of $2 \log B$ equals $L_m^2 - [(df_m) \log N]$ where L_m^2 is the likelihood ratio chi-square for model m, df_m is the corresponding degrees of freedom, and N is the number of observations ($N = \Sigma_i \Sigma_j f_{ij}$). Raftery calls this statistic *bic*.

Raftery's bic statistic is most useful in a situation that is commonplace in analyses of mobility tables but is difficult to deal with in a case of classical probability theory. This situation arises when all of the models of interest produce test statistics that are too large under the rules of classical inference. Further reductions of the test statistic come at the price of adding effects that are too small to be of substantive interest. It seems illogical in such situations to reject some models because they fail to fit the data but then, in the end, to accept some other model despite the fact that it does not fit the same data. Raftery (1986b) points out that this common conundrum can be avoided in practice by using bic. Grusky and Hauser (1984), for example, reject the model of constant mobility rates in 16 countries because the fit is poor, while accepting their model of constant association despite the fact the L^2 for their model has an associated probability level of 10^{-120}. Others, including myself (Hout 1984a), routinely do the same thing. The bic statistic is useful in these situations where classical inference theory is less so because bic < 0 means that the fit of the proposed model is good enough to make it more likely than the saturated model, given the observed counts $\{f_{ij}\}$.

Furthermore, models can be compared using bic. To see how to make comparisons, think of two models m and m'. Let model m contain all of the terms of model m' plus some extra terms. Both models have unknown probabilities of being true, given the data. According to Raftery (1986a), we can estimate the ratio of this unknown probability to the (also unknown) probability that the saturated model s is true, given the data for each model. Label these estimable ratios B and B'. If we take the ratio B/B', the probability that s is true cancels out, leaving:

$$B/B' = \frac{\text{prob (model } m \text{ is true given observed counts)}}{\text{prob (model } m' \text{ is true given observed counts)}}$$

Then:

$$
\begin{aligned}
-2 \log (B/B') &= -2 [\log B - \log B'] \\
&= \text{bic} - \text{bic}' \\
&= (L_m^2 - L_{m'}^2) - [(df_m - df_{m'}) \log N]
\end{aligned}
\tag{2.3}
$$

This relationship greatly facilitates model selection using bic; the preferred model is the one with the bic that is most negative. If bic < 0 for none of the models of interest, then the saturated model is preferred.

The combination of detailed coding of occupational origins and destinations coupled with relatively strong statistical associations involving those variables results in a very uneven distribution of cases across the cells of most of the cross-classification tables analyzed here. The pattern found in most of the mobility tables is for most of the cases to be in the cells that are on or near the main diagonal of the table (i.e., in those cells that indicate immobility or short distance mobility), leaving few cases to be distributed among the other cells. Many of the cells in the lower left and upper right cells of the mobility tables have zeros in them. These are what statisticians refer to as "sampling zeros" because they arise as part of the sampling process.[10] Sampling zeros can bias the X^2 and L^2 tests (Haberman 1979), leading to the incorrect rejection of reasonable models. The chi-square approximations for these tests in most of the tables are probably invalid. Some accommodation must be made. First, the raw counts for the most important cross-classifications appear in the appendix so that statistical advances in the treatment of this topic can be applied in the future to reassess the results reported here. Second, small quantities were added to the zero cells in these tables before fitting models as a way of minimizing the problems. This technique introduces biases that shrink the parameter estimates toward zero (Clogg and Eliason 1987), but it is the best solution now available.

The small quantities added to the cells depend on the size of the table and the marginal totals for the row and column involved. The procedure used here is a generalization of the recommendation to add ½ to zero cells when the dependent variable is dichotomous (e.g., Cox 1970, p. 33). Goodman (1972b) recommends adding ½ to cells in order to improve estimates of the parameters of *saturated* log-linear models when counts are small. This solution is very good for applications involving few cells, such as constructing confidence intervals for binomial probabilities via the logit transformation (Rubin and Schenker 1987). But for a $14 \times 14 \times 2$ table (see Table A.1), adding ½ to each cell count adds 196 psuedocases to the overall sample size (an increase of about 4 percent). So a reasonable method for adding less than ½ to each cell had to be invented. My technique involves two steps. First, I add $1/R$ to each cell count (where R is the number of occupational categories used in that tabulation). The new counts are then shrunk toward independence by using iterative proportional fitting and the observed row and column totals (Clogg and Eliason 1987).

The modeling process seems so complicated. Why not simply tabulate the data and draw conclusions from the uncooked numbers and percentages? The first reason is parsimony. Sometimes a huge array of numbers can be summarized by a few parameters from a simple model. Even when the model becomes complex, it is less complex than the original data unless the model has no degrees of freedom.

The second reason in interpretability. Even when there are no degrees of freedom, the parameters will usually be informative about sociological concepts. For example, nearly all models decompose expected counts into a marginal component and an association component. The size of specific marginal effects or associations will have more substance than specific counts will.

Finally, models are more likely than counts to be replicated in repeated samples. We cannot lose sight of the fact that the data are samples of numbers from an infinite population of outcomes, only a portion of which are realized in the world of everyday existence. As such, the data are inherently variable. If we were to repeat our data collection following exactly the same procedures each time in an unchanged world, we would nonetheless obtain different counts each time. That is the nature of sampling. Unsaturated models, namely models with at least one degree of freedom, selected according to the criteria employed in this study, vary less from sample to sample than the simple counts that make up the raw data do. Unsaturated models vary less from sample to sample than the constituent data do because models average out sampling variability. Therefore, inferences from unsaturated models are inherently less risky (i.e., more likely to be replicated in repeated samples) than are inferences from raw data. The more degrees of freedom a model has, the more likely it is to be replicable.

Out in the sparse regions of a large table where the cell frequencies are small, the changes in counts from one sample to the next can be dramatic. But a well-specified model, selected according to the precepts used in this study, is replicable to within a known margin of error. The margin of error is indicated by the standard error for each coefficient. Departures of the raw data from the expected frequencies under a well-specified model cannot reliably be predicted to recur in any replication of the study at hand.

Mobility Table Methodology

The methodological commentary to this point refers to cross-classified data in general. Most of the tabulations in this study are mobility tables—

cross-classifications of a special kind. A mobility table cross-classifies workers by the combination of their occupational origins and destinations. The most common example of a mobility table arrays a sample of current workers by the occupations held by their fathers and the workers' current occupations. In such a table the occupation of the father measures occupational origins for workers in the sample while the current occupation measures occupational destinations. Of course, fathers may have more than one occupation, so a particular occupation (e.g., when the respondent was 14 or 16 years old) is analyzed. Other origins and destinations may make up the table; an occupation treated as a destination in one table may even be the origin variable in some other table. The only restriction is that the origin must precede the destination in the worker's life cycle.

A distinguishing feature of mobility tables is a one-to-one correspondence between the categories used to code occupational origins and the categories used to code destinations. This study adopts the additional convention of arraying the destination categories across the columns of the table and the origin categories down the rows.

Conditional mobility tables add a control variable (or variables) to the bivariate format of the usual mobility table. Age, education, and ascriptive variables like sex and ethnicity are frequently used as control variables. In the analysis of Irish mobility, the most natural controls are region (Republic or Northern Ireland) and religion (in Northern Ireland).

The elementary operations common to the analysis of any cross-tabulation, such as calculation of row and column percentages, can be applied to mobility tables, whether or not control variables are used. In addition, there are special methods designed to take advantage of the properties of the mobility table. Most of these techniques have received a lot of attention (see Hout 1983).

The first special statistic among the many peculiar to mobility table methodology is the occupational mobility rate itself. The mobility rate in a given table is the proportion of workers whose current occupation differs from their occupational origins. Calculation of the mobility rate takes advantage of the identical coding of origins and destinations in the mobility table. Identical coding means that the cells along the main diagonal of the table contain all of the immobile cases, namely, the cases for which origin and destination are identical. The mobility rate (M) is the number of workers in the sample (N) minus the sum of the frequencies in the diagonal cells ($\Sigma_i f_{ii}$) divided by N: $M = (N - \Sigma_i f_{ii})/N$.

A high mobility rate results if the distribution of current occupations differs substantially from the distribution of occupational origins among current workers or if origins and destinations are statistically independent, that is, if the distribution of destinations is the same for all origins. A low mobility rate, however, results if the distribution of origins among current workers is similar to the distribution of current occupations *and* if the association between origins and destinations is strong. Mobility table methodology is designed to separate these two elements: mobility due to dissimilar distributions of origins and destinations (known as structural mobility) and mobility due to a weak association between origins and destinations (an important component of what is known as exchange mobility).

Mobility studies commonly feature the concepts of structural (or forced) and exchange (or circulation) mobility. Structural mobility arises because the marginal distributions of origins and destinations typically differ, making it impossible for all cases in a mobility table to be in diagonal cells. Some authors, notably Rogoff (1954) and Kahl (1957), seek to equate differences between the distributions of origins and destinations with trends in the occupational distribution of the work force. This idea is not well suited to the study of intergenerational mobility, because the distribution of origins cannot (except by accident) correspond to the actual distribution of the work force at any definite time in the past (Duncan 1966). Therefore, following Sobel, Hout, and Duncan (1985)—referred to hereafter as SHD—structural mobility is identified with unequal origin and destination totals, without attribution to specific changes in the occupational composition of the labor force over time. There is also an understanding in prior work—which is sometimes vague (Kahl 1957) and sometimes explicit (Featherman and Hauser 1978, p. 83)—that structural mobility to a particular destination affects all origins uniformly. Again following SHD, such an understanding is carried over into this work, so that structural mobility refers to all those factors that are independent of origins but that also account for all marginal heterogeneity.

SHD define exchange mobility as that part of the mobility process that produces equal flows between pairs of cells (i, j) and (j, i) of the mobility table. Their definition is adopted here. Giving substance to exchange mobility in this way avoids the logical inconsistencies entailed in the common practice of equating all mobility not attributable to structural mobility with exchange or circulation (see Sobel 1983; Sobel et al. 1985).

In combination, these definitions of structural and exchange mobility imply the multiplicative model of quasi-symmetry (QS). SHD develop an expression of this model that contains parameters that are isomorphic to structural and exchange mobility:

$$F_{ij} = \alpha_j \beta_i \beta_j \delta_{ij} \tag{2.4}$$

under the following conditions: $\Pi_j \alpha_j = 1$ (for all j), $\beta_i = \beta_j$ (for $i = j$), $\delta_{ij} = \delta_{ji}$, and $\delta_{ij} = 1$ (for $i = j$). For a table with R rows and R columns, there will be R^2 cells, $R - 1$ independent α_j parameters, R independent β_i parameters, and $\frac{1}{2} R (R-1)$ independent δ_{ij} parameters. Therefore, the QS has $R^2 - (R-1) - R - \frac{1}{2} R (R-1) = \frac{1}{2} (R-1)(R-2)$ degrees of freedom.

Given equation (2.4), SHD show how ratios of the α_j parameters measure structural mobility and how products of the β_i, β_j, and δ_{ij} parameters measure exchange. In particular, α_j/α_i measures the extent to which structural mobility alters the flow of labor from category i to category j; a ratio greater than 1.0 means that structural mobility increases the flow from i to j; a ratio less than 1.0 means that structural mobility increases the flow from j to i. The δ_{ij} parameters measure association inversely, relative to the usual conventions defining direction of association, such as the cross-product ratio. What is generally thought of as a strong positive association will manifest itself in the form of very small δ_{ij} (close to zero), while what is normally thought of as a strong negative association will appear in this format as δ_{ij} greater than one. However, unlike applications of the cross-product ratio, this model does not require that the categories of origins and destinations be ordered (Pullum 1970). These symmetric association parameters are the geometric means of two odds: the odds on moving from i to j relative to staying in i (F_{ij} / F_{ii}) and the reciprocal odds on moving from j to i relative to staying in j (F_{ij} / F_{jj}), that is:

$$\delta_{ij} = (F_{ij} F_{ji} / F_{ii} F_{jj})^{1/2} \tag{2.5}$$

In usual applications of the concept of exchange mobility, exchange is confounded with the association between origins and destinations, an equation that leads to logical inconsistencies (Sobel 1983). Under equation (2.4) exchange mobility is the product

$$\beta_i \beta_j \delta_{ij} \tag{2.6}$$

This equation contains association parameters (δ_{ij}), but it also contains symmetric marginal parameters (β's).

If QS holds, that is, if the frequencies expected under equation (2.4) do not differ significantly from the observed frequencies according to the likelihood ratio (L^2) or Pearson (X^2) chi-square tests, then the δ_{ij} parameters account for all of the association between origins and destinations in the table.[11] In most mobility tables, $\delta_{ij} < 1$; therefore, *the volume of exchange is diminished by strong association.*

The SHD framework for studying structural and exchange mobility departs from prior approaches in three beneficial ways: SHD avoid the tendency to view either structural or exchange mobility as the residual left over when the other is accounted for, SHD provide a one-to-one correspondence between concepts and measures, and SHD reorient thinking about structural mobility by replacing a society-wide concept with one that applies to an occupational category. Regarding the last point, when structural mobility is measured via a single index for an entire mobility table, the tendency is to think of it as a unitary property of the society from which the mobility table was drawn. In fact, structural mobility operates within societies to enlarge some occupations and to diminish others. From this perspective, a structural mobility measure must not only be a parameter of a well-specified model of the mobility process but also be occupation-specific.

The usual method of assessing structural mobility by comparing the marginal distributions will tend to understate the importance of structural mobility. Usual methods, such as computing the index of dissimilarity between the origin and destination distributions are best suited to tables in which origin and destinations are independent. Empirical samples of independence are exceedingly rare. In the usual case in which destination depends on origin, the structural mobility multipliers (α_j) from the SHD parameterization are the appropriate estimates of the force of structural mobility because the equation used to estimate α_j also contains coefficients for association (δ_{ij}).

To see how the index of dissimilarity understates structural mobility when destinations depend on origins, consider the 6×6 mobility table from São Paulo, Brazil (Hutchinson 1958; SHD).[12] The origin and destination totals are reproduced in the first two columns of Table 2.7. The index of dissimilarity between origins and destinations in São Paulo is, as always, the sum of the positive differences divided by N: $[(217 - 168) + (338 - 148)] / 1,037 = .230$ (or 23.0 percent). Comparing this with the structural mobility multipliers (α_j) is difficult, because a single index of dissimilarity summarizes the pair of distributions while the α_j measure the effect of structural mobility on each occupational category. For purposes of comparison, then, consider a new set of category-specific calculations that not only use the same information as the index of dissimilarity but also result in quotients in the same metric as the α_j. First, take the natural

Table 2.7
Bias entailed in ignoring association when calculating the effects of
structural mobility: Sao Paulo, Brazil, 1956

#	Occupation	Totals Origin	Destination	$\log c_j$	$\log \alpha_j'$	$\log \alpha_j$
1	Professionals	58	72	.22	.12	1.03
2	Managers	60	108	.59	.49	1.08
3	Intermediate nonmanual	116	188	.48	.39	.54
4	Lower nonmanual	217	168	−.26	−.35	−.39
5	Skilled manual	248	353	.35	.26	−.19
6	Semi– & unskilled manual	338	148	−.83	−.92	−2.04

logarithm of the ratio of the number of cases in destination j to the number of cases in origin j (let c_j be the symbol for this ratio): $c_j = \log (n_j^d / n_j^o)$. Second, subtract the mean ($\Sigma_j c_j / 6$) from each c_j. Finally, take the antilog of results of the second step (label this result α_j'). If origins and destinations are independent, then $\alpha_j = \alpha_j'$, so the difference between the two sets of coefficients is due to the departure of the data from independence. The fourth column of Table 2.7 reports α_j' for the Brazilian data. The fifth column contains the α_j.

Figure 2.1 shows the disparity between α_j (SHD) and α_j' (biased). The large difference between SHD and biased estimates of structural mobility arises because the biased α_j', like the index of dissimilarity, are based solely on the marginal distributions; they fail to take into account the very strong association between origins and destinations in these data.[13] They therefore understate the force of structural mobility to a significant extent. In the interpretation of these results, it may prove useful to think of the association between origins and destinations as the amount of inertia in the system that must be overcome by the force of structural mobility. A strong association between origins and destinations means that a large proportion of sons are going to end up in the same occupational category as their fathers, regardless of how much structural mobility there is. In contrast, a weak association means that sons are being redistributed anyway; structural mobility does not have to operate on the residual left over from a large immobile population. Therefore, if we observe the same dissimilarity between origins and destinations in two societies, one with a strong association between origins destinations and the other with a weak association, the conclusion is *not* that structural mobility is the same in the two societies, but that the force of structural mobility must be greater in the society with a strong effect of origins on destinations than in the other society.

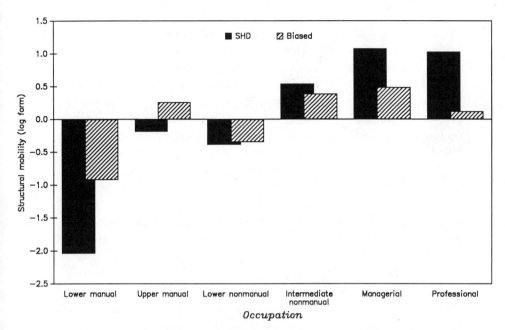

Figure 2.1 Unbiased (SHD) and biased estimates of structural mobility: men, São Paulo, Brazil, 1956.

For large mobility tables, the SHD model yields a great number of association parameters (δ_{ij}). If there are R occupational categories, then the number of δ_{ij} parameters is $\frac{1}{2} R (R - 1)$. In this study, most tables use the 14 or 16 occupational categories in Table 2.5 for origins and destinations. Fitting the SHD model to a 14 $\times$ 14 table yields 91 δ_{ij} parameters to interpret; a 16 $\times$ 16 table yields 120 δ_{ij} parameters. The more parameters that there are to interpret, the more difficult it is to make sense of the results. Therefore, many of the analyses here use the techniques of log-linear modeling to search for simpler models.

Association models (Goodman 1979a; Clogg 1982a,b; Hout 1983) are a logical place to start the search for simpler models. They use few parameters, so they are statistically efficient and conceptually simple. They accord well with the model of the stratification process employed in the status attainment literature (Duncan 1979; Logan 1983). They simplify comparisons across substrata of a single population and across populations. For many of the analyses in this study, a related model developed by Hout (1984a) is used to reduce the numbers of association parameters. The starting point for the specification of this model is the uniform association model (Duncan 1979; see also Goodman 1979a). The uniform association model specifies a single parameter for the association between origins and destinations. That parameter is related to the correlation coefficient if the categorization is a partition of an underlying bivariate normal distribution; for other, more general bivariate distributions the uniform association parameter possesses a number of desirable statistical properties, and perhaps more important, it does not have a number of undesirable properties attributed to the correlation coefficient (Goodman 1985a).

The uniform association model can be written in *multiplicative* form:

$$F_{ij} = \alpha_j \beta_i \beta_j \theta^{ij} \tag{2.7}$$

where $\Pi_j \alpha_j = 1$ (for all j) and $\beta_i = \beta_j$ (for $i = j$). Substituting equation (2.7) into equation (2.6) implies that $\delta_{ij} = (\theta^{(i-j)(i-j)})^{-1/2}$. A *log-linear* expression for equation (2.7) is

$$\log F_{ij} = a_j + b_i + b_j + u X_i X_j \tag{2.8}$$

where $\Sigma_j a_j = 0$ (for all j), $b_i = b_j$ (for $i = j$), $X_i = i$, and $\log \delta_{ij} = -\frac{1}{2} u (i-j)^2$. The logit form highlights the analogy between uniform association and a regression model:

$$\Phi_{ij} = \log (F_{ij} / F_{ij'}) \tag{2.9a}$$

$$= \alpha_j^* + \beta_j^* X_i \tag{2.9b}$$

where $\alpha_j^* = (a_j - a_{j'}) + (b_j - b_{j'})$, and $\beta_j^* = u (X_j - X_{j'})$.

Mobility tables typically have a preponderance of cases on the diagonal, at least more than uniform association or most other general models predict. For that reason special dummy variables are frequently added to models such as uniform association in order to control for excessive immobility (or "occupational inheritance," as it is sometimes somewhat erroneously called).[14] The expected frequencies under this "quasi-uniform association" model are (in log-linear form)

$$\log F_{ij} = a_j + b_i + b_j + u X_i X_j + d_i Z_{ij} \tag{2.10}$$

where $\Sigma_j a_j = 0$ (for all j), $b_i = b_j$ (for $i = j$), $X_i = i$, and $Z_{ij} = 1$ (if $i = j$) or 0 (otherwise). The logit form is

$$\Phi_{ij} = \alpha_j^* + \beta_j^* X_i + \delta_{ij}^* \tag{2.11}$$

where $\alpha_j^* = (\alpha_j - \alpha_{j'}) + (b_j - b_{j'})$, $\beta_j^* = u (X_j - X_{j'})$, and $\delta_{ij}^* = d_i (Z_{ij} - Z_{ij'})$.

As Haberman (1974; 1979, pp. 417–418) points out, the stipulation that $X_i = i$ is arbitrary. Any known scores can be substituted for the category numbers; that is, X_i can take any values that make sense. This observation can be refined even more by specifying multiple X's—one for each of the dimensions of occupational mobility to be considered (Hout 1984a). Furthermore, the independent variables (X's) can be used to scale the diagonal effects as well as the main association effects. In log-linear form the expected frequencies under a multidimensional model with an arbitrary number of independent variables (indexed by k) are

$$\log F_{ij} = a_j + b_i + b_j + \Sigma_k u_k X_{ki} X_{kj} + \Sigma_k d_k X_{ki}^2 Z_{ij} \qquad (2.12)$$

and in logit form

$$\Phi_{ij} = \alpha_j^* + \Sigma_k \beta_{kj}^* X_{ki} + \Sigma_k \delta_{kj}^* X_{ki} \qquad (2.13)$$

where $\alpha_j^* = (a_j - a_{j'}) + (b_j - b_{j'})$, $\beta_{kj}^* = u_k (X_{kj} - X_{kj'})$, $\delta_{kj}^* = d_k (X_{kj} Z_{ij} - X_{kj'} Z_{ij'})$.

The multidimensional model has a number of substantive and methodological advantages. Chief among them is the close fit between verbal and mathematical formulations of the mobility process. The dependence of occupational destinations on social origins is a continuous relationship that is disturbed by a large stochastic element—what Jencks (1972) calls luck. Duncan's formulation captures both the continuous and the stochastic aspects of the mobility process in one formulation (Duncan and Hodge 1963; Duncan 1966a,b; Blau and Duncan 1967; Duncan, Featherman, and Duncan 1972; Duncan 1979). This synthesis accounts for the appeal and power of Duncan's models. The most glaring weakness of these models is their dependence on socioeconomic status as the one and only salient dimension of occupational stratification. Yet while the socioeconomic status of occupations probably does dominate the mobility process, considerable evidence implicates other dimensions as well (Hout 1984a). The model in equation (2.13) preserves the advantages of Duncan's formulations while adding to them the prospect that dimensions other than socioeconomic status may also contribute to the association between origins and destinations. The close fit between verbal and mathematical formulations is a distinct aid in interpreting the results of fitting equation (2.13) to data. Because the parameters succinctly model the substantive concerns of the mobility researcher, their meaning is more readily apparent than is the appropriate interpretation for the parameters of other kinds of log-linear models, especially topological models (Hauser 1978, 1979; Hout 1983, pp. 46–51).

Multidimensional models of the form of equation (2.13) have advantages over multidimensional approaches that are not based on log-linear models, and certainly they have an advantage over the many multidimensional approaches that are not based on any well-specified model of the mobility process. As a statistical model, equation (2.13) specifies the process generating the statistical fit in advance of actually fitting the data. Most other methods used to examine the dimensionality of occupational mobility are not models at all; they are data reduction techniques modified for service in a theoretically informed enterprise that really requires a model. Cluster analysis, canonical correlation, smallest space analysis, and other forms of multidimensional scaling are all exploratory methods (Blau and Duncan 1967, pp. 67–75; Klatzky and Hodge 1971; Hope 1972; Horan 1974; Vannemann 1977; Featherman and Hauser 1978, pp. 30–37; Haller and Hodge 1983). They give researchers little or no control over the data analysis and search routine. Researchers can choose the number of dimensions to be extracted from the data, but they cannot specify in advance the substantive content of those dimensions. In the end, the statistical algorithm spits out coefficients leaving researchers on their own to make sense of the results.

A technical problem compounds the lack of control over the analysis, in that these methods generate second dimensions that are orthogonal to the first dimension by construction.[15] The possibility that any important variables are uncorrelated with socioeconomic status must be regarded as remote. So it is no wonder that the results are hard to interpret; the statistical algorithms provide researchers with an image that is not the second variable itself but its residual stripped of covariance with socioeconomic status. Thus, the results are hard to replicate from data set to data set or from method to method. The correlation between socioeconomic status and other factors is bound to change somewhat from sample to sample, and each method differs from the others in the way that it purges that correlation (no matter what its magnitude). Under such circumstances, interpretation of the results is closer to divination than to hypothesis testing. This limitation of prevailing methodology manifests itself in the "volatility" of interpretations offered for the results of previous research (Featherman and Hauser 1978, p. 34).

Despite researchers' difficulties in finding substantive interpretations for their results, each analysis of American data has turned up something in the pattern of mobility which suggests that the persistence of socioeconomic status from one generation to the next does not exhaust the association between occupational origins and destinations. Equation (2.13) offer a method for analyzing the dimensionality of mobility in Ireland without giving up the substance of continuous, stochastic modeling and without stumbling into interpretational difficulties.

The model in equation (2.13) offers an interpretation of *immobility* that is an advance over prior methodologies—both those that are based on log-linear models and those that are not—by scaling the relative sizes of diagonal cells to variables of interest. Many studies delete the diagonal or, equivalently, treat each diagonal cell as a special case with its own parameter (Goodman 1965, 1969b, 1972a, 1979a,b; Blau and Duncan 1967, pp. 44–48; Hauser et al. 1975a,b; Featherman and Hauser 1978, pp. 76ff; Duncan 1979; Brieger 1981; Clogg 1981; Yamaguchi 1983; Hauser 1984). Duncan (1979) and others have decried the ad hoc nature of this approach. Clogg (1981), however, argues that each diagonal cell contains a residual class of "stayers"—individuals who will not change their occupational category owing to an unspecified social inertia. This is not a viable interpretation. It has both conceptual and methodological flaws. First, the concept of social inertia, vague as it is, hardly applies to most of the excess immobility that is observed. For example, consider the occupations "judge" and "schoolteacher." In many classifications (though not in the one used here), judges and high-school teachers are coded in the same category: salaried professional, upper nonmanual, white collar. Yet in what sense is the son of a judge who becomes a high-school teacher exhibiting social inertia? In principle, statistical models could be developed to adjust somehow for this phenomenon (e.g., Spilerman 1972), but so far successful models have not appeared. The estimated proportion of stayers in the diagonal cells of a mobility table should increase as the number of occupational categories is increased, because more categories mean more homogeneity within categories (namely, a greater margin for the effects of inertia). In practice, the opposite occurs. It is no surprise that the proportion of the sample in diagonal cells increases as the number of categories decreases; what is surprising is the tendency for estimates of stayers among those immobile cases to increase as well—such as Clogg's (1981) comparison of 5 × 5 and 8 × 8 tables for Britain.[16]

The multidimensional model also provides some insight into the properties of the association parameters in the SHD model (equation 2.4). The following equation spells out the relationship between the models in equations (2.4) and (2.13):

$$\log \delta_{ij} = -\tfrac{1}{2} [\Sigma_k u_k (X_{ki} - X_{kj})^2 + \Sigma_k d_k (X_{ki}^2 + X_{kj}^2)] \tag{2.14}$$

Recall that the δ_{ij} parameters measure association "negatively" relative to the usual conventions. In view of this fact, equation (2.14) shows that a strong association ensues when a pair of categories i and j are separated by a large difference on one or more variables that affect mobility, that the impact of a difference of some given magnitude is proportional to the effect of that dimension on mobility (u_k), and that high net immobility (indexed by a significant diagonal parameter d_k) also increases association.

Another perspective on equation (2.14) might interpret log δ_{ij} as an index of exchange mobility due to weak association. This quantity is measured directly by the log δ_{ij} parameters; that is, a high value for the parameter means a high rate of exchange mobility due to weak association. Equation (2.14) means that a high rate of exchange mobility can be expected between some pair of occupations i and j due to weak association only if those occupations are close on all significant dimensions of mobility and if there is no significant net immobility in either occupation. Exchange mobility due to weak association decreases if the difference between occupational categories i and j on any significant dimension increases (the size of that effect is proportional to the size of the effect of the dimension in question on mobility process, namely on u_k). Exchange mobility due to weak association also decreases if either occupational category is high on a dimension that has a significant positive effect on immobility or if either occupational category is low on a dimension that has a significant negative effect on immobility.

Some hypothetical calculations can illuminate the complexities of the relationship between the multidimensional and QS models. Table 2.8 provides illustrative calculations, showing five hypothetical occupations with their scores on three hypothetical dimensions that are related to occupational mobilty by parameter values. Occupation 1 scores high on all three dimensions. Occupation 2 is very similar. Occupation 3 scores somewhat lower on the first dimension and much lower on the second dimension. Occupation 4 is low on the first and third dimensions but intermediate on the second. Occupation 5 is the converse of occupation 3, with very low scores on the first and third dimensions and a high score on the second dimension. The values of δ_{ij} show that exchange mobility due to weak association is highest between the pair of occupations that are most similar (1 and 2). In all other pairs, the occupations differ substantially on at low rates of exchange mobility due to weak association. Indeed, except for occupations 1 and 2, association is very strong and exchange due to association is correspondingly low.

Several vertical dimensions are measured in anticipation that the main dimension of occupational mobility in Ireland will be some aspect of

Table 2.8
Relationship between multidimensional models
and the SHD model: hypothetical data

$i \setminus j$	Scores			δ_{ij}				
	1	2	3	1	2	3	4	5
1	70	70	70	1.000				
2	65	70	65	.957	1.000			
3	50	20	70	.045	.058	1.000		
4	30	50	25	.037	.071	.134	1.000	
5	20	70	20	.013	.029	.011	.573	1.000
Parameters								
u_k	.0030	.0020	.0005					
d_k	.0005	.0030	.0040					

socioeconomic standing. The analysis includes prestige, socioeconomic status, educational credentials, and income. Prestige for occupational category *j* is the mean on the Hope-Goldthorpe scale for the combinations of occupation and employment status that fall into category *j* (Goldthorpe and Hope 1974). Socioeconomic status is the average of two other measures: the proportion of workers in category *j* who completed primary school education and the proportion of workers in category *j* with an annual income from this occupation of over £2,500.[17] Education and income enter the analysis separately as well as in combination.

There is also reason to believe that labor market segmentation plays a role in occupational mobility in Ireland (Goldthorpe 1980, pp. 39–42). Answers to the question "How did you get this job?" are used to classify each occupational group according to the kind of labor markets it recruits from. The responses are grouped into five means of obtaining jobs:

1. Bureaucratic entry (by applying at an employment or personnel office, answering advertisements, or making other unsolicited approaches to an employer)
2. Bureaucratic advancement (by promotion or recruitment)
3. Enterprise (by starting a business or buying property)
4. Personal contacts (by inheriting property, working in a family business, or being hired on the recommendation of family member or friend)
5. Miscellaneous other means

Then a 16 × 5 table cross-classifying type of recruitment by occupational category is formed to reveal the percentage of each occupation's incumbents who got their job through each of the means. The percent in row *i* and column *j* of that table is the score for occupation *i* on market dimension *j*. For example, among salaried professionals and managers in large enterprises (class Ib), 34 percent applied for their job or obtained it through a related "bureaucratic entry," 56 percent were promoted ("bureaucratic advance"), 1 percent claimed to have started the business (an apparent misclassification of either the employment status or the means of obtaining the job), 1 percent obtained the job through personal contacts, and 8 percent gave a response that did not fit any of these four categories (including men who gave no answer). Thus class Ib is scored 34 on bureaucratic entry, 56 on bureaucratic advance, 1 on enterprise, and 1 on personal contact. The scores on all dimensions are displayed in Table 2.9.

Event History Analysis

Mobility tables approach time in discrete intervals. They make it possible to view a social process at the beginning and the end of some period of interest. This approach is well suited to the usual social-science data on origins and destinations. The Irish Mobility Study is much richer in detail about timing and number of events than is the usual mobility study. The work history component of this study allows a continuous view of time from first job to interview. A mobility table is still needed to view the transition from origins to first job, but subsequent shifts can be modeled for all time points from one month to many years. These data free the researcher from the beginning-and-ending approach of mobility table analysis (although the beginning and ending still occupy a prominent place in the analysis scheme). To take advantage of this richness, we need a different statistical approach. This approach is known as event history analysis.

Statistically, as in everyday language, an *event* is a change from one condition to another in continuous (real) time. In the Irish study, each job change of each subject is an event.[18] The dependent variable in an event history analysis is the *rate* at which events occur; the independent variables include all of the substantive variables of interest plus time itself. The objective of event history analysis is to estimate the net effect of each independent variable on the rate, controlling for time (Coleman 1981; Carroll 1983; Tuma and Hannan 1984; Allison 1985).

To be precise about event history analysis, we must give mathematical expression to some terms. Also, for ease of reference, certain recurrent

Table 2.9
Scores for dimensions of occupational mobility

Occupation	Code	SES	Prestige	Primary education	Income >£2500	Bureaucratic		Enterprise	Personal contact
						Entry	Advance		
Professionals & proprietors I[a]	Ia	92	76	96	89	10	20	55	15
Professionals & managers I	Ib	88	69	93	83	34	56	1	1
Professionals & managers II	II	78	60	91	65	34	50	0	12
Clerical & sales workers	IIIa	72	42	89	54	47	36	0	12
Proprietors with employees[a]	IVa	59	51	61	56	8	3	66	20
Proprietors without employees[a]	IVb	34	48	38	31	15	1	73	10
Service workers	IIIb	43	31	52	34	41	24	0	34
Unpaid workers, nonfarm	VIInf	21	31	70	24	0	0	0	99
Technicians & foremen	V	52	47	64	39	31	56	0	11
Skilled manual workers	VI	45	38	55	35	47	26	0	22
Semiskilled manual workers	VIIss	32	30	36	28	55	21	1	20
Unskilled manual workers	VIIus	21	18	18	24	66	14	0	18
Farmers with employees[a]	IVc	48	58	44	53	8	7	26	57
Farmers without employees[a]	IVd	16	37	18	14	3	3	25	61
Agricultural workers	VIIf	12	31	6	18	35	8	0	54
Unpaid workers, farm	VIIIf	12	31	36	18	0	0	0	99

a.   Self–employed workers.

relationships between rates and time are given names, so that the equations do not have to be hauled out every time a reference is needed. One of the most imposing parts of event history analysis is learning this new vocabulary.

To begin, think of an individual (represented by the letter h) who has a job. Assign a number to each of the jobs that the individual has worked, using integers from 1 for the first job to some number K for the last job that the individual will ever take.[19] Include in the count spells of unemployment and spells out of the labor force. Use the letter k to represent the number of any specific job.[20] In this scheme, an event is the movement of individual h from one job to the next, that is, from job k to job k' (where k' is short for $k + 1$). When an event occurs, a clock starts. The time elapsed on that clock at any point is represented by t_k; the time elapsed on the clock when the next event occurs is represented by T_k. The clock keeps running after the shift from k to k' occurs, that is, $t_k > T_k$ exists, but a new clock with elapsed time $t_{k'}$ starts at zero when $t_k = T_k$.[21] The period between one event and the next is called a *spell*; T_k is the duration of the kth spell.

The terms t_k and T_k measure time relative to an event in an individual's life. Sometimes a measure of real time is needed. Let the symbol τ represent real time measured from some arbitrary point before the first event in the data set, such as midnight of 1 January 1900. The formal definitions below require a symbol that relates the job count k to real time. Let $Y_h(\tau)$ be that symbol so that $Y_h(\tau) = k$.

Although individual h actually moves from job k to job k' at time T_k, there is no reason to think that things were certain to turn out that way. Other events might have been just as likely or even more likely to occur. In fact, it is useful to think about an individual's having a distribution of probabilities of experiencing an event at each time from $t = 0$ (that is, the time when he entered his kth job) until $t = \omega$, the time of his retirement from the work force or death.[22] Because time is continuous, it is conventional to refer to the continuous time probability distribution as a *density* function. The only constraint on the probability density function is that the accumulated density over all time (that is, integrated over the range from $t = 0$ to $t = \omega$) is less than one.[23] Let $f_{hk}(t)$ be the symbol for the density at time t, that is, for the probability of an event during the infinitesimal time interval between t and Δt for individual h in his kth job. Formally:

$$f_{hk}(t) = \lim_{\Delta t \to 0} \frac{\text{prob}\,[t < T_k < (t + \Delta t)]}{\Delta t} \qquad (2.15)$$

The formal definition of the *rate* is closely related to the probability density:

$$r_{hk}(t) = \lim_{\Delta\tau\to0} \frac{\text{prob}\,[Y(\tau + \Delta\tau) = k' \mid Y(\tau) = k]}{\Delta\tau} \tag{2.16}$$

The event history analysis consists of the multiple regression of $\log r_{hk}(t)$ on a set of independent variables (Cox 1975):

$$\log r_{hk}(t) = \alpha(t) + \Sigma_p\, \beta_p\, X_{hp} + \Sigma_q\, \delta_q\, Z_{hq}(t) \tag{2.17}$$

where $\alpha(t)$ is a time-varying baseline rate that may be estimated by imposing some constraints (such as $\alpha(t) = \phi + \theta t$ [for $\theta < 0$]) or may be treated as a nuisance function and partialed out of the estimation routine (Cox 1975); $p = 1, \ldots, P$ is an index for the independent variables that are constant throughout the spell (such as the prestige of job k, the educational credentials of individual h, the employment status of individual h in job k); $q = 1, \ldots, Q$ is an index for the independent variables that vary with time through the spell (such as the marital status of individual h, the amount of work experience h has, the initiation of some economic reform at real time τ); and β_p and δ_q are parameters to be estimated.

Equation (2.17) is interpreted as a regression equation, but ordinary regression techniques do not apply. In particular, while we observe $Y(\tau)$, T_k, the X_{ph}, and the $Z_{qh}(t)$, we do not observe $r_{hk}(t)$. $Y(\tau)$ and T_k are related to $r_{hk}(t)$, but usual regression procedures have to be altered in order to take those relationships into account. Furthermore, every individual h in the sample is in the labor force by definition of the sampling frame. That simple fact means that nobody in the sample has reached ω (their ultimate date of labor force participation), so the interview interrupts an ongoing job spell (k^*) for every individual h at some time (t^*). For these spells we know that $t^* < T_{k^*}$. This incomplete but useful information must also be entered into the estimation procedure.

The phenomenon of interrupting the event history in the course of gathering observations, usually by interviewing current job holders, is referred to as *censoring*. To understand how information about censored observations are entered in the estimation procedure, we must define a function based on $r_{hk}(t)$. To this point, job change has been the focus of discussion. What about the men who are left unchanged at some time t? The function that describes the "stayer" part of the process is called the *survival* function or the *survivorship*. Formally, the survival function at time t_k is the probability that T_k is greater than t_k, which works out mathematically to:

$$\lambda_k(t) = \text{prob } [T_k \geq t_k] = \exp\left[-\int_0^t r_{hk}(s)ds\right] \qquad (2.18)$$

where λ_k is the label for the survivorship. This equation makes good sense. The higher the rates for times preceding t_k, the lower the probability of surviving as long at t_k without an event.

The survival function is important for estimation in event history analysis in three ways. First, nonparametric estimates of $\lambda_k(t)$ are available on the computer package SPSS[X] (Kaplan and Meier 1958). Second, parametric models that estimate the β and δ coefficients in equation (2.17) use $\lambda_k(t)$ in the estimation procedure (Cox 1975). Finally, the distribution of $\lambda_k(t)$ over time indicates the relationship between the rate of change $[r_{hk}(t)]$ and time. If $r_{hk}(t)$ is constant, then the plot of log $\lambda_k(t)$ against t will look like a straight line. Similarly, the cumulative hazard function (also called the cumulative mobility rate) will be linearly related to t because $H_k(t) = -\log \lambda_k(t)$.

Most treatments of the application of event history analysis do not give as much special attention to the event count (k) as is the case here. In particular, most treatments of event history analysis do not use the k subscript. The k appears in this exposition because it helps keep the time references clear by distinguishing between the durations of different jobs, and between duration in a job and real time (τ). In the substantive analyses in this study, as in substantive work by others, spells of different number but the same duration are combined; that is, $r_{hk}(t_k) = r_h(t)$ for all k (e.g., Sorenson and Tuma 1981; Carroll and Mayer 1986; Mayer and Carroll 1987). This means that transitions from first jobs to second jobs are combined with shifts from second jobs to third jobs, and so forth, in order to estimate a single set of $r_h(t)$, ignoring k.

However, the rate of movement into some destinations might differ from movement into other destinations. This is an important source of heterogeneity in the analysis of job shifts in Ireland. At that point mobility into some occupations is viewed as being a different process with different β coefficients than is mobility into some other occupations. This kind of heterogeneity is captured by defining a new censoring variable that treats job spells as incomplete if either they are interrupted by the interview (as usual) or they involve a shift to an occupation other than one under study. In particular, eight destination strata are distinguished in the analysis: upper nonmanual employee, lower nonmanual, self-employed lower nonmanual, upper manual, lower manual, farmer, farm worker, and unemployed. A job spell for a worker who moves from being a clerk in a store to being the store manager (a move from lower nonmanual to upper non-manual) would be treated as a completed job spell when the dependent variable is the rate of movement into upper nonmanual occupations but as a censored job spell for all of the other dependent variables, that is, for the rates of movement into other occupational strata. The logic is that the risk of moving from his clerk's job into a job in a stratum other than upper non-manual was interrupted for worker h when he moved into the managerial position. If there are many cases of clerk-to-manager moves and few clerk-to-laborer moves, presumably the rate of movement from lower nonmanual to upper nonmanual is higher than the rate of movement from lower nonmanual to lower manual. But the fact that a move from lower nonmanual to upper nonmanual occurred before a move to lower manual in this case does not mean that individual h would never move to a lower manual position. Given enough time, he might have. In this sense, the move to an upper nonmanual job censored the ability to observe the process of moving from lower nonmanual to lower manual. Therefore, the move is treated as a completed job spell for one outcome and as a censored job spell for all of the other outcomes.

3   Exchange, Structure, and Mobility

The Republic of Ireland greeted the 1970s with a national sense of accomplishment. The Irish of the South expressed a justifiable pride in the economic gains of the 1960s and the reversal of emigration (Walsh 1979). As they prepared to join the EEC in 1973, the Irish sensed that their society had been transformed. Growth had brought prosperity to many occupations. Significantly, this transformation had redistributed the labor force away from traditional pursuits in the direction of a more modern economy of services and manufacturing.

The mood and sense of place in Northern Ireland offered a somber contrast. The "troubles"—the euphemism for unionist-nationalist warfare—draped the province in mourners' black crepe. The political struggle overwhelmed economic considerations in setting the mood of the times. Yet ironically, there was as much reason for hope for a bright employment outlook in the North as in the Republic. If one cared to look beyond the car bombings, signs of growth, development, and industrial restructuring could be seen. Northern Ireland had shared in some of the dynamism of a very prosperous decade for the United Kingdom, especially between the mid-1950s and the onset of the troubles in 1968.

With 20/20 hindsight, the astute observer could probably also see the signals of economic hardships to come for both parts of the island. Inflation and unemployment were on the rise in both the Republic and Northern Ireland as the 1960s drew to a close. But it was not until the Arab oil embargo in 1973–1974, with its disastrous consequences for the world economy, that prospects throughout Ireland ebbed.

Regardless of the outlook for the late 1970s, the 1960s had brought unprecedented growth to the island as a whole and to the Irish Republic in particular. The fundamental question for this study concerns the theoretical link between growth and mobility. As a case in point, what are the implications of Irish economic growth for the work lives of Irish people? How had the economies of the two parts of the island distributed the spoils of growth?

By 1973 Ireland had the semblance of a modern division of labor. A professional service class had emerged to complement the old middle class of shopkeepers and employing farmers. An industrial working class outnumbered the agricultural working class of small farmers, farm laborers, and urban low-skill service workers. Who occupied the new positions? It would be naive to think that the salaried professional and managerial positions went to a cross-section of workers proportionately drawn from the array of social origins. Nonetheless, inequality of opportunity is a matter of degree. The task here is to quantify the inequality, to use mobility data to answer the rhetorical question, Was privilege in the Irish social structure of the 1950s bankable in the Ireland of the 1970s? Or had modern Ireland so restructured the division of labor that privilege in the old system brought no advantage in the new?

Only a pollyanna would believe that economic growth obliterated privilege altogether. Yet the theoretical proposition to be tested is that industrial development is accompanied by a leveling of privilege. The competitive bases of modern industrial and professional employment are thought to undermine the ascriptive bases of property privilege in traditional Ireland (Smelser and Lipset 1966). A detailed examination of that proposition begins by measuring the association between socioeconomic origins and destinations for Irish workers at the peak of Ireland's economic growth in the winter of 1973–74. Workers employed during that winter got to their current positions amid the greatest economic advance in Irish history.

The descriptive account of mobility in Ireland is based on some of the more commonly used measures of mobility. Because these indexes leave the fundamental questions unanswered or ambiguously answered, the analysis then turns to more complicated but more realistic models of mobility processes that make it possible to assess the important questions of distribution and inequality in Ireland at the peak of modern prosperity.

Descriptive Measures of Occupational Mobility

The occupations of Irish workers in 1973 differ markedly from their origins.[1] The economic and demographic changes in Irish society (perhaps accompanied by other changes) contribute to a readily apparent dissimilarity between the contemporary opportunity structure and the backgrounds of contemporary workers. Most obvious is the "surplus" of farmers' sons. In both the Republic and Northern Ireland the number of opportunities in farming falls far short of the number of men with backgrounds in farming. There are also fewer farm laborers than sons of farm laborers. These figures may actually understate the shortfall of contemporary opportunities in agriculture if farmers' sons made up the bulk of the emigrants who did not subsequently return to Ireland to work.

In contrast with declining rural pursuits, urban proprietorships show relatively little net change, especially in Northern Ireland. Independent professional practice also shows little dissimilarity between the origin and destination totals.

The shortfall of farming opportunities is balanced by a surplus of white-collar positions. The number of salaried professional, managerial, sales, and clerical positions far exceeds the number of men with white-collar backgrounds. There is also a net gain in technical, supervisory, skilled, and semi-skilled manual occupations, especially in the Republic.

A summary index of these countervailing changes in common use is the index of dissimilarity (Δ) between the distribution of origins and the distribution of destinations. The sum of positive differences, Δ, between the percentage distribution of origins and the percentage distribution of destinations (Hout 1983, pp. 12–13). It contains no information about the increase or decrease found in particular categories, but it is useful as a summary because it reduces all of the differences to a single number which is easy to remember. For the Republic of Ireland, Δ is 20.8 percent; for Northern Ireland Δ is 18.1 percent.[2] These numbers reflect the minimum amount of mobility in Northern Ireland and the Republic. In that sense, roughly one worker in five (in both societies) must find an occupation different from his father's. Substantially more did so. The gross mobility rates are 69.5 percent for the Republic and 76.0 percent for Northern Ireland.

Gross mobility rates are higher in Northern Ireland than in the Republic regardless of which classification scheme is used. Table 2.6 showed that the difference ranges from a high of 14 percent obtained by using the full detail of unit group and employment status for paid workers (UG/ES) to a low of 8 percent obtained by using the 16-category PREF + scheme.

Differences in gross mobility rates—even differences of greater magnitude than those observed here—are frequently related to differences in the distribution of occupations in the labor forces being compared (Featherman, Jones, and Hauser 1975; Erikson, Goldthorpe, and Portacarero 1982; Grusky and Hauser 1984; Hauser 1984; Erikson and Goldthorpe 1987b). The most obvious difference between the occupational structure of Northern Ireland and that of the Republic is the preponderance of farming in the Republic. Since farming typically contributes disproportionately to immobility (Erikson and Goldthorpe 1987a,b), a high concentration in farming in the Republic (relative to the concentration in farming elsewhere in Europe) is good grounds for expecting a lower gross mobility rate in the Republic than in Northern Ireland.

As a first approach to assessing the contribution of occupational structure to the difference between the Republic and the North in gross mobility, a simple log-linear analysis relating the odds on being immobile (that is, in an occupational group other than one's father) to origin and region is presented in two tables.[3] Table 3.1 shows the proportion of men from each region and origin category who are immobile.[4] Table 3.2 presents some chi-square statistics that test the hypothesis that occupational structure accounts for regional differences in immobility.

Table 3.1
Immobility rates by origin and region (including unpaid workers):
men aged 18–65, Ireland, 1973

Origin		Observed Republic	Observed Northern Ireland	Expected[a] Republic	Expected[a] Northern Ireland
Professionals & proprietors I[b]	Ia	35	20	30	25
Professionals & managers I	Ib	28	34	35	30
Professionals & managers II	II	25	32	31	27
Clerical & sales workers	IIIa	19	19	21	17
Proprietors with employees[b]	IVa	21	20	23	19
Proprietors without employees[b]	IVb	14	15	16	13
Service workers	IIIb	11	10	12	10
Technicians & foremen	V	16	14	17	14
Skilled manual workers	VI	36	29	35	30
Semiskilled manual workers	VIIss	22	26	28	23
Unskilled manual workers	VIIus	21	14	19	16
Farmers with employees[b]	IVc	28	23	28	23
Farmers without employees[b]	IVd	43	31	41	35
Agricultural laborers	VIIf	22	12	19	16
Total		30	24	30	24

a. Expected under the model of proportional differences between regions.
b. Self–employed workers.

Table 3.2
Fit of selected models to $14 \times 2 \times 2$ immobility tables:
men aged 18–65, Ireland, 1973

#	Model[a]		L^2	df	p	bic
0	[O][R][M]		395.35	40	<.01	60
1	[OR][M]		198.77	27	<.01	−28
2	[OR][MR]		180.79	26	<.01	−37
	Subtotal:	Republic	111.14	13	<.01	12
		North	69.65	13	<.01	−31
3	[OR][OM]		30.67	14	<.01	−87
4	[OR][OM][RM]		19.40	13	.11	−90

a.   O = origin; R = region; M = mobility/immobility.

Immobility varies substantially more between origin categories than it does between regions. Indeed, when contrasted with the very wide range of immobility across origin categories, the regional difference seems small.[5] It is nonetheless significant, as shown in Table 3.2.[6] The tests show that both region (R) and origins (O) affect mobility-immobility (M). Their effects are additive in the sense that the regional difference is a single adjustment downward as one moves from the Republic to Northern Ireland; the magnitude of the adjustment does not depend on origin.

In the Republic of Ireland immobility is strikingly high (43 percent) among the sons of farmers without employees. The sons of craftsmen and of self-employed professionals and large proprietors are also more immobile than average. The sons of clerical and sales workers, technicians and foremen, shopkeepers without employees, and service workers are least likely to pursue their father's occupation.

In Northern Ireland immobility is less overall than it is in the Republic of Ireland. Immobility among farmers' sons is notably less there than it is in the Republic, although still above the average for all occupations in the North (31 percent). The greatest immobility is in the salaried professions and among managers. Low immobility is found among technicians and foremen and service workers, just as in the Republic. Low immobility is also found among unskilled workers on and off farms.

There is no one comprehensive reason for high (or low) immobility in an occupation. High immobility may occur in a desirable occupation if sons have ample opportunity to enter their fathers' line of work; it may also occur in undesirable occupations if there are few opportunities for advancement. Some occupations may have structural attributes favorable to inheritance, while others clearly do not.

Proprietorial occupations tend to have high immobility for reasons related to legal inheritance and to socialization, a kind of "social inheritance" related to lifestyle and upbringing (e.g., Miller and Swanson 1958; Kohn 1969). Together these factors tend to produce high immobility, except where opportunities are limited (Hout 1984a). The importance of inheritance is abetted by the tendency for small farms and shops to rely on unpaid labor by family members who then presumably may make future claims on the farm or business.[7] Even those family members who assist on the farm or in the shop but who are not among the inheritors may be affected by the experience of farm or shop work. They may well pursue the autonomy that comes with the proprietorial way of life through some other means, typically by "marrying a farm" or shop (that is, by marrying a woman who will inherit her family's farm or business), or by buying a piece of land or a shop for which there are no heirs. In the United States sons of proprietors who do not enter self-employment nonetheless tend to enter occupations that offer at least some measure of on-the-job autonomy (Hout 1984a).

There is less inheritance—legal and social—in Northern Ireland than there is in the Republic. This is due to the smaller share of small farming in the economy of the North, not to a weaker tendency to pass on the farm among Northern farmers.

A low immobility pattern prevails in technical and supervisory occupations. This pattern is in many ways the converse of that in proprietorial occupations. The high ratio of destinations to origins suggests that these occupations may have high immobility, yet they are relatively unlikely to be passed from father to son. The key to low immobility is likely to be tied to the fact that technical and supervisory occupations lack physical capital. Instead, bureaucratic advancement that is not easily passed from father to son dominates access to these positions.

To see this in a striking way, compare technical and supervisory occupations with skilled crafts. The crafts have much higher immobility than technical and supervisory occupations. Fathers can teach their sons the trade, and then use connections to win for their sons positions in apprenticeship programs. In some circumstances they may even be able to get their sons union cards or other necessary credentials. This clout is two-edged: it can ease the passage of sons of craftsmen into crafts (whether the same craft or a different craft is not revealed in the PREF classification scheme), whereas the absence of clout handicaps men of different origins who might otherwise pursue a career in skilled manual work.

In contrast, the bureaucratic apparatus of accession to technical and supervisory positions limits these kinds of discretionary effects on immobility. Perhaps in another generation or so, the technical occupations will also acquire the traits associated with crafts. But it seems unlikely that the supervisory positions will ever show a high rate of intergenerational immobility because access to them is not under the control of the supervisors themselves. Control of hiring and promotion of supervisors rests with upper management, not with incumbent supervisors. Furthermore, the labor market for technical and supervisory positions tends to operate within firms; they are so-called internal labor markets. New positions are filled not by workers who have a skill that can be acquired outside the job setting but by workers from inside the company who are singled out by upper management for responsibility and authority. This control of access to the occupations by managers who are not themselves engaged in the occupation militates against immobility because a father is obviously constrained in the degree to which he can either train or sponsor his son.[8]

In contrast to these kinds of factors that are related to the proprietorial, technical, and supervisory occupations per se, the high rate of immobility for professions and management and the low rate of immobility for unskilled positions are related to changes in the opportunity structure. The growing number of professional and managerial positions fosters immobility among the sons of professionals and managers, while contraction at the low end of the occupational prestige scale fosters mobility. This is the contribution of structural mobility to relative rates immobility, namely, increasing immobility for some occupations and decreasing it for others.

Among sons who are mobile, there are clear patterns of movement. The model of quasi-perfect mobility is rejected for both the Republic and Northern Ireland (L^2 = 894.46; df = 209 in the Republic; and L^2 = 723.36; df = 209 in Northern Ireland).[9] There are a number of ways of discerning the patterns of movement. Table 3.3 shows a set of summary calculations that aid in finding the patterns: the destinations of mobile workers are classified into five broad strata:[10]

Stratum	PREF category
1. White collar (WC)	Ib, II, IIIa, IIIb
2. Proprietorial (P)	Ia, IVa, IVb
3. Manual (M)	V, VI, VIIss, VIIus, VIIf
4. Farm (F)	IVc, IVd
5. Unpaid (UP)	VIIIf, VIIInf

Table 3.3
Interstratum mobility rates by origin and region:
men aged 18–65, Ireland, 1973

Origin	*Republic*[a]					*Northern Ireland*[a]				
	WC	P	M	F	UP	WC	P	M	F	UP
Professionals & proprietors I[b]	55	5	0	0	5	40	15	15	10	0
Professionals & managers I	51	0	14	0	7	44	2	20	0	0
Professionals & managers II	36	9	28	3	0	35	2	29	8	1
Clerical & sales workers	39	6	34	3	0	37	10	34	0	0
Proprietors with employees[b]	41	7	25	1	6	34	6	33	4	3
Proprietors without employees[b]	21	7	48	4	5	27	11	46	0	2
Service workers	20	6	60	3	0	30	11	46	3	0
Technicians & foremen	23	9	50	3	0	30	14	40	2	0
Skilled manual workers	24	2	36	0	1	24	8	38	0	0
Semiskilled manual workers	24	6	45	2	1	20	6	47	0	1
Unskilled manual workers	13	4	58	2	2	17	4	64	1	1
Farmers with employees[b]	13	7	18	24	11	23	15	21	14	4
Farmers without employees[b]	12	6	27	4	9	10	9	39	4	6
Agricultural laborers	9	10	52	7	0	14	5	67	2	0
Overall	20	6	36	5	4	23	8	42	2	2

a. WC = white collar; P = proprietor; M = manual (including farm labor); F = farm; UP = unpaid. The totals for the rows (within region) fall short of 100 percent because immobile workers are tabulated in Table 3.1.

b. Self–employed workers.

The outflow percentages from each origin to these five destination strata show a strong class gradient. This is most clearly seen by comparing high and low prestige origins that fall within the same strata. The odds on a man's achieving one of the white-collar and proprietorial destinations are proportional to the prestige of the origin. For example, with respect to origin classes that belong to the white-collar stratum, the proportion of mobile sons attaining white-collar occupations ranges from 51 percent for sons of salaried professionals to 20 percent for sons of service workers.[11]

For the most part, upward interstratum mobility exceeds downward interstratum mobility. Within the farm stratum, however, downward mobility from IVc to IVd exceeds upward mobility from IVd to IVc.[12] With one exception (a man whose father was a salaried dentist in the Republic), unpaid work is a destination exclusive to the sons of proprietors.

Table 3.4 shows significance tests based on a log-linear analysis of the 14 × 6 × 2 table of origin by modified destination (including immobility as a sixth destination category) by region. Unlike the log-linear analysis of

Table 3.4
Fit of selected models to 14 × 6 × 2 interstratum mobility tables:
men aged 18–65, Ireland, 1973

#	Model[a]		L^2	df	p	bic
0	[O][R][M]		1225.54	148	<.01	−17
1	[OR][M]		1028.96	135	<.01	−104
2	[OR][MR]		946.14	130	<.01	−145
	Subtotal:	Republic	539.46	65	<.01	41
		North	406.68	65	<.01	−95
3	[OR][OM]		140.51	70	<.01	−447
4	[OR][OM][RM]		91.65	65	.02	−454

a.   O = origin; R = region; M = interstratum mobility.

the immobile-mobile dichotomy, this analysis uncovers a three-way inter-action among origin, destination, and region. Finding a three-way interaction like this implies that, strictly speaking, a simple summary statement, such as "There is more upward mobility in Northern Ireland," will not suffice to characterize the regional differences between the destination distributions of the origin groups. These differences are not constant. The interaction effects, however, are extremely small. Furthermore, there is no clear pattern to them, so they are ignored here. Support for ignoring the interaction effects comes from the fact that Raftery's bic chooses the model of constant regional differences—[*OR*][*OM*][*RM*].

Occupational Supply and Recruitment

Related to immobility and interstratum mobility is the issue of occupational supply and recruitment. Immobility refers to the proportion of men from a given social origin class who arrive in that class as adults. Some occupations send many sons to other occupations while taking in few sons from other origin classes. These "self-recruiting" occupations are also of special interest. Typically they have a high proportion of current incumbents who are drawn from a single occupational origin, even though a majority (or at least a large proportion) of the men from that origin class may be mobile to other occupations. Farming in the United States is such an occupation (Featherman and Hauser 1978, pp. 166–173): most farmers' sons work outside of agriculture, but nearly all farmers are farmers' sons. Table 3.5 presents the percentage of each occupational destination that is self-recruited as well as the percentage of each occupational origin that is immobile. In the absence of structural mobility, the proportion self-recruited equals the proportion immobile because in that case origin and destination totals are equal. In Ireland structural mobility is important, so the structural mobility multiplier (α_j; Sobel, Hout, and Duncan 1985) is also presented. Off-diagonal cells also contribute to differences in supply and recruitment. An occupation that serves as a channel for upward mobility might very well have a low proportion self-recruited and a low proportion immobile, but for different reasons. Most of the men recruited to such an occupation would come from occupations that have lower socioeconomic status or prestige, whereas most of the men with origins in an occupation of this type would have destinations of high standing. For that reason the index of dissimilarity between the origin distribution and the destination distribution for each occupational class is also presented. Occupational classes with low values on this index recruit from the same occupational classes to which they send their sons; occupational classes with high values on this index have divergent patterns of supply and recruitment. The minimum value for this index is the index of dissimilarity

Table 3.5
Indexes of supply and recruitment by origin and region:
men aged 18–65, Ireland, 1973

Origin	Republic[a]					Northern Ireland[a]				
	SR	IM	α_j	Δ_j	Δ_j/Δ_t	SR	IM	α_j	Δ_j	Δ_j/Δ_t
Ia	30	35	1.71	55	2.62	14	20	2.20	22	1.22
Ib	8	28	5.38	60	2.86	13	34	4.55	40	2.22
II	13	25	2.57	37	1.76	17	32	2.95	35	1.94
IIIa	12	19	1.96	37	1.76	12	19	2.31	29	1.61
IVa	29	21	.77	38	1.81	22	20	1.12	33	1.83
IVb	19	14	.66	43	2.05	14	15	1.03	33	1.83
IIIb	5	11	2.43	39	1.86	7	10	1.76	28	1.56
V	8	16	2.00	33	1.57	9	14	1.96	32	1.78
VI	29	36	1.44	28	1.33	26	29	1.36	22	1.22
VIIss	17	22	1.26	33	1.57	25	26	1.12	27	1.50
VIIus	25	21	.75	34	1.62	18	14	.76	28	1.56
IVc	63	28	.12	34	1.62	68	23	.09	52	2.89
IVd	77	43	.15	40	1.90	75	31	.13	55	3.06
VIIf	38	22	.37	34	1.62	29	12	.30	52	2.89
Overall	30	30	1.00	21	1.00	24	24	1.00	18	1.00

a. Symbols for the columns are: SR = self–recruited; IM = immobile; α_j = structural mobility multiplier; Δ_j = index of dissimilarity between origins and destinations for occupation j; Δ_t = index of dissimilarity between origins and destinations for total labor force. See Table 3.1 for category labels.

between the origin marginal and the destination marginal, so the ratio of the occupation-specific indexes to the index for the entire population is also presented.[13]

Self-recruitment patterns in the Republic of Ireland and in Northern Ireland are very similar ($r = .95$). Farming (classes IVc and IVd) and agricultural labor (class VIIf) are big self-recruiters. The first two of these also have high immobility. The rapidly growing white-collar and technical occupations cannot rely on self-recruitment; they score low on this index. Self-recruitment and immobility are strongly correlated in the Republic of Ireland ($r = .60$). They are less so in Northern Ireland ($r = .36$), but with so few cases, the difference is not statistically reliable at the .05 level. The regional differences in immobility are slightly greater than the regional differences in self-recruitment.

Structural mobility leaves little margin for self-recruitment in growing occupations and leaves little room for any but the offspring of incumbents in declining occupations. Evidence supporting this proposition can be found in the strong negative correlation between self-recruitment and structural mobility in both regions; that is, growing occupations have much lower levels of self-recruitment than do declining occupations. The correlation between the additive coefficient of structural mobility ($\log \alpha_j$) and percent self-recruited is $-.90$ in the Republic and $-.89$ in Northern Ireland.

The distributions of supply and recruitment within particular occupations differ far more than do the origins and destinations per se in each region (compare the overall index of dissimilarity with indexes for specific occupations). The indexes of dissimilarity between supply and recruitment for the Republic are uncorrelated with those in the North, so the discussion will have to distinguish between region at each point. In the Republic the highest prestige occupations (classes Ia and Ib) have the most dissimilar patterns of supply and recruitment because the sons of professionals are highly concentrated in professions, while contemporary professionals are drawn from a very diverse combination of social origins. Skilled manual occupations have the most similar origin and destination distributions, but dissimilarity is still quite high for this class (28 percent). In Northern Ireland it is the agricultural occupations (classes IVc, IVd, and VIIf) that have the most dissimilar patterns of supply and recruitment. The occupations with the most similarity are independent professions and crafts; both of these occupations come close to the minimum of 18 percent (the dissimilarity of the origin and destination marginals).

These data bear on the so-called closure thesis (Goldthorpe and

Llewellyn 1977) that posits an upper limit to mass mobility imposed on self-recruitment by upper management and the independent professions. Goldthorpe (1980, pp. 42–46) criticizes this view, associated with Bottomore, Miliband, Giddens, and others who argue that British society is closed at the top. The self-recruitment of Goldthorpe's class I (which includes classes Ia and Ib of the present scheme) is 25 percent; the remainder of the British elite appears to be drawn from nonelite origins. Over a quarter (28 percent of nonfarm origin men) are from working- class backgrounds. Whelan and Whelan (1984, pp. 52–58) find less openness in their Dublin samples of 1969 and 1972. Their figure for elite self-recruitment is 35 percent. They find an even higher proportion self-recruited among independent professionals and industrial managers (51 percent and 41 percent, respectively) when they subdivide class I. This is substantial self-recruitment, but not the absolute closure that some writers envision. The national sample of Irish workers under study here reveals less elite self-recruitment in the Republic-as-a-whole than Whelan and Whelan found in Dublin— less than Goldthorpe found in Britain when classes Ia (30 percent self-recruitment) and Ib (8 percent) are combined. Small numbers of elites in the sample make inferences tenuous, but in the national sample the numbers of elites from class Ia or class Ib origins are as follows: 3 of 14 self-employed professionals of higher grade, 10 of 51 salaried professionals of higher grade, 5 of 37 administrators and officials of higher grade, 1 of 11 managers in large industrial firms, and neither of the 2 self-employed professionals of lower grade. In Northern Ireland self-recruitment of elites is even less pronounced: 14 percent for class Ia and 13 percent for class Ib. The occupational and industrial structures of Dublin probably account for at least part of the relatively high degree of closure within the Irish capital. Thus the Irish elite is not as closed, the closure theorists argue, as elite ranks in capitalist societies are. Outside Dublin elite positions in Irish society are no more closed to men of nonelite backgrounds than are elite positions in British society. In fact, Ireland is probably less closed in this respect.

Structural Mobility

Structural mobility creates opportunities in some destinations and limits them in other destinations for all workers, regardless of their social origins. This type of mobility results from the disparity between the distribution of contemporary occupations and the distribution of social origins among contemporary workers. In this report, as in Sobel, Hout, and Duncan (SHD), structural mobility is defined as those forces that redistribute workers of fixed origins into the contemporary distribution of occupational niches in a way that is independent of social origins.

Two related indexes of structural mobility are structural mobility multipliers (α_j, for occupation $j = 1$ to 14) and structural mobility ratios (log [α_j/α_i], for pairs of occupations i and j). The structural mobility multipliers are the parameters of the SHD expression for the model of quasi-symmetry (QS). A value of $\alpha_j > 1$ means that structural mobility favors occupation j; conversely $\alpha_j < 1$ means that structural mobility depletes the ranks of occupation j. The α_j reflect the overall tendency of structural mobility. But mobility is ultimately a relational concept. The forces of structural mobility affect each occupation, but the effects are reflected more than anywhere else in the relative flows of manpower from i to j and back from j to i. In the absence of structural mobility, QS devolves into the model of symmetry, in which case the flows from i to j equal the flows back from j to i; that is, $F_{ij} = F_{ji}$. The departure from symmetry due to structural mobility is reflected in the significance and magnitude of the α_j, but ratios of the form log (α_j/α_i) measure more clearly the effect of structural mobility on flows between pairs of occupations. If log (α_j/α_i) > 0, then the flow from i to j exceeds the flow back from j to i; if log (α_j/α_i) < 0, then the converse is true. Because log (α_j/α_i) $= -$log (α_i/α_j), half of the structural mobility ratios for any data set are redundant. In the following tables only the positive ratios are reported.

Application of the SHD framework for studying structural mobility depends on the symmetry of the association between origins and destinations. The hypothesis of symmetric association is tested by the fit of QS to the observed mobility table. If the fit of QS is acceptable, then the inferences based on the SHD parameterization are valid (pp. 363–365). If the data depart significantly from QS, then some of the difference between the marginal distribution of origins and the marginal distribution of destinations is due to asymmetric association; that is, there must be some unreciprocated mobility that cannot be attributed solely to structural mobility. Therefore, testing QS is the first step in applying the SHD framework to Irish data. QS fits the data for the Republic ($L_{qs}^2 = 77.63$; $df = 78$; $p = .49$; bic $= -520$) very well. A case could be made for rejecting QS for Northern Ireland ($L_{qs}^2 = 101.48$; $df = 78$; $p = .04$; bic $= -500$), although examination of the residuals reveals no obvious asymmetries and the bic statistic shows the fit for Northern Ireland to be both acceptable and close to the fit for the Republic. Furthermore, the combined, "all Ireland" fit tested with the conditional QS model (CQS) is acceptable on the basis of both p-level and bic ($L^2_{cqs} = 179.11$; $df = 156$; $p = .10$; bic $= -1,130$).[14] Therefore, the hypothesis of symmetric association in each region is not rejected for purposes of further analysis.

Examination of the association parameters for Northern Ireland (δ_{ijn}) and the Republic (δ_{ijr}) reveals few differences, so a special case of CQS that constrains $\delta_{ijn} = \delta_{ijr}$ is considered. This model of CQS with homogeneous association (CQSHA)[15] has a full set of 14 β_i parameters for each region, a full set of 13 α_j parameters for each region, but only one set of 91 δ_{ij} parameters that apply to each cell (i, j) in each region. CQSHA fits well ($L^2_{cqsha} = 289.38$; $df = 247$; $p = .46$; bic $= -1,818$); the increase in L^2 over CQS is not significant ($L^2_{cqsha} - L^2_{cqs} = 95.19$; $df = 91$; $p = .41$; bic $= -669$). Therefore, most of the rest of the analysis in this chapter will ignore regional variation in the association between origins and destinations.

Table 3.6 shows the parameter estimates for CQSHA. The coefficients are supplemented by a graphic representation of the δ_{ij} parameters. The darker the rectangle for cell (i, j) in the bottom panel of the table, the higher the rate of exchange mobility due to weak association. The absence of shading indicates a low rate of exchange due to strong association, and the degree of shading in between gauges the intensity of intermediate levels of exchange and association.

As might be expected, structural mobility redistributes the work force into professional, managerial, white-collar, technical, and skilled occupations, and away from more traditional pursuits in farming, shopkeeping, and unskilled labor. Structural mobility most strongly affects farming (negatively) and salaried professional and managerial occupations (positively). In both Northern Ireland and the Republic, the α_j parameters for farming (classes IVc, IVd, and VIIf) depart from 1.0 on the low side by a wide margin. The large positive α_j parameter for class Ib in each region stands out. Other white-collar positions benefit from substantial structural mobility as well, their multipliers range from 1.9 to 2.9. Technical, supervisory, skilled, and semi-skilled manual positions all increase through modest structural mobility (multipliers between 1.2 and 2.1). Proprietors show almost no net change in three of four instances; the exception is a decline among proprietors without employees in the Republic. Unskilled labor shows a small relative decline in both regions ($\alpha_{viius} = .72$ for the Republic and .75 for Northern Ireland).

A large volume of exchange mobility (due either to size effects or to weak association) can keep an occupational group from declining as much

Table 3.6

Estimates of the parameters of the model of conditional quasi–symmetry with homogeneous association by region: men aged 18–65, Ireland, 1973

Param- eter	Region/origin	Destination													
		Ia	Ib	II	IIIa	IVa	IVb	IIIb	V	VI	VIIss	VIIus	IVc	IVd	VIIf
Marginal parameters[a]															
α_j	Republic	2.19	7.81	2.87	2.15	.76	.61	2.73	2.10	1.45	1.25	.72	.08	.11	.31
	Northern Ireland	2.77	5.80	3.36	2.56	1.15	1.03	1.91	2.08	1.42	1.14	.75	.05	.09	.25
β_j	Republic	.86	.59	1.69	1.39	3.00	2.82	.68	1.29	3.95	3.51	4.58	14.74	27.13	6.00
	Northern Ireland	.69	.83	1.63	1.24	2.60	1.86	.88	1.42	4.65	4.86	3.52	14.16	16.46	3.81

Association parameters ($\delta_{ij} = \delta_{ijn}$)

	Ia	Ib	II	IIIa	IVa	IVb	IIIb	V	VI	VIIss	VIIus	IVc	IVd	VIIf
Ia	1.00	.51	.25	.12	.11	.07	.06	.06	.06	.06	.02	.02	.02	.01
Ib		1.00	.67	.42	.29	.12	.20	.22	.18	.15	.05	.03	.02	.03
II			1.00	.60	.29	.22	.36	.45	.32	.31	.13	.06	.06	.06
IIIa				1.00	.30	.21	.58	.45	.31	.29	.29	.02	.06	.06
IVa					1.00	.43	.33	.37	.22	.23	.11	.09	.08	.06
IVb						1.00	.28	.37	.24	.40	.29	.08	.13	.26
IIIb							1.00	.42	.55	.57	.34	.05	.07	.19
V								1.00	.70	.59	.48	.03	.09	.18
VI									1.00	.71	.59	.02	.07	.18
VIIss										1.00	.90	.05	.12	.35
VIIus											1.00	.04	.14	.49
IVc												1.00	.29	.08
IVd													1.00	.13
VIIf														1.00

a. $L^2 = 289.38$; $df = 247$; $p = .03$; bic $= -1784$. [blank] $0 \le \delta_{ij} < .20$; ▨ $.20 \le \delta_{ij} < .30$; ▨ $.30 \le \delta_{ij} < .40$; ■ $.40 \le \delta_{ij} < .50$; ■ $.50 \le \delta_{ij} < 1.00$.

as its structural mobility multiplier indicates. At the same time, high exchange mobility between rapidly growing groups can amplify the effects of structural mobility.

A researcher might be tempted to simplify the calculation of structural mobility multipliers by taking the ratio of the number of workers with destination j to the number of workers with origin j; that is,[16] $c_j = n_{+j}/n_{j+}$. These ratios will systematically understate the force of structural mobility unless destinations are independent of origins. As long as there is some association between origins and destinations, the α_j will reveal more structural mobility than the c_j parameters reveal. Figure 3.1 plots the α_j and the c_j statistics for the Republic and Northern Ireland.[17] The α_j are labeled "SHD"; the c_j are labeled "biased." The steeper slope of the SHD line shows the bias of the c_j very plainly.

The source of the bias is the association between origins and destinations. In this context the association is like friction. A given force of structural mobility in one society in which destinations do not affect origins will result in a larger difference between the marginal distributions of origins and destinations than will be observed in a society with the same force of structural mobility but a strong association between origins and destinations. Or in a complementary view, more structural mobility is needed to produce a given change in marginals when association is strong than when association is weak or absent. Therefore, inferring structural mobility from marginal change alone leads to false inferences. Estimates of the force of structural mobility must control for the strength of association in order to be unbiased.

Table 3.7 gives the structural mobility log-ratios [log (α_j/α_i)], showing the mobility channels that benefit from structural mobility. The presence of a number in a cell of this table is evidence of an inflow due to structural mobility. An empty cell means that structural mobility forces an outflow from that cell; the magnitude of that outflow is equal to the magnitude of inflow into the corresponding cell on the other side of the diagonal. For example, the number in the first row, second column [cell (1,2)] is 1.27; there is no number in the second row, first column [cell (2,1)]. The (suppressed) value for cell (2,1) is -1.27. The log-ratios range from .01 (virtually no structural mobility) to nearly 5.0 (massive structural mobility). The scale of these log-ratios is probably unfamiliar to many readers. To get a sense of the changes described, note that a log-ratio of 1.0 for some cell (i, j) means that expected mobility from class i to class j is $(e^{1.0} =)$ 2.72 times greater than expected mobility in the opposite direction. For example, the log-ratio of 1.27 in cell (1,2) means that structural mobility

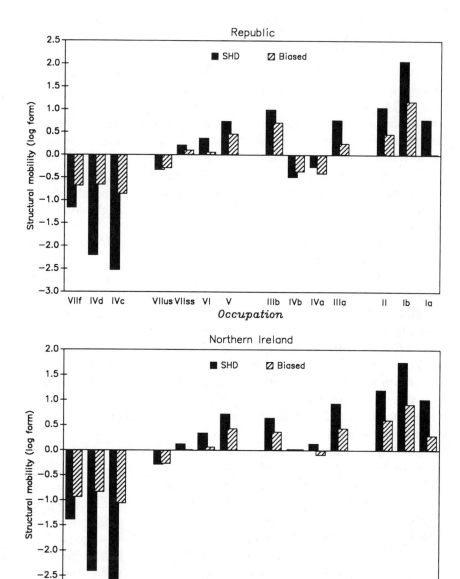

Figure 3.1   Unbiased (SHD) and biased estimates of structural mobility by region: men aged 18–65, Republic of Ireland (*above*) and Northern Ireland (*below*), 1973.

makes the flow from origin 1 to destination 2 ($e^{1.27}$ =) 3.57 times greater than the counterflow from origin 2 to destination 1.[18]

The log-ratios less than 0.2 for several combinations of white-collar occupations indicate that mobility in one direction exceeds mobility in the opposite direction by (at most) 22 percent ($e^{0.2}$ = 1.22). The log-ratios for manual-to-manual mobility that range from .37 to 1.07 gauge the modest amounts of upward mobility within the working class due to the redistribution of manual positions within the Irish economies in the direction of more skill and authority. The log-ratios of 3.0 or more for mobility out of farming indicate that structural forces are moving men out of farming into selected other occupations at a rate about 20 times greater than the back channel flow from those other occupations into farming ($e^{3.0}$ ≈ 20).

Because CQSHA fits the data reasonably well, these log-ratios can be equated with structural mobility.[19] All of the changes implied by these figures are due to structural mobility, and all of the effects of structural mobility are captured by these ratios (SHD 1985).

Exchange Mobility

Exchange mobility is the equal flow of workers between a pair of occupations.[20] For every worker who moves from origin *i* to destination *j*, exchange mobility returns a worker from origin *j* to destination *i*.[21] In societies that are relatively open, exchange should be an important component of mobility. Indeed, this is the prevailing notion behind most mobility research, namely, that a society's openness can be assessed by measuring the ease with which members of that society move from one class to another. Closed societies, however, can be expected to exhibit little exchange. Because of the influence of structural mobility, gross mobility rates do not necessarily give an accurate picture of the extent of openness in society. For example, Brazil (or at least São Paulo) exhibits very high gross mobility, but that high rate results from massive structural mobility moving workers through a very rigid class system (SHD 1985, p. 367). On the other hand, Great Britain—as revealed by a 1949 study (Glass 1954)— exhibits appreciable mobility without much push from structural mobility (SHD, p. 369), suggesting that in the immediate postwar era, Britain was more open than Brazil. In this study, then, openness is used in a refined sense to mean the genotypic flow of workers between occupations, not the phenotypic flow that may be subject to structural disturbances. More specifically, openness is equated with a high degree of exchange that is

Table 3.7

Estimates of structural mobility [log(α_j / α_i)] from the model of conditional quasi–symmetry with homogeneous association by region: men aged 18–65, Ireland, 1973

Origin (i)	Destination $(j)^a$													
	Ia	Ib	II	IIIa	IVa	IVb	IIIb	V	VI	VIIss	VIIus	IVc	IVd	VIIf
Republic of Ireland														
Ia	–	1.27	.27		.22									
Ib		–												
II	1.00		–											
IIIa	.02	1.29	.29	–	.24									
IVa	1.06	2.33	1.33	1.04	–	1.28	1.02	.65	.50					
IVb	1.27	2.54	1.54	1.25	.21	–	1.49	1.23	.86	.71	.16			
IIIb	1.05	.05					–							
V	.04	1.31	.31	.02	.26	.37		–						
VI	.41	1.68	.68	.39	.63	.52	.15		–					
VIIss	.56	1.83	.83	.54	.78					–				
VIIus	1.11	2.38	1.38	1.09	.05	1.33	1.07	.70	.55		–			
IVc	3.35	4.63	3.63	3.34	2.29	2.08	3.58	3.32	2.95	2.80	2.24	–	.40	1.41
IVd	2.96	4.23	3.23	2.94	1.90	1.69	3.18	2.92	2.55	2.40	1.85		–	1.01
VIIf	1.95	3.22	2.22	1.93	.89	.68	2.17	1.9	11.54	1.39	.84			–
Inflow	10	13	12	9	5	3	11	8	7	6	4	0	1	2

Northern Ireland

	Ia	Ib	II	IIIa	IVa	IVb	IIIb	V	VI	VIIss	VIIus	IVc	IVd	VIIf
Ia	—	.74	.19											
Ib	.55	—	.27											
II	.08	.82	—											
IIIa	.88	1.62	1.07	—	.11	.33								
IVa	.99	1.73	1.19	.80	—	.11	.60							
IVb	.37	1.11	.56	.91	.51	—	.62							
IIIb	.29	1.02	.48	.29			—							
V	.67	1.41	.86	.20	.38	.30	.21	—						
VI	.89	1.62	1.08	.59	.52	.01	.71	.60	—					
VIIss	1.31	2.04	1.50	.81	.31	.42	.08	.22	.64	—				
VIIus				1.22				1.02	.42	.94	—			
IVc	3.96	4.70	4.15	3.88	3.08	2.97	3.59	3.68	3.29	3.08	2.66	—	.58	1.56
IVd	3.38	4.12	3.57	3.30	2.50	2.39	3.01	3.10	2.71	2.49	2.08		—	.98
VIIf	2.40	3.14	2.59	2.32	1.52	1.40	2.03	2.11	1.73	1.51	1.09			—
Inflow	11	13	12	11	6	4	8	9	7	5	3	0	1	2

a. Only positive structural mobility is shown. See Table 3.1 for category labels.

attributable to a weak association between occupational origins and destinations.

While the association between origin and destination contributes to the rate of exchange mobility, size plays a role too. To see how size affects exchange, imagine a society in which 90 percent of contemporary workers were farmers and a similarly high share, say 88 percent, of workers were from farm origins. That society may have a very weak association between origins and destinations but not much exchange mobility simply because the nonfarm occupations would lack sufficient numbers of workers to exchange among themselves and with farming. Immobility in such a society could be quite high even if origins and destinations were statistically independent. Thus, as Sobel (1983) first showed, the common practice of equating exchange and association is wrong (e.g., Garnier and Hazelrigg 1974; Goldthorpe 1980, p. 60; Hope 1982).

In the SHD framework, exchange mobility is the product of size (β_i and β_j) and association (δ_{ij}) parameters. Estimates of these parameters, along with the α_j parameters, appear in Table 3.6. The size parameters are not very interesting. Their one noteworthy aspect is their contribution to immobility. The association parameters range from .01 (very strong association) to .90 (near independence). The estimates of δ_{ij} very close to .01 for several pairs of occupational categories that mix white-collar occupations with agricultural occupations show odds of about 1 percent on moving between white-collar work and farming relative to staying immobile. Yet the odds are right around 90 percent on moving between unskilled and semi-skilled manual occupations relative to immobility.

Other exchanges that are greater than 50 percent are between pairs of classes: (Ia, Ib), (Ib, II), (II, IIIa), (IIIa, IIIb), (IIIb, VI), (IIIb, VIIss), (V, VI), (V, VIIss), (VI, VIIss), and (VI, VIIus). The barriers between other pairs of occupational classes limit exchange. Even between the two types of farm proprietorships the internal stratification of agriculture ($\delta_{ivc,ivd}$ = .29) limits exchange mobility between farming on a plot prosperous enough to support paid labor and small holdings. Presumably part of this effect is due to the fact that the succession of generations tends to split family holdings. This tendency is apparently not overcome by the trend toward larger holdings and land consolidation in Ireland, perhaps because farmers buy tractors before they hire hands for the farm, thus improving their standard of living in a way that is invisible, given the present data.

The pattern of homogeneous association for the Republic and Northern Ireland estimated using the CQSHA model repeats itself in each region. Table 3.8 presents the region-specific estimates of δ_{ij}. Homogeneity like this is not a foregone conclusion. The difference between L^2s for CQSHA and CQS tests all 91 δ_{ij} at once. Isolated pairs of differences could exist in the data but be missed by the summary test used before. Table 3.8 is very reassuring on that count. No substantial regional differences are in evidence.

Dimensions of Occupational Mobility

Summarizing the 91 association parameters in Table 3.6 is a formidable task. Five points are important. First, a single pattern of association applies in the Republic of Ireland and Northern Ireland. Second, the estimates of association are independent of the substantial structural mobility out of farming and unskilled labor into white-collar work and skilled manual work. Third, the values of δ_{ij} parameters tend to decrease (indicating stronger association) as the differences between the prestige of the categories being compared increase. There are several exceptions to this tendency, however. Fourth, a self-employment effect appears to compound the prestige effect. For example the prestige of class IVb is nearly equal to that of class V (see Table 2.9), yet exchange between classes II and V is easier ($\delta_{ii,v} = .45$) than exchange between classes II and IVb ($\delta_{ii,ivb} = .22$). Finally, farm and nonfarm occupations are separated by strong association parameters.[22]

Mobility research has produced an impressive array of parsimonious models that facilitate tests of these generalizations (Hout 1983). One of these parsimonious models—a multidimensional model for American data (Hout 1984a)—is used here to interpret the Irish data. The original model is altered to fit the Irish context and to take advantage of some data on labor markets that are available for Ireland (but were not available for the American study).

Mobility analysis typically features a concern with upward and downward mobility. The "up" and "down" refer to the socioeconomic hierarchy of positions. Occupations that are high on the list get there because they command substantial economic resources and return substantial economic rewards. These pecuniary concerns influence public perceptions of the relative desirability of pursuing one occupation rather than another (Duncan 1961; Hope and Goldthorpe 1972; Treiman 1977). Public

Table 3.8

Estimates of association parameters from the model of conditional quasi-symmetry with heterogeneous association by region: men aged 18–65, Ireland, 1973

Origin (*i*)	Ia	Ib	II	IIIa	IVa	IVb	IIIb	V	VI	VIIss	VIIus	IVc	IVd	VIIf
								Destination (*j*)						
Ia	1.00	.50	.22	.20	.07	.12	.17	.10	.04	.08	.02	.02	.02	.02
Ib	.58	1.00	.84	.61	.32	.18	.37	.17	.20	.13	.05	.04	.04	.05
II	.33	.61	1.00	.67	.41	.30	.24	.51	.35	.39	.12	.09	.09	.02
IIIa	.12	.36	.57	1.00	.27	.14	.51	.60	.28	.39	.24	.02	.08	.09
IVa	.25	.33	.24	.37	1.00	.41	.27	.36	.13	.24	.11	.08	.07	.07
IVb	.12	.12	.20	.33	.47	1.00	.35	.36	.14	.44	.31	.09	.15	.35
IIIb	.09	.17	.45	.67	.45	.28	1.00	.33	.45	.67	.41	.06	.10	.23
V	.12	.30	.44	.36	.42	.43	.53	1.00	.64	.58	.36	.04	.08	.16
VI	.13	.20	.32	.35	.31	.35	.63	.75	1.00	.68	.53	.03	.10	.12
VIIss	.09	.18	.29	.25	.24	.38	.51	.60	.74	1.00	.73	.08	.13	.34
VIIus	.07	.09	.18	.37	.13	.29	.31	.65	.65	1.07	1.00	.06	.14	.59
IVc	.06	.05	.09	.06	.14	.12	.09	.05	.03	.06	.06	1.00	.30	.09
IVd	.03	.01	.05	.07	.10	.14	.06	.13	.06	.14	.16	.28	1.00	.13
VIIf	.04	.05	.13	.06	.08	.17	.22	.27	.29	.41	.34	.10	.17	1.00

a. Republic above the diagonal; Northern Ireland below the diagonal. See Table 3.1 for category labels.

perceptions also reflect the "goodness" of the people staffing the occupational positions; occupations filled by "better-educated" people are better than other positions. These factors get reflected in occupational prestige scales. The conjecture that the rate of exchange due to weak association declines as the distance in relative prestige between two occupational groups increases hardly surprises anyone. Time and again prestige and socioeconomic standing have been shown to be the dominant factors in occupational mobility (Hout 1984a). The goals here are to establish the strength of this effect—more or less taking for granted that it is not zero— and to determine what, if anything, is left in the way of systematic association between origins and destinations that might be explained by other factors of interest.

The metaphor of the labor market provides clues to the sources of mobility barriers not attributable to prestige, namely, to the so-called nonvertical dimensions of mobility that might be important. The two essential elements of the labor market metaphor are a differentiated set of "sellers"—workers with time and skills to sell—and perfectly informed "buyers"—prospective employers, knowledgeable about the range and supply of skills among the sellers and willing to pay money for the time and skills of workers. According to the metaphor, the short supply of some kinds of skills relative to demand bids up the wages of the workers who have those skills, while the wages of other workers are depressed by oversupply and slack demand. The market metaphor is useful not because it describes the process of matching workers to jobs (it does not) but because it fails in informative ways. Both workers and employers strive to organize labor markets to their own advantage. The social organization matching worker with occupation limits the extent of direct competition between men and women, majority and minority group members, immigrants and natives. The existence of these cleavages not only demonstrates that the labor market is differentiated just as the workers in it are differentiated, but also suggests the possibility that different norms may govern hiring in different labor markets. For example, labor markets may differ in the extent to which they conform to the norms of universalism. Blau and Duncan (1967, p. 430) hypothesize that these norms are expanding under industrial capitalism. It might well be the case that new labor markets created by manufacturing or service growth are more likely to adopt new, more universalistic norms, while more traditional labor markets adhere to other, more particularistic norms. This view holds universalism to be a factor in occupational mobility into and within some labor markets but not others. As such, universalism is an attribute of occupations and the labor markets in which they reside, not of whole societies, as Blau and Duncan propose (most writers on this topic tend to share the society-wide view).

Self-employment further complicates the market metaphor. Most Irish workers sell their labor, but about one-fifth do not. The self-employed segment of the working population creates its own jobs without clearing the market. This does not deny that market forces apply. Self-employed people need credit, wares, and space. They evaluate the utility of self-employment relative to working for wages. But they do not participate in the labor market, except perhaps as buyers.

The blending of traditional and modern pursuits in a developing economy further complicates the market metaphor. In the Irish economy, government subsidies help farmers to persist in the traditional way of life while the same budget allocates money for the construction of new industrial parks that encourage multinational corporations to site their plants in Ireland, injecting the modern way of life into the rural setting.

These failings of the market metaphor raise the prospect of many hierarchies that may or may not be related. An origin position that is privileged in one hierarchy may offer no advantage in another sphere. This effect, if substantial, should direct advantaged workers toward destinations that allow them to cash in on their origins and away from destinations that offer little return on the assets of their origin. To estimate the effect of labor market segmentation on occupational mobility, occupational categories are scored on four dimensions of occupational recruitment. The scores are based on the workers' responses to the question "How did you obtain your current job?" The responses are coded into four categories: bureaucratic entry, bureaucratic advancement, enterprise, and personal contact.

Socioeconomic measures of the mean prestige, proportion of workers who completed primary school, proportion with an annual income from this occupation of over £2,500, and socioeconomic status (SES) index obtained by averaging the income and education indexes are also covered in the analysis. The variables are included in a modified version of the multidimensional model devised by Hout (1984a). Both general and specific (diagonal) effects are considered for each variable. Table 3.9 summarizes the search for a preferred model. The table includes region-specific goodness of fit statistics and association parameters for selected multidimensional models.[23]

The first model considered includes each of the four market variables and the socioeconomic index. Even though L^2 implies rejection of this model on classical grounds, bic is negative for both the Republic and Northern Ireland. More important, bic for the multidimensional model is more negative than bic for QS in both regions. Furthermore, the model accounts for all but $(360.89/1,624.11 =)$ 22 percent of the baseline L^2 in the Republic and all but $(256.10/1,270.47 =)$ 20 percent of the baseline L^2 in Northern Ireland. So even though QS fits at conventional levels of significance for the Republic and for both regions combined while the multidimensional model fails on these conventional criteria of fit, the multidimensional model is preferred in this context because of its parsimony.

Examination of the coefficients for the general and specific diagonal effects in the first column of Table 3.9 shows that enterprise does not affect mobility or immobility (at the .05 level). The second model considered deletes enterprise. The increase in L^2 occasioned by this change is not significant, and bic goes down, so that market dimension is dropped from further analysis.

The search for a preferred multidimensional model continues with the consideration of other hierarchical dimensions. The original model contained the SES measure. Prestige is a closely related concept. Including both variables in the equation may or may not be informative because of their high correlation—a problem analogous to the problem of multicolinearity familiar to users of multiple regression. As seen in Table 3.9, there are problems of inference in the model typical of multicolinearity with both prestige and SES at once. When prestige is added to the original model, L^2 goes down significantly in the Republic of Ireland but not in Northern Ireland; bic goes up in both regions. Parameter estimates also demonstrate the problem of separating these variables. Large standard errors make inferences difficult: the diagonal effect of SES and the main effect of prestige are insignificant in the Republic, while both diagonal effects and the main effect of prestige are insignificant in Northern Ireland. The parameter estimates also indicate similar multicolinearity problems with the bureaucratic entry and advance variables. Dropping bureaucratic advance from the model somewhat improves the situation. Adding educational credentials compounds the inference problem.

There are several changes to the model that might reduce multicolinearity at this point. By definition an inference problem is a question to which the data cannot give an unambiguous answer. Criteria other than data must be invoked. SES is a rather arbitrary average of two other

Table 3.9a
Fit and parameter estimates for selected multidimensional models by region:
men aged 18–65, Republic of Ireland, 1973

				Model			
Dimension	1	2	3	4	5	6	7

Goodness of Fit

L^2	360.9	364.1	349.1	359.3	337.4	341.4	344.9
df	159	161	159	161	159	161	162
bic	−858	−870	−869	−875	−881	−892	−897

General Effects[a]

Status	6.841	6.626	5.951	6.302	−4.559	—	—
	(.724)	(.711)	(1.027)	(.928)	(2.493)		
Prestige	—	—	3.379	3.037	6.686	3.936	4.921
			(2.431)	(2.346)	(2.558)	(2.143)	(2.077)
Education	—	—	—	—	7.366	4.712	4.400
					(1.597)	(.595)	(.573)
Bureaucratic entry	6.155	6.605	6.013	6.312	5.954	6.355	6.217
	(.800)	(.703)	(.829)	(.808)	(.807)	(.784)	(.780)
Bureaucratic advance	.466	1.275	.994	—	—	—	—
	(1.198)	(1.047)	(1.098)				
Enterprise	.656	—	—	—	—	—	—
	(.708)						
Personal contact	4.835	4.663	5.009	4.909	4.544	4.377	4.612
	(.979)	(.942)	(1.007)	(1.001)	(1.006)	(.998)	(.989)

Specific Diagonal Effects[a]

Status	2.417	2.919	.041	1.496	1.646	—	—
	(.520)	(.417)	(.996)	(.869)	(2.384)		
Prestige	—	—	4.221	5.021	5.520	4.757	2.970
			(1.362)	(1.322)	(1.420)	(1.037)	(.381)
Education	—	—	—	—	.007	.962	—
					(1.452)	(.523)	
Bureaucratic entry	−.060	−.099	−.102	−.336	−.878	−.651	−.796
	(.322)	(.321)	(.322)	(.313)	(.337)	(.317)	(.308)
Bureaucratic advance	−3.192	−4.377	−3.599	—	—	—	—
	(1.383)	(1.197)	(1.161)				
Enterprise	.454	—	—	—	—	—	—
	(.652)						
Personal contact	3.169	3.145	1.589	1.484	1.641	1.700	2.444
	(.391)	(.387)	(.654)	(.638)	(.636)	(.576)	(.415)

a.   Standard errors in parentheses.

Table 3.9b
Fit and parameter estimates for selected multidimensional models by region: men aged 18–65, Northern Ireland, 1973

Dimension	1	2	3	Model 4	5	6	7
Goodness of Fit							
L^2	256.1	260.1	254.0	257.4	256.1	264.6	264.6
df	159	161	159	161	159	161	162
bic	−974	−986	−976	−988	−974	−981	−989
General Effects[a]							
Status	7.048	6.697	5.852	6.128	7.015	—	—
	(.713)	(.690)	(1.025)	(.947)	(2.522)		
Prestige	—	—	3.148	2.718	2.898	6.386	6.330
			(2.343)	(2.276)	(2.464)	(2.019)	(1.984)
Education	—	—	—	—	.667	3.405	3.426
					(1.558)	(.590)	(.574)
Bureaucratic entry	6.122	6.989	6.283	6.542	6.530	5.959	5.961
	(.840)	(.713)	(.850)	(.827)	(.837)	(.799)	(.799)
Bureaucratic advance	−.427	−.720	−.648	—	—	—	—
	(1.113)	(.940)	(.982)				
Enterprise	1.153	—	—	—	—	—	—
	(.637)						
Personal contact	7.544	7.093	7.504	7.432	7.551	7.665	7.650
	(1.210)	(1.182)	(1.226)	(1.213)	(1.221)	(1.219)	(1.216)
Specific Diagonal Effects[a]							
Status	1.689	2.019	.499	.189	2.343	—	—
	(.482)	(.384)	(.930)	(.853)	(2.160)		
Prestige	—	—	2.414	2.665	3.224	2.406	2.550
			(1.360)	(1.336)	(1.428)	(1.024)	(.348)
Education	—	—	—	—	1.414	.076	
					(1.300)	(.505)	
Bureaucratic entry	−.640	−.675	−.668	−.792	−.846	−1.034	−1.023
	(.303)	(.301)	(.300)	(.293)	(.318)	(.299)	(.290)
Bureaucratic advance	−1.019	−1.791	−1.752	—	—	—	—
	(1.184)	(.998)	(.979)				
Enterprise	−.084	—	—	—	—	—	—
	(.601)						
Personal contact	3.418	3.333	2.397	2.434	2.293	2.748	2.685
	(.521)	(.518)	(.760)	(.741)	(.746)	(.673)	(.529)

a.   Standard errors in parentheses.

variables, whereas prestige is a carefully constructed scale (Goldthorpe and Hope 1974), so prestige is given precedence whenever the choice is unclear on statistical grounds. SES and the diagonal effect of education produces an acceptable model for the Republic and a plausible contender for that title in Northern Ireland. The main competitor in Northern Ireland is the model with SES, prestige, bureaucratic entry, and personal contact as the dimensions. The fit is comparable relative to degrees of freedom (the bic statistics differ by only one point). In the end, model 7 emerges as the preferred model, both because it contains no insignificant coefficients in either region and because it is clearly superior in the Republic and the plausible alternative is not unambiguously superior to model 7 in Northern Ireland.

Tests of the difference between each coefficient in the Republic and the corresponding coefficient in Northern Ireland turn up only one significant difference.[24] The general effect of personal contacts in Northern Ireland exceeds the corresponding effect in the Republic. Tests for differences in the size and structural mobility coefficients show that none of the marginal parameters differ significantly by region.

The interpretation of the coefficients of the multidimensional model parallels the interpretation given to partial regression coefficients; this parallel constitutes part of the appeal of this kind of model. A positive coefficient for dimension X means that the odds on attaining a destination occupation that is high on X relative to some other destination that is lower on X increases as the X-score of the origin occupation increases. Unlike partial regression coefficients, however, these coefficients are not pure slopes. The effect of origin on destination is proportional to the difference in X-scores between the destinations being compared. For example, when calculating the effect of origin prestige on the odds on attaining a destination in class IVc relative to class IVd (farmer with employees compared to farmer with no employees), a pair of destinations separated by 21 prestige points, the prestige coefficient (.0004921) is multiplied by 21 to yield .0103. Thus the odds on being a farmer with employees relative to being a farmer without employees go up .0103 for every point increase in origin prestige. The range of prestige in the data is $(76 - 18 =)$ 58 points, so the range in the odds on having employees due to prestige is $(.0103 \times 58 =)$ .599.

Table 3.10 shows further calculations of this type, designed to help sort out the several effects in the model. The calculations in the table decompose the odds on a lower-grade professional occupation relative to an unskilled manual one. In principle the calculation could be used to contrast any pair of occupations; it is just that some combinations are more interesting than others. This contrast highlights the mechanics of the model because classes II and VIIus differ substantially on three of the four significant dimensions. Most extreme is the vertical difference reflected in both prestige (42 points) and education (73 points). On bureaucratic entry, the rank of the two destinations being compared reverses and the magnitude of the difference diminishes somewhat (to 32 points). Neither occupation scores very high on personal contacts, with a difference of 6 points. The first column of the table arrays the logits expected under the model separated by origin category and region. The other columns show the contribution of each independent variable to that logit. The results are similar in the two regions, as might be expected given the good fit of CQSHA.[25] A convenient summary of the magnitude of each effect is the range of individual contributions. This summary range varies according to the magnitude of the effect parameter itself, the difference between the score of classes II and VIIus on that dimension, and the range of the independent variable. In these comparisons education differs most on the dependent variable and manifests the widest range on the independent variable, so its range of contributions is the greatest.

For further illustration, consider four cases: a son of a roofer, a man whose father was a glassblower at the Waterford crystal factory, a man who grew up under the roof of a family-run shop in which there was no hired help, and a man whose father was a lawyer for the Dublin County Council. These cases are men from the Republic with origins in classes VIIss, VI, IVb, and Ia, respectively. Consider their odds on attaining a lower-level professional position, such as schoolteacher, draftsman, journalist, or priest, relative to unskilled manual positions, such as general laborer, porter, or truck driver's assistant. The odds are just slightly better than three to one against the son of a roofer's attaining a professional position—even a lower-level (class II) professional position—relative to his chances of arriving in unskilled labor.[26] The glassblower's son sits on the fence between white-collar and lower-blue-collar destinations; his chances are nearly even at ten to nine against class II. The middle-class backgrounds of the shop owner's son and the lawyer's son stack the odds on middle-class employment in their favor. The logits for origin classes IVb and Ib are both positive. For the shopkeeper's son the odds on lower professional employment versus an unskilled destination are about five to four in favor; for the lawyer's son, the odds are an impressive eight to one in favor.

Table 3.10
Decomposition of log–odds on a lower–level professional destination
(class II) relative to an unskilled manual destination (class VIIus)
according to model 7: men aged 18–65, Ireland, 1973

Origin	Logit	Prestige b_1	d_1	Education b_2	Bureaucratic entry b_3	d_3	Personal contact b_4	d_4
Republic of Ireland								
Ia	2.78	1.57	—	3.08	−.19	—	−.04	—
Ib	2.09	1.43	—	2.99	−.68	—	−.00	—
II	2.82	1.24	1.07	2.92	−.68	−.09	−.03	.04
IIIa	1.11	.87	—	2.86	−.94	—	−.03	—
IVa	1.15	1.05	—	1.96	−.16	—	−.06	—
IVb	.24	.99	—	1.22	−.30	—	−.03	—
IIIb	−.25	.64	—	1.67	−.82	—	−.09	—
V	.73	.97	—	2.06	−.62	—	−.03	—
VI	−.09	.79	—	1.77	−.94	—	−.06	—
VIIss	−1.02	.62	−.10	1.16	−1.09	.35	−.06	−.08
VIIus	−1.89	.37	—	.58	−1.31	—	−.05	—
IVc	.65	1.20	—	1.41	−.16	—	−.16	—
IVd	−.53	.76	—	.58	−.06	—	−.17	—
VIIf	−1.66	.64	—	.19	−.70	—	−.15	—
Range	4.71	1.20	1.17	2.89	1.24	.44	.17	.12
Northern Ireland								
Ia	2.98	2.02	—	2.40	−.19	—	−.07	—
Ib	2.33	1.83	—	2.33	−.65	—	−.00	—
II	2.84	1.60	.92	2.28	−.65	−.12	−.06	.04
IIIa	1.22	1.12	—	2.23	−.90	—	−.06	—
IVa	1.47	1.36	—	1.53	−.15	—	−.09	—
IVb	.73	1.28	—	.95	−.29	—	−.05	—
IIIb	.02	.82	—	1.30	−.78	—	−.16	—
V	1.04	1.25	—	1.60	−.59	—	−.05	—
VI	.22	1.01	—	1.38	−.90	—	−.10	—
VIIss	−.61	.80	−.08	.90	−1.05	.45	−.09	−.09
VIIus	−1.30	.48	—	.45	−1.26	—	−.08	—
IVc	1.06	1.54	—	1.10	−.15	—	−.26	—
IVd	−.07	.98	—	.45	−.06	—	−.28	—
VIIf	−1.11	.82	—	.15	−.67	—	−.25	—
Range	4.28	1.54	1.00	2.25	1.20	.57	.28	.13

These calculations quantify the appreciable differences in life chances experienced by men of diverse social origins. The fact that all of these differences mimic the intuition of the informed observer of the social scene should not obscure the significance of their magnitude. As for the difference in life chances for the son of a roofer compared with the son of a lawyer, of the total difference in logits of 3.11, the prestige difference in their origins accounts for .81, the educational difference for 1.83, bureaucratic entry for .41, and personal contact for .06. Clearly, in this comparison of origins separated by a great vertical distance, the effects of the socioeconomic aspects predominate. In contrast, origins in classes VI and IVb are not separated by much vertical distance. In fact, the prestige of shop owners is contradicted by the greater education of craftsmen. The greatest difference is in market dimensions, where the effects of bureaucratic entry work to the disadvantage of craftsmen. The difference in personal contacts between the two origin groups would benefit craftsmen if the effect of personal contacts were greater than it is.

Carrying through similar comparisons for cases drawn from Northern Ireland reveals a similar pattern of differential life chances among the four origin groups. The odds on lower-grade professional employment compared with unskilled work are uniformly higher for all men in Northern Ireland because of the relatively greater preponderance of professional jobs and the smaller share of unskilled positions among the blue-collar jobs available in the North.

The comparisons in Figure 3.2 further underscore the point that the differential life chances separate distant origins but not proximate ones. This figure plots the expected logits from Table 3.10 along with the expected logits for two proximate destinations. The differences between clerical and sales workers (class IIIa) and technicians and foremen (class V) on the four significant dimensions of mobility do not stand up to the differences between lower professionals and unskilled laborers: 5 points on prestige, 25 points on education, 16 points on bureaucratic entry, and 1 point on personal contact. The narrower range of logits (1.57 in the Republic, 1.24 in Northern Ireland) in the IIIa: V line corresponds to this restricted range of comparison. If we acknowledge this narrower range of effects, a noteworthy departure from the pattern of the II: VIIus logit centers on the contribution of immobility (relative to mobility to class V) among clerical and sales workers.

An important component of the overall structure of opportunity in Ireland is the pattern of immobility. All elements of the multidimensional model contribute to immobility: size, structural mobility, general effects, and specific effects. The size effects (β_i parameters) contribute the bulk of immobility in most origin groups. Structural mobility works against many of these size effects, redistributing workers away from some of the traditional, large occupations like farming toward professional, manage-

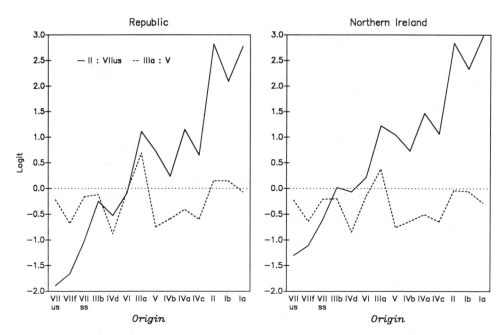

Figure 3.2   Expected log-odds on a lower professional or managerial destination
(relative to unskilled manual) and clerical or sales destination
(relative to technical or supervisory), by region: men aged 18–65,
Ireland, 1973.

rial, and technical occupations. Each of the dimensions of mobility contributes to immobility in the occupational categories that are high on the
dimension in question. Most of the immobility is the function of general
effects. Many mobility models rely on special treatment of the diagonal
cells in order to achieve an acceptable fit to the data. The multidimensional model includes specific diagonal effects, too, but the magnitudes of
these effects are definitely smaller than the magnitudes of the corresponding general effects.

   The specific diagonal effects in the multidimensional model do not produce a perfect fit along the diagonal of the mobility table. Significant residuals show up with some consistency in both the Republic and Northern
Ireland. The correlation between the residuals for the Republic and the
corresponding residuals in Northern Ireland is .63. The model fails to
account for all of the immobility among service workers (class IIIb),
skilled manual workers (class VI), and medium-sized proprietors (class

IVa). Immobility is less than expected among high-status salaried workers (classes Ib and II). This pattern suggests the possible influence of the autonomy factor that is so important in mobility in the United States (Hout 1984a). Two of the three classes with large positive residuals have high autonomy relative to their prestige and education (classes VI and IVa), and the converse is true for the two classes with large negative residuals. Irish data on autonomy are lacking, and the attempt to apply an American autonomy scale to the Irish mobility data was unsuccessful (Hout and Jackson 1986), so the autonomy idea must be considered to be conjecture until a suitable autonomy scale is developed for Ireland.

Conclusion

How does intergenerational mobility in Ireland correspond to the sense of change that was prevalent in Ireland at the beginning of the 1970s? First, it validates the spirit of growth by reflecting the scale of the changes. Many workers were far from their origins in 1973. Structural mobility propelled many men from traditional backgrounds into industrial jobs and even into the postindustrial service class. In the Republic, salaried professional, managerial, and technical occupations are twice as large a share of current occupations as they are of origins (9 percent of origins, 20 percent of destinations). In Northern Ireland, professional, managerial, and technical occupations are also twice as common among destinations as among origins, and the level of postindustrial employment is 25 percent higher than it is in the Republic (24 percent of destinations in Northern Ireland are postindustrial).

The Irish elite is impressive in its broad base of recruitment: over three-fourths of the salaried professionals, managers, and technicians are from nonelite backgrounds (82 percent in the Republic, 75 percent in Northern Ireland). Not only has a new, modern class emerged in Ireland, but that class also draws overwhelmingly from more traditional origins.

The changes of the 1960s and early 1970s marked a turning point for Irish economic development. Structural mobility in Ireland is about average by European standards. Yet by Irish standards of comparison the mere fact of keeping abreast of the rest of Europe is a significant departure from the past. Through most of Irish history growth has been languid at best. For a century and a half Ireland—especially the twenty-six counties of the Republic—lagged behind Europe in manufacturing and the standard of living associated with economic development. When Europe was depressed, Ireland was also depressed. When the rest of Europe was growing, Ireland was either mired in civil war or for other reasons failed to achieve sufficient investment. To keep pace during the decade of the most rapid growth in the century is an estimable accomplishment.

Despite opportunity and growth in the 1960s and early 1970s, inequalities of opportunity persist. Some social backgrounds are advantaged and others are disadvantaged in the Irish class structure. Despite hopes and predictions that economic development would be accompanied by more equal opportunity for all classes, the changes brought about in Ireland in the 1960s improved living standards without altering the rank order of the Irish social classes. By and large, the men who grew up in privileged circumstances in the 1940s were in the top positions in the 1970s. The dimensions of advantage include the vertical dimensions so important in other Western societies; prestige and educational credentialism are the most salient dimensions in the Irish case, as they are elsewhere. Advantage in Ireland also includes the rationalization of occupational placement and its converse, the personal imperative in traditional occupations. These two nonvertical dimensions of mobility contribute to the association between origins and destinations in Ireland in a definitive way that is not so evident elsewhere.

The contribution of nonvertical aspects of mobility to the apparent difference between Irish mobility and that in other European countries is unclear at this point (Whelan and Whelan 1984; Erikson and Goldthorpe 1987b). Unclear also is the extent to which mobility changed between 1959 and 1973. It is known by now, however, that the dissimilarity between origins and destinations in Ireland is not the same thing as change in occupational structure over a specific period of time (Duncan 1966). Nor does the importance of the various dimensions of mobility in 1973 indicate whether inequalities in Ireland were increasing or decreasing.

Several things are already obvious. Foremost is the importance of structural mobility. In this regard, Ireland echoes the experience of industrialization elsewhere. William Sewell, Jr. (1985, p. 268), draws conclusions about mobility in Marseilles during the nineteenth century that apply equally well to Ireland and the rest of contemporary Europe: "Social mobility patterns are governed as much by structural constraints arising from demographic conditions and patterns of economic growth as by a society's intrinsic degree of openness." Structural mobility comes about because the distribution of social origins among contemporary workers is inconsistent with the distribution of occupations in the current labor market. For example, the number of farmers' sons typically exceeds the current number of viable farms, while the number of engineers' sons falls short of the current number of engineering jobs. Discrepancies of this sort guarantee a minimal level of intergenerational mobility. Under these circumstances some sons cannot follow in their fathers' footsteps; structural conditions force a certain amount of mobility. In Ireland, as elsewhere, this structural mobility affects workers with farm origins more than it affects workers from other backgrounds. Technological, economic, and demographic forces line up against a-farm-for-every-farmer's-son. Mechanization increases the amount of land an individual farmer can work, and economic realities pressure farmers to take advantage of technology and expand. Meanwhile, farm families typically have more than one child. These realities of agrarian life create a great disparity between the supply and demand of farmers' sons, inducing great structural mobility in any society with a dynamic agrarian sector.

Matters down on the farm get even more complicated. Farmers' children who are in line to inherit the family farm typically reach maturity long before the father is ready to retire. In some societies this results in a period of nonfarm work followed by a return to farming later in life. In other societies the farm passes to every other generation. The grandchild inherits the family farm. A third adjustment entails a period of waiting, a limbo of unpaid assisting on the family farm. Agrarian limbo is the most prevalent adjustment in Ireland. It contributes to high rates of social disorganization, including mental illness among bachelor farmers-in-waiting (Scheper-Hughes 1979).

Farmers' daughters feel these constraints even more than their sons. Opportunity for women in traditional Irish agriculture does not range much beyond "the good match," which brings with it a secure career caring for husband and children. Work outside the home requires migration to urban centers. Although the movement of Irish women of farm origins to cities and towns of Ireland, England, and elsewhere is invisible in this study, it is a substantial source of structural mobility in Ireland (Kennedy 1973, pp. 66–87).

These processes accumulate to induce mobility for sons. In the past, the displaced farmers' sons sought opportunity offshore—in England, North America, and Australia. In the generation covered by this study, the opportunity at home increased. More and more young men and women stayed in Ireland, where they found employment in newly opened industrial and service sectors. This pattern reveals itself in the models presented throughout this book as strong negative structural mobility for farming and positive structural mobility for blue-collar and white-collar occupations in manufacturing and services.

Does this huge structural mobility mark a historical turning point for Ireland? It does and it does not. The outflow is not new; the inflow is. The economic and demographic pressures on Irish farmers did not arise for the first time in 1959. Arensberg and Kimball (1940) made structural adaptations to pressure the cornerstone of their analysis of Irish country life in the 1930s. The emigration record verifies that Irish farms (and the off-spring of Irish farmers) were under economic and demographic pressures even before the famines of the 1840s (Kennedy 1973; Goldstrom and Clarkson 1981). The new element in Ireland since 1959 has been the option of leaving the farm without leaving Ireland. Structural mobility takes on the strength it does in part because the men of farm origins who responded to the force of structural mobility in the 1960s and 1970s did so in Ireland instead of taking their labor power to England, Canada, Australia, or the United States.

In Ireland, as elsewhere, growth of some positions complements the contraction of farming.[27] The growth of the service economy, especially in the professions, makes it impossible for the privileged of one generation to fill all the available positions while blocking the ascent of people from working-class and farm origins. As a consequence, substantial class barriers fail to impede upward mobility altogether. Management and the professions draw people from all origins into the upper middle class. This engine of upward mobility may be running low on fuel in the 1980s, but the changes of 1960s and 1970s were a major source of mobility.

High rates of mobility into elite occupations can be found in other Western European and English-speaking societies (Erikson and Goldthorpe 1987a,b). In the richer coutries this inflow comes from industrial working-class and lower-service-sector origins. In Ireland, the deficient stock of working-class origins and persistent class barriers suppress the flow from the working class to the upper middle class. A different kind of flow from traditional to modern occupations distinguishes the Irish case, giving it a special character, even though higher rates of mobility can be found elsewhere. In this regard mobility in Ireland has a character one might expect to find in earlier periods elsewhere.

Structural mobility not only boosts the overall rate of mobility substantially but also accounts for the surplus of upward over downward mobility. The structural changes in Ireland since 1959 have expanded positions that rank higher than the positions that have shrunk in prestige and social status. In the absence of structural mobility every move upward would have to be compensated with a move downward. In a society without structural mobility there can be no move without an equal and opposite countermove. This symmetry is the essence of exchange mobility.

The absence of structural mobility does not imply, however, that a society is closed. Nor does high structural mobility imply anything about equality of opportunity. The degree of openness is determined by the strength of association between origins and destinations in occupational mobility. On this score, Ireland does not fare well relative to other parts of the Western world. The class barriers to mobility in Ireland exceed those in other societies (Whelan and Whelan 1984; Hout and Jackson 1986; Erikson and Goldthorpe 1987b). By factoring the total association between origins and destinations into partial associations along several dimensions, this study reveals the contours of that low degree of intrinsic openness. As elsewhere, the hierarchy of social classes limits mobility by granting privilege to the workers with upper-status origins while rationing access to good jobs for workers with lower-status origins. This vertical dimension of occupational mobility dominates the pattern of exchange mobility in Ireland.

Although class affects life chances, this aspect of exchange mobility in Ireland is not so distinctive. The important dimension that differentiates Ireland from other countries, except perhaps Eastern European ones, is the contribution of informal labor markets to overall inequality. Informal labor markets are by nature laden with inequalities of access. Their informality shields them from public scrutiny. They are not subject to reviews of their fairness. The patterns of unpaid apprenticeships within the traditional sectors of the economy create obvious channels for restriction of opportunity. Farming is a prime example. Only those born on farms have a reasonable chance of making a career of farming. The links between farmers and their sons are of course not unique to Ireland. What is special in Ireland is the way this personal imperative in the traditional economy spills over into the modern sector. Personal contacts reveal themselves in the data as a heavy weight in occupational immobility at all prestige levels in both parts of Ireland. Independent of its effects in traditional sectors of the Irish economy, personal contact weighs heavily on occupational mobility throughout Irish society.

4 The Gap between Working Class and Middle Class

The distinction between manual and nonmanual forms of work lays the foundation of nearly every discussion of mobility and social stratification across all points of view from Blau and Duncan (1967) to Poulantzas (1973, 1975). Classical theory sees the white-collar–blue-collar (or manual-nonmanual) distinction as fundamental (Sorokin 1927). Contemporary approaches make finer distinctions among occupations, giving no special attention to the gross distinction between manual and nonmanual occupations. Critiques, especially by British Marxists, have faulted the contemporary approach. The approach taken here is contemporary. The models presented score occupations on several dimensions relevant to occupational mobility. Nonmanual occupations score higher than manual occupations on a number of these dimensions, notably prestige and education, but no special attention is given to the so-called boundary between classes. In fact, the prestige of upper manual occupations is not as far below the lower nonmanual occupations as it is above the lower manual occupations.

The traditional concerns with a qualitative difference between working class and middle class have not disappeared, nor should they. Parkin (1971), Giddens (1973), Poulantzas (1973, 1975), Goldthorpe (1980), and Wright (1985) raise questions predicated on the differences between nonmanual and manual workers as classes with distinct social and political interests that grow out of their working conditions and "relations of production." If the manual-nonmanual distinction is, in fact, fundamental, then the models used here will fail in predictable ways. Thus, the models generate a test of the proposition that the distinction between manual and nonmanual work is unlike distinctions within those broad classes. The test involves an examination of mobility across the manual-nonmanual border.

Issues in Previous Research

Early mobility studies attend to a variety of occupational distinctions, but the classification schemes employed in those studies have little in common except the middle-class–working-class distinction (Sorokin 1927, pp. 416–417). Researchers had done little to standardize classification techniques by the 1950s. As a consequence, Lipset and Zetterberg collapse the 1950s data into simple 2 × 2 (nonmanual-manual) and 3 × 3 (nonmanual-manual-farm) tables (Lipset and Bendix 1959, pp. 14–17). The data differ in details that preclude any other basis of comparison.[1] Their dichotomy accords well with the concerns that those authors and others express regarding the distinction between the working class and the middle classes of industrial societies. Discussions of the proletarianization of the lower nonmanual strata (Wright 1985, pp. 40ff; Wright and Martin 1987) and of embourgeoisement (Goldthorpe and Lockwood 1963; Goldthorpe et al. 1968, 1969) question the salience of this boundary for social stratification and class formation, but most discussions take for granted that the manual-nonmanual distinction embodies the boundary between the middle class and the working class in advanced societies.

Since the work of Blau and Duncan, the use of a much finer grain to analyze mobility in the United States and elsewhere has spread. Nonetheless, nearly every classification scheme retains the distinction between blue-collar and white-collar occupations in constructing the categories. For Blau and Duncan this traditional distinction proves to be critical to understanding the mobility patterns of the American mobility tables. Amid the detail of those tables, they discern "two semi-permeable class boundaries that limit downward mobility between generations as well as within life-time careers, though they permit upward mobility" (p. 59). Subsequent analyses of the 1962 data collected by Blau and Duncan and of the 1973 replicate survey lead Featherman and Hauser (1978) to reject the idea of semipermeable class boundaries. They report significant differences between the life chances of men with white-collar origins and those with blue-collar origins, but they uncover a pattern of asymmetries that diverges substantially from the pattern implied by the semipermeable membrane thesis. Their image emphasizes the symmetry of mobility chances upward and downward across the white-collar–blue-collar boundary. The apparent asymmetry of the tables in Blau and Duncan (as well as the Featherman-Hauser replicate tables) reflects the dissimilarity of origins and destinations (SHD, pp. 368–371). Featherman and Hauser's model reveals immobility of occupations at the extremes of the socioeconomic hierarchy and the existence of transitional zones—broad strata that include upper-manual and lower-nonmanual occupations—"within which there are relatively homogeneous chances of immobility and of exchange with adjacent extreme strata" (p. 179). But "once the boundaries of the transitional zones have been crossed, no social distance gradient seems to underlie variations in long-distance mobility chances" (p. 79). Hauser's (1978) analysis of mobility in Britain accords well with the conclusions drawn from the American data, although the data are not comparable enough to test the hypothesis that the structure of opportunity or the pattern of social fluidity (namely, the association between origins and destinations, controlling for the marginal distribution of origins and destinations) is the same in Britain and the United States.[2]

English writers also emphasize transition zones that straddle the middle-class–working-class boundary (e.g., Bottomore 1965; Parkin 1971; Giddens 1973). But while they locate a "buffer zone" near the middle of the class structure, just where the transition zone of Featherman and Hauser is, these theorists assert a sharp gradient within the buffer zone that is inconsistent with the lack of a gradient in Featherman and Hauser's findings. According to Goldthorpe (1980, p. 47), the buffer zone theory claims that the preponderance of short-distance mobility in Britain and the United States "effectively blocks off longer-range mobility." One implication of this thesis is that the chances for upward mobility from working class to middle class should be much greater for men with origins in the upper reaches of the working class (classes V and VI) than for men with lower origins (classes VIIss, VIIus, and VIIf).[3] Another implication is that the chances of downward mobility from middle class to working class should be greater for men with origins in the lower strata of the middle class (classes IIIa, IIIb, IVa, and IVb) than for men with origins in the "service class." In England and Wales, these implications are incorrect. The expected gradient does not appear: "The buffer zone, in the form in which it has been advanced, appears to give rise to some specific propositions which are empirically invalid, and to be in general somewhat inapt to the nature and extent of the intergenerational movement [in Britain]" (p. 50).

Whelan and Whelan (1984) replicate Goldthorpe's analysis, using data for Dublin. These Irish data approximate the pattern expected under the buffer zone thesis: "Unlike the English case, sons of skilled manual workers are twice as likely [as men with lower working class origins] to achieve a higher professional and managerial position" (p. 45). Yet "in the case of the white collar origins we may observe . . . that there is no tendency towards concentration of downwardly mobile men in skilled rather than non-skilled [manual] grades" (p. 48; see also Breen and Whelan 1987).

Goldthorpe does not abandon the buffer zone idea; he recasts it: "It is in fact possible for the closure and buffer zone theses still to retain some merit if they are reformulated so as to refer to fluidity rather than to absolute mobility rates (p. 114)."[4] This conclusion is based on the pattern of association between origins and destinations according to the levels of topological models (Hauser 1978; Hout 1983). The topological approach is particularly well suited to the testing of the buffer zone thesis. It presumes discontinuous mobility chances in a way that mimics the conceptualization of the buffer zone. The results offer some support for the buffer zone thesis, certainly greater support than it garnered from the pattern of absolute rates. The key is the gradation of the levels parameters from the topological model in a way that is consistent with both the closure thesis and the buffer zone thesis. In particular, the closure thesis finds support in the density of immobility in the elite (class I), which is extremely high compared with other densities in the model.[5] Furthermore, density drops to its lowest level for mobility downward from elite origins to blue-collar destinations. Support for the buffer zone thesis takes the form of definite gradation in the odds on white-collar destinations for men of blue-collar origins; short-range moves into clerical and service positions are far more likely than are moves into more prestigious white-collar occupations. Even more important for the buffer zone thesis, downward mobility of men from middle-class origins to blue-collar destinations is clearly graded according to the skill level of the destinations. Apparently the pattern of structural mobility in Britain obscured the rigidity of the underlying association between origins and destinations.[6] In other words, this rekindled support for hypotheses about closure and buffer zones reflects latent tendencies inherent in the class structures of Irish, British, and American societies. It appears that the structural differentiation of occupational positions works against tendencies to concentrate privilege. In this way structural mobility hides class boundaries from those workers (and researchers) who observe only the gross movements from lower to upper classes. At the same time, the imbalance between the number of elite destinations and the number of men from elite origins in contemporary Ireland, England, and the United States frustrates the elites in these three societies who seek to exclude men of lower origins from access to positions of power and prestige but actually aids them in their aim to pass advantage on the next generation. At issue is the extent to which the scaled association models miss this important interaction of interests and immobility.

Head and Hand in Ireland

The Irish data speak to a number of these issues. First, interstratum mobility negates the closure thesis, at least as it applies to absolute rates of mobility. The Irish data are mixed—much more so than the English data appear to be—on the issue of a buffer zone. On the negative side, the buffer zone thesis, at least as rendered by Goldthorpe, implies differential chances of mobility upward from working-class origins, depending on where in the working class those origins fall. In particular, men from technical, supervisory, or skilled backgrounds (the upper working class) can be expected to move into white-collar occupations more often than men from semiskilled or unskilled backgrounds do. The English data and the Dublin data do not distinguish between semiskilled and unskilled workers. In the effort to evaluate the buffer zone thesis in the Republic, this proves to be a crucial distinction because, while the men from semiskilled backgrounds have the same chances of arriving in the middle class as do men from the upper working class, the chances of men from unskilled backgrounds are significantly less than other men's chances (see Table 3.3). The pattern in the national data is not as strong as the pattern in the Dublin data (Whelan and Whelan 1984, p. 43).

In Northern Ireland, the pattern of differential working-class mobility supports the buffer zone thesis. The odds on mobility into the middle class increase with skill level of origins.

The buffer zone thesis also generates a related expectation that downwardly mobile men from middle-class origins will be disproportionately drawn from origins within the buffer zone, namely, from clerical, sales, or proprietorial origins. This is certainly the case in both parts of Ireland (see Table 3.3).

On both counts, then, the Irish data show the plausibility of a buffer zone easing mobility from manual to nonmanual origins, so long as the incursion into the middle class does not carry too great a distance into the middle class. Few men of working-class origins move beyond the ranks of clerical and sales workers and the petit bourgeoisie. The relation is symmetrical, in keeping with the overall symmetry of intergenerational exchanges in Ireland. The extent of net downward mobility from white-collar origins to blue-collar destinations depends on the status of both origins and destinations. In general, short-distance mobility prevails in both directions (and also within strata).

Wright (1985) would regard this evidence in a very different light. His class schema locates clerical workers in the working class, along with manual workers. He distinguishes the petit bourgeoisie on the basis of their control of property. The categorization used here cannot be translated into his 12-class schema, so determination of the extent to which the pattern of mobility resembles class mobility in the sense that he means is impossible.

Analyzing interstratum mobility obscures differences in destinations among the white-collar occupations attained by men from different working-class origins. Many of the inferences on the topic that one might want to draw from the frequencies in Table A.1 must be carefully qualified, because so many of the numbers are small. Without a large data base it is difficult to distinguish between real patterns in the data and psuedopatterns caused by nothing more than sampling error. The preferred strategy is to smooth over the sampling error with a model. That aim is accomplished by multidimensional models. The significant effects of prestige and education produce the preponderance of short-range over long-range moves that Goldthorpe is looking for as evidence of the buffer zone's existence. Scaled effects of the type included in the multidimensional model imply that workers move toward destinations like their origins and away from destinations very different from those origins.

If the buffer zone is understood in these simple, mechanical terms, then the model results support it. But Giddens (1973), at least, seems to have a stronger effect in mind. His theory of class-specific resources (property, qualifications, and manual labor power) implies that the buffer zone, if it exists—and he believes that it does—exaggerates short-distance mobility over and above the constraints of a linear effect. He suggests a departure from linearity of some kind—an *excess* of short-distance mobility and a surfeit of long-distance mobility relative to the expectations of the linear model. He argues that there is a qualitative shift in the odds on clerical and sales destinations for men from working-class origins (relative to upper nonmanual destinations) due to the displacement of one type of resource by another.

The residuals from the multidimensional model will reflect those nonlinearities, if they exist. If the buffer zone thesis—in this stronger expression—is true, then the residuals near the diagonal of the mobility table will be positive, and the residuals for cells that indicate long-distance mobility will be negative.

Table 4.1 includes data that clearly refute the stronger version of the buffer zone thesis. The key regions of the table for this thesis are the upper right and lower left corners. If the buffer zone thesis is correct, the cells in the rectangles that are closest to the diagonal should be positive, and the ones farthest from the diagonal should be negative. No unambiguous pattern emerges for either the Republic of Ireland or Northern Ireland. Furthermore, there is no correlation between the residuals in one region and the residuals in another region. Thus, there are no systematic deviations that might be construed as tentative support for a buffer zone that augments the linear effects of prestige, educational credentials, bureaucratic rationalization of occupational entry, and the Irish tradition of personal imperative in some occupations.

Homogeneity within the Working Class

An important issue for Goldthorpe is the homogeneity of social origins among the working classes. Over three-fourths of the British working class (classes V, VI, VIIss, and VIIus) claim working-class origins. The percentages of working-class men of *nonfarm* origins who claim working-class origins are just as high in Northern Ireland and in the Republic: 80.6 percent and 78.1 percent, respectively. Goldthorpe was looking at men of nonfarm origin, so these are the comparable figures; they look very impressive. They do not mean, however, that the Irish working class is as culturally homogeneous or as socially closed as the British working class. The force of structural mobility that shifts farmers' sons into urban pursuits is much stronger in Ireland than in England. The "true" homogeneity of the Irish working class is reflected in the percentages of working-class men who are from working-class backgrounds when men from farm backgrounds are included. Those percentages are 65.0 percent for Northern Ireland and 56.5 percent for the Republic. More important, perhaps, is the impressive volume of mobility among working-class positions (reflected in

Table 4.1
Residuals from multidimensional model by region: men aged 18–65, Ireland, 1973

Origin		Ia	Ib	II	IIIa	IVa	IVb	IIIb	V	VI	VIIss	VIIus	IVc	IVd	VIIf
Republic of Ireland															
Professionals & proprietors[a]	Ia	.35	1.05	-1.23	-.33	-2.70	.58	1.00	-3.11	-3.13	-2.38	-1.18	-1.46	-1.34	-.19
Professionals & managers	Ib	-2.16	-.42	.85	-.04	-2.44	-2.08	1.83	.11	-.79	-.22	-1.97	-.95	-.85	-.25
Professionals & managers	II	.71	.39	-.53	.31	.48	.35	.31	.15	-.19	.21	.27	.23	.87	-1.91
Clerical & sales workers	IIIa	.57	.40	.04	.02	-.11	.15	.02	.29	-.61	-.08	-.62	.55	-2.95	-2.05
Proprietors with employees[a]	IVa	-.89	.35	.18	.10	.32	.26	.78	-.20	-.88	.01	-.39	-3.69	-1.55	-.59
Proprietors without employees[a]	IVb	-.35	-.09	.05	-1.02	.24	.13	-.04	-.25	-.33	.39	.24	-.14	-.55	.38
Service workers	IIIb	-1.45	-.49	-1.09	.68	-.19	-.19	.32	.05	.08	.16	-.68	.55	-2.95	.65
Technicians & foremen	V	-.16	-1.84	-.16	-.06	.15	-.05	-1.02	-.12	.67	.10	.05	-2.73	.16	-2.74
Skilled manual workers	VI	-.67	-.22	.01	-.41	-.21	-4.69	-.06	-.04	.37	.14	-.04	-1.00	-4.36	-1.54
Semiskilled manual workers	VIIss	.69	-.48	.35	-.01	.26	-.17	.22	.21	.15	-.04	-.41	-3.47	-.12	.17
Unskilled manual workers	VIIus	-1.93	-.88	-.41	.14	.05	.06	.07	.14	.22	-.18	-.15	-3.19	-.14	.80
Farmers with employees[a]	IVc	-.87	-.16	.08	-1.79	-.18	-.44	-.78	-.83	-1.33	-.35	.17	.14	1.03	.13
Farmers without employees[a]	IVd	.11	.27	.57	.54	-.38	-.01	-.31	.16	-.35	.08	.47	.21	-.05	-.61
Agricultural workers	VIIf	-1.89	.28	-1.51	.26	-.34	.77	-.24	.16	-.29	-.03	.26	-.68	-.47	.11
Northern Ireland															
Professionals & proprietors[a]	Ia	-.09	.51	-.29	-2.96	.73	-2.41	-1.58	-3.23	.04	.01	-1.06	1.81	2.25	.44
Professionals & managers	Ib	1.39	-.16	.36	.32	-.66	-2.98	-2.33	-.63	-.49	.23	.28	-.81	-.38	-.05
Professionals & managers	II	.60	.38	-.16	.31	-1.65	-.56	.70	-.10	-.40	-.00	.41	-2.10	.88	2.27
Clerical & sales workers	IIIa	-.20	-.18	.14	.32	.54	-.21	1.00	-.67	-.13	-.39	-.27	-1.57	-1.53	-1.51
Proprietors with employees[a]	IVa	-.45	.45	-.12	.22	.13	-.01	-.70	-.52	-.19	.16	-.70	-.47	.64	.69
Proprietors without employees[a]	IVb	-.36	-.48	-.25	.45	.34	.14	.31	-.32	-.00	.01	.34	-2.54	-2.96	-2.53
Service workers	IIIb	-1.99	.14	.48	.39	.47	-.12	.30	.01	.02	-.35	-1.64	.56	.04	-2.61
Technicians & foremen	V	-.58	-.21	-.18	-.22	.43	.12	.36	-.16	.30	-.39	.37	.38	.23	-2.25
Skilled manual workers	VI	-.11	-.21	-.09	-.49	.16	-.12	.30	.19	.12	-.05	-.00	-3.51	-3.85	.33
Semiskilled manual workers	VIIss	-.02	-.03	.05	-.63	-.49	.05	.06	.30	.07	.01	-.04	-.66	-3.96	.41
Unskilled manual workers	VIIus	.63	-.28	.01	.33	-.04	-.35	-.23	.55	.02	.01	-.19	.26	-.61	-4.01
Farmers with employees[a]	IVc	-.38	.18	.25	.13	.17	.21	-.33	-1.36	-1.36	-.06	-.02	.11	.91	.23
Farmers without employees[a]	IVd	-.76	-.51	.05	.55	-.35	.16	-1.01	-.31	.03	.21	.51	.13	-.05	-.16
Agricultural workers	VIIf	-1.87	.11	.40	-.50	-1.51	.07	-.26	.53	.08	.10	.08	-3.50	-.75	-.04

a.   Self–employed workers.

the self-recruitment and immobility calculations). All in all, it appears that the Irish working class is more heterogeneous than the working class of England and Wales because of the influx of farmers' sons into working-class occupations over the past generation.

Conclusion

The life chances of men born into working-class origins are inferior to those of men born into middle-class origins in Ireland. Thus the pattern seen in Ireland is common to all industrial societies, at least in broadest outline (Erikson and Goldthorpe 1987a,b). This pattern reveals no special "boundary" between middle class and working class other than what can be attributed to the hierarchy of status and prestige that divides occupational groups in industrial and postindustrial society. The divide between the old classes is quantitative, not qualitative. According to the scales used in this research, the spread in prestige and educational credentials *within* the broad nonmanual and manual strata exceeds the spread *between* the highest manual and lowest nonmanual occupations. Indeed, as in the United States (Featherman and Hauser 1978, p. 26), the upper end of the working class ranks above the lower reaches of the middle class.[7] Thus the continuous operation of the several dimensions of occupational mobility identified here—not the discontinuous influence of deep interclass boundaries, as through the shift from labor power to credentials—governs differential life chances for men of working-class and middle-class origins.

5　The Occupational Mobility
of Farmers' Sons

In "Digging," Seamus Heaney expresses the ambivalence of many Irish farmers' sons when they think about their roots. As sons of the land, they are born into a noble heritage that they may or may not be able to claim. Those who leave the farm break the generational succession. Those who stay have to do the hard work of cultivating the soil. At the end of the day, farming is an honorable pursuit that brings with it the esteem of one's fellows but less material reward than one might hope for.

Changes in Ireland since the late 1950s have diminished the role of farming in the economy of the island. In the Republic there were 342,000 male farmers and relatives assisting in 1951; by 1971 the number was down to 213,000 (Whelan and Whelan 1984, table 2.1). According to the 1981 census, there were 131,000 male farmers and 21,000 male relatives assisting (Central Statistics Office 1986, table 2). Comparable statistics for Northern Ireland are not available; in 1973, however, 8.5 percent of Northern Irish men worked in agriculture (O'Dowd 1986). This figure may mark a long-standing low level of employment in agriculture or a downward trend. The statistics do show that the mobility chances of farmers' sons are more subject to the forces of social change in Ireland during the lifetime of the workers under study than are the mobility chances of men from other social origins. This inference is reinforced by the strong negative structural mobility for both the Republic and Northern Ireland. The rich detail in the work histories of farmers' sons provides additional insight into the microdynamics of these changes.

Aggregate decline does not necessarily mean individual mobility. For example, farmers can continue to farm until death or retirement, but if their sons do not stay on to inherit the farm, then the aggregate concentration of the labor force in farming will go down. Both the intergenerational mobility and the intragenerational mobility of farmers' sons are important for identifying the source of agricultural decline. And, of course, farmers must have sons. In particular, three probabilities are important for the persistence of farming: the probability that a farmer's son will take up farming, the probability that a farmer's son who has taken up farming will remain in farming throughout his work life (and not subsequently change to a nonagricultural occupation), and the probability that a farmer's son who takes up farming will also marry and reproduce himself. A decrease in any of these probabilities will contribute to the overall decline in farm employment.

Despite the importance of the farm sector for inequality in Ireland, the process of farm immobility has been invisible in past investigations of occupational mobility in Ireland. Earlier Irish mobility studies sampled from the Dublin metropolitan area (Hutchinson 1969, 1973; Whelan and Whelan 1984). Some inferences could be drawn from the mobility of farmers' sons who moved into the Dublin region, but questions of selectivity hampered the interpretation of those results (e.g., Whelan and Whelan 1984, pp. 28–30, 35, 96–97).

Types of Agricultural Employment

Over three-fourths of farmers' sons in the Irish Mobility Study had worked at some type of agricultural job as of December 1973. Table 5.1 breaks down that experience by type of agricultural employment. Three occupations are distinguished: farmer, relative assisting on a farm, and paid farm worker.[1] Farmers' sons are classified according to whether or not they have ever held each of the occupations. Farming and assisting are far more common than are working on a farm for wages.

Social and economic factors influence the distribution of farmers' sons by type of agricultural employment. Farms are family enterprises, so farmers who need extra labor tend to recruit within the family before looking to others. Furthermore, "relative assisting" is a holding category for farmers' sons waiting for the opportunity to begin farming on their own. This wait frequently comes to an end when the father turns over the farm to his son, but some farmers' sons enter farming by marrying into another family that has a farm but no male heir, by purchasing land from someone else, or by taking over from a bachelor farmer who has no heir.[2] Among the economic factors, scale and productivity of farms affect agricultural employment. Succinctly put, few Irish farms are large enough to

Table 5.1
Types of farm employment experience: farmers' sons, Ireland, 1973

Farm laborer	Farm owner	Republic[a]		Northern Ireland[a]	
		Farm helper	Not a farm helper	Farm helper	Not a farm helper
Yes	Yes	4%	4%	3%	3%
	No	6	6	4	8
No	Yes	37	4	29	4
	No	21	18	22	26
Total		68	32	58	42
(N)		(563)	(261)	(307)	(218)

a. Percentages sum to 100 percent within regions (exceptions are due to rounding).

employ many workers, especially in an era when mechanization has greatly enhanced the productivity of each hand.

Irish farming is dominated by families and family interests. This has been the pattern for generations (Arensberg and Kimball 1940; Hannan 1982). Landownership and access to land rights are vested in families. Few men get into farming on their own; they depend on their families. The modal pattern is to work as an unpaid relative assisting and then to move to a farm of one's own. Thirty-seven percent of farmers' sons now living in the Republic have followed this path; 29 percent of farmers' sons living in the North have done so. Another large group (roughly one-fifth in each region) are those whose only farming experience is as a relative assisting. About 10 percent of current workers are relatives assisting, indicating that half of this group has left farming, while the other half is still assisting.

The preponderance of unpaid work on farms underscores the importance of family for farming in Ireland. It also reflects the poverty and marginal existence that farming offers in rural Ireland. Labor-intensive farming methods survive to this day in the Irish countryside because of a surplus of labor and a surfeit of material capital. These economic realities caution against overemphasizing the barriers to farming. It is probably fair to say that most Irishmen of nonfarm origins do not confront those barriers head-on because, for them, farming is not a very attractive occupation, even if the opportunity were somehow to open to them.

The fact that some of those who assist on farms eventually leave agriculture does not undermine the importance of assisting as a gateway to farming. Eleven farmers in twelve began work as a relative assisting. Less than 5 percent of farmers worked as paid laborers, and the rest moved directly into farming as their first job. In the Republic, the odds on being a farmer are 7.2 times greater for farmers' sons who have assisted on a farm than for men who have no such experience (among men who were not paid workers); in Northern Ireland, the corresponding odds ratio is 8.5. Among men who have experience as paid workers, assisting has no effect on whether or not they eventually become farmers. However, being a paid worker *decreases* the odds on becoming a farmer among men with experience as family members assisting (the odds ratios are .40 in the Republic and .69 in Northern Ireland). Finally, for men with no experience assisting, the effect of working for pay on the odds on becoming a farmer are positive (2.7 in the Republic and 2.8 in Northern Ireland).

The Life Cycle of Farmers' Sons

Farmers' sons work as unpaid helpers because they reach working age before their fathers reach retirement age. The fathers of the vast majority of men in the sample—85 percent—were still farming when the respondent took his first job. Ten percent of the fathers had died; the remainder (5 percent) had left farming for another job or retirement. In the family-based system of agriculture, it is difficult to retain one's claim on the farm without working for it. So for many young men who aspire to farming as a life's work, an apprenticeship period precedes their accession to the title of farmer. These men work without pay as their father's assistant until the father dies or retires. This life cycle is visible in the distribution of occupations held by farmers' sons at different ages. Table 5.2 shows the distribution of employment of farmers' sons across several occupational categories at selected ages and dates.[3]

In both the Republic and Northern Ireland a substantial proportion of farmers' sons are employed in agriculture at each point in the life course. The relative numbers of farmers and relatives assisting, however, changes dramatically with age. At young ages, assisting predominates; as fathers retire and die, the balance shifts, so that by age 30 (in the North) or 35 (in the Republic), farmers outnumber assistants. The rate of increase in the proportion working as farmers is greatest between the ages of 25 and 30 in Northern Ireland and between the ages of 30 and 35 in the Republic.

Self-employment outside of farming also manifests a distinct life cycle. The proportion of farmers' sons who own their own business or professional practice is low relative to the whole population at each age

Table 5.2
Occupations of farmers' sons at selected ages and dates by region:
men aged 18–65, Ireland, 1973

Age/ date	*Destination*[a]									
	F	FH	FT	FL	SE	WC	BC	U	Total	(N)
Republic of Ireland										
First	2%	67%	69%	9%	1%	10%	11%	0%	100%	(801)[b]
20	4	52	56	10	1	10	19	3	100	(769)
25	12	41	53	8	3	12	21	3	100	(717)
30	25	31	56	7	4	10	22	2	100	(639)[b]
35	36	23	59	5	5	8	20	3	100	(560)[b]
40	47	13	60	4	5	7	21	3	100	(489)[b]
45	51	9	60	3	6	8	20	4	100	(410)[b]
1959	33	27	60	4	4	10	20	3	100	(631)[b]
1973	47	8	55	2	6	11	19	6	100	(814)[b]
Northern Ireland										
First	3%	55%	58%	12%	1%	13%	16%	0%	100%	(509)
20	6	47	53	9	2	11	24	2	100	(485)
25	15	34	49	6	5	13	24	3	100	(452)
30	27	21	48	6	9	12	23	2	100	(402)
35	31	16	47	5	9	13	22	4	100	(342)
40	33	10	43	6	9	11	27	4	100	(293)
45	37	6	43	6	11	12	26	2	100	(243)
1959	27	22	49	6	6	13	23	2	100	(403)
1973	35	5	40	2	11	14	26	7	100	(522)

a. F = farmer; FH = farm helper; FT = family total (the sum of F and FH); FL = farm laborer; SE = self–employed; WC = white collar; BC = blue collar; U = unemployed.
b. Regional difference significant at the .05 level.

(compare appendix Tables A.1 and A.2). Nonetheless, the upward trend over the life cycle cannot be mistaken. These data do not disclose the course of events that lead these men into self-employment. Some are employees who save up and eventually go into competition with former employers; some are craftsmen who strike out on their own after a period of journeyman work; and a few are farmers who sell off their holdings to seek a different, maybe even better, life in town. The data in Table 5.2 are entirely rates of net change. Since some moves are canceled out by observations of this kind, the rising rates of self-employment in the table understate the true level of mobility into and out of self-employment.

The life cycles of white-collar and blue-collar occupations show almost no net shift. This aggregate equilibrium also hides some mobility.

The changes in Irish agriculture may well have altered some of the life cycle patterns in Table 5.2. In particular, one might expect lower rates of farming for more recent cohorts and a higher rate of mobility from farm to nonfarm employment over the life cycle. To investigate such a prospect, we divide the sample into four birth cohorts: 1908–1925, 1925–1935, 1936–1945, and 1946–1955. Data from Northern Ireland and the Republic are pooled for this part of the analysis because there are not enough cases to control for region and cohort at the same time.[4]

The median age at first job (with cohort in parentheses) increased for farmers' sons in the two more recent cohorts, as shown by the following figures: 14.9 years (1908–1925), 14.9 years (1926–1935), 15.6 years (1936–1945), and 16.2 years (1946–1955). Recent cohorts have delayed entry into the work force at a rate averaging two-thirds of a year per decade. Thus the average member of the oldest cohort began working in 1931 or 1932, the average member of the 1925–1935 cohort began working in 1945, the average member of the 1936–1945 cohort began working in 1956, and the average member of the 1946–1955 cohort began working in 1966—after the important changes that began in the Republic in 1959. Similar changes in the countryside of Northern Ireland were in process even earlier.

Table 5.3 presents the data on occupational distributions of the different cohorts by age. The transition from farm helper to farmer is evident as an important pattern in these data, just as in Table 5.2. Controlling for cohort reveals a parallel decline in paid agricultural labor over the life course, which was not clear in Table 5.2.

Cohort is controlled in this analysis not merely to reconfirm the life cycle effects but also to investigate the shift away from farming for farmers' sons in successive cohorts. The evidence in Table 5.3 reveals that just such a shift occurred, starting with the 1936–1945 cohort and continuing with the most recent, 1946–1955, cohort. All but a few members of the older of these cohorts reached the age of 20 in the late 1950s, 1960s, or early 1970s—after the redistribution of both Irish economies was well under way.

Consider the changes in family farming as a whole. Combining for the moment farmers and farm helpers, the third column of the table shows that, for the oldest two cohorts, the proportion of farmers' sons working in family-based agriculture is 8 to 10 percentage points higher at each age than the corresponding figure for the next youngest cohort, and 17 to 21 percentage points higher than the corresponding figure for the youngest cohort.

The cohort differences show further that the employment experiences of the oldest two cohorts differ from one another at each age beyond 25 years. Men from the 1926–1935 cohort transfer from farm helper to farmer

Table 5.3
Occupations of farmers' sons at selected ages and dates by cohort:
men aged 18–65, Ireland, 1973

Age/date	F	FH	FL	SE	WC	BC	U	NLF	Total	(N)
					Destination[a]					
1908–1925										
First	4%	66%	12%	0%	8%	9%	0%	0%	100%	(561)
20	5	54	12	1	6	16	2	4	100	(561)
25	11	44	9	2	9	20	3	0	100	(561)
30	22	32	9	5	9	21	2	0	100	(561)
35	31	23	6	5	9	22	3	0	100	(561)
40	39	14	5	6	8	24	3	0	100	(561)
45	45	9	5	6	8	23	3	0	100	(561)
1973	53	2	2	7	8	20	8	0	100	(555)
1926–1935										
First	3%	68%	9%	1%	11%	8%	0%	0%	100%	(275)
20	4	52	9	2	10	19	2	3	100	(275)
25	14	40	6	4	13	21	2	0	100	(275)
30	28	28	4	6	11	22	1	0	100	(275)[b]
35	40	16	2	8	11	19	4	0	100	(275)[b]
40	48	7	2	7	10	20	4	0	100	(221)[b]
45	51	3	2	12	14	16	1	0	100	(92)[b]
1973	52	3	2	10	11	17	5	0	100	(271)
1936–1945										
First	2%	58%	8%	0%	13%	18%	0%	0%	100%	(256)[b]
20	7	43	6	2	12	21	2	6	100	(256)
25	16	28	4	6	17	28	2	0	100	(256)
30	34	12	2	8	15	27	2	0	100	(206)[b]
35	36	9	5	12	17	20	2	0	100	(66)
1973	39	8	2	10	15	23	3	0	100	(252)[b]
1946–1955										
First	1%	50%	9%	1%	16%	23%	0%	0%	100%	(246)
20	3	35	6	3	18	24	7	4	100	(218)[b]
25	16	22	7	10	14	20	10	1	100	(83)[b]
1973	12	25	4	7	21	28	4	0	100	(232)[b]

a.   F = farmer; FH = farm helper; FL = farm laborer; SE = self–employed; WC = white collar; BC = blue collar; U = unemployed; NLF = not in labor force.

b.   Difference between this row and the corresponding row for preceding cohort is significant at the .05 level.

at a younger age than do men from the 1908–1925 cohort. At each age the proportion of men from the 1926–1935 cohort working as farmers exceeds the corresponding proportion among men born 1908–1925. At ages 40 and 45, differences in the distribution of men into middle-class or working-class occupations contribute to the overall difference; men from the 1926–1935 cohort are more likely to be middle class than their counterparts in the earlier cohort.

The 1936–1945 cohort differs from the preceding cohort in the distribution of first occupations, occupations at age 30, and current occupations. Men from this cohort are substantially less likely than their predecessors to begin their careers as helpers or to remain helpers for long if they take a first job as a relative assisting. One consequence of these tendencies is the anomalous observation that the proportion of men from the 1936–1945 cohort who are farming at age 30 exceeds the proportion from the 1926–1935 cohort, despite the general tendency toward lower rates of participation in agriculture in the recent cohorts.

The 1946–1955 cohort was still very young at the time of the 1973 survey, but the available evidence through age 25 shows a continuation of the trend toward nonagricultural employment, lower levels of working as a helper, and a shorter stay in the unpaid category among those who do enter it. Self-employment outside agriculture also appears to be strong for the 1946–1955 cohort, although small numbers of cases make inferences somewhat unreliable.

Sources of Recruitment into Farming

The modal pattern is for farmers to enter farming from inheritance, either directly as a first occupation or after a period of apprenticeship as an unpaid family member assisting on the farm. Approximately one-fifth of current farmers, however, got into farming from some other route. Table 5.4 tabulates the occupation held by farmers' sons just prior to farming for each region and for Ireland as a whole. This table covers all farmers' sons who ever worked as farmers, including those who were no longer farmers at the time of the survey. These data show how some men move into farming after a period of paid labor, either in agriculture or in other industries. Particularly for men in the Republic, this avenue provides a second chance for mobility into farming; 8.4 percent of men who ever farmed in the Republic moved into farming from paid agricultural labor, and another 11.2 percent moved into farming from paid labor outside agriculture. About one second generation farmer in 20 left a middle-class job or self-employment to take up farming.

In the changing context of Irish agriculture, one can hardly expect the patterns of recruitment documented in Table 5.4 to be reproduced in all cohorts. The possibility that changes across cohorts in the accession to farming might come about because of proportional shifts in the probability of entering farming for farmers' sons in all occupations cannot be ruled out

Table 5.4
Occupation prior to farming by region:
farmers' sons aged 20–65 who ever worked as farmers, Ireland, 1973

Occupation	Republic	Northern Ireland	Total
Farmer first job	4.9%	8.4%	6.0%
Farm helper	71.3	73.3	72.0
Farm laborer	8.4	6.9	7.9
Self–employed	2.0	2.5	2.2
White collar	2.3	2.5	2.4
Blue collar	11.2	6.5	9.6
Total	100.0	100.0	100.0
(N)	(394)	(202)	(596)

on the basis of the evidence so far, but it must be considered an unlikely explanation for trends. A more plausible hypothesis is that men who enter some occupations might have stopped coming back to farming. This hypothesis might be termed the selective decline hypothesis. It views the changes in the proportion of each cohort engaged in farming as a consequence of declining rates of countermobility that may be greater for some nonfarm occupations than for others. A third alternative, called the cohort succession hypothesis, involves a compositional shift of first jobs. Suppose that opportunities for first jobs in white-collar occupations and other positions that send few men back to farming increase, while opportunities in agriculture contract. Such a situation could result in less countermobility for farmers' sons even if the occupation-specific probabilities of mobility into farming remained constant over time. Table 5.3 supports the premise of this argument: the proportion of each successive cohort taking a white-collar first job increased, while a smaller proportion of each successive cohort took unpaid first jobs as farmers' helpers. More evidence is needed to reach a conclusion.

The key to evaluating these alternative hypotheses is the rate of change over time in the conditional probability of moving from each occupational group into farming. Table 5.5 presents conditional probabilities of this type calculated for each cohort over a five-year time span.[5] These calculations clearly support the cohort succession hypothesis. The probabilities of moving from farm labor or farm help into farming actually increase with successive cohorts. Farmers' sons moved from other forms of agricultural work into farming at a faster pace from the late 1950s on. The decline of farming came about because fewer farmers' sons stayed in the countryside after leaving school. The root of this change is unclear. The data do not reveal whether those farmers' sons in later cohorts who pursued white-collar and blue-collar first jobs did so in anticipation of a slim chance of inheriting the farm. These data are not inconsistent with a scenario in which many young men leave agriculture because they expect no future in it and choose not to waste their time in paid or unpaid labor that they suspect will be a dead end. Regardless of the psychology involved, this is evidence that the microdynamics of industrialization required less individual movement than one might suppose from aggregate statistics. The macroeconomic changes in both parts of Ireland provided inducement for many young Irishmen to begin their work lives outside agriculture. Once the lot was cast and a first job was taken, however, those who began their work lives in agriculture were able to stay there. The changes of the 1960s did not force a rural exodus. Nor did they stimulate one. They did provide opportunities for nonagricultural employment for young men who could not find stable employment in the countryside of their origins.

Table 5.5
Mobility into farming in a five–year period by age at becoming a farmer,
birth cohort, and prior occupation: farmers aged 20–65, Ireland, 1973

Cohort	FH	FL	SE	Prior occupation[a] WC	BC	U	NLF
20–25 years old							
Born 1908–25	8%	3%	—[b]	3%	6%	--	8%
1926–35	15	12	—	8	2	--	--
1936–45	18	20	—	0	2	--	0
1946–55	26	--	—	2	4	--	--
25–30 years old							
Born 1908–25	20%	9%	7%	6%	1%	6%	--
1926–35	27	20	10	6	5	--	--
1936–45	55	--	9	6	3	--	--
30–35 years old							
Born 1908–25	23%	10%	11%	2%	6%	0%	--
1926–35	39	20	12	3	0	--	--
1936–45	--	--	—	0	12	--	--
35–40 years old							
Born 1908–25	34%	6%	0%	5%	6%	6%	--
1926–35	50	--	6	0	0	--	--
40–45 years old							
Born 1908–25	28%	14%	11%	0%	4%	--	--

a.   FH = farm helper; FL = farm laborer; SE = self–employed; WC = white collar; BC = blue collar; U = unemployed; NLF = not in labor force.
b.   Less than 10 cases in the denominator.

The probabilities in Table 5.5 of course leave a wide margin for mobility out of agriculture. For example, the probability of moving from farm helper to farmer is never greater than 55 percent, and it is often substantially less than 50 percent. Perhaps the men who do not move from helper to farmer leave agriculture. If true, this would undermine some of the previous conclusions. But it is not the case, as Table 5.6 shows. The vast majority of farmers' sons assisting relatives on farms who do not move into farming remain as helpers. The only appreciable cohort differences repeat the finding of Table 5.5 (men from younger cohorts make the move to farming at a younger age if they make the move at all); there is no evidence that helper-to-nonfarm mobility increased.

Unpaid work functions mainly as a holding pattern for farmers' sons who aspire to farming. There is scant indication of an "impatience effect," that is, movement out of helping into other, nonagricultural lines of work. One might expect the family farm to be something of a safety net as well, a refuge for out-of-work farmers' sons to fall back on. But there is no evidence in these data of such movement. Indeed, 94 percent of the

Table 5.6
Occupational distribution at age $(x+5)$ years by age (x) and cohort: men who ever worked as farm helpers, Ireland, 1973

Age (x) / cohort	FH	F	Occupation at age $(x+5)$[a] FL	SE	WC	BC	U	Total
20 years old								
Born 1908–25	78%	8%	2%	1%	2%	7%	1%	100%
1926–35	72	15	1	1	3	8	1	100
1936–45	62	18	2	2	4	10	2	100
1946–55	46	26	3	3	6	9	9	100
25 years old								
Born 1908–25	70%	20%	3%	1%	0%	5%	0%	100%
1926–35	66	27	1	0	1	5	0	100
1936–45	38	55	2	0	2	4	0	100
30 years old								
Born 1908–25	71%	23%	1%	1%	1%	4%	1%	100%
1926–35	58	39	0	0	0	0	2	100
35 years old								
Born 1908–25	58%	34%	2%	1%	0%	4%	2%	100%
1926–35	44	50	0	0	0	3	3	100
40 years old								
Born 1908–25	63%	28%	1%	3%	1%	4%	0%	100%

a. FH = farm helper; F = farmer; FL = farm laborer; SE = self–employed; WC = white collar; BC = blue collar; U = unemployed.

farmers' sons who assisted on family farms without pay took this "helper" role as a first job.

Who Stays in Farming?

The first occupation a farmer's son takes after leaving school determines his access to the farm thereafter. Because the first job is so important, it is necessary to distinguish between those farmers' sons who go into farming and those who do not.

First jobs are classified into six categories (1) farmer, (2) farm helper, (3) farm laborer, (4) self-employed, (5) white collar, and (6) blue collar. The independent variables do not distinguish between farm helper and farm laborer, so these two categories are here combined.[6] Furthermore, the number of self-employed workers is extremely small, so the self-employed are here combined with white collar. These changes leave a four-category dependent variable.

The first independent variable is education.[7] It affects placement into white-collar versus blue-collar occupations among those farmers' sons who leave agriculture (Whelan and Whelan 1984). Whether or not it affects other aspects of first job placement remains to be seen. On the one hand, farmers' sons who expect to inherit the farm may forgo schooling, anticipating that it will do little to enhance their success on the farm. On the other hand, farmers' sons who do go to school may well have to wait less time for their inheritance. The other three independent variables are region, number of siblings, and a dummy variable that indicates whether or not the subject's father was alive at the time he took his first job. The population for this analysis is all farmers' sons in the sample. There are 29 cases with data missing on one or more of the variables, leaving 1,307 cases for analysis.

Hierarchical log-linear models are used to assess the effects of these variables on first job placement (Goodman 1970, 1972b; Fienberg 1980). All models fit the four-way association among the independent variables. In the notation of Goodman (1970, 1972b), that term is represented as $[RSAE]$, an acronym for Region, Siblings, Alive, and Education. The baseline model includes a term for the marginal distribution of first occupations, $[J]$, but it includes no effects for any of the independent variables on occupation at first job. Table 5.7 shows in the first line that the baseline model does not fit the data. The search for more plausible models begins with education. Education is the one factor known to be important; it is also a more proximate cause of occupation at first job than are the other

Table 5.7
Goodness–of–fit statistics for models of the effects of region, number of siblings, whether or not father is alive, and educational level on first occupation: farmers' sons aged 18–65, Ireland, 1973

Model[a]	L^2	df	p	bic
1 [RSAE][J]	471.38	189	<.01	−885
2 [RSAE][EJ]	196.57	177	.15	−1073
3 [RSAE][EJ][RJ]	183.61	174	.29	−1065
4 [RSAE][EJ][SJ]	174.75	168	.34	−1031
5 [RSAE][EJ][RJ][SJ]	162.01	165	.55	−1022
6 [RSAE][EJ][RJ][AJ]	180.12	171	.30	−1047
7 [RSAE][EJ][RJ][SJ][AJ]	158.55	162	.56	−1004
Differences between models				
[1]–[2]	274.81	12	<.01	−188
[2]–[3]	12.96	3	<.01	8
[2]–[4]	21.82	9	<.01	42
[3]–[5]	21.60	9	.01	43
[4]–[5]	12.74	3	<.01	9
[5]–[7]	3.46	3	.28	18

a.   R = region; S = number of siblings; A = father alive; E = educational level; J = first occupation.

factors, as they pertain more to social background. Adding the effect of education on occupation at first job, [EJ], to the model substantially improves the fit. According to the likelihood ratio ($L^2 = 196.57; df = 177$), the model is acceptable; according to Pearson ($X^2 = 239.21$), it is not. The effects of region, [RJ], and number of siblings, [SJ], on occupation at first job are also significant. Surprisingly, the absence of a living father has no affect on first occupation. Model 5 is the preferred one.[8]

Table 5.8 shows the parameter estimates under model 5. The coefficients are presented in the form of three logit regressions (see Goodman 1981b for equivalences among different expressions of log-linear models).[9] The dependent variables in the logit regressions are the odds on three destinations: being a farmer, being self-employed or employed in a white-collar occupation, and being employed in a blue-collar occupation—each relative to being a family member assisting ("farm helper") or a paid farm worker. The coefficients are read the same way that coefficients for dummy variables in ordinary least squares regressions are read, as deviations of the dependent logit from the logit expected in the deleted category of the independent variable. The deleted category for education is incomplete primary; for siblings, it is seven or more; for region, it is Republic of Ireland. This form of presenting the coefficients suits these results well because of the lack of three-way interactions involving the dependent vari-

Table 5.8
**Effects of education, number of siblings, and region on first occupation
(in logit form): farmers' sons aged 18–65, Ireland, 1973**

	Dependent logit		
Independent variable	White collar: farm helper	Farmer: farm helper	Blue collar: farm helper
Education			
Postsecondary	4.90	1.99	2.65
Complete secondary	3.45	−.40	1.58
Incomplete secondary	1.58	−.54	1.46
Complete primary	.64	−1.11	−.06
Incomplete primary	—	—	—
Number of siblings			
0 – 1	.08	1.18	−.36
2 – 3	.46	.03	−.38
4 – 6	.34	.37	.25
7 or more	—	—	—
Region			
Republic	—	—	—
Northern Ireland	.51	.46	.50

able. When three-way and four-way interactions complicate the model, other forms, especially graphic forms, of presenting data might be more informative (Duncan and Duncan 1979).

The odds on a middle-class first occupation increase as length of schooling increases. Middle-class first occupations include self-employment or work for wages or salary in a professional, managerial, sales, service, or clerical occupation. The odds are measured relative to first jobs as an unpaid assistant on a family farm or a paid agricultural laborer. Considering the difference in socioeconomic status between middle-class employment and paid or unpaid agricultural labor, this result seems reasonable. The effect of education estimated here does not depend on the effect of social origins, as all of the men in this analysis have farm origins. The parameter estimates show that the effect of each successive educational threshold up to completion of secondary school has a bigger effect on the odds on middle-class employment than the preceding educational threshold had. A farmer's son increases his odds on being middle class by .64 (in log scale) with the completion of primary school. He increases his odds on being middle class by an additional .94 over that by starting secondary school, and he increases his odds a further 1.87 log-points by finishing secondary school. Attainment of at least some postsecondary schooling adds a bonus of 1.45 points, to produce a net gap of 4.90 in the logit of a middle-class first job between men with postsecondary education and men with incomplete primary education. This is an enormous effect. If the probability (not logit) of a middle-class first job for some farmer's son with an incomplete secondary education is .10, then the model predicts that a farmer's son who has a postsecondary education but matches the first man in all other respects will have a probability of a middle-class first job of .94.[10]

The effect of education on the odds on a blue-collar first job is also positive, but this working-class attainment process lacks the bonus payoff for completion of each successive level. The odds on a blue-collar first job jump faster for enrollment at the next level than for completion of the level already started; that is, the odds on blue-collar employment increase more between primary and incomplete secondary and between complete secondary and postsecondary enrollment than between incomplete and complete primary or between incomplete and complete secondary.

Education has a distinctly curvilinear effect on the odds on farming versus merely working on a farm (with or without pay). The group with the highest odds on farming is the most educated segment. A postsecondary education raises a farmer's son's expected odds on farming in his first job from fifteen to two against (if he has minimal education) to even odds; that is, it raises the expected probability from .135 to .500. Intermediate levels of education actually depress the odds on farming as a first job. Apparently the later phases of primary education and all of secondary education provide human capital that is marketable in the towns but not on the farms. Completing the primary cycle without going on minimizes one's chances of moving directly into farming, although the substantial mobility from unpaid farm helping into farming per se makes this effect more one of timing than one of ultimate destination. This result should in no way be interpreted as a claim that men with complete primary education do not engage in farming. On the contrary, this result simply means that men with primary education conform to the modal pattern of helping for a while prior to farming on their own. Entering secondary school raises the odds on farming in the first job as compared with those who stop at the end of primary school, but not as compared with those who leave primary school prior to finishing.[11] Completing secondary education raises the odds on farming to a modest extent over that expected among those who fail to complete secondary education, but again, the odds on farming in the first job for men with complete secondary educations fall short of the odds among men with the lowest education.

The relationship between number of siblings and first occupation boils down to one simple effect: the only child and the son with one sibling are substantially more likely than are other farmers' sons to move directly into farming as a first occupation. Inheritance in Ireland is impartable, but primogeniture is not practiced widely. The heir gets the whole farm, but the eldest son is not necessarily the heir. Traditionally, a "stem family" system prevailed, in which one son and one daughter were endowed—the son with the farm and the daughter with a dowry (Arensberg 1937, p. 79; quoted in Hannan 1982, p. 143). Selection of whom to endow was left to the father's discretion. The unendowed siblings were left without land or dowry to tend to their own futures in the towns and cities of Ireland, on the road, or overseas.

The contemporary system echoes the stem family practice, but much less is at stake. Over time the land has become less a gem than a burden on the prospective heirs, at least in the West of Ireland, as shown by this quote on a community on the Dingle peninsula: "For at least three decades the selection of an heir for the land has been governed by the process of elimination rather than by choice [on the part of the father]. That is, the last one to escape (usually the youngest son) gets stuck with an unproductive farm and saddled with a lifestyle of almost certain celibacy and service to the old people" (Scheper-Hughes 1979, pp. 41–42). In the sense that having a large number of brothers and sisters might spread one's risk, it seems surprising that the number of siblings does not affect the odds on nonagricultural employment.

Finally, all three alternatives to helping on the family farm or working on farms for pay are more favored in the North than in the Republic. Living in Northern Ireland raises the odds on a middle-class first job, a working-class first job, or farming as a first job by a modest amount over what those odds might be in the Republic.

To determine the factors that distinguish the farmers' sons who enter agriculture from those who do not, we need to recognize that those who go into farm help or paid farm labor have a substantial probability of farming someday, while those who do not enter agriculture when they take their first job have almost no chance of ever farming. The Irish data recapitulate the familiar finding that education predominates in this distinction. The well-educated farmers' sons are the ones who have substantial chances of going into white-collar employment away from farming. Part of the effect is status. The general principle that increased education enhances the probability of moving into a higher-status destination occupation holds true here as well. But part of the effect of education on first job is surely prospective as well (Jackson and Miller 1983). Those farmers' sons who want to avoid being "the last one to escape" seek an advantage over their siblings and fellows in the schools. In parallel fashion, those who expect to inherit the farm may well drop out of school at a stage that many might consider premature simply because they fail to see the relevance of further schooling for their prospective lives as farmers.

The most serious issue facing Irish farms is the problem of succession. A study of farmers' *sons* misses this significant issue, but it should not be ignored. Farmers per se, especially bachelor farmers, are an important part of rural decline in Ireland (Scheper-Hughes 1979). Hannan (1982, p. 155) estimates the farmer replacement "rate" by taking the ratio of farmers' sons and sons-in-law living with the farmer to the number of married farmers. This rate has several imperfections, most notably the fact that a farmer with four sons or sons-in-law at home could mask the want of a successor on three other farms. Nonetheless, the trend is unmistakable. The farmer replacement rate fell by 60 percent between 1951 and 1971, from 80 percent of farms expecting replacement to 30 percent. Hannan (p. 156) notes that the "rapid decline in the retention of farmers' sons is not so much due to fewer sons entering farming in their teens but rather to much higher rates of off-farm migration in the post-war period."

The farmer replacement rate uses *married* farmers in the denominator, so it suffers from the same shortcomings as does the Irish Mobility Study. Bachelorhood is at once a cause and a consequence of the rural decline in Ireland. Bachelor farmers contribute to decline by failing to secure the continuation of farming on their land. When they pass away or retire, the land goes to relatives who may or may not continue to farm it. But of course, remaining a bachelor is the last resort of an impoverished farmer. Most single, young farmers expect to marry, but the serious imbalance of the sexes in rural Ireland presents them with few prospective mates (Kennedy 1971; Scheper-Hughes 1979).

The serious problem of bachelorhood among farmers prompted the Roman Catholic bishops of western Ireland to establish a marriage bureau in 1968. The scale of the problem is awesome. In 1926 one-third of the male farmers between the ages of 35 and 44 were single; the range between small farmers (<15 acres) and larger farmers (≥100 acres) was only 6 percentage points. By 1971 over half of farmers on plots smaller than 15 acres were single; bachelorhood had not increased on larger farms (Hannan 1982, table 7.5). The "family failure rate"— namely the percentage of farmers on farms of 15–30 acres, aged 55 and over, who are single—more than doubled from 7 percent in 1926 to 18 percent in 1971 (Hannan 1982, figure 7.3). By 1981, the family failure rate had reached an astounding 43 percent (Central Statistics Office 1986, table 10A).

Less has been written about bachelorhood among Ulster farmers than about bachelorhood among their counterparts in the Republic. The Irish Mobility Study reveals no differences between the marital status of farmers of the Republic and farmers of Northern Ireland. One-fourth of the farmers over 40 years of age in both parts of Ireland are bachelors (see Table 5.9). Other agricultural workers appear to have even more difficulty in finding a mate. The very small number of observations

Table 5.9
Aspects of relationship between farming and marital status:
men aged 40–65, Ireland, 1973

A. Marital status and timing of marriage
among farmers' sons who ever worked as farmers
by current farming status and region

| | Current farmers | | Former |
Martial status/timing	Republic	Northern Ireland	farmers
Ever married	72%	76%	70%
Timing:			
Before farming	20	36	26
Same year as began farming	14	8	17
Year after began farming	6	4	4
2 years after began farming	4	5	<1
3–5 years after began farming	10	7	4
6+ years after began farming	17	15	17
Never married	28	24	30
Total	100	100	100
(N)	(303)	(135)	(46)

B. Marital status among men who never
worked as farmers by experience in agriculture
(as farm helper or farm laborer) and origins

| | Farmers' sons | | Nonfarm |
Marital status	Experienced	Not	origins
Ever married	41%	86%	93%
Never married	59	14	7
Total	100	100	100
(N)	(17)	(247)	(685)

frustrates any attempt to get a precise estimate of marriage rates for farm helpers and farm laborers, but 10 of the 17 men over 40 who are employed in these two occupations have never married. Former farmers who now work in other occupations have a high rate of bachelorhood as well. In fact, the estimate of 30 percent never married among former farmers is slightly higher than the rate for current farmers. The marriage chances of farmers' sons who have never farmed exceed those of their brothers and cousins who stay in farming; 14 percent of men in this group over age 40 never married. In comparison, only 7 percent of men with nonfarm origins who are older than 40 have never married.

Conclusion

Irish agriculture remains an important component of the economy of the island. It contributes to exports and, in the North, to the exchange between Ulster and the rest of the United Kingdom. Compared with the rest of the EEC, rates of agricultural employment in both parts of Ireland are very high. From the Irish perspective, however, a contraction in agriculture is evident over the 1959–1973 period. Ireland's share of both GNP and exports declined dramatically. Part of the deline was relative; that is, agricultural growth simply failed to keep up with growth in manufacturing and services. An example of relative but not absolute decline can be found in the income of family farms of all sizes between 1955–1958 and 1972–1975 (Commins 1986, table 2). But real declines occurred.

Among the more dramatic was the drop in agricultural employment. Labor power in the countryside contracted steadily from 1951 on. There were fewer farmers in Ireland in 1973 than in 1951. There were also fewer relatives assisting on farms and fewer paid farm laborers.

Aggregate changes like these portend a major increase in mobility from agricultural to nonagricultural work. The reasonable observer of Irish social structure would expect such an outflow, as would the scholarly reader of the sociological literature on modernization and mobility. The facts confound these expectations. The Irish Mobility Study reveals only a modest decrease in the odds that a farmer's son will himself become a farmer, either by inheritance or by other means. Even more important, only 10.5 percent of farmers' sons who took up farming subsequently left their fields to take a nonagricultural job.

Apparently, Irish agricultural employment has fallen since 1951 because of an acceleration of "family failures." A combination of more bachelors and childless couples has left many farms without heirs. Agricultural employment falls when these farmers die (or occasionally retire) because there is no one from the next generation to replace them. This "rural crisis" can be seen in the growth in the number of Irish farmers who never marry. Bachelorhood has been prevalent in Ireland for at least a century, but in the last 20 years it has increased dramatically among the rural poor. In 1926, one in five of the Republic's farmers never married; that is, 20 percent of farmers between 45 and 54 years of age were single. By 1966, the bachelorhood rate was 33 percent. Most of the increase was among poor farmers on small farms. The farmers with over 200 acres were slightly more likely to be married in the 1960s than the farmers in similar conditions had been in the 1920s. Yet bachelorhood among farmers with 30 acres or less doubled. The bachelorhood rate for 1966 reached 39 percent of farmers 45–54 years old working 15–30 acres and 43 percent of farmers 45–54 years old working less than 15 acres (Kennedy 1973, table 54).

These bachelorhood rates, high as they are, underestimate the actual number of farms that have no heirs. Childlessness among married farmers, the emigration of the children of some farmers, and the permanent migration to Ireland's cities of other farmers' children add to the succession problem. A 1972 survey of County Kerry farmers over age 50 reported that 23 percent definitely had no heirs, another 12 percent were rated "doubtful," while the prospective heirs of an additional 6 percent had moved away and were rated "unlikely" to return, for a total family failure rate of 41 percent (Commins and Kelleher 1972; cited in Scheper-Hughes 1979, p. 39).

The land of a farmer with no heirs passes to kin who may or may not live in the community, and who may or may not farm the parcel. Because most of the failures involve small farms that offer few of the material or spiritual incentives that might induce even a dissatisfied factory worker to return to his roots on the farm, virtually every death of a farmer with no heir reduces the agricultural work force by one.

The failure of cohorts of farmers to replace themselves in the countryside appears to be the principal means by which agricultural employment has contracted in Ireland. Many Irish farmers have no heirs. A growing proportion of prospective heirs pursue nonagricultural careers. These downward trends are offset somewhat by a trend toward a faster transition to farming among those farmers' sons who stay in agriculture. The transition from the status of family member assisting on a farm to farmer has accelerated, with the result that a larger proportion of those sons who stay in agriculture move into farming per se at a younger age. Although this tendency nearly offsets the decline in the proportion of farmers' sons who enter agriculture as a first job, it does not offset the succession problem of the bachelor farmers.

6   Scales, Levels, and Dimensions
of Mobility

Duncan and his associates captured the relationship between origins and destinations in a single parameter by scaling occupations according to their socioeconomic standing (Duncan and Hodge 1963; Duncan 1966a,b; Blau and Duncan 1967; Duncan, Featherman, and Duncan 1972). This development spawned a tremendous amount of progress in the scientific study of social stratification by facilitating both a parsimonious comparison of the dependence of origins on destinations among subgroups and an assessment of how other variables influence social inequality (see Bielby 1981 for a review).

At about this time, Goodman (1972a) showed the utility of log-linear models for the analysis of mobility tables per se. This methodology led to a number of valuable contributions, but the very fruitfulness of Goodman's approach focused attention too narrowly on the bivariate relationship between origins and destinations. More important, the capacity to examine mobility tables on a cell-by-cell basis threatened to divert the study of mobility away from the task of specifying the dependence of occupational destinations on occupational origins as a causal relation.

Duncan (1979) brought the issue of causality back to the center of attention in the form of his uniform association model. Uniform association is a powerful model. It includes a single association parameter that "shifts the destination distribution upward or downward [in socioeconomic status] as the origin is shifted up or down" (p. 802). The bridge between uniform association and path analysis is the fact that the single uniform association parameter has a number of characteristics in common with the familiar regression coefficient that is the bedrock of path analysis (Haberman 1979, pp. 396–397; Logan 1983).

Uniform association and related linear and quasi-linear approaches to analyzing mobility tables promise to be powerful tools for the further advancement of knowledge about the social stratification process (Goodman 1979a,b, 1984; Logan 1983; Hout 1983, 1984a). The distinction between general and specific effects and the link between heterogeneity models of individual mobility chances and uniform association allow the incorporation of additional independent variables into the analysis (Yamaguchi 1982; Logan 1983). All of this gets stratification back onto the trail blazed by Blau and Duncan (1967, p. 10): it "enables us to dissect the process of occupational mobility by determining how various factors condition the influence of origins on occupational success."

Limitations and Pseudolimitations of the Unidimensional Approach

The power of the socioeconomic ranking approach is also its weakness. Its power comes from its parsimony: scaling occupational origins and destinations creates the opportunity to summarize the dependence of destinations on origins with a single parameter. Its weakness is that this kind of parsimony does not accord well with the complexity of social mobility. As Hodge (1981) argues, the data reduction entailed in the socioeconomic ranking approach is extreme. Occupations differ in many ways in addition to their obvious socioeconomic differences. Any of these differences may lead to distinctions that are important for occupational mobility. Limiting inquiry to a single distincton—no matter how crucial—thwarts that inquiry. The proper goal of stratification research is the identification of relevant dimensions of cleavage within the occupational structure and (among related goals) the quantification of how those dimensions affect occupational mobility.

The negative reaction among critics of unidimensional models like path analytic models of socioeconomic achievement or uniform association models of occupational mobility is in proper proportion to the loss of information in such a model. Unfortunately, while the criticism rings true, the proposed solutions are excessive. The most extreme attacks eschew all models. This approach is destructive; it offers no constructive advice or insight. A potentially more profitable critique takes the tack of modeling without presupposing a rank ordering of occupational categories—a kind of agnosticism about the nature of the hierarchy within the division of labor. A comprehensive picture of the stratification process, which is more complete than the distilled view of unidimensional models, is possible without resort to agnosticism and certainly without abandoning the modeling approach altogether. The appropriate response to the limitations of unidimensional models is to build multidimensional models. To give up modeling or to give up ranking flies in the face of the tremendous increments to understanding social stratification that both have produced. The reasoned response to the limitations of earlier approaches is constructive. Multidimensional models can be combined with the most sophisticated example of the agnostic approach—the topological model of Erikson and Goldthorpe (1987a,b)—to assess what is gained and what is lost in sticking to either course exclusively.

The point of this approach is not to overturn well-articulated critiques of unidimensional approaches, such as Goldthorpe (1980, p. 115):

> One must be led to question the predominant practice in recent mobility research of taking scales of occupational prestige or socioeconomic status as the sole basis of analysis—and to question this practice not so much on ideological grounds as on the grounds, rather, that in this way significant features of mobility processes must tend to be overlooked. While analyses made in terms of such synthetic scales may be able to display certain hierarchical effects in great detail, they would seem likely to blur or obscure distinctions that we have shown to be of substantial importance: for example, those between self-employed and employee groupings, even within the same occupational area; or between groupings differentiated in their market and work situations on the lines that we have labelled white-collar and blue-collar. For occupations that are distinct in these ways will to quite a large extent be bracketed together by a synthetic scale, in the process of all occupations being ordered on the single dimension that the scale represents.[1]

Rather, the goal of this approach is to subvene on behalf of both sides of the controversy, that is, to advance the cause of the critics by improving on the models of the criticized.

Specification of Topological Models of Mobility

Goldthorpe makes his point as part of a proposition that mobility be studied without reference to hierarchy and ranking through the lens of topological models developed by Hauser (1978, 1979; Featherman and Hauser 1978, chap. 4). That topological models contribute to our understanding in a number of ways is clear (Hout 1983). What is less clear is the extent to which they contribute information not contained in the multidimensional models. Resolution of this point will decide the controversy between scaled and topological models.

Hauser (1978, 1979) explicitly frees the specification of topological models from the presuppositions engendered in an ordering of the origin and destination categories, as when he says: "Unlike Goodman's (1972a) multiplicative models, this model does not assume ordinal measurement of occupations. Of course, the assumption of ordinality may help us interpret results, or our findings may be used to explore the metric properties of our occupational classification" (1978, p. 930). By making no assumptions about order, Hauser minimizes the overlap between topological and multidimensional models. Unless a single hierarchy does in fact dominate the pattern of interaction, the models will produce distinct results. If multidimensional models overstate the importance of hierarchy, topological models will obviously be superior.

Results of topological modeling vindicate those who assume a hierarchical order among occupations. Clues to the importance of hierarchy in the levels effects of topological models abound in American, British, French, Irish, and Scandinavian data. First of all, there are references to the socioeconomic hierarchy of positions in the verbal descriptions offered by researchers using the topological models (e.g., Featherman and Hauser 1978, pp. 152–156; Goldthorpe 1980, pp. 109–114; Erikson et al. 1982, pp. 14–17; Whelan and Whelan 1984, pp. 87–96; Erikson and Goldthorpe 1987a,b).[2] Then there are explicit comparisons between topological models and models that presuppose an order among the categories. For example, Pöntinen (1982) demonstrates that the Featherman and Hauser model can be transformed into a crossings-parameter model (which presupposes order) that is adjusted to accommodate the asymmetric association that their model includes. For this reason, Pöntinen argues that researchers will be unable to choose between vertical and nonvertical representations of the mobility process on the basis of fit between model and data.[3] This may be so for tables with small numbers of occupational categories. When the number of categories is large, however, the outcome considered by Hauser (1984, p. 105) must be regarded as more likely:

> In a model of some complexity, each theory adds some contrasts that have been neglected by the other, but most contrasts in each will overlap those in the other . . . If this view of vertical and non-vertical models of class mobility as transformations or near transformations of one another is correct, then it does not really matter which view one adopts, so long as one communicates the perspective taken in the analysis. Debate on the relative merits of one or the other concept of class mobility will be resolvable only by evidence from other sources, outside the mobility process per se.

Yet in the analysis from which these passages are taken, Hauser finds that the vertical dimension of mobility in the English, French, and Swedish data is related to educational composition of the occupational categories but not to prestige or income. How is one to decide which hierarchical or vertical variables are important for mobility without expressly incorporating a variety of measures in the model? The "verbal analog to a multiple regression analysis" that Hauser (p. 106) ascribes to Goldthorpe is not sensitive enough to detect such a subtle difference of effects—between a significant education effect but nonsignificant prestige and income effects. For most analysts one vertical variable taps pretty much the same concept as any other vertical variable. Some distinctions enter consciousness, such as the well-known difference between socioeconomic indexes and prestige scales in the ranking of farmers. But by and large, the analyst treats "vertical" as a generic concept. When education but not prestige and income matter for mobility, "verbal multiple regression" is likely to be taxed to its limits (or beyond).

The key is to incorporate both vertical effects and topological levels in a single model. Hout (1984a) includes a weak version of this hybrid model; the status, autonomy, and training model includes special terms for agricultural occupations. Hout and Jackson (1986) present a more systematic approach, which begins with the topological "common social fluidity" model of Erikson, Goldthorpe, and Portocarero (1982). Scaled effects are added in sequence to the model. The final model contains the effects of prestige, education, and bureaucratic advance. However, five of the six topological levels effects are also significant. More important, including the scaled effects does not substantially reduce the size of the levels effects.

Topological modeling has recent become more sophisticated, requiring new work integrating scales and levels. Erikson and Goldthorpe (1987a,b) modify the strategy of topological modeling. They abandon the usual approach of using a variety of criteria to assign cells of the mobility table to levels in favor of a layered approach. Instead of specifying a single levels matrix, they propose several separate effects matrices, "each of which is designed to capture a specific effect that we see as playing an important part in shaping the pattern of fluidity within a class structural context" (p. 2). Their layers are *hierarchy, inheritance, sector,* and *affinity.* Each layer contains multiple levels defined by dummy variables that apply to specified cells of the 7 × 7 mobility table that they analyze.[4]

The hierarchy effects are formed by creating three occupational strata:

(Ia + Ib + II), (IIIa + b, IVa + b, V + VI), and (IVc + d, VIIss + VIIus, VIIf) for origins; (Ia + Ib + II), (IIIa + b, IVa + b, IVc + d, V + VI), and (VIIss + VIIus, VIIf) for destinations.[5] The two hierarchy effects limit mobility across stratum boundaries. The first (HI1) applies to cells separated by at least one stratum boundary; the second (HI2) applies to cells separated by two stratum boundaries. The scoring of hierarchy effects makes operational the hypothesis that mobility across two stratum boundaries is limited by the combined effects of HI1 and HI2; that is, HI2 measures the extent to which mobility across two boundaries is less than expected on the basis of HI1. This kind of "distance" (Haberman 1979) or "diamond" (Hope 1982) modeling of the vertical effect has the same logical standing as the more common regression-based formulations of hierarchy effects (derived from Duncan 1979), but empirical results for England, France, and Sweden indicate that diamond models understate the vertical effect (Hauser 1984). Including diamond effects and regression effects in one model will allow an assessment of their relative efficacy in the Irish case.

The inheritance effects give special attention to the diagonal cells of the table. The first inheritance effect (IN1) applies to all diagonal cells. The second (IN2) applies to I + II, IV a + b, and IVc. The third (IN3) applies to IVc uniquely. Because I + II, IVa + b, and V + VI are collapsed categories, these effects are not strictly inheritance effects, for cases of mobility between I and II, between IVa and IVb, and between V and VI are treated as immobility.

The sector effect separates the agricultural and nonagricultural sectors. The one and only sector effect (SEC) is scored one in cells involving mobility between farm and nonfarm occupations and zero for mobility among nonfarm occupations or between IVc and VIIf.

The affinity effects add to or subtract from the other effects in selected cells of the table. The first affinity effect (AF1) applies to extreme mobility between agricultural labor (VIIf) and "the service class" (I + II). It is expected to be negative, reflecting the very low rates of long-distance mobility usually observed. This effect might well be considered a kind of hierarchy effect. The second affinity effect (AF2) applies to several near-diagonal cells. These are areas of higher than otherwise expected mobility (the coefficient for AF2 is expected to be positive). In their analysis Erikson and Goldthorpe (1987a,b) found that including mobility between professional and managerial occupations (class Ia + Ib + II) and farming (class IVc + d) produced better results in the Republic than their original formulation did. So they modified AF2 when analyzing the data for the Republic of Ireland. In this analysis, the modified AF2 term is used for both regions. The variable AF2 is difficult to work with. It appears to be based mostly on a ransacking of the British and French mobility tables by Erikson and Goldthorpe (1987a,b). For example, it is unclear what principle of "affinity" organizes this term. In many ways it overlaps HI1 within classes, but it does not include exchanges between white-collar and blue-collar positions. There are too many notable exceptions to this generalization, however. In short, this variable lacks a coherent interpretation.

Erikson and Goldthorpe (1987a,b) propose two additional affinity terms that they label AFX and AFN. These are ad hoc effects that they added to their common model to remedy its poor fit to the data for the Republic of Ireland and for Northern Ireland. The term AFX applies to mobility between farming (class IVc + d) and farm labor (class VIIf) and to mobility between less-than-skilled nonfarm labor (class VIIss + VIIus) and farm labor (VIIf). These mobility flows are higher than expected under their common model in the Republic. The term AFN applies to mobility between farming (class IVc + d) and other kinds of proprietorship (class IVa + b) in Northern Ireland. This effect is also positive in Erikson and Goldthorpe (1987a, b). Exploratory runs adding AFX and AFN as well as the vertical effects to the common model failed to converge when either the GAUSS or GLIM statistical programs used for the rest of the log-linear analyses in this report were utilized. Apparently the multi-colinearity of these special effects with effects already captured by the main levels and scales effects destabilized the minimization routines in the programs. For this technical reason, results for the AFX and AFN effects are not reported here.

The design matrices for hierarchy, inheritance, sector, and affinity effects appear in Appendix Table A.22. The rows of this table represent the combinations of origins and destinations in the 7 × 7 collapsed table that is the basis of the Erikson and Goldthorpe specification; the columns record the presence or absence of each levels effect in a given cell. A "1" in a given row and column of Table A.22 indicates the presence of the effect; a "0" indicates its absence.

Scales and Levels Models for the Irish Data

The data analysis for the Republic and Northern Ireland begins with the topological model of Erikson and Goldthorpe (1987a,b). Vertical scales are then added to the model. The modeling strategy is to try to eliminate levels effects by including scales that are related to the "verbal multiple regression" that defines the levels effects. The first scales to be introduced are the vertical measures: prestige, then education. If the levels simply reflect socioeconomic barriers to mobility, then the only significant coefficients in the combined model will be the ones for vertical scales. If at least some of the levels effects are significant when the vertical effects are in the model, then nonvertical scales will be introduced. If the levels effects are diminished by the inclusion of these effects, it can be safely concluded that the multidimensional model captures the same barriers to mobility as the Erikson and Goldthorpe model. The same conclusion will be reached if all of the levels effects are significant and none of the scales have significant effects. Yet if both levels and scales are significant, then each approach can be said to add statistical value that is at least partially independent of the information conveyed by the other, especially if the introduction of scaled effects into the topological model of Erikson and Goldthorpe (1987a,b) yields significant scaled effects without diminishing the size of levels effects.[6] Interpreting the combined models is a matter that is best left until a final model has been arrived at.

The upshot of all this is that Hauser is right to assert that the difference between the fit of levels models and the fit of scaled models, taken separately, cannot arbitrate disputes between vertical and nonvertical theories of class mobility. However, once hybrid models are considered, it is not self-evident that "debate on the relative merits of one or the other concept of class mobility will be resolvable only by evidence from other sources, outside the mobility process per se" (Hauser 1984, p. 105). On the contrary, hybrid models seem to be a logical method for resolving the debate about the relative merits of continuous conceptions of multidimensional mobility processes.

Table 6.1a gives the resulting coefficients and fit statistics for the Republic of Ireland data; Table 6.1b, the same for the data from Northern Ireland. Coefficients in parentheses are not significant. The first column of each panel shows the outcome of fitting the Erikson and Goldthorpe model to the 14 × 14 tables. The model does not fit by classical criteria, but the bic statistic is negative in both regions. As Table 3.9 shows, the preferred multidimensional models fit better than these topological models in each region (Republic: $L^2 = 344.9$; $df = 162$; bic $= -897$; North: $L^2 = 264.6$; $df = 162$; bic $= -989$). If a choice had to be made, the multidimensional model would be preferred on the basis of fit and parsimony.[7] But the two kinds of effects can be included simultaneously, so a choice is not necessary.

Table 6.1a
Goodness–of–fit and parameter estimates for selected
topological and combination models of occupational mobility:
men aged 18–65, Republic of Ireland, 1973

Effect	Model 1	2	3	4	5
Goodness–of–fit					
L^2	407.9	267.1	261.1	310.2	222.9
df	161	159	158	158	158
bic	−826	−959	−950	−900	−987
Levels effects					
Hierarchy 1	(−.07)[a]	(.00)	(−.02)	(<.01)	—
Hierarchy 2	−.26	(.21)	(.16)	(.13)	—
Inheritance 1	.89	.49	.49	—	.40
Inheritance 2	.63	(.17)	(.28)	—	—
Inheritance 3	1.55	1.81	1.53	—	2.12
Sector	−.41	−.56	−.52	−.66	−.67
Affinity 1	−1.65	(−.07)	—	—	—
Affinity 2	.53	.54	.52	.25	.41
General effects					
Prestige	—	16.57	15.76	6.81	8.73
Education	—	—	—	4.27	3.67
Bureaucratic entry	—	—	—	5.18	(1.34)
Personal contact	—	—	—	(.02)	(−4.75)
Diagonal effects					
Prestige	—	2.67	2.12	3.30	2.69
Bureaucratic entry	—	—	(−.11)	−.66	(−.41)
Personal contact	—	—	1.06	2.07	(.60)

a.   Coefficients in parentheses are not significant at the .05 level.

Looking past the fit statistics to the coefficients, those familiar with Erikson and Goldthorpe (1987a,b) can see that the results for the 14×14 tables closely resemble the results for the 7×7 tables. In the Republic the main hierarchy effect, HI1, is not significant. Erikson and Goldthorpe (1987a,b) report the same finding. This does not negate the inference that Irish society is stratified by hierarchy effects in the form of scaled prestige and education effects. On the contrary, it means only that HI1 is a poor index of hierarchy. Hauser (1984) reaches a similar conclusion about Hope's (1982) diamond specification of the vertical dimension of the effect of origins on destinations in England, France, and Sweden.

The second column of each panel shows what happens when prestige is included in the model proposed by Erikson and Goldthorpe. Both the general effect of prestige and its diagonal effect are substantial. The fit of the model improves dramatically with the addition of prestige. Expending just

Table 6.1b
Goodness–of–fit and parameter estimates for selected
topological and combination models of occupational mobility:
men aged 18–65, Northern Ireland, 1973

			Model		
Effect	1	2	3	4	5
Goodness–of–fit					
L^2	323.7	223.9	209.0	237.4	196.6
df	161	160	158	159	158
bic	–922	–1014	–1013	–992	–1025
Levels effects					
Hierarchy 1	–.19	–.14	–.16	–.24	—
Hierarchy 2	–.31	(.13)^a	(.07)	(.01)	—
Inheritance 1	.69	.41	.47	—	.49
Inheritance 2	.63	(.24)	(.21)	—	—
Inheritance 3	1.64	1.91	1.58	—	1.54
Sector	–.63	–.73	–.66	–.68	–.49
Affinity 1	–.27	(.06)	—	—	—
Affinity 2	.46	.45	.43	.23	.31
General effects					
Prestige	—	13.54	12.94	6.87	8.08
Education	—	—	—	2.42	2.42
Bureaucratic entry	—	—	—	5.00	2.45
Personal contact	—	—	—	(3.97)	(2.84)
Diagonal effects					
Prestige	—	1.88	1.66	2.35	2.06
Bureaucratic entry	—	—	–.79	–.68	–1.06
Personal contact	—	—	1.61	2.38	1.32

a.   Coefficients in parentheses are not significant at the .05 level.

two degrees of freedom shrinks L^2 by 140.8 in the Republic and 99.8 in Northern Ireland. Prestige, however, fails to supplant hierarchy as the representation of the vertical component of mobility, at least in Northern Ireland, as HI1 remains statistically significant in the North when prestige is in the equation. Evidence of the redundancy of vertical and levels effects comes in the form of AF1, an insignificant vertical "affinity" effect.[8] The diagonal effect of prestige eliminates the need for a special term (IN2) to capture the extent to which white-collar immobility exceeds blue-collar immobility, inasmuch as the introduction of prestige renders IN2 insignificant. The other two inheritance effects, the sector effect, and AF2 are still significant in the revised equation that includes prestige.

Bureaucratic entry and personal contact are important for immobility—what Erikson and Goldthorpe call inheritance. The next step in exploring the overlap between vertical and nonvertical models of mobility process is the introduction of these two variables with an eye toward eliminating the remaining inheritance effects: IN1 and IN3. Adding the diagonal effects of bureaucratic entry and personal contacts to the model achieves mixed results. Bureaucratic entry is an insignificant net of the overall inheritance effect (IN1) and specific farm inheritance (IN3). Apparently an important component of the (negative) bureaucratic entry diagonal effect stems from the immobility of farmers' sons.

The remaining variables from the multidimensional model (the main effects of education and bureaucratic entry) are added to the model in the fourth column of each panel. The hierarchy effects from the Erikson and Goldthorpe model are eliminated when these terms are in the model, as are IN2 and AF1 because their effects are insignificant. Excluding them reduces the standard errors of several other coefficients, so the more precise estimates obtained without HI1, HI2, IN2, and AF1 are reported in the table. The main effects of bureaucratic entry (in the Republic) and personal contact (in either region) are also not significant. Nor is the diagonal effect of either variable in the Republic. These variables are included in the final model because it is the only one that reports coefficients for all of the variables in Model 7. The combination of inheritance, sector, and affinity effects accounts for the important bureaucratic entry effects from the multidimensional model (and then some). Yet the scaled effects of prestige and education do a better job than the distance-coded hierarchical levels effects.

Conclusion

Socioeconomic differences among occupations restrict mobility. This much is not in dispute. The controversy concerns the form, magnitude, and exclusivity of these vertical effects. The class structure may be characterized as a series of steps or as a continuous gradient; the effects may be strong or weak relative to other aspects of stratification; factors that are independent of vertical barriers may also contribute to the pattern of occupational mobility. Erikson, Goldthorpe, and their associates emphasize discontinuous and multifaceted effects (Goldthorpe 1980; Erikson et al. 1982; Erikson and Goldthorpe 1987a,b). They formulate topological models of mobility processes and stress the variety of constraints that contribute to the pattern of topological levels effects as they interpret empirical results. Others stress the lack of clear-cut breaks in the socioeconomic hierarchy (Duncan 1979; Haller and Hodge 1982; Hope 1982; Hout 1984a; Sobel, Hout, and Duncan 1985). They propose models with continuous (or integer) scores for the effects of social distance on mobility patterns. A third group takes both continuous and discontinuous models as basically interchangeable descriptions of the same reality (Pöntinen 1982; Hauser 1984; Whelan and Whelan 1984; Whelan and Breen, 1985). According to this ecumenical view, the important point is that class structure limits the life chances of workers from disadvantaged backgrounds, and current data and methods are insufficient to distinguish between a class structure that operates as a gradient and one that is basically a discontinuous series of steps of varying heights.

The approach taken here is ecumenism of a different sort. While the particular models proposed by each side of the controversy are not reconcilable in the sense that the parameters of one cannot be transformed into a function of the parameters of another—as Pöntinen and others point out— a hybrid model can include terms of both kinds. The original model of Hout (1984a) and its modification (Hout and Jackson 1986) incorporate both scaled and levels effects. When levels effects are added to the multidimensional model, both kinds of effects are significant. The scaled effects are smaller, particularly the effect of bureaucratic entry. The combination of inheritance, sector, and affinity effects in Erikson and Goldthorpe's (1987a,b) model accounts for the pattern of market divisions in Irish mobility better than the scaled term does. But the effects of hierarchy and middle-class inheritance do not stand up to the scaled effects of prestige and education. Indeed, for the Republic, Erikson and Goldthorpe (1987b, table 6) delete one of their hierarchy effects (HI1). Their model therefore understates the importance of hierarchy in Ireland much as the model of Hope (1982), on which their HI1 and HI2 are based, understates the importance of hierarchy elsewhere in Europe.

The vertical dimension of Irish mobility is extremely important. It not —only accounts for much of the differential mobility in Ireland, but also accounts for a sizable portion of the differential immobility.

As to methodological considerations, these results indicate that the overlap between topological and vertical models may well have been overestimated by some writers. The results here argue strongly for a consideration of scales. Topological models are very difficult to interpret anyway, and without controls for well-understood vertical effects, an exclusive reliance on topological models can lead to seriously misleading results.

7   Religion and Mobility in Northern Ireland

Equal social opportunity for Catholics and Protestants in Northern Ireland invokes nationalist, sectarian, and familial issues that run to the core of social relations.[1] Not surprisingly, this terrain is also contested by theories of social stratification, minority relations, and political sociology. At issue are the relative effects of religion and class on the social fortunes of Catholics in Northern Ireland. They are a minority within the province, outnumbered by Protestants in roughly the same two-to-one ratio since before the division of Ireland in 1921.[2] Their unemployment and underemployment exceeds that of Protestants (UK Office of Population Censuses and Surveys 1974; Equal Opportunity Commission 1981). They perceive themselves as the victims of Protestant discrimination in the skilled trades and professions (O'Malley 1981). Is their poverty due to discrimination against Catholics, to class forces that generate cycles of poverty in the face of opportunity, or to a cycle of privilege that perpetuates the middle class from generation to generation?

Measuring differences in occupational achievement between Catholics and Protestants is straightforward. Assessing the meaning of the measured differences is much more difficult. A difference may or may not be attributable to prior differences on the well-known determinants of occupational achievement. If Catholics and Protestants from identical backgrounds have identical economic fortunes, then discrimination can be ruled out as the source of gross differences. Such a definitive outcome is unlikely.

Class and Religious Discrimination

The literature on Northern Ireland has produced three different images of discrimination. Each of them implies a pattern of statistical interaction that can be compared with the observed pattern. If the data conform to one of the models, it is then possible to rule out the other models and concentrate on the empirically verified model as a likely depiction of religious stratification in Northern Ireland.

The case for discrimination, statistical or otherwise, against Catholics in Northern Ireland seems clear enough at first glance. Protestants dominate the economic life of the province. In particular, the large employers are Protestants who are alleged to prefer hiring Protestants. In contrast, the Catholic middle class is mostly a petit bourgeoisie that provides few jobs (Hout 1986). These two conditions mean that semiskilled and unskilled Catholics (a majority of Catholic workers) must seek employment from firms that have jobs to offer but a bias against Catholics, or from small entrepreneurs who have no objection to hiring Catholics but very few jobs to offer.

This is the focus of the first model of discrimination in Northern Ireland. Some writers, particularly Marxists (e.g., Farrell 1969), stress what they see to be a perfect correlation between religion and class. They write of the conflict between working-class Catholics and middle-class Protestants.

But do claims of discrimination stand up to closer scrutiny? Protestant leaders were quick to point out in the 1960s that some of the absence of Catholics in high places in the civil service and professions was self-imposed. Catholics avoided entanglements with the Protestant state because they feared that their participation might lend it legitimacy. That policy included an avoidance of state jobs (Buckland 1981, pp. 66–67).

Catholics' qualifications can also be called into doubt. Very few Catholics pursue education beyond the minimum required by law.

More to the point, Protestants might be alone at the top of the status hierarchy in Northern Ireland, but Catholics are not alone at the bottom. Many Protestants are working class (Hout 1986). The majority of the Northern working class is Protestant. Even the poorest classes—the unskilled and the unemployed—are half Catholic and half Protestant. The Sinn Fein rhetoric and writers such as Farrell (1969) suggest that a Protestant aristocracy represses a Catholic working class. This image harks back to conditions in the South and West of Ireland in the nineteenth century, but it does not hold in contemporary Northern Ireland. As many Protestants as Catholics work in marginal jobs. As many Protestants as Catholics live in substandard housing. More Protestants than Catholics leave school earlier than their counterparts in England, France, or the United States. Of course, since Protestants outnumber Catholics two-to-one, anything short of a two-to-one Protestant majority in the working class is evidence of disparity between the two groups. Nonetheless, the disparity is far less than the perfect correlation between religion and class that politicians and others assume. Poverty exists, to differing degrees, in both communities. Protestant poverty, existing as it does alongside Catholic poverty, suggests that the class structure compounds religious discrimination to account for the underachievement of Catholics.

The traveler in Northern Ireland sees the parallel poverty of Protestant and Catholic in the Belfast slums. In the United States, notorious slums like the South Bronx in New York stand in sharp contrast to white working-class areas like the ones that make up most of Queens in New York. In Belfast, the only feature of the depressed urban landscape of the Catholic ghetto of Falls Road that distinguishes it from the Protestant ghetto of Shankhill is the "cop shop," the fortified police barracks that marks the paramilitary occupation of the Catholic district. In all other respects—the red brick Victorian row houses, the idle men on street corners, the houses and shops that have been bricked up because bombs left them too damaged to repair—these slums are the same.[3] In the countryside, the traveler can safely assume that the large farms are owned by Protestants, but the small farms might be worked by families of either religion.

The poverty and unemployment of Catholics and Protestants reflect some degree of exploitation by the local Protestant elite. They also reflect the economic weaknesses of an entire region. Northern Ireland is part of the United Kingdom's industrial rust bucket. The plight of Ulster's urban and rural working classes echoes the desperate conditions found in much of the North of England, the Midlands, and parts of Scotland and Wales. Factory and mine closings throughout the UK have diminished opportunity in cities untouched by sectarian violence.

A weak or modest correlation between class and religion would contradict this model of discrimination in Northern Ireland. Perspectives that acknowledge the existence of a Protestant working class focus on the gap in living standards between Catholic and Protestant manual workers, arguing that working-class Protestants live better than working-class Catholics (e.g., McCann 1974). This perspective is consistent with a number of mobility patterns so long as the net effect of being Catholic is substantially negative—the operational definition of "substantially negative" being strong enough that middle-class Catholics do worse than working-class Protestants.

The weakness of this perspective is that it gives almost no attention to the question of the Catholic middle class. Ignoring the Catholic middle class may signal a belief that the Protestant working class lives better than the Catholic middle class or that the standard of living among Catholics in middle-class occupations is so low that it is indistinguishable from the standard of living of working-class Catholics.

A third perspective focuses less on class and views religious differences in racial terms. It borrows heavily from images that describe the struggle of blacks in the United States (Aunger 1975; Miller 1984; Hout 1986).[4] This line of argument expects weaker correlations among social class measures for Catholics than for Protestants—in line with the experience of American blacks prior to the mid-1960s.

Figure 7.1 shows what each of these points of view implies for the three-way interaction among social origins, destinations, and religion in Northern Ireland. The "perfect correlation" of Farrell would look like the first chart in Figure 7.1. The expectation here is of very little overlap between the origins or destinations of Catholics and Protestants. The impression of the class structure is of a rather straightforward pattern of social stratification that emphasizes short-range over longer-range mobility. The distinctive feature anticipated by Farrell is the redundancy of class and religion. Catholics have working-class origins and destinations; Protestants have middle-class origins and destinations.

McCann acknowledges the large Protestant working class, but asserts their advantages over Catholics. This implies a pattern of association such as that in the second chart in Figure 7.1. The achievement of middle-class Catholics still falls below that of the lowest class of Protestants according to this model.

The third chart reproduces the "inheritance of race" pattern (Duncan 1969). Here Catholics achieve less than Protestants in part because achievements of one generation are not passed on to the next. While a "normal" pattern of association between origins and destinations stratifies Protestants in this model, Catholics are an unstratified caste whose achievement is universally low.

The fourth chart is a variant on the second, with a much smaller gap between the lines for the two religions. In this chart some middle-class Catholics do better than some working-class Protestants.

All of the charts in Figure 7.1 are conjectures. The Irish Mobility Study data on Northern Ireland make it possible to test these different images of

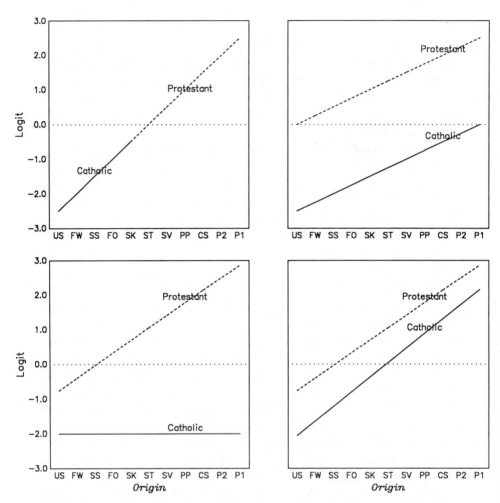

Figure 7.1   Four types of interaction among origin, destination, and religion in Northern Ireland.

religious stratification by separating the influences of class and religion on employment patterns.

The rhetoric of an analysis such as this one makes it tempting to exaggerate the possible stakes in uncovering the causes of (and solutions to) the sectarian conflict. But the issue of equal opportunity for Catholics must be seen as interesting in its own right, not as a component of sectarian struggle, because opportunity is not the central question in Northern Ireland today. Claims that Protestants had privileged access to jobs, along with other civil rights issues, fueled the tensions of the late

1950s and early 1960s. Those tensions eventually flared up into the current troubles. But after twenty years of violence, a solution in Northern Ireland will take a great deal more than jobs can hope to accomplish.

Events have pushed the conflict beyond fair treatment. If some miracle brought 100,000 well-paid, well-placed, middle-class jobs to Catholics tomorrow, the violence would continue. Too many militants on both sides now justify their acts of violence with references to blood ("The other side killed my brother; how can I turn my back on that?"); references to fair employment and civil rights have faded (O'Malley 1984). The sectarian armies will not forsake the armalite at this point. There was a time in the mid-1960s when equality of opportunity for Catholics and Protestants could have made a huge difference in Northern Ireland. That time is past.

Even though events have robbed the equal opportunity question of its strategic importance in the public life of Northern Ireland, religion affects employment in the North. The patterns revealed in this area disclose an element of social stratification that is more covert elsewhere. For the interplay of ascription and achievement is nowhere more dramatic than in the occupational attainments of individuals from disadvantaged minority groups. Almost by definition, persons from a disadvantaged minority group have the ascriptive handicap of lower-class background in the pursuit of economic success. In many societies they carry an additional ascriptive burden in the form of discrimination on the basis of their ethnic or religious heritage. Catholics in Northern Ireland are disadvantaged; they come from lower-class backgrounds. It remains to be seen whether or not they also bear the burden of discrimination.

Distribution of Occupations

Table 7.1 shows the distribution of Catholic and Protestant workers from Northern Ireland according to their origins, first occupations, and current occupations. Slightly over half of both groups come from working-class origins (counting farm laborers as working class). Two-fifths of both groups began their careers in the working class, and a clear majority are currently working class.

Differences between Catholics and Protestants in the distributions of origins, first occupations, and current occupations are all significant.[5] The index of dissimilarity provides a summary of how different the distributions are: a minimum of one Catholic worker in seven (14.2 percent or 14.8 percent) would have to change his origins and destinations in order to

Table 7.1
Distribution of occupational origins, first occupation, and
current occupation by religion: men aged 18–65, Northern Ireland, 1973

Occupation	Origins[a]		First[a]		Current[a]	
	C	P	C	P	C	P
Professionals & proprietors I	.4%	1.3%	.5%	.1%	.8%	1.4%
Professionals & managers I	.9	2.9	.9	3.1	1.8	7.4
Professionals & managers II	4.6	5.9	3.1	3.2	7.2	11.3
Clerical workers	3.0	3.7	4.7	8.5	4.6	6.2
Proprietors with employees	5.8	6.1	.1	.3	6.3	5.2
Proprietors without employees	5.1	3.0	.5	.2	4.8	3.6
Service workers	2.6	2.6	10.9	8.7	5.4	3.2
Unpaid helpers, nonfarm	.2	.3	2.4	2.7	.4	.3
Foremen & technicians	3.9	5.3	4.3	6.1	7.9	7.6
Skilled manual	13.8	17.1	16.9	19.3	18.0	18.0
Semiskilled manual	17.1	17.1	17.7	17.0	20.0	17.0
Unskilled manual	12.4	8.7	11.3	8.0	11.5	6.0
Farmers with employees	4.8	9.0	.0	.3	1.0	3.5
Farmers without employees	19.3	11.8	.4	.5	6.9	5.7
Unpaid helpers, farm	.5	.2	16.0	12.7	1.1	1.5
Farm laborers	5.6	5.1	10.2	9.2	2.4	1.9
Total	100.0	100.0	100.0	100.0	100.0	100.0
(N)	(846)	(1504)	(786)	(1463)	(835)	(1488)
χ^2 $(df=15)$	71.08		49.12		92.23	
Dissimilarity	14.2		11.2		14.8	

a.   C = Catholic; P = Protestant.

equalize the distributions. The distributions of first occupations are slightly less dissimilar (11.2 percent). By way of comparison, the dissimilarity between origins and destinations in Northern Ireland is greater than any of these differences (18.9 percent; see Table 2.6). The distinction between commercial farmers and family farmers contributes about two-fifths of the dissimilarity in origins. Catholics are only slightly more likely than Protestants to come from farm backgrounds. However, the fathers of Protestants were nearly twice as likely as the fathers of Catholics to have employees. Farming contributes much less to dissimilarity in current occupations. However, this difference in the propensity to have employees recurs. The relative advantage of Protestant farmers (3.5 percent to 1.0 percent) interacts with their numerical advantage so that, among the rural middle class of employing farmers, Protestants outnumber Catholics by nearly seven-to-one. Among family farmers, Protestants still outnumber Catholics, but the margin is just 1.46-to-one.

Protestants outnumber Catholics in every category of working-class origin and four of the five categories of working-class destination. In relative numbers, however, Protestants have a higher average status that contributes to the index of dissimilarity. Protestants are more likely than Catholics to have origins among the technical, supervisory, and skilled positions, while Catholics are more likely than Protestants to come from unskilled backgrounds. Catholic disadvantage more aptly characterizes the distribution of current working-class occupations than does any claim of Protestant advantage. Protestants and Catholics are proportionately represented in the technical, supervisory, and skilled destinations; Catholics are overrepresented in semiskilled and unskilled occupations.

Protestants have a slight advantage in each of the upper nonmanual origin categories that contributes 2.1 points to the overall dissimilarity of origins. This small contribution contradicts claims that the Protestant majority is universally advantaged. On the contrary, it shows that privilege is restricted to a small elite within the majority. A Protestant advantage in the attainment of upper-middle-class destinations contributes over one-third of the total dissimilarity between the current occupations of Protestants and Catholics. Protestants outnumber Catholics in professional and managerial occupations by nearly four-to-one.

Two other sources of dissimilarity between Catholics and Protestants in Northern Ireland are hidden within the classification used in Table 7.1. The first has to do with the segregation of Protestants and Catholics within the same detailed occupation. The distributions of Catholics and Protestants across broad occupational categories is not the same thing as occupational segregation on the basis of religion. In principle at least, Protestants and Catholics can be proportionately represented in a given occupation without coming in contact with members of another faith, because work places are segregated. For example, Protestant ministers and Catholic priests do not share the same space as they go about their jobs. They practice their occupations among their coreligionists exclusively. Schoolteachers are likely to be segregated on the basis of religion as well. To a large extent schools are segregated by religion in Northern Ireland. Catholic schools hire Catholic teachers; state schools and Protestant schools hire Protestant teachers. For this reason, primary- and secondary-school teachers are highly segregated on the job in a way that is not obvious from data such as those in Table 7.1.

The churches and schools are organized on the basis of religion, so segregation in the clergy and teaching is no scandal. However, it is possible that other occupations are also segregated at the work site in a way that contributes to the poverty of the Catholic population. If Protestant brick-layers, for instance, work for large construction companies that work on major projects that provide continuous employment, while Catholic brick-layers work for small firms that provide sporadic employment, then equal proportions of Catholics and Protestants in the skilled trades might hide an important difference. Or consider barristers and solicitors. If Protestants work for corporate law firms representing business clients and for the public prosecutor representing the state, while Catholics work as trial lawyers representing individuals who lack resources, a discrepancy in earnings and status could hide within the proportions in Table 7.1. Unfor-tunately, neither the Irish Mobility Study nor other available data sources are designed to tap this aspect of religious differences in employment. Data on firms would be needed to study the extent of on-site segregation (as in Bielby and Baron 1986).

Another form of occupational differentiation by religion that is missed by the data in Table 7.1 is occupational specialization within broad occu-pational categories. Dozens of specific occupations make up each cate-gory, and it would be surprising indeed if the distribution of Catholics across specific categories was identical to that of Protestants. Analyzing white ethnic groups in the United States, Lieberson (1980) notes that Ital-ians dominate the occupations barber and hairdresser, while dispropor-tionate numbers of Irish are police officers and fire fighters.

Sample data are insufficient to investigate specific occupations. With observations on only 835 Catholic workers, it is not possible to infer that Catholics do not follow a given occupation just because that occupation is not represented in the sample. Many occupations are too small to show up consistently in repeated samples of 800 cases. A tabulation of workers by detailed occupation and religion from a complete enumeration of the pop-ulation is needed (OPCS 1974, table 8).

In the OPCS data, overall dissimilarity between Protestants and Catholics appears to be 9.6 percent for the Census's major groups (com-pared with 14.8 percent in Table 7.1). Of course, dissimilarity of occupa-tional location does not necessarily imply dissimilar stratification out-comes. Occupations may mark different positions within the division of labor that are, in a sense, parallel if they do not differ in factors such as earnings, prestige, educational requirements, chances for advancement, and autonomy. It seems unlikely that the differences between Protestants and Catholics in Northern Ireland are merely parallel differences, but the truth of the matter remains to be seen.

These limitations aside, dissimilarity within major groups reflects the importance of different pursuits for Catholics and Protestants within broad occupational categories. The range of dissimilarity goes from zero for farmers and farm managers (there is only one category in this major group) to 34.4 percent among service workers.[6] To understand the differences reflected in these figures, we need to know which specific occupations contribute to them.

The differences between Protestants and Catholics in the professions and management divide along a line distinguishing community service from business, finance, and engineering. The proportion of Catholic professionals who are clergymen, nurses, and teachers exceed the corresponding proportions for Protestants by more than two percentage points. In contrast, the proportion of Catholic professionals who are engineers or draftsmen falls short of the corresponding proportions for Protestants by more than two percentage points. In management, Catholics are concentrated in local trade, managing public houses and shops; Protestants manage mines and factories.

The service occupations divide neatly into protective services and other services. Protective services are strategically important in a violent state. Furthermore, they require more skill and offer greater reward. This distinction contributes the largest portion of the greatest intragroup dissimilarity found in the Census. Protestants dominate in the protective services; they are police officers, security guards, and fire fighters. Catholics provide other kinds of services. Among Northern nonprotective service workers the largest religious difference is in the occupation of barman. Disparities also occur for hairdressers, barbers, and cooks.

The most notable difference between Protestants and Catholics in skilled trades is among the millwrights, fitters, and machine erectors (a single category in the OPCS scheme). This occupation is dominated by Protestants, who outnumber Catholics in the occupation by a four-to-one margin. It is an extremely important craft for Protestants, employing one-fourth of the skilled Protestant men who are not foremen and one-fifth of all Protestant foremen, technicians, and craftsmen. Shipbuilding employs most of the men in this category—62 percent of all millwrights (etc.) in Northern Ireland work in shipbuilding according to a cross-classification of occupation by industry, which regrettably is not broken down by religion (OPCS 1974). Shipbuilding is arguably the most important heavy industry in Northern Ireland, and exclusion of Catholics from the shipyards has long been a contentious issue (Lyons 1978, pp. 753–754).[7]

This pattern of religious segregation implies that comparisons which are primarily socioeconomic will understate the differences between majority and minority in Northern Ireland. Understanding the differences in prestige or earnings between Catholics and Protestants is not the same as understanding the whole picture of sectarian segregation separating the two groups. Of course, any study of detailed occupations will uncover differences that less detailed classification schemes might miss. The differences under study here are of more than mere methodological interest because of the pattern that emerges. These differences disclose something important about the process of ascriptive stratification, not only in Northern Ireland, but also in other societies that have disadvantaged minority populations (Hout 1986).

Most discussion of disadvantaged minority groups addresses intergroup dissimilarity—the kind of inequality expressed in Table 7.1. The queuing theory of ethnic stratification provides the most coherent account of ascriptive differences between groups (Hodge 1973; Thurow 1975). But not every member of a disadvantaged minority group ends up underpaid, underemployed, or out of work. Some queue jumpers make it into the middle class. For blacks in the United States, Lieberson (1980, p. 297) notes: "Among other factors, as a group gets larger, it is likely to develop certain internal strengths that will support some occupational activities even if outsiders are totally against their holding the position. Hence, if the black population base is large enough, there will be support for black doctors, black clergy, and so on, even if they remain totally unacceptable to others. Likewise, there will develop certain entrepreneurial possibilities and other employment shifts will occur." In short, a sizable minority community, if sufficiently segregated, can support a number of service professionals, proprietors, and tradesmen. Residential segregation may also create support for other occupations like schoolteaching and community service if majority members are reluctant to work in predominantly minority neighborhoods or towns. This general tendency gets a boost in Northern Ireland from the tradition of parochial education. Catholic schools everywhere favor Catholic teachers, hiring members of religious orders and Catholic lay persons.

A minority middle class emerges in these niches created by segregation. A basis in community services distinguishes this minority middle class from the middle class of business people, professionals, engineers, managers, and clerks of the majority. The majority middle class produces goods more than services. Majority professionals produce services that support goods production or produce community services for the majority community.

Minority niches require residential segregation. The existence of neighborhood ghettos like Falls Road and Shankhill in Belfast give testimony to the residential segregation of Protestants and Catholics in Northern Ireland. Data from the Irish Mobility Study can be used to confirm or reject the hypothesis that segregation spreads throughout the North. The sampling unit for this study was the designated electoral district (DED). The segregation in the DEDs is nearly complete: 82 percent. The DEDs do not constitute neighborhoods. Their boundaries are manip-ulated to blunt the electoral impact of Catholics. Despite the gerrymandering, the pattern of residential segregation by religion is unmistakable.

The distribution of middle-class Catholics and Protestants according to detailed occupation shows that the minority middle class is in fact more bound up in community service. Half of middle-class Catholics and one-third of middle-class Protestants work in designated community service occupations. Members of both groups are represented in each of the occupations. Surprisingly few of the occupations stray far from the overall ratio of three-to-two for Protestant percentages compared with the Catholic percentages. Exceptions to the three-to-two rule include legal professionals (barristers, solicitors, and judges), garage proprietors, physicians, and social workers, all of which show parity or a proportion of Protestants that exceeds the proportion of Catholics. Exceptions to the three-to-two rule also include occupations that have a higher than overall percentage of Catholics, including nurses, publicans, and teachers. This pattern of queue jumping within the sectarian enclave generalizes the American finding that the isolation of minorities from the majority creates ecological niches that tend to be filled by in-group members (Lieberson 1980, pp. 496–499).

Crude Differences in Mobility

A key issue in deciding the relative importance of religion and class in the distribution of occupational rewards in Northern Ireland is the association between origins and destinations. Only if Protestants and Catholics from similar backgrounds arrive at similar occupational destinations can it be inferred that religion plays a small or insignificant part in the process of social stratification in Northern Ireland.

Inferences about mobility processes require some synthesis of the raw data (see Appendix). Two kinds of calculations are undertaken here. One is simple percentages that disclose general tendencies in the data. Inferences from these percentages are tenuous, because variability due to sampling can produce swings as large as those produced by substantively important effects. The other kind of calculation is Goodman's (1979, 1984) system of modeling association in cross-classifications of variables with ordered categories which takes account of sampling variability.

Table 7.2 presents some summary percentages calculated from the raw data on overall mobility, mobility to first occupations, and from first to current occupations by religion. For each origin category, the upper panel lists the percentage of men from that origin whose current job is in the same category (percent immobile), the percentage whose current job is in one of the upper nonmanual categories, and the percentage whose current job is in one of the lower manual categories. The lower panel lists the corresponding percentages for each category of first job. The percentages do not sum to 100 across the row because the categories "immobile," "upper nonmanual," and "lower manual" are neither mutually exclusive nor exhaustive.

The immobility of men from middle-class origins differs by occupation, but not appreciably so by religion. The higher-status origins show very high rates of immobility; the lower-status origins within the middle class show less. The lack of clear immobility differences between Catholics and Protestants does not rule out the prospect that Catholics suffer a disadvantage in overall mobility. In fact, the proportion of Catholics from middle-class origins who move to upper nonmanual destinations is appreciably below that of Protestants. Catholic sons of clerks and salesmen have a particularly large disadvantage with respect to the Protestants from similar backgrounds. Catholic disadvantage also appears in the rates of downward mobility between upper nonmanual origins and lower manual destinations that are higher than the rates for Protestants.

The pattern of Catholic disadvantage is more pronounced among men from working-class backgrounds. Since half of the labor force in Northern Ireland has working-class origins, this difference between religions affects more men than does the smaller difference found among men from middle-class origins. In particular, Catholics from skilled or semiskilled backgrounds are more likely than Protestants of comparable origins to be downwardly mobile. Among those Catholics who are not downwardly mobile from semiskilled origins, the tendency to be immobile is greater than it is among Protestants. Catholics have less than half the chance of moving up from working-class origins to upper-middle-class destinations than Protestants from the same origins have. A noteworthy exception to this picture of Protestant advantage is the case of Protestants from the lowest working-class category—sons of unskilled workers. They have virtually no advantage over their Catholic counterparts. Both groups face enormous odds against occupational accomplishment.

The mix of class and religion effects among men from farm origins is striking. For men of both religions, coming from a middle-class farm that employs agricultural workers constitutes a substantial advantage over coming from a subsistence farm. Immobility for men from farms without employees is greater than that for men from more prosperous farms. Small holdings are very likely to be passed on from one generation to the next. Despite the economic marginality of such enterprises, inheritance is one of the best options for men who grew up on subsistence farms. Very few of the sons of subsistence farmers who leave farming end up in the middle class. One-fourth of Catholics and one-sixth of Protestants from subsistence origins are currently working in lower manual occupations; lower manual workers are two-fifths of the Catholics and one-third of the Protestants who left farming. In contrast, one-fifth of Catholics from upper agricultural origins who left farming and one-third of Protestants from upper agricultural origins who left farming are currently working in upper nonmanual occupations.

Catholics from agricultural origins are thus at a disadvantage compared to Protestants. These disadvantages are compounded for Catholics because they are far less likely than Protestants to inherit farms with employees.

Intragenerational mobility repeats many of the patterns found for intergenerational mobility to current occupations. Both class and religion affect the relative rates of immobility, mobility to upper nonmanual destinations, and mobility to lower manual destinations.

Among men with middle-class first jobs, higher-prestige jobs are more stable (have higher immobility rates) than lower nonmanual first jobs, which tend to be clerical, sales, and service jobs rather than proprietorships. The unstable lower-middle-class jobs lead in different directions. Clerical and sales first jobs lead upward to professional and managerial current jobs, especially for Protestants. Service jobs lead outward but not always upward. For Protestants, half of those who leave service jobs move downward to a lower-status current occupation. For Catholics, downward career mobility from a service first job exceeds upward

Table 7.2

Percentage of workers who are immobile, in an upper nonmanual current occupation, and in a lower manual current occupation by occupational origins and first occupations by religion: Northern Ireland, 1973

Origin/first job	Immobile[a]		Upper nonmanual[a]		Lower manual[a]		N[a]	
	C	P	C	P	C	P	C	P
Origin								
Professionals & proprietors I	(50)%	(18)%	(50)%	(60)%	(0)%	(6)%	2	17
Professionals & managers I	(20)	37	(60)	71	(20)	7	5	41
Professionals & managers II	33	31	54	51	15	9	39	78
Clerical & sales workers	12	22	12	35	32	4	25	54
Proprietors with employees	20	20	22	25	18	12	49	88
Proprietors without employees	14	9	14	16	21	26	42	43
Service workers	(9)	10	18	20	4	23	22	39
Unpaid helpers, non farm	(0)	(0)	(0)	(40)	(0)	(0)	2	5
Technicians & foremen	16	14	9	24	19	16	32	80
Skilled manual workers	29	29	7	18	32	24	117	254
Semiskilled manual workers	31	24	5	15	48	35	144	254
Unskilled manual workers	17	11	4	8	45	46	102	131
Farmers with employees	7	29	12	18	20	10	41	133
Farmers without employees	29	34	2	8	25	16	160	176
Unpaid helpers, farm	(25)	(0)	(0)	(0)	(50)	(33)	4	3
Farm laborers	11	12	4	10	44	36	46	73
Total	23	24	10	20	32	23	832	1469

First occupation

	(75)%	(100)%	(75)%	(100)%	(0)%	(0)%		
Professionals & proprietors I	(57)	74	(100)	91	(0)	4	4	1
Professionals & managers I	83	64	83	81	4	4	7	46
Professionals & managers II	27	32	32	45	11	5	24	47
Clerical & sales workers	(100)	(75)	(0)	(0)	(0)	(25)	37	123
Proprietors with employees	(50)	(67)	(0)	(0)	(25)	(33)	1	4
Proprietors without employees	16	12	14	24	27	21	4	3
Service workers	(0)	3	(16)	18	(16)	15	85	126
Unpaid helpers, nonfarm							19	39
Technicians & foremen	50	36	12	11	12	11	34	88
Skilled manual workers	47	40	5	17	19	22	133	282
Semiskilled manual workers	36	31	4	13	55	39	137	247
Unskilled manual workers	14	14	6	7	42	40	87	115
Farmers with employees	(0)	(40)	(0)	(20)	(0)	(20)	0	5
Farmers without employees	(100)	(75)	(0)	(12)	(0)	(0)	3	8
Unpaid helpers, farm	5	11	1	5	21	11	125	186
Farm laborers	12	12	2	6	47	42	79	130
Total	27	28	10	20	30	23	779	1450

a.   C = Catholic; P = Protestant. Numbers in parentheses indicate that fewer than 20 cases are in the denominator.

mobility by a two-to-one margin. Catholics and Protestants in service occupations are actually working at very different jobs (Hout 1986). Protestants dominate in the protective services. These positions have a strong civil service tradition; they are likely to lead to advancement (or at least stability) through the seniority system. Catholics in services have jobs like bartender and busboy. Clearly these are not stalwart middle-class jobs that lead upward to management or proprietorship. They are far more like the lower manual occupations into which many of the men who leave them move.[8]

Among men with working-class first jobs, the better occupations are more stable, especially for Catholics. The higher immobility of Catholics in the technical, supervisory, and skilled manual positions does not negate the pattern of Protestant advantage because a large part of the difference in immobility by religion is due to the higher upward mobility of Protestants into the upper nonmanual positions. Many Catholics who take skilled or semiskilled first jobs subsequently take unskilled jobs in a pattern that might be labeled "career deskilling."

Models of Class and Religion

The percentage differences in mobility highlight several important differences between Protestants and Catholics and between men from different classes. Care must be taken in interpreting these differences because religion and class are confounded in many of the comparisons. Some of the differences based on few observations might well reflect sampling variability instead of substantively important differences.[9] Models developed by Goodman (1979, 1984) serve to disentangle class and religion. They are statistical models that take sampling variability into account. Although the models are much more complicated than are the percentage differences, they provide sharper evidence for inferences. For example, the tendency for Catholics to have lower manual current jobs than Protestants do might result from Catholics' disadvantaged origins. It might just as well result from a disadvantage for Catholics of all origins. If disadvantage took such a form, it could make a current occupation in the lower manual stratum a likely outcome for all Catholics, as it did for American blacks prior to the mid-1960s (Duncan 1969; Featherman and Hauser 1976).

In all likelihood, both class and religion affect occupation. It would not be surprising if Catholics from each origin class were to have a lower current class position than Protestants from similar origins, while men from higher-status backgrounds are likely to have, within each religion, higher current status than are men from disadvantaged backgrounds.

Size of occupational groups is important for understanding stratification everywhere, no less so in Northern Ireland. In part, Catholics work in lower manual jobs because the economy of Northern Ireland generates a lot of unskilled jobs and relatively few jobs in skilled trades, management, and the professions.

Association models (Goodman 1979, 1984) express the mobility between an origin (i) and a destination (j) for each religion (k) as the product of size and occupational composition (β_{ik}), structural mobility (α_{jk}), vertical distance (μ_{ik} scores), net immobility (δ_{ik}), and association (ϕ_k). The analysis of association proceeds in two steps. First, a preferred model is chosen from among several alternatives on the basis of fit and parsimony. As with log-linear models, the idea is to find a model that includes all of the significant effects but no extraneous ones (Goodman 1979; Clogg 1982). When a preferred model has been selected, its parameters estimates are interpreted. The large number of zero cells in detailed tabulations lead to imprecise estimates of many of the parameters, including the crucial ϕ_k, δ_{ik}, and μ_{ik} scores. The remedy is to collapse some of the categories. This surely introduces its own form of imprecision, but it proved to be the only workable solution. The distinctions lost to this maneuver are those between salaried and self-employed upper-grade professionals (classes Ia and Ib), proprietors with employees and without (classes IVa and IVb), paid and unpaid service workers (classes IIIb and VIIInf), farmers with and without employees (classes IVc and IVd), and paid and unpaid farm workers (classes VIIf and VIIIf).

Table 7.3 reports the searches for preferred models for the 11 × 11 versions of the intergenerational and intragenerational mobility tables. On classical criteria, none of the models fit the data. However, the bic criterion selects homogeneous uniform association for mobility from origins to destinations and homogeneous row-and-column effects for mobility from origins to first jobs and first jobs to current jobs. Including μ_{ik} scores in the model for mobility from origins to current occupations significantly improves the fit by classical criteria, and although it brings bic somewhat closer to zero, the lower bic is comparable to the bics for other forms of mobility, so the same model—homogeneous row-and-column effects—is used here. Table 7.4 presents the parameter estimates for homogeneous row-and-column effects for each form of mobility. These coefficients differ from one type of mobility to another, so each is discussed in turn.

Table 7.3
Goodness–of–fit statistics for association models for 11 × 11 × 2 mobility tables by religion: Northern Ireland, 1973

Model[a]	df	*Origin to current*		*Origin to first*		*First to current*	
		L^2	bic	L^2	bic	L^2	bic
0 Independence	200	1317.96	−224	1205.99	−342	1842.68	301
1 Quasi–independence	178	483.25	−895	1005.16	−367	856.48	−516
2 Homogeneous UA	188	347.53	−1108	683.56	−766	463.62	−986
3 Heterogeneous UA	176	341.52	−1021	660.00	−697	440.96	−916
4 Homogeneous RC	178	316.54	−1061	332.16	−1040	322.62	−1050
5 Mixed RC	167	312.52	−980	309.80	−978	297.95	−990
6 Heterogeneous RC	157	293.77	−922	293.82	−916	290.23	−920

a. Quasi–independence, heterogeneous uniform association (UA), heterogeneous row × column (RC), and mixed RC fit the diagonal cells exactly; homogeneous UA and homogeneous RC fit the "class–specific" diagonal parameters, i.e., each occupational category has a different diagonal parameter but these parameters do not differ by religion.

The first two columns of Table 7.4a, 7.4b, and 7.4c show the structural mobility multipliers for Catholics (α_{jc}) and Protestants (α_{jp}). Overall the force of structural mobility for Catholics exceeds that for Protestants, as evidenced by the larger standard deviation of the log α_{jc}. Especially high structural mobility into upper-grade professional and managerial occupations and out of farming account for most of the larger standard deviation for Catholics. Differences between other log α_{jc} are actually smaller than the differences between the corresponding log α_{jp}. This is not immediately evident in Table 7.4, so the differences [log (α_{jc} / α_{ic}) − log (α_{jp} / α_{ip})] are reported in Table 7.5.[10] A coefficient of ±.40 indicates that structural mobility in one group exceeds that in the other group by 50 percent. Of the 55 coefficients shown, 27 exceed .40 in absolute value. Ignoring the other numbers in the table leads to three conclusions about differential structural mobility in Northern Ireland: mobility from service and blue-collar origins to white-collar destinations is more likely for Protestants than for Catholics; mobility out of farming is more likely for Catholics than for Protestants (and highly likely for both groups); and upward mobility from lower to higher professions is more likely for Catholics than for Protestants.

The impressive structural mobility for both Catholics and Protestants works in opposition to substantial class barriers to exchange mobility. The μ_{ik} scores vary substantially across occupational categories, scaling categories in a familiar order that distinguishes manual from nonmanual

Table 7.4a
Parameter estimates for homogeneous RC (model 4) for mobility from occupational origins to current occupation by religion: men aged 18–65, Northern Ireland, 1973

Occupation	Structural mobility[a]		Scores μ_j	Diagonal effects δ_j
	C $\log \alpha_{jc}$	P $\log \alpha_{jp}$		
Professionals & managers I (Ia,b)	2.56	2.22	5.00	1.95
Professionals & managers II (II)	1.67	1.88	2.87	1.67
Clerical workers (IIIa)	1.55	1.52	1.78	2.21
Proprietors (IVa,b)	1.03	.79	.13	2.78
Service workers (IIIb,VIIInf)	1.72	.89	−.22	1.65
Foremen & technicians (V)	1.71	1.01	−1.48	1.69
Skilled manual (VI)	1.20	.65	−2.38	1.69
Semiskilled manual (VIIss)	1.00	.48	−4.26	1.06
Unskilled manual (VIIus)	.77	.06	−5.37	.93
Farmers (IVc,d)	−2.18	−1.85	−2.69	46.14
Agricultural workers (VIIf,VIIIf)	.23	.05	−5.00	2.78
Uniform effect (100ϕ)	7.75	7.16	—	—
σ (logα)	1.23	1.09	—	—

a.   C = Catholic; P = Protestant.

Table 7.4b
Parameter estimates for homogeneous RC (model 4) for mobility from occupational origins to first occupation by religion: men aged 18–65, Northern Ireland, 1973

Occupation	Structural mobility[a]		Scores μ_j	Diagonal effects δ_j
	C $\log \alpha_{jc}$	P $\log \alpha_{jp}$		
Professionals & managers I (Ia,b)	3.77	2.61	5.00	11.21
Professionals & managers II (II)	2.74	2.30	4.66	2.46
Clerical workers (IIIa)	3.86	3.90	6.65	1.23
Proprietors (IVa,b)	−.30	−.58	3.37	7.04
Service workers (IIIb,VIIInf)	4.74	4.26	3.59	1.30
Foremen & technicians (V)	3.32	3.00	3.77	1.81
Skilled manual (VI)	3.41	3.01	3.74	1.53
Semiskilled manual (VIIss)	3.22	2.86	3.58	1.85
Unskilled manual (VIIus)	3.12	2.72	2.58	2.04
Farmers (IVc,d)	−5.51	−4.65	−1.22	372.42
Agricultural workers (VIIf,VIIIf)	4.01	3.63	−5.00	.04
Uniform effect (100ϕ)	10.51	9.71	—	—
σ (logα)	2.92	2.56	—	—

a.   C = Catholic; P = Protestant.

Table 7.4c
Parameter estimates for homogeneous RC (model 4) for mobility from
first occupation to current occupation by religion:
men aged 18–65, Northern Ireland, 1973

	Structural mobility[a]		Scores	Diagonal effects
	C	P		
Occupation	$\log \alpha_{jc}$	$\log \alpha_{jp}$	μ_j	δ_j
Professionals & managers I (Ia,b)	1.84	2.93	5.00	13.74
Professionals & managers II (II)	2.58	3.13	3.90	6.31
Clerical workers (IIIa)	.99	.54	3.64	3.47
Proprietors (IVa,b)	4.41	4.20	.85	11.68
Service workers (IIIb,VIIInf)	−.34	−.85	.32	2.42
Foremen & technicians (V)	1.49	.77	.28	7.40
Skilled manual (VI)	.58	.20	−.52	3.66
Semiskilled manual (VIIss)	.52	.23	−1.11	1.82
Unskilled manual (VIIus)	.28	−.15	−1.96	1.22
Farmers (IVc,d)	3.01	2.30	−9.17	.40
Agricultural workers (VIIf,VIIIf)	−2.84	−2.60	−5.00	3.09
Uniform effect (100ϕ)	8.54	7.94	—	—
σ (logα)	1.90	1.99	—	—

a.   C = Catholic; P = Protestant.

occupations and makes skill, training, income, and education distinctions within the manual and nonmanual strata. The difference between the first two μ_{ik} scores shows a very large gap between the status of upper and lower professional and managerial positions; it is the largest difference between adjacent scores in this set of coefficients. Two other differences that are substantially greater than 1.0 are the distance from clerical occupations to proprietorship and from farming to semiskilled manual work. Occupations that come out close together on the scale of μ_{ik} scores are proprietorships close to service jobs (including unpaid work as shopkeeper's assistant) and skilled manual jobs close to farming.

Substantial immobility effects for many occupational categories compound the general barriers to mobility captured by the μ_{ik} scores. As elsewhere, farming is the most inheritable occupation by an overwhelming margin. The only two occupational categories that show no significant net immobility are semiskilled and unskilled manual occupations. The absence of significant immobility among the lowest-status occupations is extremely important for understanding stratification in Northern Ireland. The expanse of the working-class and lower-class neighbor-

Table 7.5
Difference between structural mobility from origins to current occupation for Catholics and Protestants: men aged 18–65, Northern Ireland, 1973

Origin[a]	Ia Ib	II	IIIa	IVa IVb	IIIb VIIInf	V	VI	VIIss	VIIus	IVc IVd	VIIf VIIIf
Ia, Ib	—										
II	.54	—									
IIIa	.29	−.24	—								
IVa,IVb	.09	−.44	−.21	—							
IIIb, VIIInf	−.50	−1.03	−.79	−.59	—						
V	−.37	−.90	−.66	−.46	.13	—					
VI	−.21	−.74	−.50	−.30	.29	.16	—				
VIIss	−.19	−.73	−.49	−.28	.31	.18	.02	—			
VIIus	−.37	−.92	−.67	−.47	.13	−.01	−.16	−.18	—		
IVc, IVd	.67	.12	.37	.57	1.16	1.02	.88	.85	1.04	—	
VIIf, VIIIf	.16	−.39	−.14	.06	.65	.51	.37	.35	.53	−.51	—

a. Ia = self–employed professionals I and proprietors with 25 or more employees; Ib = salaried professionals I and managers I; II = professionals II and managers II; IIIa = clerical and sales workers; IIIb = service workers; IVa = proprietors with 1–24 employees; IVb = proprietors without employees; IVc = farmers with employees; IVd = farmers without employees; V = technicians and foremen; VI = skilled manual workers; VIIss = semiskilled manual workers; VIIus = unskilled manual workers; VIIf = agricultural laborers; VIIIf = unpaid farm helpers; VIIInf = unpaid nonfarm helpers.

b. Coefficients greater than zero indicate more mobility for Catholics; coefficients less than than zero indicate greater mobility for Protestants.

hoods, Protestant and Catholic, tempt observers to describe conditions in those neighborhoods in terms of a cycle of poverty or to use some other metaphor of lack of opportunity. These δ_{ik} coefficients contradict that image. Poverty is not self-sustaining in Northern Ireland. Poverty persists from generation to generation not because of inaction by the poor, which would show up in the data as large δ_{ik} coefficients for semiskilled and unskilled manual occupations. The substantial differences in resources between the working class and the middle class (reflected in the μ scores) coupled with the large δ_{ik} coefficients for professional and managerial positions, mean that it is privilege (however modest) that is self-sustaining.[11]

The system in Northern Ireland is structured not so much to block the ascent of the underclass as to block the descent of the middle class. In the absence of structural mobility, the consequences of blocked ascent or blocked descent are the same. But there is significant structural mobility in the North that allows more movement out of the lower working class than would be possible if the δ_8 and δ_9 parameters were large.

Figure 7.2 displays how the ϕ_k, μ_i, and δ_i coefficients combine to model the dependence of current occupational standing on social origins. A pair of occupational categories widely different in status—lower-grade professional and managerial occupations (class II) and unskilled manual work (class VIIus)—are selected as alternative destinations. The odds on having a current occupation in the higher-status category instead of one in the lower-status category are arrayed by origin and religion. The odds on a higher-status destination climb sharply with rising origins for both Catholics and Protestants. Differential structural mobility (see Table 7.5) and the conditional distribution of occupations by religion (captured by the log β_{ic} and log β_{ip} parameters) give Protestants an advantage over Catholics at each level of origin, that is, the line for Protestants is higher than the line for Catholics throughout the range of origins. The gap between lines would be smaller in most alternative comparisons.

Although the Protestant advantage is evident, it does not cancel the effect of class. The Protestant son of a semiskilled manual worker has an even chance of arriving at a high-status or a low-status destination (the logit is on the zero line). If religion canceled the effect of class, then the odds on a high-status versus a low-status destination would be less than even for all Catholics, not just those from working-class backgrounds. In fact, all Catholics whose fathers were employed at or above the level of supervisory or technical workers (class V) have better than even odds on attaining the higher-status job.

In less technical terms, Catholics with middle-class backgrounds (an admittedly small group) have an advantage over Protestants with working-class backgrounds. This is not to gainsay the importance of religion for stratification in Northern Ireland; the Protestant-Catholic effect is very clear. However, focus on the religious conflict in the North cannot obscure the role of class in that society.

Class dominates career beginnings as well. Structural mobility is more extreme for Catholics, mainly because of a massive exodus from farming, which is a more important origin for Catholics than for Protestants. Upward structural mobility from working-class origins to a middle-class first job is greater for Protestants than for Catholics. Protestants have an advantage over Catholics with the same origin status.

The principal departure of these findings from form is in the μ_{ik} scores. The major portion of the association between origins and first occupations

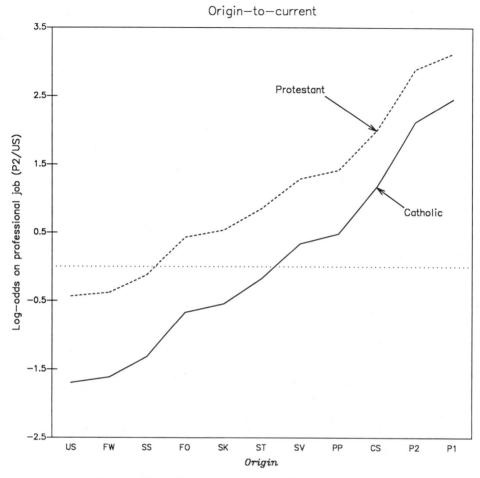

Figure 7.2 Expected log-odds on a lower professional or managerial destination (relative to unskilled manual) and clerical or sales destination (relative to technical or supervisory) for mobility from origin to current job, by religion: men aged 18–65, Northern Ireland, 1973.

is in the δ_i parameters. The μ_{ik} scores fail to distinguish among occupations in the middle of the status hierarchy. All five occupational categories between proprietors and semiskilled manual workers all score between 3.37 and 3.77 on a scale that ranges from -5 to 5. The ϕ_k coefficients are relatively large (about 60 percent larger than the ϕ_k for mobility from origin to current occupation), but in this important middle range of the status hierarchy that spans the white-collar–blue-collar divide, the large

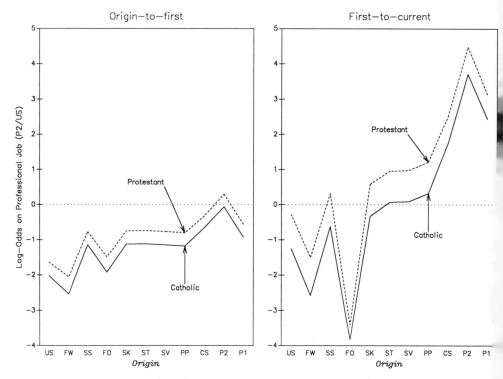

Figure 7.3 Expected log-odds on a lower professional or managerial destination (relative to unskilled manual) and clerical or sales destination (relative to technical or supervisory) for mobility from origin to first job and first to current job, by religion: men aged 18–65, Northern Ireland, 1973.

ϕ_k has little variation in status to affect. In compensation for this lack of variation, the extremes of the status scale are truly extreme. The μ_{ik} scores appear to be modeling a farm-nonfarm distinction rather than a set of status distinctions.

Structural mobility within the career reflects the life-cycle switch from paid work to self-employment in Northern Ireland. Protestants do not have the advantage in structural mobility from the working class to the middle class that was found in the pattern of intergenerational mobility. Class barriers to intragenerational mobility are evident in the μ_{ik} scores, the large ϕ_k coefficients, and the large δ_i parameters.

Figure 7.3 clearly shows the class barriers to mobility in the steep slope of the lines for both Catholics and Protestants. Not so clear is the fact that the two lines for intragenerational mobility would be more similar to the intergenerational lines in the absence of the large δ_i parameter for lower-grade professionals and managers, and that the odds on professional employment for men who begin their careers as farmers are very low. (As noted in Jackson and Miller 1983, very few men who begin farming ever leave.) Aside from those two exceptions, the lines for mobility from origins to current occupations and for mobility from first occupations to current occupations coincide to a surprising extent, illustrating a complementarity between intergenerational and intragenerational mobility.

Intragenerational Mobility and Countermobility

Intergenerational and intragenerational mobility express the main features of the mobility process one step at a time. Unless mobility is a Markov process—and there is much information to the contrary (see Featherman 1972)—details about the intersection of the various mobility patterns add useful information. If the men with upper nonmanual origins who took middling first jobs are subsequently upwardly mobile to prestigious current jobs, whereas the men from lower origins who took middling first jobs subsequently regress toward their lower origins in the course of taking their current jobs, then the step-by-step approach taken above misses a component of the stratification process.

For example, some of the men who began their careers with first jobs in a service occupation proceeded to higher-status current jobs by 1973; others who began in services moved to manual current jobs. If the men from nonmanual origins are disproportionately upwardly mobile from service first jobs while men from working-class origins are disproportionately downwardly mobile, then the association models (and Figures 7.2 and 7.3) understate the effect of class on mobility in Northern Ireland.

Mobility out of an origin class at first occupation and subsequently back to those origins by the time of current job is known as "countermobility" (Bernard and Renaud 1976; Goldthorpe 1980). Lifetime mobility can be divided into four main types, and three of those main types can be subdivided. Because the four-way tabulations of origin by first occupation by current occupation by religion leave even more zero cells than the three-way tabulations, only six broad occupational strata are used. The strata (with the roman numeral codes for the original categories that compose them in parentheses) are upper nonmanual (Ia, Ib, II); lower nonmanual

(IIIa, IIIb, IVa, IVb, VIIInf); upper manual (V, VI); farm owner (IVc, IVd); lower manual (VIIss, VIIus); and farm worker (VIIf, VIIIf). This list ranks the strata in order of descending prestige, which is the order used in reckoning upward and downward mobility. The countermobility typology is as follows:

Immobile: Men whose first and current occupations are both in the same stratum (using the six strata) as their origin.

Countermobile: Men whose current occupation is in the same broad occupational stratum as their origin but who have a first occupation that falls in some other stratum. In the analysis of men from all occupations, this category is subdivided into countermobility from *above,* namely from an occupation that has higher prestige than the current occupation, and countermobility from *below,* namely from an occupation that has lower prestige than the current occupation.

Upwardly mobile: Men whose current occupation is more prestigious than their origin. Some of these men moved upward to their first occupation and stayed there; these men are of the *directly upward* subtype. Some men took a first job that had less prestige than their current job but the same or more prestige than their origin; these men are of the *indirectly upward* subtype. Finally, some men took a first job that had less prestige than both their current occupation and their origin; these men are of the mixed *down then up* subtype.

Downwardly mobile: Men whose current occupation is less prestigious than their origin. Within this general type, *directly downward, indirectly downward,* and mixed *up then down* subtypes are defined in a manner analogous to the subdivisions of upwardly mobile men.

The population for this analysis is men who began work prior to 1959. Men with less experience are too close to their career beginnings for the forces of countermobility to have had sufficient chance to work themselves through. Of course, limiting the sample in such a way excludes men who may have benefited from employment changes during the 1959–1973 period.

Table 7.6 cross-classifies men from Northern Ireland according to their countermobility status, origin stratum, and religion. Three important conclusions follow from these data. First, Catholics from upper manual origins are *less* likely than Protestants to be directly or indirectly upwardly mobile. Second, Catholics from upper manual origins are *more* likely than Protestants to be directly downwardly mobile (that is, to get inadequate first jobs and not subsequently recover). Third, Catholics from lower manual origins are *more* likely than Protestants to be immobile within the lowest stratum. Protestants who get lower manual first jobs do no better than Catholics, but Catholics are more likely than Protestants to get low-status first jobs. The Protestant advantage consists in being directly upwardly mobile. Despite these differences, the countermobility pattern does not differ substantially by religion. More important, nothing in the data suggests that the foregoing analysis was misleading in any fundamental way.

Workers pass through many statuses in their lifetimes. Limiting attention to the prime stages in the socioeconomic life cycle captures the most important aspects of the stratification process but does not guarantee that no aspects have been missed until all of the moves have been investigated. Most mobility studies lack data on occupational careers. Not so the Irish Mobility Study, which has complete work histories. The interviews with 1,488 Protestants and 835 Catholics yield data on 14,594 job spells: 2,323 spells were censored by the interview (that is, the job spell was still ongoing at the time of interview); the remaining 12,271 were closed by an observed job shift. Nonparametric methods that adjust for censoring are used to analyze both the closed and the censored job spells (Kaplan and Meier 1958).

A job shift may be good or bad for an individual. A move from entry level to supervisor would be a sure plus. A sequence of unskilled jobs sprinkled with spells of unemployment, however, would not constitute an enviable career. Whether a religious group's mobility is composed of more moves of the former type or the latter will color the interpretation of its overall rate of mobility. The job shifts show the overall rate of mobility for Catholics and Protestants and reveal whether class or religion is the source of differential mobility.

The cumulative mobility hazard $H(t)$ is the measure of overall mobility.[12] Figure 7.4 displays the rate of increase in $H(t)$ as duration of the job spell increases. The cumulative mobility hazard is displayed instead of the cumulative mobility rate because equal rates of mobility over the range $t + \Delta t$ result in parallel line segments between $H(t)$ and $H(t + \Delta t)$, but diverging line segments between mobility at t and $t + \Delta t$ (unless the cumulative mobility of Protestants and Catholics is identical at t).

The mobility of Catholics obviously exceeds that of Protestants. After twelve months the cumulative mobility hazard for Catholics is .41 (corre-

Table 7.6
Countermobility by religion and origin: men aged 25–65, Northern Ireland, 1973

			Origin			
Component[a]	Upper nonmanual	Lower nonmanual	Upper manual	Farm owner	Lower manual	Farm worker
Catholics						
Immobile	22%	14%	24%	2%	37%	10%
Countermobile	35	22	19	31	10	5
From above	—	2	1	1	4	5
From below	35	20	18	30	5	—
Upwardly mobile	—	20	23	38	51	85
Directly	—	8	5	17	24	39
Indirectly	—	4	6	<1	22	46
Down then up	—	8	12	21	5	—
Downwardly mobile	42	45	34	29	2	—
Directly	42	38	21	28	<1	—
Indirectly	<1	7	8	<1	1	—
Up then down	—	<1	5	2	<1	—
(N)	(40)	(92)	(122)	(178)	(205)	(41)
Protestants						
Immobile	24%	18%	20%	3%	24%	12%
Countermobile	36	19	20	37	14	2
From above	—	1	3	1	8	2
From below	36	17	16	36	6	—
Upwardly mobile	—	25	34	35	60	86
Directly	—	8	11	16	32	53
Indirectly	—	6	10	1	25	33
Down then up	—	11	12	18	2	—
Downwardly mobile	40	39	27	25	1	—
Directly	39	34	17	23	1	—
Indirectly	1	4	8	<1	<1	—
Up then down	—	1	2	1	<1	—
(N)	(129)	(170)	(305)	(299)	(390)	(66)

a.   Percentages in italics sum to 100 percent (except for round-off); percentages in roman type sum to the italicized percentage above them (except for round-off).

sponding to a mobility rate of 34 percent); for Protestants it is .30 (a mobility rate of 26 percent).[13] After five years the mobility hazard is up to 1.38 for Catholics and 1.16 for Protestants. These cumulated mobility hazards mean that 75 percent of Catholics and 68 percent of Protestants can be expected to change jobs every five years. Median job duration is 24 months for Catholics and 30 months for Protestants. Comparative data would help to evaluate whether these durations are long or short. However, because the Irish Mobility Study data are unique, the only comparable calculation is for the Republic of Ireland, at 37 months.

To separate the effects of class and religion on career mobility, we need to control for occupation (either the sending occupation, referred to as "current," or the receiving occupation, referred to as "next") when examining the mobility hazard. If class dominates religion in determining career mobility (as the analysis of association implies), then the difference between the mobility of Catholics and Protestants that is so evident in general should be much less evident in particular kinds of mobility.

From this perspective on mobility from current occupations, the higher mobility of Catholics could be due to either a preponderance of Catholics in occupations that have high mobility for all incumbents or a higher rate of exit for Catholics in all kinds of jobs. Figure 7.5 shows the cumulative mobility hazard for Catholics and Protestants in six current occupational strata (farm laborers are excluded because their line falls very close to the lower nonmanual line). The results show that the differences in mobility by religion are due in large part to differences between Catholics and Protestants in the kinds of jobs they begin with. Farmers are the least mobile; the unemployed are the most mobile. Within both of these occupational strata, Protestants are more mobile than Catholics. Differences between Catholics and Protestants in mobility among nonmanual workers

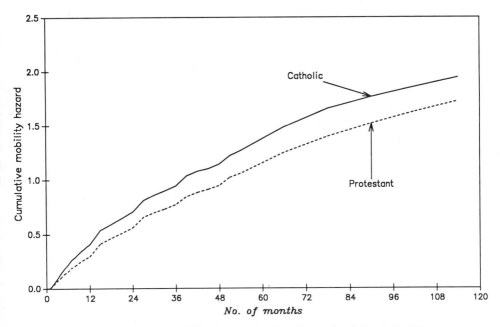

Figure 7.4   Cumulative mobility hazard, by duration and religion: job shifts, Northern Ireland, 1922–1974.

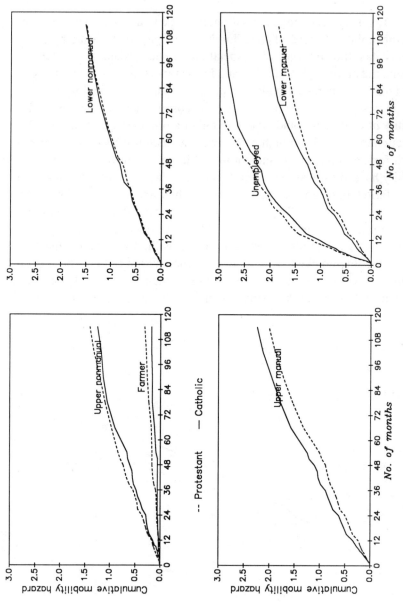

Figure 7.5   Cumulative mobility hazard, by duration, current occupation, and religion: job shifts, Northern Ireland, 1922–1974.

are very small. The greater mobility of Catholics comes from the intersection of the high concentration of Catholics in manual (especially lower manual) occupations, the high mobility among all manual workers, and the higher mobility of Catholic manual workers.

To separate religion and class further, Table 7.7 presents the cumulative mobility proportion $(1 - \lambda_t)$ at 12, 60, and 120 months for Catholic and Protestant upper or lower manual workers for each next job stratum.[14] These cumulative mobility rates differ widely by destination. Moves within the manual stratum, particularly moves within skill level, predominate. Only in one combination of current and next occupation within the manual stratum is there an appreciable difference between Protestants and Catholics. Protestants from skilled manual current jobs are more likely than Catholics to move to another skilled manual job between months 60 and 120. Otherwise, current and next occupations account for all of the religious difference in mobility from one job to another. Unemployment is another story: Catholics suffer a significantly higher risk of unemployment, especially if they are currently in a semiskilled or unskilled occupation.

Table 7.7
Cumulative mobility hazard by duration, current occupation,
next occupation, and religion: men aged 18–65, Northern Ireland, 1973

Next occupation	Upper manual		Lower manual	
	Catholic	Protestant	Catholic	Protestant
12 months				
Upper nonmanual	.01	.01	.00	.01
Lower nonmanual	.03	.02	.02	.03
Upper manual	.24	.19	.09	.09
Lower manual	.07	.05	.21	.13
Unemployed	.09	.05	.17	.08
60 months				
Upper nonmanual	.04	.06	.01	.02
Lower nonmanual	.11	.07	.09	.12
Upper manual	.53	.49	.20	.25
Lower manual	.18	.14	.53	.51
Unemployed	.22	.13	.33	.17
120 months				
Upper nonmanual	.07	.11	.03	.05
Lower nonmanual	.22	.15	.13	.16
Upper manual	.72	.71	.24	.32
Lower manual	.29	.23	.69	.62
Unemployed	.29	.23	.43	.25

Religion and Unemployment

Unemployment is the most serious differential between Catholics and Protestants encountered in this analysis. After one, five, and ten years, the risk of unemployment among Catholics in lower manual occupations is nearly twice that of comparable Protestants.

Figure 7.6 shows how important unemployment is for overall job mobility in Northern Ireland by presenting the ratio of the unemployment hazard to the hazard for job shifts of all types. During the first year in any job, the hazard of unemployment is 25 percent of the total hazard of a job shift for Catholics and 15–18 percent for Protestants. Subsequently, the unemployment hazard for Catholics drops to 17 percent of the total hazard of any job shift; the unemployment hazard for Protestants drops to 11 percent of the total. To put these figures in perspective, Figure 7.6 also shows the relative hazards for moves to a lower manual and an upper nonmanual occupation. The hazard of a move to a lower manual occupation is twice the unemployment hazard for Catholics and Protestants at all durations. The hazard of moving to an upper nonmanual occupation is a small fraction of the total hazard at short durations, but it climbs steadily. These relative hazards show clearly both the quantitative importance of spells of unemployment in job mobility in Northern Ireland and the greater impact of unemployment on Catholics.

Catholics suffer not only from higher unemployment but also from long spells of unemployment. The top line in Figure 7.6 shows the cumulative reemployment hazard by religion. While spells of unemployment are unambiguously shorter than job spells, it is also obvious that reemployment accumulates faster for Protestants than it does for Catholics. The scale hides some of the difference. The median duration of unemployment is seven months for Protestants and one year for Catholics. After five years, less than 1 percent of Protestants remain (continuously) unemployed; among Catholics 5 percent are still unemployed after ten years.

The duration of unemployment is a function of the skills the worker brings to the labor market. Therefore previous employment history might be expected to affect the chances of reemployment. Figure 7.7 presents the cumulative reemployment hazard by previous occupation (for the categories of previous occupation that contain at least 50 unemployment spells) and religion. The results are impressive. The substantial disadvantage of Catholics seeking reemployment is almost completely attributable to their prior job histories. All workers who enter unemployment

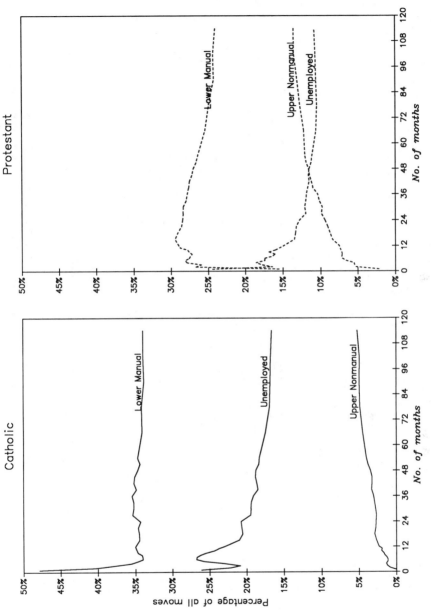

Figure 7.6   Hazard of mobility into unemployment, a lower manual job, or an upper nonmanual job (as a percentage of total hazard) by duration, destination of job shift, and religion: job shifts, Northern Ireland, 1922–1974.

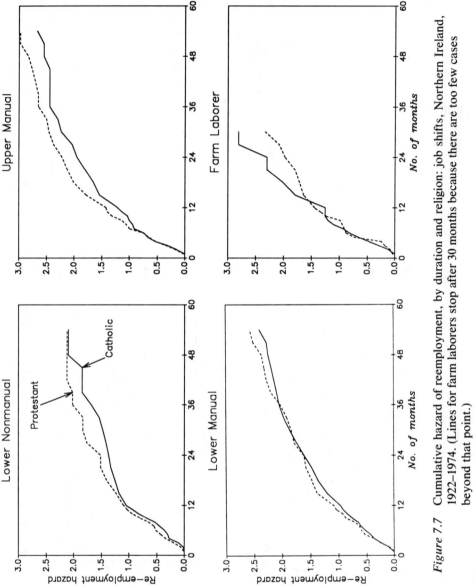

Figure 7.7   Cumulative hazard of reemployment, by duration and religion: job shifts, Northern Ireland, 1922–1974. (Lines for farm laborers stop after 30 months because there are too few cases beyond that point.)

from a lower manual occupation have more trouble finding reemployment than do workers who enter unemployment from a lower nonmanual or upper manual occupation. The largest differences between Protestants and Catholics are among upper manual workers and farm laborers. In both instances the difference between the median duration of unemployment for Catholics and Protestants is just over one week (.28 month).

Class or Values?

In *The Protestant Ethic and the Spirit of Capitalism* Max Weber (1958) spells out the links among Calvinist Protestantism, asceticism, and capital accumulation. Weber counters materialist explanations of the history of capitalism by asserting the crucial role of ideology in the economic processes that distinguish capitalism from other economic forms. By emphasizing deferred gratification, saving, and investment, he argues that ideology allowed some protocapitalists to get the full measure from their meager resources, thereby spawning a cycle of development that exceeded the return available to less thrifty entrepreneurs who may well have had similar resources at their command at some initial point. While he addresses the timing of capitalist development and differences in national income, many others have sought the implications of his theory for the wealth and prosperity of individuals. They typically begin with the reasonable corollary that individuals who profess a Protestant faith, especially Calvinists, will be more likely than Catholics to defer consumption, save, and invest (e.g., Lenski 1959). They then purport to test their derivation by observing the relative concentration of Protestants and Catholics in white-collar occupations (as if white-collar employment involved investment in anything more substantial than human capital).

Northern Ireland appears, on the surface, to be fertile ground for such a test of the microversion of the Protestant ethic thesis. The centuries of Protestant and Catholic presence in Northern Ireland overcome one of the vexing problems in research on this topic in the United States. Religion is not confounded with length of residence in Northern Ireland, so the confounding influence of migration that complicates the analysis of religious effects in many American contexts is not a factor (e.g., Lenski 1959; Thernstrom 1973). The Protestant faith prevalent throughout Northern Ireland is Calvinist Presbyterianism; it stresses the asceticism and self-control identified with the Protestant ethic. Furthermore, both Catholics and Protestants practice their religions; religious labels are not merely cultural markers left over from a more devout past, as they may be in Germany, Italy, or France.

Despite these advantages, employment in Northern Ireland makes an inappropriate testing ground for Weber's thesis or its individual-level corollary. The problem is neither Northern Ireland as a venue for such a test nor the Irish Mobility Study data. The problem is one of deduction. A logical link between the theory and the occupational data is missing. Indeed, all such "tests" based on comparisons between occupational achievements of Protestants and Catholics are irrelevant—Weber's apparent endorsement of such tests notwithstanding (Lipset and Bendix 1959, p. 49).

The missing link in deriving the microhypothesis from the macrotheory of the Protestant ethic comes at the end of the chain. The macrotheory is about savings, investment, and accumulation. The microcorollary refers to individual investment and consumption. The test refers to employment. In accepting differential attainment of white-collar occupations by Protestants and Catholics as evidence of differential consumption, savings, and investment, Weber, Lenski, Thernstrom, and even critics of the hypothesis like Lipset and Bendix, suppose a link between the outcomes of ideological asceticism—deferred gratification, savings, and investment—and white-collar employment. They implicitly assume that one attains a middle-class occupation much as the ideal typical capitalist expands his enterprise, by denying the self and investing in the business.

Is that how it is done? Does the Protestant advantage in middle-class employment in Northern Ireland arise because Protestants invest more prudently in their careers than do Catholics? Probably not, at least not in the way that Weberians assume. For example, engineering is an important white-collar occupation that contributes to the difference between Protestants and Catholics in Northern Ireland. Savings and investment have little if anything to do with attaining a job as an engineer. Perhaps investment and savings undertaken by Protestant parents on behalf of their children might foster those children's chances of attending universities that grant engineering degrees. But it seems that the Weberians—if they have any specific dynamic in mind—posit intragenerational investment. For religious differences in occupational distributions to pertain to the Protestant ethic, workers must somehow accumulate occupational success the way a firm accumulates capital assets. Otherwise, the emphasis on savings and investment in the macrotheory is meaningless at the microlevel.

This is simply not the way it works in Northern Ireland (if it works this way anywhere). In the world of salaried employment, job performance has far more to do with retaining and advancing one's position over the course of one's career than does anything related to what one does with the salary earned. If the advantage of Protestants over Catholics in Northern Ireland could be shown to originate in a career pattern that involves salaried work in youth, accompanied by prolific savings, financial independence, and self-employment for the majority of middle-class Protestants, then religious differences in achievement could be interpreted in Weberian terms. As it is, most Protestants work for pay throughout their careers. Catholics are actually slightly more likely to be self-employed than are Protestants. The accumulation analogy breaks down; the "test" is moot.

The only viable conclusion is that religious differences in occupational achievement are structural. They come from the distribution of power and rewards in Northern Irish society, not from the belief systems of Irish Catholics and Protestants. The values and material outlooks of Protestants might well differ from those of Catholics. However, their existence does not imply that religious differences in achievement stem from religious values or from secular values that reflect theological differences. In the end, to be effective, values must influence the career employment pattern. Before religion per se can be accepted as an explanation of religious differences in achievement, the causal sequence that starts with the effect of religious values on consumption and savings behavior and ends with the effect of private consumption and savings on career advancement must be affirmed. It remains to be shown that the career advancement of Irish workers depends in any way on their consumption or savings.

Conclusion

Catholics in Northern Ireland are disadvantaged by their lower-class origins, the general scarcity of opportunity in Northern Ireland, and specific, ascriptive handicaps that appear to be related to discrimination. This list of factors is not too surprising. The surprise is the importance of social-class ascription in Northern Ireland. As appalling and apparent as the religious divide in the North may be, *class* does more to limit achievement. For Catholic and Protestant alike, working-class origins are a pronounced disadvantage. Being born to the middle class brings with it a number of advantages that are passed from one generation to the next.

The clearest evidence of the importance of class is found in the effect of origin class on occupational destination (see Figure 7.2). Catholics from middle-class backgrounds have a distinct advantage over most Protestants from working-class backgrounds—a state of affairs inconsistent with the castelike images sometimes used in describing the divided society of the Northern Ireland. Indeed, none of the models of stratification in Northern Ireland has so far anticipated the overriding importance of class.[15]

The gap between Catholic and Protestant achievement is not necessarily evidence of discrimination against Catholics. The achievements of Catholics from middle-class backgrounds may lag behind those of Protestants from middle-class backgrounds because "middle-class" origins for Catholics are not as lofty as "middle-class" origins for Protestants.[16] The achievement of Catholics may fall short of that of Protestants from the same origin class because the socioeconomic origins of Catholics are overstated by their father's job title. With equal true status, the achievements of Catholics and Protestants might well coincide. But the segregation in Northern Ireland is so severe that the concept "equal true status" is a statistical one, not an empirical reality that can be measured and put to the test in order to enlighten debate about class and religion.

The religious difference in unemployment cannot be explained away. Catholics are more likely than Protestants to be unemployed at any time, to suffer a long spell of unemployment when they are laid off, and (most troubling) to remain permanently unemployed. These differences reflect differences in background and experience to some extent, but after the inclusion of appropriate statistical controls, they persist as significant (if smaller) differences.

8   Expanding Schools, Persistent Inequality

The school system bridges the gap between socioeconomic origins and destinations.[1] A student brings to school the advantages and disadvantages of class background, acquires a share of the knowledge, credentials, values, and attitudes that schools have to offer, and exits to make her or his way in the world of work. From such a strategic location in the system of social stratification, schools—and the educational system more broadly conceived—can make or break the link between origins and destinations. If schools simply mirror the class structure, they can reproduce the order of social class origins in the credentials they bestow, thereby giving a legitimacy to inequality of opportunity that it might otherwise lack (Bourdieu 1977; Bourdieu and Passeron 1977). But if schools attend to achievement, ignoring class considerations, they can break the cycle of poverty and privilege. These two views of schools contend with each other in academic debate and in society at large.

Of course, real schools are complex. They pass on inequalities while they create opportunities. Schools sort students in a way that corresponds (to a greater or lesser extent) to the order of students according to social class background. At the same time, they introduce independent variance into the stratification system by handing out credentials based on considerations that are independent of class background. This dual role of education has two constituent parts: the path from social origins to educational attainment and the subsequent path from education to occupational success (Duncan and Hodge 1963; Blau and Duncan 1967).

The Educational System in Ireland

Education expanded dramatically in Ireland during the twentieth century. The expansion resembles expansion elsewhere and probably occurred for similar reasons. Students leaving school in the 1970s and 1980s have been in school much longer than school leavers of an earlier era. Yet while the average student in the second half of the twentieth century receives far more education than the average student of fifty years ago, the structure of Irish education in the present era resembles that of long ago to a remarkable extent. The worker from the Irish Mobility Study who left school at age 16 in 1970 probably experienced the same sequence of educational transitions as his counterpart who left school at age 16 in 1930.

Irish education follows the pattern of age-graded schooling found in many parts of the world. Students enter primary school at a young age. The starting age for the average student might be 4, 5, or 6 years of age, depending on the era, because part of the expansion of education has included the enrollment of younger children. For older men in the Irish Mobility Study (those who left school before 1959), the modal age at first schooling is 6 years; for younger men (those who left school since 1959), the modal age is 5 years. Most Dublin schools offered classes for 4-year-olds in 1983–84, so the starting age for the next generation will probably be younger still. Students stay in primary school until they are between 12 and 14 years old (if they intend to complete the primary cycle). Until 1947 in Northern Ireland and 1967 in the Republic, a Primary Certificate was awarded to those students who passed an exam given to students wishing to leave primary school.

Those who successfully complete their primary careers follow one of three channels from there. Some terminate at the end of primary school.[2] Some enter an academic program in a secondary or grammar school. The remainder go on to specialized technical training and general course work at a vocational or modern school. During the course of second-level education, there are several opportunities to drop out. Some curricula terminate after two years. Other curricula go on for up to six years but require good performance.[3] Students completing six years of secondary schooling face a limited number of openings in third-level institutions that include academic universities, training colleges for teachers and other professionals, polytechnic institutes, and technical colleges.

For most of the men in the Irish Mobility Study, the selection of a channel of further education beyond the primary level was not altogether voluntary. Entry into a second-level institution of any sort required not only a Primary Certificate and further evidence of academic achievement, but also money. Although primary schooling was free, secondary and vocational schools charged tuition until 1944 in Northern Ireland and 1967 in the Republic. In view of this important change in the economic conditions of secondary schooling, it seems reasonable to expect a diminished class effect on educational outcome among more recent cohorts. Of course, actual experience occasionally confounds expectations, even ones as reasonable as expecting class differences in secondary schooling to disappear when the financial burden of secondary education is removed. For example, Halsey, Heath, and Ridge (1980) expected the establishment of free secondary schooling in England to reduce class differences in educational attainment, but they found no evidence to confirm their expectation.

How could such a logical relationship between egalitarian social policy and egalitarian outcome fail to materialize? One hypothesis is that fees for secondary schooling taxed the means of many middle-class families as well as the means of most working-class families. Secondary schooling was by no means universal among the middle classes of England, Wales, and Ireland before the states assumed the costs. In England and Wales, Halsey et al. (1980, p. 63) report that 25–30 percent of the sons of professionals and managers from the cohorts who reached the secondary-school age prior to 1944 did not attend academic secondary schools. In Ireland, the range is 20–35 percent of sons of professionals and managers not continuing in school beyond the primary level during the era when fees were required. Perhaps the fees had something to do with these high dropout rates in Ireland and the high rates of attendance in nonselective schools in England. If they did, then maybe free secondary school can aid the middle classes as well as the working classes. If the probability of attending secondary school was affected for middle-class children as much as it was for working-class children, then free education could achieve its purpose of opening opportunities for children from families who otherwise could not afford schooling without erasing class differentials in attendance rates.

This "rising tide" hypothesis implies higher rates of enrollment in (selective) secondary school for all classes after the establishment of free secondary schooling (1944 in England, Wales, and Northern Ireland; 1967 in the Republic of Ireland). In England and Wales, the evidence is negative. Although overall enrollment rates in selective secondary education increased from 29 percent for the 1913–1922 cohort to 38 percent for the 1933–1942 cohort, there was very little growth in the proportion of sons attending selective secondary school *within* any of the classes in Britain (Halsey, Heath, and Ridge 1980, table 11.1, p. 63). Apparently all of the growth in attendance at selective secondary schools was due to a redistribution of the social origins in a way that favored educational attainment. The British program did not abolish fee-paying schools; it simply established a parallel state-supported, equally selective system. Without the state-supported schools, private education may not have absorbed the growing numbers of applicants and may instead have become more selective. The state-supported system took the pressure off the private schools, while it gave some middle-class parents a choice between paying or not paying for their children's education. Many chose not to pay. Ironically, instead of creating new opportunities for the working class by removing financial burdens, the Education Act of 1944 appears to have mainly expanded the number of positions available for educating the offspring of the rapidly growing British middle class.

The data from Ireland reveal rising opportunity for middle-class and working-class children alike. Enrollment in secondary schools grew in both the Republic and the North. More important, all classes participated equally in the growth of secondary enrollment.

Changes in Educational Attainment and Transition Rates

Table 8.1 shows the upward trend in Irish education. Educational attainment is divided into nine categories arrayed separately for each cohort and region. The cohort breakdown departs from the common practice of dividing workers according to their year of birth. Instead, cohorts are defined according to the year in which the respondent began working. The divisions among the three cohorts correspond to the timing of educational reforms in Northern Ireland (1945) and economic reforms in the Republic (1959).

Three-quarters of Irish men who began working before 1945 received no more than a primary education. Half of the men who began working in the late 1940s and the 1950s received at least some postprimary education; the other half followed the older pattern of early school leaving. The two parts of Ireland differed in the distribution of postprimary education by type during this period. Postprimary education was more likely to be academic in the Republic, where 62 percent of those continuing went to academic secondary schools, than in Northern Ireland, where 46 percent of those continuing enrolled in academic schools. Since secondary education was free in Northern Ireland but not in the Republic when the men in this cohort were ready to move from primary to secondary school, it is sur-

Table 8.1
Distribution of educational attainment by first job cohort and region:
ever–employed men aged 18–65, Ireland, 1973

Education	Republic			Northern Ireland		
	Prior to 1945	1945–1958	1959–1973	Prior to 1945	1945–1958	1959–1973
Primary						
Incomplete	5%	2%	<1%	3%	1%	<1%
Complete	70	47	24	72	49	9
Secondary						
Nonacademic	9	19	30	12	27	55
Incomplete academic	8	14	15	4	7	8
Complete academic	3	9	15	3	8	9
Postsecondary						
Nonacademic	2	4	5	2	3	6
Incomplete academic	<1	1	4	<1	1	5
Complete academic	1	2	6	2	3	4
Postgraduate	1	2	2	1	2	4
Total	100	100	100	100	100	100
(N)	(930)	(651)	(686)	(1016)	(647)	(727)

prising that the Republic was keeping up with the secondary school expansion in the North.

Perhaps the Republic's secondary schools do not deserve quite so much credit. It is possible that selective emigration, which was extremely high during these years, drew off a large share of primary school leavers from the Republic. If the poorly educated were more likely than their better-educated counterparts to leave Ireland, then their absence from this sample of Irish residents biases upward the estimate of the school-leaving pattern of the immediate postwar era. The best evidence on the point is from the Oxford Mobility Study (Goldthorpe 1980). The Irish-born workers born 1921–1940 (roughly the same cohort) drawn from the Oxford data tapes show only 40 percent with primary education ($n = 42$). This figure suggests that, if any difference exists between emigrants and other men, it is the emigrants who were better educated than the men they left behind.

After 1967 secondary schooling in the Republic was free, and the proportion of men in the post-1958 cohort who stopped their education after primary school was only half what it was for the preceding cohort. But in Northern Ireland, an even more dramatic expansion of second-level education took place, so that less than one-tenth of this cohort never went to secondary school. Most of the growth was absorbed by the nonselective, nonacademic schools.

Because few respondents dropped out of school before completing primary schooling or continued their education after secondary school, some of the categories of educational attainment are combined here. Any collapsing of categories results in a loss of information. Nonetheless, some distinctions are more important than others. The minimum classification distinguishes primary, secondary, and higher education. Two other kinds of distinctions are made within levels of education: complete versus incomplete and academic versus nonacademic. There are too few men at the extremes—that is, with incomplete primary or postgraduate educations—to make reliable generalizations. Accordingly, the distinctions between complete and incomplete primary and between complete third-level and postgraduate work are dropped. There are also too few college dropouts in the sample to generalize about, so they are combined with men with nonacademic higher educations to form a heterogeneous category composed of men wth some higher education but no academic degree. This leaves a six-category classification that is cross-tabulated with social origins, cohort, and region (see Appendix Tables A.15–A.16). The principal findings are the following:

Pronounced differences in educational attainment among social origin categories.

Clear cohort differences in educational attainment, reflecting the expansion of secondary education.

Comparatively small differences between the Republic and Northern Ireland, except in the last cohort, where attainment in Northern Ireland is clearly higher.

Probably less effect of social origins for the most recent cohort than for the other two cohorts, especially in Northern Ireland. This is a difficult effect to tease out, both because it is probably a small improvement and because the main source of diminished differentials seems to be the fact that the proportions cannot drop below zero in the primary category.

Education is a sequential process. Young people do not arrive immediately at university. They progress through each level of the school system. To separate the independent effect of social class, cohort, and region, a statistical model must correctly specify this sequence (Mare 1980). The building block of this kind of model is the transition rate: the proportion of students at level k who go on to the next level $(k + 1)$.

The most important change in Irish education is the increase in transition rates to secondary school. The proportion continuing from primary to secondary school rises from 24 percent of the pre-1945 cohort to 91 percent of the 1959–1973 cohort in Northern Ireland, and from 24 percent to 76 percent in the Republic. The differences among classes in transition rates are huge. In the first cohort, the range of transition rates in Northern Ireland is 64 points; in the Republic, the range is 72 points. In the second cohort, the range of transition rates in Northern Ireland is 64 points, similar to the 68 point range in the Republic. In the last cohort, the range is down to 28 points in Northern Ireland and 41 points in the Republic. Ceiling effects may be responsible for the compressed range in the last cohort, as all of the sons of large proprietors, professionals, and managers in that cohort went on to the second level. In each cohort the sons of large proprietors, professionals, managers, clerks, and salesmen (classes Ia, Ib, II, and IIIa) are most likely to continue their educations beyond the primary level; the sons of small farmers (class IVd) and unskilled manual laborers on and off farms (classes VIIus and VIIf) are most likely to drop out at this point. The sons of employers do significantly better than the sons of men with the same occupation but no employees. Petit proprietors with employees (class IVa) give their sons as much as a 33-point advantage over the sons of petit proprietors without employees (class IVb); the advantage of sons of employing farmers (class IVc) over sons of small holders (class IVd) ranges from 10 to 25 points. Internal stratification of the working class in the Republic is also pronounced: sons of skilled manual workers have between 20 and 50 points advantage over sons of unskilled manual workers. Differences among working-class categories are not as evident in Northern Ireland: sons of skilled manual workers are significantly more likely than sons of unskilled workers to continue beyond primary school in the pre-1945 cohort but not in the more recent cohorts.

Among men who start secondary school, the probability of attaining a complete (academic) secondary education increased from cohort to cohort in the Republic but not in Northern Ireland. Completion rates went up from 28 percent to 41 percent in the Republic but down slightly from 36 percent to 31 percent in Northern Ireland. The differences among classes at this level may not be quite as large as the differences at the primary level, especially in the earliest cohort. Furthermore, there is no sign of a decrease in the class effect over time; if anything, the effect of origin class may have actually increased.

The probability of making the transition from secondary to higher education shows no change in the Republic: it seems to have dropped off somewhat between the pre-1945 and 1945–1958 cohorts in Northern Ireland, but it rebounded to the pre-1945 level in the most recent cohort. Evidence regarding class effects at this level is somewhat tenuous, given the small number of observations, especially in the first two cohorts. The effect of class is probably weaker here, considering the small differences between classes Ia + b and IVa, IVb, and IVc. Eyeballing the raw data is insufficient to decide whether class differentials vary by level of education. Some detailed tests will be required to say what is going on at the transition to third level.

Models of Transition Rates

Tables 8.2 and 8.3 present the results of a log-linear analysis of the transition rates in logit form. There are five variables in the analysis: cohort (3 categories), region (2), origin (13), level of education (3), and the transition itself (2). For many of the models, origin is treated as a set of continuous variables: prestige, educational credentials, bureaucratic entry, and personal contact.

The baseline model reproduces the association among the independent variables—cohort, region, level and origin—but specifies the transition as independent of all of them. The data clearly contradict this model ($L^2 = 2,602$; $df = 229$; $p < .01$; bic $= 669$). The main interest is in the effect of origins on transitions, so all interactions among cohort, region, level, and transition are fit next, without any examination of the significance of individual effects. Together the 17 effects that make up this four-way interaction reduce L^2 by 1,529.

The first model to include a term for origin class is model 2. This model scales fathers' occupations according to the percent of current incumbents in the occupation who have completed primary schooling (see Table 2.9), and it fits a simple linear term for this dimension of occupation. This main effect of origins is very powerful, reducing L^2 by 670 with a single degree of freedom. Adding a similar linear term for prestige (again see Table 2.9) reduces L^2 by 32 more points. The other two dimensions of occupation that were significant in the analysis of mobility—bureaucratic entry (B) and personal contact (F)—are not significant dimensions for educational

Table 8.2
Goodness–of–fit statistics for selected models of educational
transitions: ever–employed men aged 18–65, Ireland, 1973

Terms in the model[a]	L^2	df	bic
0 [CRLO][Y]	2602	229	669
1 [CRLO][CRLY]	1073	21	–716
2 [1] + [EY]	403	211	–1378
3 [1] + [EY][PY]	371	210	–1402
4 [1] + [EY][PY][BY]	370	209	–1394
5 [1] + [EY][PY][FY]	371	209	–1393
6 [1] + [EY][PCY]	370	208	–1386
7 [1] + [ECY][PY]	353	208	–1430
8 [1] + [ECY][ELY][PY]	274	206	–1465
9 [1] + [ELY][PY]	276	208	–1480[b]
10 [1] + [OY]	189	176	–1297[c]
11 [1] + [ELY][ERY][PY]	275	207	–1472
12 [1] + [ELY][BLY][PY]	262	205	–1468
13 [1] + [ELY][PY][EY.C3]	272	207	–1475

a. C = first job cohort; R = region; L = level of education; O = occupational origins; E = educational dimension of occupational origins; P = prestige dimension of occupational origins; B = bureaucratic entry dimension of occupational origins; F = family contact dimension of occupational origins; Y = transition. The notation is that of Goodman (1970), i.e., [CRLO] indicates a four–way interaction among variables C, R, L, and O; [PY] indicates a two–way interaction between P and Y; etc. [EY.C3] is a special three–way interaction effect involving the educational dimension of social origins, educational level, and a contrast between the third cohort and the other two.

b. $p = .001$.

c. $p = .243$.

transition rates. From this result it appears that the hierarchy of occupational positions is very important for schooling, but the other dimensions of social class that are important for mobility do not affect education.

Changes in class differentials are explored in models 6–9. These models introduce cohort differences in the effects of the educational and prestige dimensions of social origins on educational transitions. Cohort does not interact with prestige in the determination of transition rates; L^2 goes down by only one point when the prestige × cohort × transition (PCY) term is added to the model (bic gets closer to zero). The effect of the educational dimension does appear to change; L^2 decreases by 18 and bic moves 37 points further from zero when the education × cohort × transition term (ECY) is added to the model. The range of percentage differences in transition rates suggests that the transition from second to third level is less strongly affected by social class. Model 8 supports that inference; introducing the education × level × transition term (ELY) reduces L^2 by 79 and moves bic 35 points further away from zero. Surprisingly,

Table 8.3
Estimates of the parameters of the preferred model (model 9) of
educational transitions by region, first job cohort, and level:
ever–employed men aged 18–65, Ireland, 1973

First job cohort	*Republic*			*Northern Ireland*		
	Constant	Education	Prestige	Constant	Education	Prestige
Entry to secondary						
Pre–1945	−2.937	.031[a]	.017[b]	−3.192	.031[a]	.017[b]
1945–58	−1.811	.031[a]	.017[b]	−2.066	.031[a]	.017[b]
1959–73	.810	.031[a]	.017[b]	.555	.031[a]	.017[b]
Completion of secondary						
Pre–1945	−2.734	.020[c]	.017[b]	−2.498	.020[c]	.017[b]
1945–58	−2.468	.020[c]	.017[b]	−2.507	.020[c]	.017[b]
1959–73	−2.018	.020[c]	.017[b]	−2.505	.020[c]	.017[b]
Entry to postsecondary						
Pre–1945	−.362	−.001[b]	.017[b]	−.220	−.001[b]	.017[b]
1945–58	−.807	−.001[b]	.017[b]	−.655	−.001[b]	.017[b]
1959–73	−.600	−.001[b]	.017[b]	−.008	−.001[b]	.017[b]

a.   Standard error: .0020.
b.   Standard error: .0029.
c.   Standard error: .0021.

dropping (ECY) at this point improves the model. Indeed, model 9—a model that specifies effects of two dimensions of occupational origins: prestige (which has the same effect in all cohorts, at all levels, and in both regions) and education (which affects the transition from primary to secondary school more than it affects other transitions)—is preferred for these data.

Models 10–13 show that further reasonable modifications of the preferred model do not improve fit. For example, using education and prestige to capture the whole effect of origins on schooling may understate the effects of origins. To check out such a possibility, model 10 removes the linear constraints on the effect of social origins; it fits all possible effects of origins at each level. Although L^2 goes down by 87, model 10 uses 32 degrees of freedom to accomplish this improvement in fit. The fact that bic moves 183 points closer to zero after this change implies that the better fit is not worth the loss of parsimony.[4] Model 11 tests the significance of regional differences in the effect of origins on educational transitions. Adding the education × region × transition term (ERY) to the preferred model does not improve fit. Model 12 gives a reprieve to the bureaucratic entry effect by adding the bureaucratic entry × level × transition term

(BLY) to the preferred model. L^2 and bic give contradictory advice on model selection at this point; L^2 prefers model 12 while bic prefers model 9. The simpler model (model 9) is chosen here. However, the parameter estimates for model 12 show that the effects of bureaucratic entry are significant only for the completion of secondary schooling. Men from origins with high proportions of bureaucratic entrants (classes IIIa, IIIb, VI, VIIss, and VIIus) are 5–8 percent *less* likely to finish secondary school than would otherwise be expected, considering the educational and pres-tige scores for those origins. Model 13 gives one last chance to cohort interactions by adding a special interaction term that allows the effect of the educational dimension of origins on transition to higher education to be weaker for the 1959–1973 cohort than for the earlier cohorts. The change in L^2 is not quite significant by classical criteria ($L^2 = 3.69$; $df = 1$; $p = .07$), and bic is five points closer to zero.

The parameter estimates in Table 8.3 highlight the effects of origins on transition rates. The other effects are reflected in differences among the constant terms for the various combinations of level, region, and cohort. The effect of the prestige dimension is the same in all combinations of level, region, and cohort: .017. Comparing lower-grade professionals and managers (class II) with semiskilled laborers (class VIIss) covers a range of 30 prestige points, so the coefficient of .017 is enough to produce a dif-ference of ($.017 \times 30 =$) .51 in the log-odds on moving from primary to secondary school. If the transition rate to second level is 20 percent for semiskilled workers, then the expected rate for lower-grade professionals and managers is 29 percent plus the effect of the educational dimension of origins.[5]

The effect of the educational dimension of origins decreases with rising educational level. The effect of origins is strongest for the transition from primary to secondary school, its strength is diminished by 33 percent at the level of completing secondary education, and it is virtually zero for the transition from secondary to higher education.[6] This is somewhat sur-prising, given the evidence of very large differences among socioeconomic groups in participation in higher education in Ireland (Clancy 1982; Rottman et al. 1982). These results show that the class differences in third-level enrollments found in other research are attributable to the cumula-tion of class effects at low levels in the educational system and not to extraordinary class bias in the advancement to third level. In order to reach third level, working-class and middle-class children alike must sur-vive the early cuts—at entry to second-level and during second-level education—that limit the number of would-be third-level students. It is at these early cuts that class effects have their greatest efficacy. Working-class students are less likely than middle-class students to make their way through the entire system of second-level education. The few working-class survivors left at the point of transition to third-level education have already surmounted the class barriers that felled most of their counterparts. When they reach the point of entry to third level, they encounter a class barrier that is not as steep as the barriers that they passed at lower levels.

The regional differences are remarkably small, as evidenced in Table 8.3 by the small differences between each constant in the left panel and the corresponding constant in the right panel. Of particular interest is the positive regional difference between the constants for the transition to secondary school among men of the 1959–1973 cohort. The proportion of men making this transition is much higher in Northern Ireland than in the Republic. The positive difference in constant terms indicates that the transition rate is higher in Northern Ireland because the distribution of social origins in the North favors the transition to secondary schooling (more fathers who were in the service class or skilled manual workers; fewer fathers who were farmers, farm laborers, and unskilled manual workers). Most of the substantial cohort differences are concentrated at the lower end of the educational spectrum. By comparison, the increases in the chances of transition higher up the educational ladder are quite small. In fact, the transition from second to third level was somewhat less likely for men of the 1945–1958 cohort than for men of the pre-1945 cohort, given achievement of a complete secondary education. Thus university enrollments grew during this time, despite the fact that universities were selecting smaller proportions of qualified school leavers because there were so many more men with the prerequisite level of education.

These results produce an anomaly. Class differences in educational attainment were more pronounced in the oldest cohort than in the most recent one. Yet this model reveals no change in the effect of class on transition rates. How can this be? The explanation lies in two facets of the model results. First, the constants for the transition from primary to secondary school show a strong upward trend in both Northern Ireland and the Republic. Second, the effect of educational origins is much stronger at this transition than at subsequent transitions. Together, these trends imply that educational developments *independent of social class* passed men of all classes along into secondary schooling at ever-increasing rates. In

Table 8.4
Educational outcomes for classes II (salaried professionals and managers, lower grade) and VIIus (unskilled manual workers) expected under model 9 by first job cohort and region: ever–employed men aged 18–65, Ireland, 1973

| | First job cohort | | | | | |
| | Prior to 1945 | | 1945–1958 | | 1959–1973 | |
Education	II	VIIus	II	VIIus	II	VIIus
A. Expected transition rates (per 1000)[a]						
Republic						
Entry to secondary	699	110	878	277	960	560
Completion of secondary	512	111	578	135	682	203
Entry to postsecondary	632	480	524	372	575	421
Northern Ireland						
Entry to secondary	643	88	847	229	987	803
Completion of secondary	570	136	568	135	569	135
Entry to postsecondary	664	<1	561	408	710	568
B. Expected educational attainment (%)[b]						
Republic						
Primary	30%	89%	12%	72%	4%	44%
Incomplete secondary	34	10	37	24	30	45
Complete secondary	13	1	24	2	28	7
At least some higher	23	1	26	1	38	5
Total	100	100	100	100	100	100
Northern Ireland						
Primary	36%	91%	15%	77%	1%	20%
Incomplete secondary	28	8	37	20	43	69
Complete secondary	12	1	21	2	16	5
At least some higher	24	<1	27	1	40	6
Total	100	100	100	100	100	100

a. Number of men (per 1000) expected to advance from one level of education on the basis of model 9.
b. Percentage of men in each educational category expected under model 9.

doing so, these forces were circumventing the highest class barriers in the educational system. By advancing to secondary education many men who would have been mustered out on the basis of class, the social forces reflected in the constants reduced class differences in the overall distribution of educational attainments without affecting the class selectivity at any particular transition point.

Table 8.4 presents some illustrative calculations. The comparison is between sons of lower-level professionals and managers and sons of unskilled laborers. The first two lines compare these origin groups for the pre-1945 cohort from the Republic; other pairs of lines compare other cohorts in the Republic and Northern Ireland. The expected transition rates reflect the probability of continuing from one educational level to the next; the educational attainment distributions on the right show the outcome of these transition rates.[7] So, for example, the transition rate from primary to secondary school of .699 for men with class II origins from the earliest cohort in the Republic leaves behind a remainder of 30.1 percent (that is, 100% − 69.9 %) with only a primary school education. The secondary school completion rate of .512 leaves 48.8 percent of the men who survived enter into second level with incomplete secondary education— that is 34.1 percent (i.e., 48.8% × 69.9%) of the cohort total. The transition rate from secondary to higher education (.643) leaves 13.2 percent of these men with complete secondary educations and passes 22.6 percent on to university. By way of comparison, the transition rate from primary to secondary school for men from this first cohort with lower working-class origins (.110) leaves behind 89.0 percent of the cohort with only primary educations.

These calculations show how unchanging class effects in a context of overall educational upgrading resulted in diminished class differentials in educational outcomes. The results provide clear support for the rising tide hypothesis. In both parts of Ireland greater educational opportunities opened up for men of working-class backgrounds, just as the framers of the educational reforms of the 1940s and 1950s had hoped. The mechanism was one that they undoubtedly had not anticipated. Increased attendance at secondary school for students from all classes promoted equality, because continuation in secondary school was not as selective by social class as was entry into secondary education. Once the transition from primary to secondary school was not as problematic as it had once been, for reasons unrelated to social class, a growing proportion of students from working-class backgrounds could complete secondary schooling and even proceed to university.

What does this say about meritocracy in Irish education? It shows that there is no *necessary* connection between meritocracy and equality among social classes. The increased equality of outcomes came about not because merit replaced class in the selection of who got ahead but because selection itself diminished. More pupils were admitted to the second level of education under the same pattern of class selectivity as before. But by excluding a smaller absolute number, the educational system gave rise to greater equality among the social classes.

To use the word *select* perhaps connotes more activity by the educational system than actually occurs. Fees were an important selection device; make no mistake about that. Nonetheless many young Irishmen would have been likely to leave school at an early age regardless of whether secondary education was free or expensive. The demand for academic skills beyond basic literacy and numeracy was very low before 1945. In fact, secondary education was not widespread anywhere. In Britain 38 percent of men born before 1926 had only primary education (Halsey, Heath, and Ridge 1980, p. 63). In the United States secondary education was free throughout the twentieth century, yet 20 percent of men born before 1926 stopped going to school before ninth grade (Duncan 1965, table C).

In the context of falling class barriers, it is important to keep in sight the substantial effect of social class on educational attainment even in the 1959–1973 cohort. These cohorts benefited from an approach to the goal of equal educational opportunity, but the Irish educational system approached equality from a great distance and did not reach it. Perhaps more important, the approach to equality was made without any increase in the importance of meritocratic selection relative to class selection at any of the crucial educational transitions. Irish education simply became less selective. In the process the upper and middle classes lost some but not all of their competitive advantage.

From a public policy standpoint an across-the-board increase in access to schools (either secondary or higher) is probably easier to implement than a change that requires a reordering of selection criteria. Advancing merit and retracting class as bases of selection in a system that remains highly selective are likely to rankle entrenched interests. Those losing privileges could be expected to fight for them. In the case of Irish educational reform in the 1950s and 1960s, little conflict ensued because interests were not threatened. Equality was advanced by giving education to those classes that had formerly been excluded while expanding the capacity of the system so much that it also absorbed the growing demand for its services from the traditional clientele.

Meritocracy and Class Selection

Resolving the issue of meritocracy in educational selection is very difficult without access to test scores. The most complete study of class and educational selection that includes the requisite test score data is the Drumcondra study (Greaney and Kellaghan 1984). Some of the data from that study illuminate the interplay between meritocracy and class-based selection in the Republic (no comparable data are available for Northern Ireland).

Of course, the equation of test scores with "ability" is a crude empirical device. There is much speculation and some evidence that class biases in tests may foster erroneous inferences about the role of merit in educational selection. In particular, if students with class advantages are favored on the tests, then the use of test scores as selection devices may simply legitimate what is essentially class-based allocation of educational resources. To solve this complex problem of inferring meaning from the effects of class and ability, it is necessary to settle the issue of just how big the relative effects of class and ability are.

Greaney and Kellaghan (1984, p. 263) conclude that "the meritocratic ideal is at least being approached if not quite attained" in the Irish educational system. The meritocratic ideal that they refer to is an educational system in which progress is determined by educationally relevant attributes such as ability, and not by other, educationally irrelevant attributes such as class and gender. Their surprising conclusion has engendered widespread controversy in Ireland (Whelan and Whelan 1984, 1985; Greaney and Kellaghan 1985; Lynch 1985; Raftery and Hout 1985; Clancy 1985, 1986). It overstates the case of ability as a basis of selection in the schools while downplaying the important role of social class as a factor in selection.

So the question remains: What is the interplay of ability and class that determines progress in Irish schools? Attempts to rectify the situation by Whelan and Whelan (1984, 1985) improve our understanding of class biases in educational selection in Ireland, but their rhetoric on the importance of class is as overblown as the rhetoric of Greaney and Kellaghan on the importance of ability.

Greaney and Kellaghan's data make it possible to display unambiguously the relative effects of class and ability on educational selection in Irish schools. This reanalysis also includes effects for aspects of school organization (principally type of school attended) and gender.

Greaney and Kellaghan drew a stratified random subsample of 500 11-year-old students from a larger sample of 2,164 students studied in 1967. The researchers maintained contact with 494 of these students until they took their first jobs—some as late as 1980.[8] The original sample of 2,164 students was drawn by sampling schools within strata defined by region and type of school and including all 11- and 12-year-olds in the selected schools. The subjects for the longitudinal study were randomly selected from this group within strata.

Dozens of measures are available for each student. Five are used in this reanalysis: Highest educational level attained, father's or head's occupation (hereafter simply father's occupation), academic ability, type of second-level school attended, and gender.[9] There are some differences between the procedures used here and originally (Raftery and Hout 1985). Father's occupation is missing or too imprecisely recorded for 26 students, so these cases are also excluded, reducing the sample size to 468.

The statistical model used to model educational transitions for older cohorts is modified here to incorporate additional variables not available in the Irish Mobility Study data. The dependent variable is the transition rate from one level of education to the next higher level. For those students who achieve a given level of education, some go on to the next level, others do not. The transition rate is simply the probability of going on. Five transitions are analyzed (the population "at risk" of such a transition is given in parentheses):

Entry to postprimary school (all students)
Completion of junior cycle (students who entered junior cycle)
Entry to senior cycle (students who completed junior cycle)
Completion of senior cycle (students who entered senior cycle)
Entry to higher education (students who completed senior cycle)

To estimate the effects of the independent variables on this transition rate, a logit transformation is used (Cox 1970; Raftery and Hout 1985).[10]

The first phase of the analysis is the simplest. Table 8.5 documents the persistence of class-based selection in Irish schools during the 1970s. The proportion of students who finish the senior cycle drops from a high point among those with upper-middle-class backgrounds (78 percent) to a nadir among the offspring of farm workers (16 percent). The other classes rank from lower middle class (57 percent completing) to farm (50 percent) to upper working class (36 percent) to lower working class (27 percent). The vast majority of all students, regardless of origins, complete junior cycle in contemporary Ireland (schooling is compulsory for 5–15-year-olds). The greatest class-based selection occurs at entry to senior cycle. Four-fifths of students from the middle classes who sit the intermediate certificate exam enter senior cycle; two-thirds of students from farm backgrounds do so; half of the urban working class does so; and just over a quarter of the rural working class attends senior level after the intermediate certificate.

Table 8.5
Education by social origins: birth cohort of 1956, Ireland, 1980

Education	Upper nonmanual	Lower nonmanual	Upper manual	Lower manual	Farmer	Farm laborer
			Origin[a]			
Primary	0%	2%	5%	13%	5%	17%
Incomplete junior cycle	5	17	16	23	12	25
Complete junior cycle	15	18	41	32	27	42
Incomplete senior cycle	2	6	2	5	6	0
Complete senior cycle	46	41	26	23	36	8
Postsecondary	32	16	10	4	14	8
Total	100	100	100	100	100	100
(N)	(59)	(88)	(39)	(159)	(111)	(12)

a. The social origin categories are composed of the following classes: upper nonmanual (Ia, Ib, II), lower nonmanual (IIIa, IIIb, IVa, IVb), upper manual (V, VI), lower manual (VIIss, VIIus), farmer (IVc, IVd), agricultural laborer (VIIf).

Tables 8.6 and 8.7 contain statistics on the *direct effects of class and ability*. Goodness of fit suggests that all of these class differences are not due to ability differences among classes.[11] The preferred model for entry into postprimary schooling includes *both* class and ability effects, as does the preferred model for transitions within second-level education.[12] Entry to third level is an exception to this general pattern. Among students who *successfully complete the leaving certificate exam,* entry into third-level institutions is not related to class.

The probability of going on to a secondary or vocational school increases with both prestige of social origins and ability (as indicated by test scores). To appreciate the magnitude of the class effect on continuation beyond the legal minimum amount of education, consider the following hypothetical example. Suppose that there are two students of equal ability but from different origin classes. Let each student have a score of 100 on the DVRT (the standardized average for the test). Suppose that one student's father has the lowest observed occupational score, 18, a social standing shared by the bottom 20 percent of the fathers in the sample.[13] Suppose that the other student's father has an occupation with a prestige score of 75, a social standing shared by the top 2 percent of the sample.[14] The model predicts a dropout rate of 6.4 percent for the lower-class student and a dropout rate of 0.6 percent for the higher-class student. Both rates are low, meaning that the vast majority of students from either background go on to a second-level school if they have average ability. But the dropout

Table 8.6
Goodness–of–fit of selected models for educational transition rates
by level of education: birth cohort of 1956, Republic of Ireland, 1980

Terms in model	L^2	df	bic
Entry to secondary			
Grand mean only	239	467	−2633
Class effects	222	46	−2643
Ability effects	188	466	−2678
Class and ability effects	180	465	−2679
Transitions within secondary[a]			
Grand mean only	1010	1023	−6082
Class effects	966	1022	−6120
Ability effects	944	1022	−6142
Class and ability effects	914	1021	−6165
Entry to postsecondary			
Grand mean only	252	210	−872
Class effects	248	209	−870
Ability effects	217	209	−902
Class and ability effects	216	208	−897

a. The transitions within secondary are (1) completion of junior cycle, (2) entry into senior cycle, and (3) completion of senior cycle. The models employ constraints that set the effect of each independent variable on each transition to be equal to the effect of that independent variable on the other transitions within secondary school.

rate for the student from the low-status background, though it is below 9 percent, is over *ten* times greater than is the dropout rate for the student from the higher-status background. This fact becomes very important for students with marginal ability. Suppose that these hypothetical students have ability that is one standard deviation below average (DVRT = 85) instead of average. This time the model predicts dropout rates of 20.9 percent for the lower-class student and 2.2 percent for the higher-status student. The gap in dropout rates between average and marginal ability students from lower-class origins is 14.5 percentage points, compared to a gap of only 1.6 percentage points for higher-class students. The convergence of ability groups in the higher classes is due to a "floor effect," by which dropout rates cannot get much lower than they are for higher-class students with below-average ability.

Another way of looking at these results is to note that virtually every student with average ability or above gets into a second-level school of some sort, regardless of social class, and that virtually every higher-class student gets into a second-level school of some sort, regardless of ability.

Table 8.7
Parameter estimates for total and direct effects of origins
and direct effects of ability on educational transitions:
birth cohort of 1956, Republic of Ireland, 1980

Model	Constant	Class	Ability
		Independent variable[a]	
Entry to second level			
Total effect	.641	.573	—
	(.494)	(.159)	
Direct effects	−7.138	.430	.905
	(1.433)	(.162)	(.160)
Completion of junior cycle			
Total effect	.178	.372	—
	(.240)	(.059)	
Direct effects	−3.710	.325	.414
	(.608)	(.062)	(.059)
Entry to senior cycle			
Total effect	−.869	.372	—
	(.252)	(.059)	
Direct effects	−4.878	.325	.414
	(.638)	(.062)	(.059)
Completion of senior cycle			
Total effect	.807	.372	—
	(.318)	(.059)	
Direct effects	−3.241	.325	.414
	(.660)	(.062)	(.059)
Entry to postsecondary			
Total effect	−1.765	.186	—
	(.152)	(.099)	
Direct effects	−9.680	.108	.752
	(1.711)	(.106)	(.149)

a.   Approximate standard errors of the coefficients are in parentheses.

The educational system selects among students of marginal ability on the basis of social class and among working-class and lower-class students on the basis of ability.

For transitions within the second level (j = 2, 3, and 4), the effects of class and ability are, once again, both substantial and significant. The effect of father's occupational prestige is nearly as large for transitions within second level (.325) as for the transition into second level (.430). Ability effects, however, are much smaller within second level (.414) than for entry into second level (.905). Consider again the two hypothetical students of average ability but widely differing class backgrounds. The expected probability of entering the senior cycle for a student with average ability (mean DVRT = 103 at the end of the junior cycle) is 49 percent for the lower-class student and 86 percent for the higher-class student. For lower-ability students, entry to senior cycle ranges from 33 percent for lower-class students to 77 percent for higher-class students. The class effect is just as strong for the first and third transitions within second-level education.

The effect of father's occupation does not carry over to the transition to third-level education. Ability has its strongest effect at this transition point. The preferred model is one that includes ability as the only predictor. Thus, it appears that third-level institutions select students solely on the basis of ability. The data on university enrollment among older cohorts, however, are cause for caution on this point. Comparing the coefficient for the effect of prestige of origins on entry to third level in the three earlier cohorts (.017) with the total effect obtained here for the more recent cohort (.0186) reveals virtually no difference. In light of the combined data on all four cohorts, the most reasonable conclusion is that while origins are much less a factor in third-level matriculation than in earlier educational transitions, they are a factor nonetheless. This result does not negate the need for policies aimed at improving equal access to education for all students, regardless of class background, to focus their attention on the crucial transitions into and through the second level.

Test scores are designed to measure ability, but few social scientists doubt that other influences are present as well. The most serious objections to interpreting the effects of test scores on educational selection as evidence of meritocracy are based on the concern with "cultural capital," a concern that stems from evidence that the educational system is sensitive to values, attitudes, linguistic practices, and styles of interaction that differentiate social classes (Bernstein 1977; Bourdieu 1977). This kind of cultural selection would not necessarily be pernicious to the interests of able students from working-class and lower-class backgrounds if the schools distributed cultural capital as well as using it to sort out students. However, the key contention of Bernstein, Bourdieu and others is that families, not schools, are the source of cultural capital. As a consequence, selection based on cultural capital favors children from families that are well endowed with it already—presumably families that already possess class advantages. So, the argument goes, at the end of the day schools perpetuate class advantages in the name of meritocracy, thereby giving legitimacy to inequality of opportunity that would otherwise be missing.

In the debate over class and ability in Irish schools, Lynch (1985, p. 87) raises this issue forcefully:

> Greaney and Kellaghan, of course, never refer to the idea of cultural capital in outlining the abilities which one needs to succeed within the educational system. Their failure to do so means that a whole range of cultural (and class related) attributes which are widely recognized as being significant in determining success within the educational system are not examined. Their failure to recognize too that verbal ability, as they define it, is but part of such cultural capital leads them to draw false dichotomies between ascribed and achieved qualities, and therefore, to make unwarranted claims about the influence of the achieved quality (ability) as opposed to the ascribed quality (social class) on educational attainments. In so far as social class itself is ascribed at birth, so too is the class culture within which early socialization occurs.

This argument also appears in Whelan and Whelan (1985) and Clancy (1986).

If the reproduction of cultural capital is the key to inequality of opportunity in Irish schools, then the "direct effects" of class are only the tip of the inegalitarian iceberg. For if test scores are proxies for cultural capital, and if cultural capital merely reproduces material and social capital, then the greater portion of the effect of class origins on educational attainment will be indirect via test scores. It is certainly true that any one indicator of social class origins will understate the total correlation between origins and test scores. Nonetheless, the same is true of the correlation between origins and educational attainment. Relying on one indicator of origins will understate the total effect, indirect effect, and direct effect of origins on attainment to the same extent. Therefore, attention is given here to both the absolute size of the indirect effects of origins on educational attainments and the size of those indirect effects relative to the estimated total effects.

The indirect effect of class is the difference between the total effect and the direct effect (Alwin and Hauser 1975). For entry into second level, the indirect effect is .143 (.573 − .430), a quantity that is one-fourth of the total effect. For transitions within second-level education, the indirect effect is .047 (one-eighth of the total effect). For entry into third level, the indirect effect is .078 (two-fifths of the total effect). None of these effects is very large in an absolute sense; only the first one (the indirect effect of class on entry to second level) is statistically significant at the .05 level. In a relative sense, only the indirect effect of class on entry to third level is large, but its size is relative to a rather small baseline (and an insignificant direct effect).

Attrition of the students with lower test scores at each stage of the educational system reduces the correlation between class origins and test scores at each successive transition. Prior to sitting the leaving certificate exam, this process eliminates the correlation between class and ability among the survivors; among students completing the senior cycle, the null hypothesis of no correlation between father's occupation and DVRT score cannot be rejected.

These results do not necessarily mean that cultural capital is not the basis of educational selection in Ireland. They do, however, untie the neat little bundle of class, capital, test scores, and educational attainment that advocates of reproduction theory have put together. To salvage the notion that cultural capital is the basis of educational selection in Ireland in light of these results, it is necessary to concede one of the following:

Working-class and lower-class students have access to cultural capital, too, which breaks the correlation between class origins and cultural capital. Such resources might include popular media and middle-class kin or friends. This perspective maintains the position that test scores reflect cultural capital assets.

Schools offer remedial cultural capital to students who lack it, breaking the link between family and cultural capital. This perspective also maintains the position that test scores reflect cultural capital assets.

Schools select on the basis of cultural capital, but it is class background, not test scores, that index access to cultural capital. This perspective breaks the link between cultural capital and test scores.

Adopting any of these positions weakens the theoretical power of cultural capital as a theoretical device and raises serious questions about reproduction theory more generally. But real life is usually more complex than theory, and the theoretical elegance that each of the alternatives lacks is compensated for by the prospect that it is true. Cultural capital is not a pot of gold horded by the haves and hidden from the have-nots. On the contrary, if the middle classes of advanced societies are guilty of anything, they have been guilty of trying to foist their values, tastes, beliefs, and linguistic practices onto the working and lower classes with all the zeal and tact of missionaries.

Reproduction theory is an explanation for the perfect correlation between class origins and educational attainment. In Ireland (as well as England, Wales, Scotland, France, and the United States) the association is strong but much less than perfect. Classes are not that segregated from one another (except perhaps in Belfast). The Catholic Church in the Republic and the churches in Northern Ireland exert important cultural influences that transcend class barriers. Economic development, imported media, and indigenous trends all work against the easy transfer of cultural capital from one generation to the next by redefining the grounds on which assets are distinguished from deficits. In the end, "cultural capital" becomes a black box for all the unmeasured assets correlated with class background (much like "human capital," which preceded it).

We are left with an image of an educational system that weights both relevant and irrelevant factors in the process of selecting and certifying a new generation of educational elites. Some students make it through the system to university because they have brains; others do so because their parents have the resources to overcome their intellectual shortcomings. In the end, the correlations among test scores, class background, and educational attainment are all positive, but none are perfect. Most of the inequality of opportunity for working-class and lower-class students arises through the selection and sorting of younger students.[15] Selection to the university is much less subject to the influence of class background than are selection at the postprimary level or selection within the second level. The key to increased equality of educational opportunity earlier in this century was a postponement of selection until students were older. A move to diminish differences among second-level institutions might achieve a further reduction in class effects on educational outcomes. But less differentiation of second-level education does not seem to be in the offing. The comprehensive schools proposed in the 1960s offered less internal selection among second-level students, but they never caught on (Clancy 1986).

Vocationalism and Class in Second-Level Education

With primary education virtually universal, the focus of educational selection has shifted to the second level and beyond. Mandatory attendance up to age 15 means that all but the students who are repeatedly held back a grade will attain at least some second-level education. Second-level education in both Northern Ireland and the Republic is divided between academic (selective) and vocational (nonselective) schools, with only a few comprehensive schools in both regions. Finishing second-level education—attaining a Leaving Certificate in the Republic or an "O-level" or "A-level" certificate in Northern Ireland—is the main source of educational differentiation in contemporary Ireland. The kind of second-level school that one attends has a tremendous influence on the odds on attaining certification. Over half of the students from academic schools finish with certificates; almost no vocational students do. The role of internal differentiation among second-level institutions in educational stratification is indicated by the extent to which class origins affect type of second-level enrollment (academic or vocational).

In other countries internal differentiation of second-level education is an important part of educational stratification. In England and Wales, the major component of inequality of educational opportunity is the correlation between class and placement in a selective or nonselective secondary school (Halsey, Heath, and Ridge 1980). The correlation between class of origin and overall educational attainment is greater in France than in the United States, largely because curricula are more class segregated in France (Garnier and Hout 1976, 1982). The growth of differentiation among types of third-level institutions in the United States may have led to an increase in class-based selection to colleges (Brint and Karabel 1989).

The Irish Mobility Study shows a strong positive association between origin class and the odds on an academic enrollment among men who entered second-level schooling in either the Republic or Northern Ireland. Figure 8.1 shows that this effect is present in each cohort. There has been no significant change in the effect of class at this important sorting point. The only significant change is a decrease in the odds on an academic education for men from the most recent cohort in Northern Ireland. The rapid expansion of vocational and technical schools has reduced the share of academic pursuits in second-level education in Northern Ireland for men from all classes.

The class effect for the transition from entry into secondary education to completion of secondary education is the product of the effect of class on selection into an academic curriculum and the effect of class on finishing, given enrollment in an academic track. About two-thirds of the total effect of class on finishing secondary school is mediated by type of school placement.

Vocational schools attract more boys than girls. This is true in Ireland and elsewhere (Hout and Garnier 1979; Greaney and Kellaghan

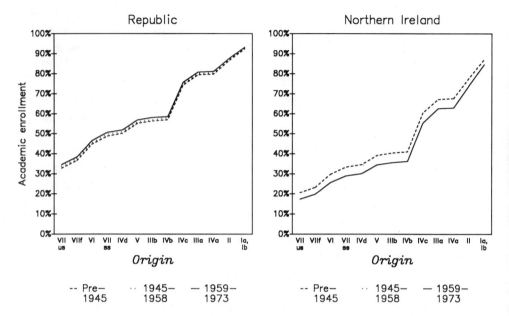

Figure 8.1   Academic enrollment as a percentage of all secondary school
enrollment, by origin: birth cohort of 1956, Ireland, 1980.

1984). Girls also tend to do better than boys on tests. Therefore, estimates
here of the effects of class and ability on attendance in an academic school
are controlled for gender. Table 8.8 shows the search for preferred models
of academic placement and educational transitions. Table 8.9 shows in the
top row the coefficients from the linear logistic regression of school type
on class, ability, and gender.[16] The effect of class is about the same as its
effect on entry to second level (compare with the top rows of Table 8.7
and the second row of Table 8.9); the effect of ability is intermediate
between its effects on transitions within the secondary system (namely, on
completion of junior cycle, entry to senior cycle, and completion of senior
cycle) and its effect on entry to the second level. The coefficient for gender
shows the clear advantage of girls in type of school placement. To translate this effect into probabilities, if a boy had the right combination of
ability and class so that his expected probability of attending an academic
secondary school was .50, then a girl with the same combination of ability
and class would have an expected probability of attending an academic
secondary school of .77.

To determine the extent to which the influence of class and ability on
educational attainment works through type of school placement, the rest

of Table 8.9 repeats the analysis found in Table 8.7 with gender and type of school included as additional independent variables. Type of school comes after entry to second-level education, so only gender is added to that equation. The preferred model contains only the variables that have significant effects. Gender (the only new variable) does not affect entry to second-level education, so the preferred model in the second row is the same as the "direct effects" model in Table 8.7.

Academic students are much more likely than vocational students to finish the junior cycle. If a vocational student has a combination of ability and class that results in an expected probability of finishing junior cycle of .50, then an academic student with the same combination of ability and class has an expected probability of finishing junior cycle of .79. This advantage grows as the students move through the second level. Should a vocational student survive the 50/50 break at the end of junior cycle, a boy would have the same chance (50/50) of entering senior cycle; a girl would have only a 35/65 chance of entering senior cycle because, at this transition, being female carries a negative effect. However, an academic student would probably finish the junior cycle and now have an excellent

Table 8.8
Goodness-of-fit of selected models for educational transition rates
by level of education: birth cohort of 1956, Republic of Ireland, 1980

Terms in model	L^2	df	bic
Entry to secondary			
Gender only	238	466	−2627
Class and ability effects	180	465	−2679
Academic vs. vocational secondary			
Gender only	522	439	−2151
Gender, class, and ability	442	437	−2219
Transitions within secondary[a]			
Type of school only	847	1020	−6225
Gender only	1006	1020	−6066
School, class, and ability	804	1017	−6247
Entry to postsecondary			
Type of school only	247	209	−872
Gender only	249	207	−870
Ability only	217	209	−902

a. The transitions within secondary are (1) completion of junior cycle, (2) entry into senior cycle, and (3) completion of senior cycle. The models employ constraints that set the effects of class and ability on each transition to be equal to the effect of that variable on the other transitions within secondary school.

Table 8.9
Parameter estimates for preferred models of entry to academic
secondary school and for transition rates within secondary school:
birth cohort of 1956, Republic of Ireland, 1980

| Transition | Type of school | Independent variable[a] | | | |
		Gender	Class	Ability	Constant
Academic school	—	1.185	.437	.531	– 6.602
		(.244)	(.090)	(.087)	(.956)
Completion of junior cycle	1.303	—	.206	.295	– 2.872
	(.276)		(.066)	(.065)	(.659)
Entry to senior cycle	2.324	–.602	.206	.295	– 4.606
	(.334)	(.288)	(.066)	(.065)	(.735)
Completion of senior cycle	3.319	—	.206	.295	– 4.138
	(.587)		(.066)	(.065)	(.831)

a.   All coefficients significant at the .05 level (standard errors in parentheses).

chance of entering senior cycle if he is male (91 percent), but only a so-so chance if she is female (50 percent). A boy from a vocational school and a girl from an academic school have the same transition rate to senior cycle (if they have the same social class and ability). Once in the senior cycle, the vocational student (male or female) once again has a 50/50 chance of finishing; the academic student with the same ability and social class has a 97 percent chance of finishing.

Ability is the only significant influence on admission to third level. All other effects—class, gender, and type of school—drop out of the preferred model for entering third level.

This collection of results leads to something of a conundrum regarding the role of gender in educational stratification in Ireland. Girls are more likely than boys to enroll in the privileged type of school, the academic secondary schools, but then they are more likely to drop out after the end of junior cycle. The conundrum lies in the lack of a significant difference between the overall postjunior dropout rates of boys and girls.[17] The explanation lies in the differing gender composition of vocational and secondary schools. Boys outnumber girls in the vocational schools where dropout rates are high; girls outnumber boys in the secondary schools where dropout rates are low. By attending schools with high general dropout rates, boys in vocational schools wipe out their advantage over their female counterparts in the academic secondary schools. One inference that may be drawn is that academic secondary schools are not as selective in their admissions of girls as they are in their admissions of boys, but they proceed to wash out a larger proportion of girls—presumably the ones of marginal ability or class background who might well have been denied admission in the first place if they were male.

This analysis is designed to assess how the academic-vocational split in Irish education mediates the effects of social class and ability. For social class, 37 percent ($.325 - .206 = .119$) of the total effect is indirect by way of the academic vocational distinction. For ability, 29 percent ($.414 - .295 = .119$) is indirect.[18] Therefore school placement transmits slightly more than one-third of the influence of class on progress through the second level and slightly less than one-third of the influence of ability on the same process.

Conclusion

Educational outcomes became more equally distributed among social classes in both the Republic of Ireland and Northern Ireland after World War II. Although reforms were enacted, the most important factor in rising educational equality was the expansion of secondary education. The educational systems of both Northern Ireland and the Republic simply became less selective as they grew. The degree to which class affected educational selection at any given point in the educational career did not change. But the relative importance of the several selection points was altered. For the men who entered the work force before 1945, the transition from primary to secondary school was the crucial selection point. Over time, selection at the beginning of secondary school became less important, as most students were expected to attend some kind of secondary school. The crucial selection points shifted to the determination of what type of secondary school the student would enroll in and whether or not he would finish second-level education with some kind of academic certificate.

Class was a significant factor in selection at both of these points. However, class effects are not as strong at these points in the secondary system as they are at the transition from primary to secondary school. Therefore, because of exogenous shifts upward in transition rates into secondary schooling for everybody, regardless of class, class became less important for educational attainment overall. The Drumcondra study indicates that the selectivity at entry into primary schooling is still the greatest among important educational transitions. As the upward trend in attending secondary school has continued, the distribution of educational outcomes has probably continued to equalize among social classes.

Investigation of the potentially competing roles of social class and ability in educational selection uncovered little competition. Both factors are important for advancement through the educational system. Yet no support emerged for the version of reproduction theory that hypothesizes strong correlations among class, test scores, human capital, and educational outcomes. The correlations in Ireland are not that strong. Instead, the results support a weaker definition of the role of cultural capital in educational attainment, which recognizes both that some of the effects of class work in ways that are not tied to cultural capital and that test scores measure more than just cultural attributes.

All of these changes are structural in nature. They have come about through expansion of the available positions in secondary schools, not from changes in the criteria for selection into higher education. There has been no change in the underlying, genotypic pattern of social inequality. As university enrollments grew in the 1970s, there was probably further equalization, since class-based selectivity is least at the third level. But as secondary schooling becomes universal while university enrollments level off, the margin for future structural contributions to greater equality of educational outcomes becomes very slim indeed. Progress on this front in the future will have to confront the selection process itself.

This pattern of structurally induced educational growth impinges on two theoretical and substantive issues. First, American writers have speculated that mass education in the United States may have outstripped the ability of the labor market to provide technical, professional, and administrative jobs commensurate with the educational attainments of new cohorts (esp. Berg 1970; Freeman 1975, 1976). The educational expansion in Ireland documented here might conceivably lay the groundwork for an overtraining or "mismatch" crisis in the Irish labor markets (Sullivan 1978; Clogg 1979; Clogg and Sullivan 1983; Clogg and Shockey 1984).

Second, Goldthorpe (1980, pp. 54–57) addresses what he calls the "counterbalance thesis." The key contention of the counterbalance thesis is that the formalization of the British labor market makes upward advancement less likely for those who lack educational credentials. The argument is that in prior eras, when (presumably) the link between education and job placement was weaker, career mobility through bureaucratic advancement, effort, or luck could promote some working-class men into the middle class.[19] As labor markets become more formal, the effect of education on job placement presumably increases, thereby shifting the locus of upward mobility for working-class men from career mobility to first-job placement. Failure to gain entry to a white-collar occupation straight out of school because of inadequate educational preparation will seal off the prospects for future advancement. Although working-class men with higher educational certificates and degrees could benefit from such a system, it cancels out hope for another segment of the working class that relies on career mobility as a channel into the middle class. The only working-class men who have a chance for upward mobility, according to the counterbalance thesis, are those who attain an advanced formal education. Goldthorpe concludes that no such process has been in operation in England and Wales. Career mobility is just as important for upward mobility of men from working-class origins in recent cohorts as it is in earlier cohorts.

The Irish Mobility Study casts serious doubt on whether any such thesis can hold true in Ireland. The counterbalance thesis implicitly assumes that class differentials in educational credentials are static. A hidden premise of the thesis is the existence of a large pool of men from working-class origins whose only resource for upward mobility is the openness of class boundaries regarding career mobility. In Ireland at least, the net outcome of educational restructuring since World War II has been to make higher education more available to young men (and women) from working-class origins. The educational process still selects on the basis of social class when it selects. But Irish education is less selective, overall, than it used to be. As a result, more students from working-class backgrounds enter the labor force with competitive educational credentials. More to the point, the pool of working-class youth with no advantage other than a loose structure of career mobility opportunities continues to shrink in Ireland.

It is therefore unclear whether a more formal labor market, if one is emerging in Ireland, will work to the advantage or disadvantage of workers from blue-collar origins. After all, the formalization of labor markets might well do more to negate the advantages of the well-to-do than to blunt the career mobility prospects of working-class aspirants who lack educational credentials. Blau and Duncan (1967, pp. 428–431) argue as much. Their "expanding universalism" thesis sees formalization as a guard against undue exercise of privilege by those with lofty origins. The erosion of formal advantages among the upper classes, North and South, suggests that expanding universalism, not counterbalance, is the main consequence of whatever formalization of labor markets might be occurring in Ireland.

9   The Socioeconomic Life Cycle

The first job that a worker takes after he finishes his education influences the rest of his career. On the one hand, for many workers contacts and promotion opportunities that come with that first job improve the prospects for subsequent achievement. On the other hand, the lack of contacts and opportunity constitute a disadvantage that some workers never overcome. The career dynamics of men in the Irish Mobility Study—the progression from school to first job and on to current job—reveals the existence of class boundaries and other barriers that affect men's careers. Analyzing this progression makes it possible to assess precisely how early career placements affect subsequent achievement.

To aid in understanding the details of career mobility, consider the distinction between occupations that are connected to many others and occupations that have links to only a few others. The prime examples of the first type are the service occupations. Jobs in service recruit workers who have more education than average. But the jobs themselves do not pay well. The disparity between education and income constitutes a "mismatch" that will motivate many workers to leave service for occupations that offer earnings more in line with high education. The urge to leave is facilitated by the tendency for service workers to come in contact with a broad array of other kinds of workers as they go about their duties. Sometimes the service worker has more prestige than the person he is working with; sometimes not. But the broad base of contacts brings with it the opportunity to make contacts in many other occupations. The combination of mismatch and contacts provide both motive and opportunity for mobility. The payoff of this combination is a high rate of mobility out of service work and into many other types of employment.

By way of contrast, the prototype of an occupation with few links to other forms of employment is unpaid work assisting on a family farm. The lack of pay is an obvious incentive to seek other work, but the limited sphere of activity offers unpaid farm workers few chances to make contacts that might lead to lucrative employment outside farming. The trade-off for unpaid farmer's helpers is inheritance. Slightly more than half of the farmers' sons who begin their work life as an unpaid worker eventually take over the family farm on their own or find another opportunity in farming. In short, workers who take unpaid first jobs subsequently move into a narrow range of occupations—primarily farming and unskilled labor. There are few moves into other occupations.

The distinction between occupations with diffuse versus circumscribed opportunities proves to be important for understanding career mobility. Workers who start their careers in occupations with diffuse opportunities have more jobs than other workers; they also have more kinds of jobs. Workers who start their careers in occupations with circumscribed opportunities have fewer jobs, and their careers tend to be more articulated, that is, they tend to follow a clear line of promotion and advancement.

Career Beginnings

School leaving and job taking mark the transition to adulthood in most modern nations. These events typically occur during the person's late teen years or early twenties. In Ireland, the teen years are particularly important. As in other European countries, school attendance is mandatory up to a certain age in both the Republic of Ireland and Northern Ireland. And as in other places, the mandatory minimum age of school leaving has risen during this century. Many of the men in the Irish Mobility Study left school as soon as they could—when they reached the age at which leaving was legal. Because the mandatory school leaving age has always been rather low in both parts of Ireland, many men left school at a rather young age. Recent reforms in secondary education have prolonged formal schooling into late teen years for the majority of recent cohorts (Greaney and Kelleghan 1984), but schooling beyond the age of 16 was the exception rather than the rule throughout the period covered by this study.

Table 9.1 shows that the modal school-leaving age in both parts of Ireland is 14 years. Nearly 10 percent of the men in this study left school at 13 years of age. Only a small minority of the men from each region attended school beyond age 18: 17 percent in the Republic and 14 percent in Northern Ireland. Regional differences in the distribution of school-

Table 9.1
Age at school leaving, at first job, and at first full-time job
by region: men aged 18–65, Ireland, 1973

Age	School leaving		First job		Full-time job	
	Republic	Northern Ireland	Republic	Northern Ireland	Republic	Northern Ireland
10 or less	.3%	.1%	.9%	.1%	.7%	.1%
11	.6	.3	.4	.2	.3	.1
12	2.5	.8	1.4	.7	1.1	.6
13	9.8	9.6	4.5	2.1	4.1	1.9
14	34.8	39.3	29.4	34.5	27.7	34.1
15	14.5	21.2	19.2	26.6	19.1	26.8
16	12.3	9.9	14.8	14.8	15.1	15.3
17	8.5	5.3	10.0	6.5	10.2	6.8
18	7.2	3.8	9.1	5.7	9.3	5.4
19	2.9	1.9	4.5	2.4	4.6	2.1
20	1.4	1.1	2.1	1.5	2.4	1.5
21	1.1	1.7	.9	1.5	1.2	1.4
22	.6	1.5	.7	1.4	1.1	1.3
23	1.3	1.2	1.0	.8	1.2	1.0
24	.7	.7	.5	.4	.5	.4
25 or more	1.5	1.6	.8	.8	1.4	1.1
Total	100.0	100.0	100.0	100.0	100.0	100.0
(N)	(2290)	(2415)	(2291)	(2415)	(2260)	(2377)
Median	15.1	15.0	15.7	15.5	15.8	15.5
L^2 (df = 15)	129.20		146.27		148.39	

leaving age are small but statistically significant. The median school-leaving age is about one month higher in the Republic (15.1) than in Northern Ireland (15.0). The spread in school-leaving ages is also slightly greater in the Republic than in the North: slightly fewer Northern men left school before age 13, and substantially fewer after age 16. The key to the regional difference appears to be the higher incidence of school-leaving at age 15 in Northern Ireland (21.2 percent) than in the Republic. The proportions of men leaving school at ages 16, 17, and 18 are correspondingly less in Northern Ireland than in the Republic.

Very little time lapses between leaving school and starting a job. The age distribution for taking a first job closely parallels the age distribution for school leaving. The medians in each region are about a half-year higher for first jobs than for school leaving, mainly because many men who left school very young apparently had some difficulty finding a first job. As with school leaving, the regional difference in the timing of first job is significant. Once again, the difference seems to revolve around the slight clustering of Ulstermen around age 15, with significant numbers of men from the rest of Ireland staying in school and out of the labor force until ages 17 or 18. Most men move into the labor force as *full-time* workers upon completion of schooling. This can be seen in the nearly identical age distribution for first job and first full-time job.

As for employment patterns, the first jobs that Irishmen take upon leaving school tend to be of lower skill and autonomy than their current jobs. Many men take unpaid first jobs, even if they work full time. Unpaid assistance on a family farm is the modal pattern for farmers' sons. Table 9.2 shows the distribution of first jobs and first full-time jobs by occupation and region. First and first full-time occupations closely resemble one another. The index of dissimilarity between first and first full-time occupation is 3.6 percent for the Republic and 2.2 percent for Northern Ireland. The difference between Northern Ireland and the Republic has to do with

Table 9.2
Occupation at first job and at first full–time job by region:
men aged 18–65, Ireland, 1973

Occupation	Code	First job		First full–time job	
		Republic	Northern Ireland	Republic	Northern Ireland
Professionals & proprietors I[a]	Ia	.1%	.2%	.1%	.2%
Professionals & managers I	Ib	2.1	2.4	2.1	2.5
Professionals & managers II	II	3.3	3.4	3.5	3.4
Clerical & sales workers	IIIa	6.5	7.2	6.9	7.3
Proprietors with employees[a]	IVa	.1	.2	.1	.2
Proprietors without employees[a]	IVb	.5	.3	.5	.3
Service workers	IIIb	7.6	9.6	7.2	9.3
Unpaid helpers, nonfarm	VIIInf	2.8	2.6	2.7	2.4
Technicians & foremen	V	4.4	5.5	4.4	5.6
Skilled manual workers	VI	12.5	18.5	13.3	18.8
Semiskilled manual workers	VIIss	10.7	17.1	10.9	17.1
Unskilled manual workers	VIIus	8.3	9.1	9.4	9.6
Farmers with employees[a]	IVc	.4	.2	.4	.2
Farmers without employees[a]	IVd	.6	.5	.8	.5
Unpaid helpers, farm	VIIIf	26.7	13.7	25.1	13.1
Farm laborers	VIIf	13.4	9.5	12.7	9.3
Total		100.0	100.0	100.0	100.0
(N)		(2187)	(2288)	(2287)	(2412)
L^2 (df = 15)		183.42		172.48	

a.   Self–employed workers.

the prevalence of agricultural labor, whether paid or unpaid.[1] Farm work—but not farm ownership in a first job—is more common in the Republic than in Northern Ireland. The proportion of first jobs in agriculture in the Republic exceeds the proportion of first jobs in agriculture in Northern Ireland by nearly a two-to-one margin (40.1 percent versus 23.2 percent).

Most Irishmen start their work lives in the employ of others. Self-employment at the time of first job is rare. All but 2 percent of Irish workers are employees (paid or unpaid) in their first job. Such a low rate of self-employment would not be surprising in a country like the United States where only 3 or 4 percent of current workers are self-employed, but self-employment is very common in both parts of Ireland: 29 percent of workers in the Republic and 20 percent in Northern Ireland are currently self-employed (see Table 2.5). The obvious inference is that the transition into self-employment is a crucial part of the socioeconomic life cycle in Ireland. Because the level of current self-employment in Ireland is so high by European and American standards, this aspect of intragenerational mobility has not previously been accessible for study. France has a high rate of current self-employment, but most of the research on French mobility has focused on intergenerational mobility.

First jobs also differ from current jobs in socioeconomic status and prestige. Upward career mobility is a stalwart of mobility studies. Consider here only the gross characteristics of first occupations as distinct from current occupations, without attention to the way in which individual career mobility links the two. The difference between the mean socioeconomic status of first jobs and current jobs is 8.4 in the Republic and 9.0 in Northern Ireland; the difference in prestige is 5.8 and 6.5, respectively.[2] Within the white-collar occupations, professional and managerial occupations (classes Ib and II) are more common as current occupations than as first occupations; the routine nonmanual occupations (classes IIIa and IIIb) are more common as first than as current occupations. Among the blue-collar occupations, the patterns differ by region. In the Republic, the only blue-collar occupations that are more common as current occupations than as first occupations are the technical and supervisory occupations of class V. In Northern Ireland, skilled and semiskilled manual occupations are also more common as current occupations than as first occupations. Given the lag in industrial development between the two regions, this difference might seem to be due to a low concentration of skilled and semiskilled *current* jobs in the Republic. In fact, the regional difference stems from the relatively low percentages of men from Northern Ireland who start out in skilled and semiskilled positions.

The search for a first job is a matter of crucial importance. With the large self-employed sector, the Irish labor market tends to be less formal than the bureaucratized labor markets of more highly industrialized nations. Indicative of the informality, the search for a first job centers on primary connections—on family and friends. A majority of workers in the Republic (56 percent) got their first job through family and friends; nearly as large a share of Northern workers (47 percent) did so. The large number of unpaid first jobs contributes to the preponderance of primary connections. Nearly all unpaid workers are relatives assisting on a family farm or in a family-run business. But there is more to primary connections than can be accounted for by this link between family and no pay. Excluding unpaid occupations, family and friends connect more workers to their first jobs than they do to current jobs. Table 9.3 shows the relationship between recruitment and occupation by region.[3] The most extreme instance of an "excess" of primary connections is the case of recruitment to upper-grade professional and managerial positions (class Ia). In the Republic, family and friends account for 41 percent of the job contacts for men entering these high-status occupations immediately upon leaving school, compared with only 1 percent of the job contacts for men currently in them. In Northern Ireland, the discrepancy is between 31 percent recruited to higher-level professional and proprietorial first jobs by family and friends and 4 percent recruited to similar current jobs by the same kinds of contacts. Blue-collar occupations also show a much higher incidence of primary connections in placement into first jobs than for placement into current jobs. Family and friends account for 37–52 percent of first placements in blue-collar occupations but only 11–22 percent of current placements in similar occupations.

Bureaucratic entry accounts for most of the first job placements not attributable to family and friends. Bureaucratic advance and enterprise are negligible sources of placement, even in positions where promotion and starting one's own business normally predominate. Keep in mind, however, that jobs such as proprietor and foreman, that is, jobs that typically involve career advancement, are (by nature) rare as first jobs. The high rate of family contact among the exceptional workers who start out in these sought-after positions confirms the working man's suspicion that it takes connections to short-circuit the usual cycle.

Table 9.3
Occupation at first full–time job by method used to obtain job
by region: men aged 18–65, Ireland, 1973

				Method used to obtain job				
Occupa-tion[a]	Family	Friend	Promoted/recruited	Asked for a job/answered an ad	Started own business	Other/missing	Total	(N)
Republic of Ireland								
Ia	0%	0%	50%	0%	50%	0%	100%	(2)
Ib	13	28	11	43	0	6	100	(47)
II	10	9	17	49	1	14	100	(78)
IIIa	22	19	13	37	0	9	100	(156)
IVa	33	67	0	0	0	0	100	(3)
IVb	67	0	0	17	0	16	100	(12)
IIIb	18	32	7	34	0	9	100	(162)
VIIInf	88	3	2	3	0	3	100	(60)
V	12	21	16	46	0	5	100	(100)
VI	25	27	9	33	1	6	100	(299)
VIIss	19	28	6	39	0	9	100	(246)
VIIus	16	23	7	42	0	12	100	(211)
IVc	67	0	0	11	22	0	100	(9)
IVd	68	0	5	5	0	21	100	(19)
VIIIf	88	2	<1	<1	0	3	100	(566)
VIIf	23	18	12	43	0	5	100	(286)
Northern Ireland								
Ia	20%	20%	20%	0%	40%	0%	100%	(5)
Ib	18	13	7	52	0	10	100	(60)
II	4	10	6	69	0	11	100	(80)
IIIa	15	19	5	51	0	10	100	(174)
IVa	60	0	0	0	20	20	100	(5)
IVb	12	12	25	38	12	0	100	(8)
IIIb	20	23	4	47	0	6	100	(221)
VIIInf	93	2	0	5	0	0	100	(58)
V	20	22	3	46	0	9	100	(134)
VI	22	21	9	39	0	9	100	(447)
VIIss	18	20	5	52	0	6	100	(405)
VIIus	20	17	4	50	0	9	100	(229)
IVc	100	0	0	0	0	0	100	(5)
IVd	83	0	0	0	8	8	100	(12)
VIIIf	95	2	<1	0	<1	3	100	(331)
VIIf	26	24	8	38	0	5	100	(220)

a.　See Table 9.2 for key to category labels.

The changing circumstances of employment in Ireland have reduced the importance of family recruitment for the most recent cohort. A log-linear analysis of a table cross-classifying first occupation by recruitment, by cohort, and by region shows that the distribution of men according to recruitment type differs by cohort and region, but the association between recruitment type and occupation has not changed. The preferred model for the four-way table includes all possible two-way interactions but no three-way interactions ($L^2 = 444.95$; $df = 383$; $p = .02$; $N = 4,385$; bic $= -2,767$). Using the model selection criteria in Goodman (1970) instead of the bic criterion leads to the inclusion of region $\times$ cohort $\times$ recruitment and region $\times$ cohort $\times$ occupation terms, but still no evidence of a change or regional difference in the recruitment $\times$ occupation association ($L^2 = 354.79$; $df = 318$; $p = .08$; bic $= -2,312$). The Irish labor market is becoming more formal. The growth of occupations with an articulated career structure imposed some formality on hiring, but the importance of primary connections waned for all occupations in the 1960s. The formalization of hiring grew in part because formal education also grew. Educational credentials afforded prospective employers a source of information about job applicants from an objective realm, outside the sphere of primary contacts. This is the pattern in other societies. Interpersonal networks provide job seekers with valuable information about openings, but employers in the United States and elsewhere rely more on bureaucratic recruitment procedures than on personal networks (Granovetter 1974). This is becoming the pattern in Ireland as well.

Educational Attainment and First Occupation

The link between education and career is more than just a matter of timing. While the age at which a man begins working coincides with the age at which he leaves school, the time spent in school and the credentials earned in the process affect the kind of job he takes as much as they affect when he takes the job. An advanced academic education increases the odds on attaining a first job in a desirable occupation; lack of education increases the odds that the first job will be in an undesirable occupation. In the Republic, 80 percent of men with only primary education started their work life in one of the lower manual or agricultural labor occupations; 68 percent of the men with university degrees entered the professions or management upon leaving school. In Northern Ireland, the comparable percentages are 68 percent of primary school leavers in lower manual or agricultural labor and 63 percent of primary school leavers in lower manual or agricultural labor and 63 percent of university graduates in the professional and managerial positions. Detailed data cross-classifying men according to their education, first full-time occupation, and region are in Appendix Tables A.17 and A.18.

To determine whether the distributions of education and first jobs differ in the Republic and Northern Ireland because of differences in occupational opportunity structure alone or whether education affects occupation differently in the North and in the Republic requires a well-defined statistical model. The analysis of association (ANOAS) models developed by Goodman (1979, 1984, 1985a) and Clogg (1982a) are well suited to the task because they incorporate information about the rank ordering of educational and occupational categories.[4]

The analysis of association begins with the model of null association.[5] This model hypothesizes that the apparent association between educational achievement and first full-time occupation arose by chance. This unrealistic model seldom fits such data, and it would be surprising if it fit in this instance. However, null association is an easy-to-understand baseline against which the fit of more complicated models might be gauged. On the one hand, if a complicated model does not fit the data much better than null association, it will be necessary to look elsewhere for an account of the relationship between education and first occupation. On the other hand, if a model substantially improves on the fit attained by null association, then it will be taken seriously, even if it is quite complicated. Table 9.4 shows in line 0 that, as expected, null association provides a poor fit to these data.

The simplest alternative to null association in the ANOAS scheme is homogeneous conditional uniform association (UA). This model takes the order of the categories as given and estimates a single coefficient of association under the constraint that all odds ratios for adjacent rows and columns are equal, that is, that $\theta_{ij} = F_{ij}F_{i+1,j+1} / F_{i,j+1}F_{i+1,j} = \theta$ for all i,j and for both Northern Ireland and the Republic. This model fits the data much better than null association does (see line 1 of Table 9.4). The key assumptions of homogeneous conditional UA are that (1) the categories are ordered monotonically with respect to the principal component of the association between educational attainment and initial occupational attainment, (2) the association between education and first occupation is the same in Northern Ireland and the Republic, and (3) the distances between adjacent categories along the principal compo-

Table 9.4
**Goodness–of–fit statistics for analysis of association between education
and first occupation by region and by first job cohort: Ireland, 1973**

Control variable / model	df	L^2	p	bic
Region				
0 Null association	150	2120.31	<.01	859
1 Homogeneous conditional UA[a]	149	956.36	<.01	−296
1' Homogeneous conditional UA–P[b]	149	1032.72	<.01	−220
2 Heterogeneous conditional UA[a]	148	953.35	<.01	−291
3 Homogeneous RC[c]	131	311.15	<.01	−790
4 Heterogeneous RC[c]	112	291.51	<.01	−650
5 Homogeneous QRC[d]	125	213.20	<.01	−847
First job cohort				
0 Null association	225	2850.61	<.01	58
1 Homogeneous conditional UA[a]	224	1004.99	<.01	−878
2 Heterogeneous conditional UA[a]	222	1002.61	<.01	−863
4 Heterogeneous RC[c]	168	357.13	<.01	−1055

a.   Uniform association with occupational categories ordered as in Table 9.3.
b.   Uniform association with occupational categories ordered by prestige.
c.   Row × column effects model.
d.   Row × column effects model with structural zeros in six cells.

nents are equal. Any of these assumptions can be relaxed to produce a new model.

Consider the order among the categories first. Better fit might be obtained by reordering the categories according to some criterion variable thought to be closely associated with the principal component of the association between education and first occupation or by estimating scores for the educational and occupational categories from the data. Reordering the categories according to prestige scores (see Table 2.9) actually increases L^2 in this case (line 1' in Table 9.4). Reordering the categories according to SES and the proportion of the men currently in the occupation who completed primary education produces similar results to those reported under UA (not shown). Letting association vary by region produces a trivial improvement in L^2 and an increase in bic (line 2 of Table 9.4). Estimating the scores from the data using the RC model (originally designated row and column effects model II by Goodman) improves fit dramatically. Three forms of the RC model are fit. The first one constrains the scores to be equal in the two regions (homogeneous RC), the second one allows for the unlikely prospect that scores differ by region (heterogeneous RC), and the third one modifies homogeneous RC to take account of an interesting pattern observed among the residuals (homogeneous QRC). The homogeneous RC model improves over homogeneous UA ($\Delta L^2 = 645.21$; $df = 18$;

$p < .01$; bic $= -494$), while heterogeneous RC fails to improve over homogeneous RC ($\Delta L^2 = 19.64$; $df = 19$; $p = .47$; bic $= +140$). The residuals from homogeneous RC indicate that there are excess flows of young workers from nonacademic secondary schools into skilled manual (class VI) and lower-level technical (class V) positions and from the graduation ceremonies at academic secondary schools to clerical and sales jobs (class IIIa). Blocking the cells of the table pertaining to those combinations of educational attainment and first occupation and refitting homogeneous RC yield a model that substantially improves fit according to both L^2 and bic (homogeneous QRC). At this point the search for a preferred model of the effects of education on first job is halted. The result is a model that estimates homogeneous scores for educational and occupational categories, specifies a separate slope for Northern Ireland and the Republic, and includes special parameters for the affinity between nonacademic secondary education and higher manual employment and between academic secondary education and clerical and sales employment.[6] Table 9.5 presents the estimated values of these parameters.

The μ parameters order the first-occupation categories in a way that is familiar in outline but distinctive in particulars. The professional and managerial occupations form the top of the scale, and agricultural labor constitutes the bottom. The order among the occupational categories according to the μ parameters closely follows the order of the SES scores and primary education scores from Table 2.9; there are some notable deviations of the μ parameters from the order of the prestige scores.[7] The correlation between the μ parameters and SES scores is not perfect. There are few (minor) disagreements between the μ parameters and the SES scale regarding the ordering of categories that fall in the middle of both scales. More important, the SES scale produces more variation among these middle categories than do the μ parameters. The prestige scale generates an order that is distinct from that found among the other scales and the μ parameters. Prestige ranks farming and agricultural labor relatively higher than do the μ parameters.

The ν parameters order the education categories from "primary school only" to "university graduate" with distinctions between complete and incomplete, academic and nonacademic, falling in line with what might be interpreted as a status or credential line. The only surprise is the lack of difference between complete academic secondary education and miscellaneous or incomplete third-level education. Apparently the first occupation does not yield much of a return to third-level education (over what could

Table 9.5
Parameter estimates of the effect of education on first occupation
by region or cohort and model: Ireland, 1973

Category	Region RC[a]	Region QRC[b]	Cohort RC[a]
First occupation (μ_i)			
Professionals & proprietors I[a]	.54	.54	.54
Professionals & managers I	.52	.52	.53
Professionals & managers II	.35	.35	.36
Clerical & sales workers	.15	.13	.15
Proprietors with employees[a]	−.09	−.08	−.13
Proprietors without employees[a]	−.10	−.09	−.07
Service workers	−.08	−.07	−.09
Unpaid helpers, non farm	−.06	−.05	−.05
Technicians & foremen	−.02	−.03	−.05
Skilled manual workers	−.07	−.09	−.09
Semiskilled manual workers	−.17	−.17	−.17
Unskilled manual workers	−.17	−.17	−.20
Farmers with employees[a]	−.05	−.03	−.01
Farmers without employees[a]	−.21	−.21	−.18
Unpaid helpers, farm	−.24	−.25	−.24
Farm laborers	−.30	−.31	−.30
Educational attainment (ν_j)			
Primary	−.75	−.73	−.74
Nonacademic secondary	−.16	−.19	−.16
Incomplete academic secondary	−.08	−.06	−.08
Complete academic secondary	.20	.16	.20
Miscellaneous or incomplete 3rd level	.22	.22	.22
Complete 3rd level or post graduate	.57	.59	.57
Association (ϕ)			
Republic of Ireland	13.73	12.22	—
Northern Ireland	11.25	10.18	—
Cohort before 1945	—	—	10.82
Cohort 1945–1958	—	—	14.15
Cohort 1959–1973	—	—	11.53

a. Row × column effects model.
b. Row × column effects model with structural zeros in six cells.

be expected from a complete academic education) unless one secures a degree.

The φ parameters indicate a stronger association between education and first occupation in the Republic than in Northern Ireland. The return to education in the Republic exceeds that in Northern Ireland by about 20 percent. These effects are independent of the direct links between non-academic secondary schools and technical and crafts occupations and between academic secondary schools and clerical and sales first occupations (controlled for in the model by fitting "structural zeros" to the relevant cells).

The important educational reforms of the post–World War II era could conceivably affect the link between education and first occupation. In particular, speculation about the deleterious effects of mass college education in the United States might apply to Ireland (Berg 1970; Freeman 1976, 1977; Welch 1979). At the least, growth in the number of college degrees in the United States engendered a "mismatch" between educational credentials and occupation (Sullivan 1978; Clogg 1979; Clogg and Sullivan 1983; Clogg and Shockey 1984). College education used to be a rare good. Those who possessed it could command high wages, salaries, and fees for their services. These rewards constituted high returns on the investment in higher education for those who had the money (and time) to make such an investment. As public colleges grew in the United States, less money was required for investment in a college education. At some point returns began to diminish. Some say that point was reached in the United States by 1970 (Berg 1970; Freeman 1976, 1977). Educational growth in Ireland expanded the prevalence of both academic secondary schooling and third-level education. Such growth may have depressed an individual's rate of return on educational investment or contributed to occupational mismatch. Proponents of the counterbalance thesis postulate an increased link between educational attainment and first job placement (Westergaard and Little 1968; Westergaard 1972; Westergaard and Resler 1975). The alternative to the overtraining, mismatch, and counterbalance theses is stasis: educational growth may well have lagged behind the expansion of opportunities for white-collar employment in administration and other services, engendering no change in rates of return.

Mismatch occurs whenever an individual finds employment in an occupation in which most of the workers have a lower level of education than he does. If, on the one hand, growth in educational attainment increases the supply of highly educated workers faster than macroeconomic changes increase the demand for workers with advanced credentials, then some highly educated workers will take jobs that normally go to people with less education. If the supply of such jobs is large relative to the supply of workers with the "traditional" amount of schooling, then the highly educated and the traditionally educated workers mix, both attaining comparable occupational status. The consequence is a depressed rate of return for investment in education because the highly educated worker presumably could have done just as well with less schooling. In such a case, higher education fails to provide occupational status, and presumably earnings, greater than the status attained by workers with less education. If, on the other hand, the demand for workers slackens at all levels of socioeconomic status, then oversupply can create a kind of domino effect, pushing workers with less education downward to positions with less occupational status. This kind of "queuing system" does not alter the rate of return for educational credentials because workers with more education retain their advantage over workers with less education (Hodge 1973; Thurow 1975). However, the floor level of attainment associated with each level of education drops lower. In the extreme, some workers who traditionally would have secure employment can experience chronic unemployment after the educational ante is raised. In the Irish context, the upshot might have been an ironic decline in individual returns to investment in education at a time when social investment in education was increasing (Irish Ministry of Education 1966; Breen 1985).

Changes of this sort are difficult to detect in the association between education and *current* occupational status because, even in their extreme applications, theories of mismatch and falling rates of return to education do not imply that employers dismiss workers with traditional levels of education in order to replace them with workers who have more education. Mismatch and falling returns to education occur through worker replacement and job creation. Workers get their first jobs because the need to replace exiting workers and the creation of new jobs open vacancies that can be filled with new workers, so mismatch and falling returns to education, if they occur at all, should be visible in the data on cohort differences in the joint distribution of educational attainment and first occupations. Unlike data on current occupations that involve comparisons among workers with varying levels of job tenure, some of whom moved into their current jobs years earlier and some of whom just entered the occupation, the association between education and first occupation reflects differences among workers at a point when all workers are making a transition.

Evidence for or against mismatch will come from data on cohort differences in the mean occupational standing of men at different educational levels.[8] If occupational-educational mismatch has been an important component of Irish social stratification, then at each level of education men from recent cohorts will have lower average occupational standing in their first jobs than do men from earlier cohorts who have the same amount of education. So, for example, the mismatch theory would be supported if men with primary educations who took their first jobs between 1945 and 1958 have a higher average occupational standing than do men with primary educations who took their first jobs between 1959 and 1973. Evidence for or against falling rates of return for investments in education will come from data on cohort differences in the slope of the line relating educational attainment to the occupational standing of first jobs.

Appendix Tables A.19–A.21 tabulate workers according to first full-time occupation, education, and first job cohort. Three cohorts are identified: first worked before 1945, first worked 1945–1958, and first worked 1959–1973.[9] The lower panel of Table 9.4 reports the search for a preferred association model. A search like the one for a preferred model of regional differences in the association between education and first occupation leads to the homogeneous RC model as preferred. The bic criterion leads directly to homogeneous RC, and other considerations also favor it.

The homogeneous RC model preferred for cohort differences produces educational and occupational scores that are nearly identical to the ones obtained in the analysis of the regional differences. The occupational scores (μ parameters) can be used to assess the extent of mismatch between education and occupation that emerged in Ireland during the post–World War II years. Table 9.6 presents the mean of the μ parameters for each educational level and first job cohort.[10] If mismatch is important, then the mean μ will decrease over time. This does not happen. The biggest intercohort change in mean μ is $+.08$ between the pre-1945 and 1945–1958 cohorts for men with complete academic secondary educations. This change is in the wrong direction. The second largest intercohort change is

Table 9.6
Mean occupational μ scores by education and first job cohort:
men aged 18-65, Ireland, 1973

| | *First job cohort* | | |
Educational attainment	Before 1945	1945– 1958	1959– 1973
Primary	−.20	−.19	−.18
Nonacademic secondary	−.11	−.11	−.11
Incomplete academic secondary	−.11	−.09	−.09
Complete academic secondary	−.02	.06	.01
Miscellaneous or incomplete higher	.07	.03	.02
Complete higher or postgraduate	.25	.27	.29

−.05 between the 1945–1958 and 1959–1973 cohorts for men with complete academic secondary educations. This change might be interpreted as
evidence supporting some degree of educational-occupational mismatch if
it were corroborated by similar changes for other cohorts or other educational levels, but here it is suspicious because it is so clearly a simple
reversal of the previous change. It might simply result from an overesti-
mate of the true mean for the 1945–1958 cohort. In short, there is no substantial evidence of a growing mismatch between education and occupation in Ireland, even though this was a period of rapid growth in the supply
of well-educated Irishmen. Apparently the growth in educational credentials was in stride with the other changes taking place in the Irish work
force—the downturn in unpaid work and low-skill employment generally
at a time when professional and managerial opportunities flourished.

The tests in Table 9.4 also reject the hypothesis that expanding education in Ireland diminished the rate of return on educational human capital.
Heterogeneous UA does not improve over homogeneous UA, and heterogeneous RC does not improve over homogeneous RC. An important consideration that holds out some hope to the proponents of a falling rate of
return is the inability of the homogeneous RC model to constrain the φ
coefficients. Thus, homogeneous RC has some built-in heterogeneity. The
φ coefficients in Table 9.5 are inconsistent, however, with a hypothesis of
falling returns to education. The φ estimate for the pre-1945 cohort is
10.82. The increase to 14.15 in the 1945–1958 cohort shows that if returns
to education changed at all, they increased during this time. The rise then
reversed in the 1959–1973 cohort, which experienced a rate of return to
educational credentials that registers a φ of 11.53. If the difference
between the 1945–1958 cohort and the 1959–1973 cohort is significant,
then that 18.5 percent drop in the effect of education on occupational
standing would support the theory of falling returns to education. However, there is no way of testing for the significance of this difference or of
estimating the precision of the estimated φ coefficients for different
cohorts with existing computer software. All of the requisite data for more
analyses are in Appendix Tables A.19–A.21, so when technology
advances a bit, a definitive test can be run. At present, it is doubtful that
such a test will support the theory of falling returns to education, because
the homogeneous UA model fits as well as the heterogeneous UA model.[11]

In sum, educational credentials influence occupational achievements in
Ireland as they do elsewhere. Those men who stay in school longer,
amassing educational credentials, enter the work force as white-collar

workers, many working in professions or entry-level management. Access to these positions is restricted to men with credentials. Men who attain only the minimum amount of education enter unpaid and unskilled occupations. First job is a crucial contingency for the rest of a worker's career. Men who do not begin their work lives in agriculture, for example, have virtually no chance of entering farming later in life. Occupations that do not involve inheritance of property are not quite as restrictive as that, but the effect of education on first occupational standing is an important component of the overall pattern of social stratification in Ireland.

Social Origins and First Occupation

First occupations are linked to social origins directly and indirectly through the effect of origins on educational attainment. Appendix Tables A.3 and A.4 cross-classify men according to their origins and first occupations by region. Mobility to first occupations is quite distinct from mobility to current occupations in a number of ways (compare Tables A.3 and A.4 with Tables A.1 and A.2). The two forms of mobility differ most obviously in the degree of clustering on the main diagonal of the table. In the Republic, the percentage of men whose first occupation is the same as their father's is half as large as the percentage immobile between origins and current occupation. Only 15 percent of men from the Republic took first jobs that fell into the same category as their fathers' occupation, compared with 29 percent immobile to current jobs. In Northern Ireland, the difference between immobility to first and current occupations is not as pronounced as the difference in the Republic; 18 percent of first occupations fall on the main diagonal of the intergenerational mobility table, compared with 24 percent of current occupations.

High rates of immobility to first jobs are found for sons of clerical and sales workers (class IIIa) and sons of manual workers (classes V–VIIf), including farm laborers. But men from other origins—notably high-prestige origins in which work involves autonomy or authority—first move into forms of employment that involve less prestige, autonomy, and authority. This sets up a sharp contrast between the pattern of immobility to first and current occupations. Prestige and personal contacts are important contributors to overall immobility. The occupations that show low immobility are the ones that are high on these correlates of overall mobility. Career mobility must be operating in a way that returns many men from upper nonmanual and farm backgrounds to their origin statuses.

Sons of farmers (classes IVc and IVd) move into unpaid work on farms in large numbers. Many eventually move into farming on their own. Men from proprietorial origins move into clerical, sales, and service work (classes IIIa and IIIb), skilled manual work (class VI), and unpaid assistance in the family business (VIIInf). Sons of professionals and managers move into other (lower-prestige) white-collar work, lower-grade technical occupations (class V), and even into manual labor. The movement of sons of lower-grade professionals and managers (class II) into manual first jobs is particularly high (39 percent in the Republic and 47 percent in Northern Ireland). The converse movement of men of working-class origins into nonmanual first occupations reflects the internal stratification of the working class along skill lines: sons of foremen and technicians have more mobility into white-collar employment than do sons of craftsmen, who in turn have an advantage in this regard over sons of semiskilled and unskilled workers.

Nearly all of the men who take unpaid first jobs are sons of self-employed fathers. For the most part, these men work with their fathers in a family business or on a family farm. This complicates the analysis of first jobs enormously by blurring the distinction between mobility and immobility. The son working in an unpaid first job works alongside his father, presumably performing many of the same tasks. He lives at home in exchange for his labors. Most unpaid workers, especially those on farms, go into the father's occupation, either by inheritance or by enterprise. This makes mobility into unpaid work seem like immobility. At the same time, the son is clearly subordinate to the father on the job. The father is the farmer or the shopkeeper; the son is the farmer's helper or the shopkeeper's assistant. Because of this subservience, mobility to unpaid work more nearly resembles other forms of (downward) mobility.

Structural mobility usually refers to the disjuncture of origins and current destinations, but this is a matter more of convention than of substance. There is no logical basis for favoring mobility from origins to current occupations over mobility involving first occupations in the study of structural mobility. Whenever the marginal distributions of origins and destinations differ, some cases in a mobility table must lie off the cells of the main diagonal. As long as the source of unequal marginal totals affects all men uniformly, regardless of origins, structural mobility becomes a factor.

The distributions of origins and first occupations differ substantially—more so than do those of origins and current destinations. More important, the sources of dissimilarity between origins and first occupations undoubtedly differ from the sources of dissimilarity between origins and current occupations. However, structural mobility is identified with unequal origin and destination totals from all kinds of sources. The only stipulation is that structural mobility to a particular destination affects workers from all origins uniformly. Sources of mobility that increase the odds on arriving at some destination, such as farming, for workers from some origins more than for workers from other origins are not structural mobility. The model of Sobel et al. (1985) tests whether or not marginal differences can be attributed to structural mobility. The key is the symmetry of the association in the mobility table, as indicated by the fit (or lack of fit) for the model of quasi-symmetry (and special cases of quasi-symmetry like conditional quasi-symmetry with homogeneous association).

Table 9.7 shows the goodness of fit for quasi-symmetry and related models applied to the counts in Tables A.3 and A.4.[12] These statistics show that the association between origin and first occupation is symmetrical, as required by the formulation of Sobel et al. (1985). Therefore, the marginal differences in mobility from origins to first jobs stem from structural sources, not from semipermeable class boundaries, one-way buffer zones, or other hypothetical images of unreciprocated mobility. This means that the α_j parameters can be interpreted as measures of the force of structural mobility on each destination. The fit statistics also show that the association between origins and first jobs is the same in Northern Ireland as in the Republic.

Not surprisingly, the α_j parameters in Table 9.8 show a different pattern of structural mobility to first occupations. Current occupations capture

Table 9.7
Goodness–of–fit for selected models applied to intergenerational and intragenerational mobility: men aged 25–65, Ireland, 1973

Model	df	Father–to–first[a] L^2	bic	First–to–current[b] L^2	bic
Conditional independence	450	3687.25	−92	4780.07	1002
Conditional quasi–independence	418	2905.18	−605	2360.58	−1149
Conditional symmetry	240	2693.75	845	2529.89	682
Conditional quasi–symmetry	210	116.10	−1502	138.57	−1479
Conditional quasi–symmetry with homogeneous association	315	263.39	−2382	298.77	−2346

a. N = 4437.
b. N = 4424.

Table 9.8

Estimates of parameters of conditional quasi–symmetry with homogeneous association for mobility from origin to first job and from first job to current job by region: men aged 18–65, Ireland, 1973

Origin		Ia	Ib	II	IIIa	IVa	IVb	IIIb	VIIInf	V	VI	VIIss	VIIus	IVc	IVd	VIIIf	VIIf
															Destination[a]		

Structural mobility parameters (α_j):

Father-to-first

	Ia	Ib	II	IIIa	IVa	IVb	IIIb	VIIInf	V	VI	VIIss	VIIus	IVc	IVd	VIIIf	VIIf
Republic	.07	2.72	1.50	5.16	.03	.08	11.61	7.27	2.76	2.73	2.64	1.79	.01	.02	166.9	4.13
North	.20	1.89	1.24	5.55	.06	.09	9.19	5.35	2.70	2.91	2.72	2.38	.01	.03	51.69	5.14

First-to-current

	Ia	Ib	II	IIIa	IVa	IVb	IIIb	VIIInf	V	VI	VIIss	VIIus	IVc	IVd	VIIIf	VIIf
Republic	203.9	7.82	3.19	.37	42.84	7.84	.14	.18	.68	.39	.30	.25	2.22	10.52	.01	.03
North	118.0	11.33	6.14	.55	32.85	14.03	.14	.07	.84	.41	.31	.23	4.02	4.67	.01	.02

Association parameters (the same in Republic and Northern Ireland):

Father-to-first (upper right) / *First-to-current* (lower left)

Origin	Ia	Ib	II	IIIa	IVa	IVb	IIIb	VIIInf	V	VI	VIIss	VIIus	IVc	IVd	VIIIf	VIIf
Ia	1.00	.19	.10	.44	.15	.06	.49	.12	.03	.04	.00	.04	.00	.00	.00	.00
Ib	.53	1.00	.44	.10	.04	.05	.12	.23	.19	.19	.17	.03	.02	.07	.03	.02
II	.01	.15	1.00	.78	.09	.05	.41	.53	.56	.23	.32	.22	.04	.14	.04	.08
IIIa	.02	.13	.23	1.00	.24	.09	.54	.24	.46	.38	.34	.21	.02	.04	.03	.03
IVa	.00	.05	.06	.09	1.00	.29	.11	3.63	.15	.33	.15	.15	.06	.00	.04	.07
IVb	.00	.04	.05	.03	1.00	1.00	.08	.76	.15	.23	.17	.21	.03	.21	.04	.06
IIIb	.00	.03	.11	.24	.28	.22	1.00	.49	.60	.72	.61	.03	.11	.00	.25	.10
VIIInf	.02	.02	.07	.13	.33	.15	1.00	1.00	.06	.11	.25	.06	.05	.06	.01	.00
V	.01	.01	.07	.14	.13	.14	.10	.29	1.00	.63	.47	.51	.03	.02	.05	.22
VI	.01	.04	.07	.06	.14	.15	.16	.28	1.00	1.00	.74	.67	.01	.02	.03	.19
VIIss	.00	.03	.07	.14	.09	.05	.41	.18	.21	.40	1.00	.90	.01	.01	.05	.23
VIIus	.00	.01	.04	.09	.06	.08	.27	.10	.23	.40	.78	1.00	.05	.06	.09	.49
IVc	.00	.00	.02	.01	.05	.00	.04	.09	.03	.01	.01	.01	1.00	.22	.18	.02
IVd	.00	.00	.01	.00	.00	.07	.02	.06	.12	.09	.05	.12	.06	1.00	.80	.15
VIIIf	.00	.00	.01	.02	.00	.03	.03	.00	.01	.02	.07	.08	.14	.19	1.00	.08
VIIf	.00	.00	.01	.01	.01	.04	.10	.00	.07	.08	.22	.42	.04	.06	.08	1.00

a.   See Table 9.2 for category labels.

men at a variety of points in the life cycle. The α_j parameters for first occupations iron out life-cycle differences by focusing on career beginnings. For the most part, they are humble beginnings. The overwhelming positive flows direct men toward unpaid (classes VIIIf and VIIInf) and service (class IIIb) employment. Modest positive structural mobility favors salaried white-collar work (classes Ib, II, and IIIa) and manual work on and off farms (classes V–VIIf). The range of these structural mobility multipliers is far greater than the range for mobility from origins to current occupations. From the contrast between structural mobility to first and current occupations, it is clear that life cycle does more to shape mobility than generation does.

The regional differences in structural mobility to first occupations appear to be small in contrast to the huge life-cycle differences. The only substantial difference is in α_{15}, the multiplier for farm helpers. The coefficient for the Republic is three times larger than α_{15} for Northern Ireland.

If origins and first occupations were independent, these structural mobility multipliers would concentrate the majority of men from all origin categories in unpaid farm help. But, origins are not independent of first occupations. The δ_{ij} for exchanges between unpaid farm help and all nonfarm occupations are less than .10, setting up a barrier that keeps men from nonfarm origins away from farm help. Combinations of high exchange due to weak association include all pairs of manual occupations with other manual occupations, white-collar occupations with adjacent white-collar occupations, and most paid occupations with service work. The δ_{ij} association parameters range from .01 (very strong association) to near independence (.90) and, in one case, to a value substantially greater than 1.0 ($\delta_{57} = 3.63$). This last value indicates that, even in the absence of a strong structural mobility multiplier, the odds on moving into unpaid nonfarm work for men whose fathers are proprietors with employees exceed the odds on entering proprietorship directly.[13] The estimates of δ_{ij} less than .10 for most pairs of occupational categories that mix white-collar occupations with agricultural occupations show the odds on moving between white-collar work and farming relative to moving within the class of origin to be less than 10 percent. On the other extreme, the odds on moving between unskilled and semiskilled manual occupations relative to immobility are nearly even ($\delta_{11,12} = .90$).[14]

Other exchanges greater than 50 percent are found between pairs: (Ia,Ib), (II,IIIa), (IIIa,IIIb), (II,VIIInf), (IVb,VIIInf), (II,V), (IIIb,VI),

(IIIb,VIIss), (IIIb,VIIus), (V,VI), (V,VIIss), (VI,VIIss), (VI,VIIus), and (IVd,VIIIf). The barriers between other pairs of occupational classes limit exchange. Even between the two types of farm proprietorships and between farming with employees and unpaid farm help, the internal stratification of agriculture limits exchange mobility ($\delta_{13,14} = .22$; $\delta_{13,15} = .18$). Presumably part of this effect is due to the fact that the succession of generations tends to split family holdings.

The pattern of association between origins and first occupations closely resembles the pattern of association between origins and current occupations (see Table 3.6). The log δ_{ij} for mobility from origins to first and current occupations are highly correlated ($r = .89$). There are few large differences. The only significant ones are for exchanges between lower-grade professions and clerical and sales occupations (more exchange in mobility to first occupations), for exchanges between service occupations and semiskilled manual occupations (more exchange in mobility to first occupations), and for exchanges between proprietorships with and without employees (more exchange in mobility to current occupations).[15]

Mobility to first occupations is constrained by class boundaries that are nearly identical to those constraining mobility to current occupations. This conclusion is not obvious from the gross flows of men from their social origins to their first occupations, because the force of structural mobility on the two types of mobility differs greatly. Unpaid work is a very common first occupation, but it is rare for men over 30 years of age. Less than 10 percent of current occupations are unpaid. Therefore, the huge structural mobility multipliers that favor movement into unpaid first occupations obscure the similarity between the social structure affecting mobility to first and to current occupations. This similarity becomes evident only after the life-cycle effects get statistically separated from the association between origins and destinations.

First Occupation and Current Occupation

The existence of occupational career lines reinforces the social class boundaries evident in mobility from origins to first and current occupations. These career line boundaries make the association between first occupations and current occupations stronger than the associations for intergenerational mobility. Stronger association diminishes the volume of exchange mobility. Gross intragenerational mobility (namely, the percentage of men working at a job that falls in an occupational category different from the category of their first job) is 71 percent in the Republic and 72 percent in Northern Ireland. These figures are actually close to the gross mobility rates for origins to current occupations: 71 percent in the Republic and 76 percent in Northern Ireland.

The clear differences between career mobility and intergenerational mobility in the α_j parameters of quasi-symmetry (Table 9.8). These parameter estimates can be interpreted as structural mobility multipliers because quasi-symmetry fits the intragenerational mobility data well (Table 9.7). Structural mobility to current jobs favors self-employment, farming, and the professions. Routine white-collar occupations, manual occupations, and unpaid work all would contract if first and current occupations were independent. Since they are far from being so, some of these occupations retain about the same proportion of workers in first and current occupations, because immobility and other barriers to mobility hold many men in place while drawing others into them from exchanges with affiliated occupations. Comparing intragenerational structural mobility with intergenerational structural mobility shows that only salaried professionals and managers of both upper and lower grade benefit from positive structural mobility in both moves. No occupation has negative structural mobility for both moves.

The association parameters (δ_{ij}) in the upper right triangle of Table 9.8 are noticeably smaller than the corresponding figures for mobility from origins to first or current occupations. In none of the 90 pairs of δ_{ij} parameters is the coefficient for intragenerational mobility significantly larger than the corresponding coefficient for intergenerational mobility. In 52 cases the δ_{ij} parameter for mobility from origins to first occupation is significantly greater than the corresponding figure for mobility from first to current occupation.

While the differences in the strength of association between intergenerational and intragenerational mobility are clear, there are many important underlying similarities. In fact, strength is about the only way that the association for intergenerational mobility differs from that for intragenerational mobility. The large δ_{ij} for intragenerational parallel the large δ_{ij} for intergenerational mobility; the δ_{ij} for intergenerational mobility are, for the most part, just uniformly larger. The correlations between the δ_{ij} (in log form) for intragenerational mobility and the two kinds of intergenerational mobility are quite high: .85 for mobility from origins to current occupation and .78 for mobility from origins to first occupation.

This pattern of association—stronger for intragenerational mobility than for intergenerational mobility but structurally similar for both—argues that the two types of mobility are governed by the same class boundaries. Additional career mobility barriers supplement the strength of association between first and current occupations. Another consideration arises. The life cycle of many farmers' sons returns them to their fathers' occupation after a long spell as unpaid family member assisting on the farm. A return to origins like this increases the association between occupational origins and ultimate destinations. If men from nonfarm origins are also likely to return eventually to their origin class, then the segmented analysis of one-step mobility may miss an important component of the structure of social inequality in Ireland.

Countermobility

Moves from a first occupation that differs from social origins to a current job in the class of origin is known as "countermobility" (Bernard and Renaud 1976; Goldthorpe 1980). The existence of substantial countermobility would be evidence of further social inequality in Ireland, over and above that already evident from the analysis of two-way mobility. More important, substantial countermobility would show that the inequality in career mobility actually understates the extent to which intragenerational mobility contributes to social stratification. The figures on inequality in career mobility make no distinction between career mobility that takes the worker away from his origins and countermobility. In so doing, they mask the structured social inequality that will appear in an analysis of mobility in three steps: origins to first occupation to current occupation. Previous analysis of countermobility in the Republic and in Northern Ireland has revealed that countermobility accounts for about half of the total immobility of mature men from nonfarm origins and nearly all of the total immobility of mature men from farm origins (Whelan and Whelan 1984; Hout and Jackson 1986; Miller 1986).

The most direct way to analyze countermobility would be to examine the careers recorded in the Irish Mobility Study on a case-by-case basis. Such an analysis would be unbearably tedious. The potential for insight would be swamped by detail. Table 9.9 shows the scale and complexity of the data from a survey of 4,800 workers. This table accounts for the careers of the 28 men from Northern Ireland whose current occupation falls into class Ia: self-employed professionals (upper grade) and large proprietors. The men are sorted according to level of education completed.

The number of jobs they have had and their origins and first occupations are shown, along with their exact current occupations. Within levels of education, men are ranked according to the prestige of their social origins.

Lifetime mobility is divided into four main types, and three of those types are further subdivided (the code used to mark each case in Table 9.9 is shown in parentheses beside the name of each type):

1. Immobile (I): Men whose first and current occupations are both in the same broad stratum as their father's occupation.
2. Countermobile (C): Men whose current occupation is in the same broad occupational stratum as their father's occupation but who have a first occupation that falls into some other stratum. In the analysis of men from all occupations, this category is subdivided into counter-mobility from above (C_a), namely, from an occupation that has higher prestige than the current occupation, and countermobility from below (C_b), namely, from an occupation that has lower prestige than the current occupation.
3. Upwardly mobile (U): Men whose current occupation is more presti-gious than their father's. Some of these men moved upward to their first occupation and have stayed there; these men are of the directly upward (U_d) subtype. Some men took a first job that had less prestige than their current job but the same or more prestige than their father's occupation; these men are of the indirectly upward (U_i) subtype. Finally, some men took a first job that had less prestige than both their current occupation and their father's occupation; these men are of the mixed down then up (U_m) subtype.
4. Downwardly mobile (D): Men whose current occupation is less pres-tigious than their father's. Within this general type, directly down-ward (D_d), indirectly downward (D_i), and mixed up then down (D_m) subtypes are defined in a manner analogous to the subdivisions of upwardly mobile men.

According to this classification scheme, five of the self-employed profes-sionals (upper grade) and large proprietors in Northern Ireland are immo-bile, seven are countermobile, and sixteen are upwardly mobile.

All five of the immobile men had fathers who were professionals or man-agers. These workers take professional first jobs and retain them. The countermobile men mix several types of background and several types of first occupation. Some of the countermobility seems to be related to career lines, especially the mobility from clerk to solicitor (including law

Table 9.9

Career mobility of self–employed professionals and large proprietors by education: men aged 18–65, Northern Ireland, 1973

Case #	Current occupation (code)[a]	First occupation	Father's occupation	Job #
Higher degree				
1	Optician (I)	Optician (Ia)	Optician (Ia)	3
2	Dentist (C_b)	Gardener (VIIa1)	Executive of large firm (Ia)	14
3	Solicitor (I)	Solicitor (Ib)	Civil engineer (Ib)	4
4	Solicitor (C_b)	Clerk (IIIa)	Surveyor (II)	2
5	Solicitor (C_b)	Clerk (IIIa)	Auctioneer (II)	7
6	Pharmacist (U_d)	Pharmacist (Ia)	Farmer (IVc)	1
7	Veterinary surgeon (U_d)	Veterinary surgeon (Ia)	Farmer (IVc)	3
8	Solicitor (U_d)	Solicitor (Ia)	Funeral home owner (IVa)	2
9	Mechanical engineer (U_d)	Mechanical engineer (Ib)	Shopkeeper (IVb)	7
10	Consultant (U_m)	Soldier (VI)	Clerk (IIIa)	5
11	Professional, n.e.c.[b] (—)	Missing (—)	Farmer (IVd)	12
12	Teacher, n.e.c. (U_d)	Teacher, primary (Ib)	Police officer (IIIb)	5
13	Physician (U_m)	Soldier (VI)	Police officer (IIIb)	3
Some higher education				
14	Pharmacist (I)	Pharmacist (Ib)	Manager of factory (Ib)	5
15	Industrial designer (I)	Industrial designer (Ia)	Manager of factory (II)	1
16	Mechanical engineer (U_i)	Millwright (VI)	Millwright (VI)	10

Complete academic secondary

17	Accountant (I)	Accountant (Ib)	Accountant (Ib)	3
18	Hotel owner (C_b)	Soldier (VI)	Hotel owner (IVa)	7
19	Pub owner (U_i)	Shopkeeper's assistant (IIIb)	Pub owner (IVa)	3

Incomplete academic secondary

20	Shop owner (C_b)	Auto mechanic (V)	Manager, engineering (Ib)	8
21	Baker (C_b)	Unpaid baker (VIIInf)	Teacher, n.e.c. (Ib)	3

Nonacademic secondary

22	Accountant (U_i)	Compositor (VI)	Millwright (VI)	9
23	Building contractor (U_i)	Bricklayer (VI)	Laborer, chemical factory (VIIa2)	29

Primary

24	Lab technician (C_b)	Unpaid lab worker (VIIInf)	Dentist (Ia)	3
25	Shop owner (U_m)	Lorry driver (VIIa1)	Shop owner (IVa)	6
26	Shop owner (U_m)	Hat maker (VI)	Gardener (IVb)	9
27	Technologist^c (U_i)	Shopkeeper's helper (VIIInf)	House painter (VI)	9
28	Shop owner (U_i)	Shopkeeper's assistant (IIIb)	Shop owner (IVb)	5

a. I = immobile; C_b = countermobile from below; U_d = upwardly mobile directly; U_i = upwardly mobile indirectly; U_m = upwardly mobile by mixed route. All current occupations are class I; see Table 9.2 for codes to other classes.

b. n.e.c. = not elsewhere classified.

c. This case is probably misclassified. The coding manual says, "Only persons performing work normally requiring training of a university degree are included." This man's primary education suggests that he should probably have been in class V.

clerks with other clerical workers is a weakness of the British occupational classification system). Some countermobility is not related to any notion of an articulated career, such as case 2 in which a man who first worked as a gardener now is a dentist. In case 18, the son of a hotel owner did a hitch in the army and then worked a string of jobs (including a short stint as an unpaid helper in the family business) before becoming a hotel owner at age 47 (the same year his father retired, although the data do not say for sure that the son took ownership of the father's hotel).

Of the upwardly mobile men, five went directly from university to a profession. While some have had several jobs (case 9 is in his seventh engineering position), they have all remained in or returned to their original profession. The most common move for these men is in and out of self-employment. The upwardly mobile men who have university degrees were downwardly mobile to their first jobs in the army, but they have since acquired the status commensurate with their education. The upwardly mobile men who lack university degrees have had mixed careers involving lower-status occupations and, in most cases, a large number of jobs.

Perhaps the most intriguing cases are not those that match some clearly anticipated type but the five cases who, despite their primary educations, are employed in the occupational class with the highest prestige. In these data, however, the exceptions fit a clearly anticipated type, or they are misclassified. Regrettably, no informative exceptions show up. The shop owners (cases 25, 26, and 28) belong in class Ia because they own shops that employ 25 or more workers. Their prestige is based on their business achievements, not on their profession. The other two cases probably do not belong in class Ia. Case 24 is correctly classified according to the Hope-Goldthorpe scale, but perhaps the scale should have placed this type of lab technician in class V instead of class Ia (except in the rare instance of a self-employed lab technician who employs 25 or more workers in his lab—an exception that does not apply to case 24). Case 27 is a coder's error. According to the Hope-Goldthorpe scale, the title "technologist" is reserved for persons performing work normally requiring a university degree. Whatever this person's job, he lacks a university degree, so he should in all probability have been assigned to a unit group that gets recoded to class V.

To explore systematically each of the 16 categories for Northern Ireland and then repeat the analysis for the Republic would tax the attention and memory of even the most diligent reader. Some way of summarizing the data must be employed. First of all, to analyze the chain from origins to first occupation to current occupation requires a radical collapsing of categories. If all 16 categories were used, the 3,101 cases would be spread over $16 \times 16 \times 16 \times 2 = 8,192$ cells—an untenable proposition. The chief concern in collapsing categories here is the preservation of the nonmanual-manual-farm distinction. Within each broad stratum, higher- and lower-prestige positions are distinguished from one another. The resultant scheme has six categories (the classes from the PREF scheme that make up each category are shown in parentheses):

1. Upper nonmanual (Ia, Ib, II)
2. Lower nonmanual (IIIa, IVa, IVb, VIIInf)
3. Upper manual (V, VI)
4. Farm owner (IVc, IVd)
5. Lower manual (IIIb, VIIss, VIIus)
6. Farm worker (VIIf, VIIIf)

References to "upward" and "downward" mobility are based on this ordering of the categories.

The population for this analysis is men who began work prior to 1959. Men with less experience are too close to their career beginnings for the forces of countermobility to have had sufficient chance to work themselves through. Limiting the sample in such a way excludes men who may have benefited from the changes during the 1959–1973 period.

Table 9.10 cross-classifies men who began working prior to 1959 according to career mobility type, origin stratum, and region. The regional differences in the association between origin and mobility type are small but statistically significant; nearly all of the apparent differences between Northern Ireland and the Republic can be attributed to the regional differences in the distribution of origins.[16] Therefore, the most reliable feature is the association between origins and mobility type, averaging out regional differences.

The strongest tendency toward countermobility affects men from farm origins. Table 9.10 contributes to the understanding of this process of waiting for an opportunity to farm on one's own by showing that no other large occupational group in Ireland has a life cycle that is quite as clearly defined from origin to destination as the farm life cycle. Other occupations have clearly defined career lines from first occupation to ultimate destination, perhaps, but those lines are not visible in the three-step mobility.

The pressure toward countermobility is strong among upper nonmanual

Table 9.10
Indicators of mobility and countermobility by origin:
men who began working prior to 1959 by region, Ireland, 1973

Component	Origin[a]					
	Upper nonmanual	Lower nonmanual	Upper manual	Farm owner	Lower manual	Farm worker
Republic of Ireland						
Immobile	*26%*	*14%*	*20%*	*3%*	*30%*	*20%*
Countermobile	*31*	22	23	55	16	4
From above	—	1	3	2	7	4
From below	31	21	20	53	10	—
Upwardly mobile	—	22	23	20	48	76
Directly	—	4	6	7	22	24
Indirectly	—	11	5	0	17	53
Down then up	—	7	12	13	8	—
Downwardly mobile	*44*	*41*	*34*	22	7	—
Directly	41	34	27	21	6	—
Indirectly	2	7	6	0	1	—
Up then down	—	1	1	1	0	—
(N)	(85)	(194)	(172)	(610)	(306)	(136)
Northern Ireland						
Immobile	*16%*	*16%*	*18%*	*3%*	*31%*	*11%*
Countermobile	*44*	19	20	40	14	2
From above	—	1	2	1	6	2
From below	44	18	17	39	8	—
Upwardly mobile	—	23	30	31	53	87
Directly	—	6	7	10	24	40
Indirectly	—	6	10	1	25	47
Down then up	—	11	14	20	4	—
Downwardly mobile	*40*	*42*	*32*	27	2	—
Directly	40	35	23	25	1	—
Indirectly	0	6	7	0	0	—
Up then down	—	1	2	1	1	—
(N)	(118)	(212)	(324)	(388)	(463)	(93)

a. Percentages in italics sum to 100 percent (except for round–off); percentages in roman type sum to the italicized percentage above them (except for round–off).

occupations—just not as strong as it is for farming. Most men from upper nonmanual origins move downward to their first occupation. Only one in five retains high status in that first move. Subsequent countermobility brings half of the downwardly mobile men back to their origin status. As a consequence, once past 35 years of age, three-fifths of men from upper nonmanual origins are themselves in upper nonmanual occupations. The rate of immobility from upper nonmanual origins to current occupations is pegged at lower values for men under the age of 35 years who are engaged in clerical, sales, and service jobs while waiting for bureaucratic advancement to the upper nonmanual stratum (Table 3.1 and Appendix Tables A.1 and A.2).

Countermobility affects about one-fifth of men from the middle of the status hierarchy, namely, lower nonmanual and upper manual origins. Nearly all of the men who eventually return to their origins are downwardly mobile to their first jobs and subsequently move up to an occupation commensurate with their origins. A little over 10 percent of men from these middle origins are downwardly mobile in their first move but eventually move into an upper nonmanual occupation (men from upper manual origins are also counted as upwardly mobile if they move into a lower manual destination). However, about half of the men from middle-status origins who move downward on their first move fail to make an upward move later in life (or move up and back down between first and current occupation) and are still working at an occupation with less status than their origins. These are the men who are classed as directly downwardly mobile. Direct downward mobility is the modal pattern (among the nine detailed mobility types) for men from middle-status origins.

Countermobility is not a common pattern for men from lower nonmanual origins. Relatively few men from disadvantaged nonfarm backgrounds seek manual work in the countryside, or about one in ten. Even fewer move upward to an upper manual or nonmanual first job only to fall back to a lower manual current occupation, or about one in sixteen. Only 5 cases out of 769 involve an upward first move followed by a move to farm labor (the mixed up then down pattern). Half of the men from lower manual origins are upwardly mobile to their current occupation. This group is evenly split between direct and indirect upward mobility.

Countermobility is virtually no factor at all for men whose fathers were farm workers. The majority of men from these most disadvantaged origins took first jobs as paid or unpaid farm workers. Most of them subsequently left farm labor for other, higher-status work. About one farm worker's son in eight went directly into farm labor and currently works there.

Upward mobility is much more common for men from low-status origins than it is for men from high-status origins. While it is a trite but true observation that men from these origins have nowhere to go but up, the alternative is to go nowhere. Theories of a "culture of poverty" and class reproduction create the impression that immobility is the modal experience for men from disadvantaged origins. In Ireland the effects of class origins on subsequent achievement are undeniable but not determinative.

A substantial minority of men from disadvantaged origins are immobile. But the majority are not.

The concern with countermobility is that, over the entire life course, immobility is greater than it appears to be from analyses of the constituent moves. It is theoretically and mathematically possible that what appears (in a two-variable analysis) to be intragenerational mobility and an openness of the class structure might in fact be a social force sorting people into current positions according to their origins. Those men who fall in status between their first and current jobs might not only be moving downward to their current occupations but also be losing the ground that they gained in upward mobility to their first occupation. The men who gain status over their careers might be moving upward to claim their inheritance as members of an advantaged origin class. The force of countermobility is asymmetric. It does draw downwardly mobile members of advantaged classes upward to better current occupations; it does not drag upwardly mobile men from disadvantaged classes downward to the poverty of their origins. Nearly all of the countermobility in Ireland is from below.

Goldthorpe and Llewellyn (1977a; Goldthorpe 1980) address countermobility in the context of evaluating what they call the "buffer zone thesis" and the "counterbalance thesis." Just as the Irish data show little support for the postulate that transition zones straddle the middle-class–working-class boundary and effectively favor limited mobility over longer-range mobility, so they lend no support to the buffer zone thesis. The trivial countermobility from above among men from working-class origins contradicts the claims of the buffer zone thesis in Ireland, as it does in Britain (Goldthorpe 1980). Furthermore, the asymmetry of the mobility pattern that makes upward countermobility more likely than downward countermobility cannot be construed as evidence of a one-way buffer zone (Goldthorpe 1980, p. 53) or as a semipermeable class boundary (Blau and Duncan 1967, p. 59) because, as shown by the analysis of structural mobility, all of the asymmetry can be attributed to structural mobility. One need not invoke unequal exchange, one-way buffer zones, or semipermeable class boundaries to account for these structurally induced changes, because they affect men from all origins equally.

The counterbalance thesis says that the trend toward formal labor markets based on educational credentials will limit the career mobility of men with working-class origins. Data on the expansion of educational opportunities for working-class youth and on cohort differences in the relationship between education and first job contradict this thesis. If any questions about the validity of the counterbalance thesis remain, the counter-mobility and career mobility patterns of men with working-class origins answer them in the negative. Direct and indirect upward mobility are both important for Irish men of working-class origins. More pertinent are cohort differences in the types and extent of upward mobility for the Irish working class. Separating the 719 men of lower manual origins into an earlier (1919–1944) and a later (1945–1958) first-job cohort uncovers an increase in upward mobility but no trends in the tendency for upward mobility to be direct rather than indirect. In the Republic of Ireland, 39 percent of working-class men who first worked before 1945 were upwardly mobile as of 1973; 56 percent of working-class men who first worked in 1945–1958 were upwardly mobile. In Northern Ireland, the comparable percentages are 47 and 63 for the earlier and later cohorts, respectively. If the counterbalance thesis were correct, there would be no increases in upward mobility. Since the increases do exist, however, the counter-balance thesis might attribute such an increase to increases in direct upward mobility to higher-status first occupations while positing that the contribution of indirect upward mobility should shrink (thus the name counterbalance).

Data on cohort differences in the Republic contradict the counter-balance thesis; the data for Northern Ireland provide only superficial support for it. Both direct and indirect upward mobility increased in the Republic. In the earlier cohort, the 39 percent upward mobility was due to 17 percent of men from working-class origins taking higher-status first jobs and staying above their origins (direct upward mobility), 15 percent taking lower manual first jobs but higher-status current jobs (indirect), and 8 percent taking first jobs as farm workers and higher-status current jobs (mixed). Upward mobility in the later cohort climbed to 56 percent because all three components increased: direct upward mobility increased to 28 percent, indirect upward mobility increased to 20 percent, and the mixed mobility pattern increased to 9 percent of men from working-class origins. In Northern Ireland, indirect upward mobility for men with working-class origins fell as hypothesized. In the earlier cohort 16 percent direct upward mobility, 26 percent indirect, and 4 percent mixed mobility combined to raise 47 percent of working-class men above their origins; the later cohort achieved higher upward mobility through the combination of 35 percent direct, 24 percent indirect, and 4 percent mixed. This last finding is somewhat misleading, however. The probability of staying in a lower manual occupation, given that a man from working-class origins entered such an occupation on his first job, actually declined in Northern Ireland from .567 to .505 between the earlier and the later cohort. But because a far smaller share of the later cohort entered lower manual first jobs, that lower probability of staying did not translate into more indirect upward mobility; there were simply too few men at risk of being trapped in a lower manual occupation for the declining risk to show up as more indirect mobility. Thus, even this result contradicts the counterbalance thesis.

Mobility over the Life Cycle

The barriers that emerge most clearly from the comparison of intergenerational and intragenerational mobility are not class boundaries so much as sectors that organize moves. Within these sectors are hierarchies that closely resemble the hierarchies that constrain intergenerational mobility. Association between first and current occupations is stronger than intergenerational association because these hierarchical effects are supplemented by sectoral divisions that organize men's careers. For example, sectoral divisions separate farmers' sons who go into manufacturing from those who go into public service and from those who stay in agriculture.

Within sectors, age and status are highly correlated. The farmer's son who overstays in the young man's category of "helper" gets relegated to a perpetual young man's status of bachelorhood. More generally, the age-graded stratification system passes over those who fail to make their move at some time close to the modal time for a status change. The clearest indication of these modal times are to be found in the mobility of men of fixed age. In most mobility studies, when only first and current occupations are known for each respondent, the only way to study the life cycle is by separating the sample according to current age. An advantage of the Irish Mobility Study is the ability to pick an age and compare the mobility of all men who have reached that age.

Appendix Tables A.23–A.25 show three kinds of mobility: (1) mobility from first occupation to occupation at age 25 for men who first worked before their twenty-fifth birthday and who had reached age 25 before being interviewed, (2) mobility from the occupation held at age 25 to the one held at age 35 for men who first worked before their twenty-fifth birthday and who had reached age 35 before being interviewed, and (3) mobility from the occupation held at age 35 to the one held at age 45 for men who first worked before their thirty-fifth birthday and who had reached age 45 before being interviewed. No regional differences in the association between origins and destinations were significant, so men are not separated by region of residence. This pooling improves the reliability of the parameter estimates for mobility between ages 35 and 45, where the numbers of observations are thinly spread. Each of the mobility tables uses 14 categories instead of 16 because self-employed professionals, upper grade (part of class Ia), and proprietors with employees (the rest of class Ia and all of class IVa) rarely start their practice or hire their employees prior to reaching age 25. Excluding these categories altogether is an unnecessary waste of data; they are combined with adjacent categories—Ia with Ib and IVa with IVb.

Most men start their careers in low-prestige occupations that offer little direct reward. Many of these positions offer promise though. Most Irishmen have humble beginnings. The differences in prestige, status, and autonomy among the occupations of 25-year-olds, 35-year-olds, and 45-year-olds shown in Table 9.11 hint at the upward progress of many careers. The dominant pattern in these marginal distributions is the decrease in unpaid work and the increase in self-employment. But these percentages mix substantive and methodological factors. The structural mobility multipliers (α_j) more clearly report the life-cycle effects of interest. The patterns of mobility out of unpaid labor and into self-employment so evident in the simple percentages show up clearly in the α_j parameters, to be sure, but a number of other trends appear when the data are put in this form.

To use the SHD formulation, we must be sure that the model of quasi-symmetry fits the age-specific intragenerational mobility tables. The fit is very good at conventional levels of significance. The sum of the separate L^2 values is 239.36 with 234 degrees of freedom. The model is clearly acceptable ($p = .48$; bic $= -1,599$). Constraining the δ_{ij} parameters to be the same for all three life-cycle intervals would simplify interpretation. Conditional quasi-symmetry with homogeneous association (CQSHA) does not fit at conventional levels of significance, but bic prefers it over the model with heterogeneous association ($L^2 = 875.14$; $df = 416$; $p < .01$; bic $= -2,633$). Table 9.11 presents the α_j parameters from the heterogeneous association models. Only the estimate of α_1 for mobility from first occupation to occupation at age 25 is affected by the treatment of the δ_{ij} parameters; use of CQSHA would give more support to the conclusion reached below that α_1 and α_2 do not change appreciably over the life cycle.

First of all, the force of structural mobility favoring the expansion of self-employment over the life course varies with age. Structural mobility

Table 9.11
Occupational distribution, structural mobility, and percentage immobile for career mobility by age: men, Ireland, 1973

Occupation	Age			Structural mobility (α_j)			Percentage immobile		
	25	35	45	First–25	25–35	35–45	First–25	25–35	35–45
Professionals & proprietors I	.3%	.9%	1.3 ⌉	9.49	4.66	11.03	89%	81%	92%
Professionals & managers I	3.3	4.0	4.4 ⌋						
Professionals & managers II	6.6	6.7	6.3	4.76	3.23	3.55	76	78	76
Clerical & sales workers	5.8	4.8	4.2	.50	.86	1.26	52	51	69
Proprietors with employees	1.7	4.0	4.8 ⌉	17.99	4.78	3.14	76	78	85
Proprietors without employees	2.7	4.2	4.3 ⌋						
Service workers	4.3	3.0	3.2	.16	.40	1.33	27	44	69
Helpers, nonfarm	1.9	1.0	.4	.29	.16	.17	37	35	37
Technicians & foremen	5.9	5.9	5.9	.87	1.12	1.78	50	55	72
Skilled manual workers	19.2	15.1	12.5	.85	.44	.60	58	62	70
Semiskilled manual workers	14.6	15.7	15.8	.43	.67	.83	34	64	77
Unskilled manual workers	9.5	9.4	10.5	.40	.42	.50	27	53	70
Farmers with employees	1.0	2.6	3.5	5.38	5.03	12.06	77	83	95
Farmers without employees	3.6	10.4	14.8	36.34	33.88	1.83	96	98	91
Helpers, farm	13.0	7.2	3.3	.03	.07	.01	57	45	38
Agricultural laborers	6.5	5.2	4.7	.07	.16	.22	41	50	61
Total / L_{qs}^2 / Overall %	100.0	100.0	100.0	74.83	88.00	76.53	47	70	73
(N)/df	(3650)	(2716)	(1821)	78	78	78	—	—	—

fosters self-employment at every age, but some age intervals are more strongly favored than others. The optimal timing for a move into proprietorship comes early in the life cycle. The α_j parameter for proprietors (classes IVa,b) drops from 17.99 for mobility from first occupation to occupation at age 25 to 4.78 for mobility between ages 25 and 35. Mobility into farming without employees (class IVd) is extremely heavy at ages 25 and 35; it falls off for mobility between ages 35 and 45. Mobility into farming with employees (class IVc) has a complementary age pattern; it goes from moderately high at ages 25 and 35 to very high for mobility between ages 35 and 45.

Structural mobility drains the unpaid categories (classes VIIIf and VIIInf) as surely as it fills the ranks of self-employment. The force of negative structural mobility represented by the very small α_j coefficients is as strong as positive structural mobility into farm ownership (for example, for mobility from first occupation to occupation at age 25, $\log \alpha_{12} = 3.55$ and $\log \alpha_{13} = -3.45$).

Among wage and salary workers, structural mobility depends on prestige. The humble beginnings of these workers are reversed (to some extent) by life-cycle forces that favor upward mobility, regardless of origins. For mobility at each age, the α_j parameter for upper-grade professionals, managers, and proprietors (classes Ia,b) exceeds the other α_j while that for agricultural laborers (class VIIf) is the closest to zero. The α_j parameters for classes Ia,b and II are not as large as those for self-employment, but the coefficients for most occupational categories are strong—far greater than 1.0—relative to the corresponding parameters for intergenerational mobility (Tables 3.6 and 9.8).

The life cycle of clerical, sales, and service occupations (classes IIIa and IIIb) marks the only pronounced age dependence among paid occupations. This kind of routine white-collar work is common as a first occupation. Structural mobility between first occupation and age 25 puts strong downward pressure on both classes. If first occupation and occupation at age 25 were independent, this downward pressure would drain these occupations. They maintain high numbers because of high immobility. Structural mobility between ages 25 and 35 also fosters an outflow, but immobility is even stronger at this point. Positive structural mobility between ages 35 and 45 fails to promote more than a small amount of growth because immobility becomes even more important later in the life cycle.

Structural mobility for other kinds of paid employment varies only slightly with age. The upper nonmanual positions (combined class Ia,b) show a curvilinear pattern, but the first two parameter estimates are based on very few cases, so the differences are probably insignificant.[17] The α_j parameters for lower-grade professionals and managers (class II) change even less. The only manual occupations to show age variation are the technical and supervisory positions (class V). A slight net outflow for mobility from first occupation to occupation at age 25 is reversed for subsequent mobility. The net inflow due to structural mobility between ages 35 and 45 is relatively strong, reflecting the importance of bureaucratic advance.

Table 9.12 shows the association between earlier and later occupation over short spans of the life cycle. The δ_{ij} parameters reveal a very strong association—even stronger than the association between first and current occupation (Table 9.8). Immobility (Table 9.11) accounts for most of the strong association. Deleting the diagonal cells accounts for 84 percent of the total association between earlier and later occupation.[18] The rough correspondence between percentage immobile and structural mobility shows how the downward pressure of negative ($\alpha_j < 1$) structural mobility precludes the possibility of high immobility. The converse is not true; positive structural mobility does not guarantee high immobility. More important, the very low δ_{ij} parameters show that immobility would be even higher in the absence of structural mobility.

None of the δ_{ij} parameters are large enough to speak of "weak association," but exchange between some pairs of occupations is relatively high because of "somewhat weaker" association. The ten pairs with the highest δ_{ij} include most pairs of manual occupations (the combination of unskilled manual with technical/supervisory occupations is the exception), unskilled manual with farm labor, semiskilled manual with service, upper with lower-grade professional and managerial, and lower-grade professional and managerial with sales and clerical. These are all occupations that score close together on several of the dimensions important for overall mobility (Table 2.9), especially prestige, educational credentials, and (low) personal contact. They differ in their bureaucratic entry scores. Many pairs involve promotional relationships pairing an occupation high on bureaucratic entry with one high on bureaucratic advance.

Not all relatively high exchange comes from weak association. Exchange is the product of composition as well. Exchange mobility between occupation i and j is expressed as the product of the size parameter for occupation i (β_i), size of j (β_j), and association (δ_{ij}). Pairs of occupations that have relatively high rates of exchange because the product

Table 9.12

Association parameters (δ_{ij}) for conditional quasi–symmetry with homogeneous association for mobility from first job to occupation at age 25, occupation at age 25 to occupation at age 35, and occupation at age 35 to occupation at age 45: men aged 25–65, Ireland, 1973

$Origin^a$							$Destination^a$							
	Ia,b	II	IIIa	IVa,b	IIIb	VIIInf	V	VI	VIIss	VIIus	IVc	IVd	VIIIf	VIIf
Ia,b	1.00													
II	.10	1.00												
IIIa	.04	.10	1.00											
IVa,b	.01	.03	.04	1.00										
IIIb	.01	.04	.10	.04	1.00									
VIIInf	.01	.02	.06	.07	.05	1.00								
V	.02	.04	.05	.06	.06	.01	1.00							
VI	.02	.04	.04	.09	.07	.05	.14	1.00						
VIIss	.01	.03	.08	.04	.15	.06	.13	.20	1.00					
VIIus	.00	.01	.02	.02	.08	.02	.07	.14	.28	1.00				
IVc	.00	.01	.01	.01	.00	.01	.01	.01	.00	.00	1.00			
IVd	.00	.00	.00	.02	.01	.01	.00	.01	.01	.02	.02	1.00		
VIIIf	.00	.00	.01	.01	.02	.01	.01	.01	.02	.04	.05	.09	1.00	
VIIf	.00	.00	.01	.01	.03	.01	.02	.03	.08	.17	.01	.03	.05	1.00

a.   See Table 9.2 for category labels.

$\beta_i\beta_j$ is high are unpaid farm help with most manual occupations and service, most manual occupations with other manual occupations, and routine nonmanual occupations with manual occupations. Growth over the life cycle implies an asymmetry that is incompatible with the symmetry of exchange, association, and composition as they are defined under the SHD model. Accordingly, the growth of farming, self-employment, and professional and managerial employment comes from the one asymmetrical component of the model—structural mobility.

Career mobility thus has a number of aspects. Structural mobility leads to an increase in prestige and autonomy over the life cycle. Professional and managerial employment grow at a steady rate up through age 45. The growth of self-employment and farming on one's own accelerates early, then tapers off. Farming with employees emerges later—between ages 35 and 45—as does supervisory work. Manual labor and unpaid decline dramatically over the life course. For all declining occupations except unpaid farm helping, this erosion peaks early and diminishes somewhat by age 35. In contrast, the strongest structural outflow affects those few men left in unpaid farm help by age 35.

Most exchange mobility involves pairs of manual occupations. Some exchanges between unpaid farm help and manual occupations also occur, as do exchanges between routine nonmanual and manual occupations. For the most part, exchange mobility in midcareer is quite low because the association between occupational positions separated by only a decade is exceptionally strong. This strong association fosters unusually high rates of occupational immobility. Job shifts occur (an average of 4.3 between first occupation and occupation at age 45), but they do not necessarily involve a change of occupation (53 percent of job shifts result in an occupational change, mainly involving manual-to-manual occupations). Overall, the pattern of intragenerational mobility in Ireland arises from the interaction between the thrust of very strong structural mobility and the inertia of very strong association.

Direct and Indirect Effects of Origins

Social-class origins affect occupational success directly through inheritance, connections, and cultural resources, but they also have indirect effects through access to schooling, achievement aspirations, and other psychological factors (Hauser, Sewell, and Tsai 1983). This distinction has led to debate. Contention about the balance between direct and indirect

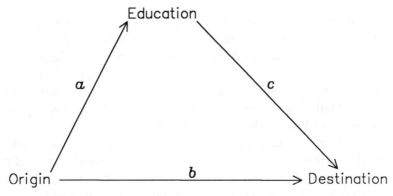

Figure 9.1 Path diagram for simple model relating origin and education to destination.

effects has focused on the role of the schools in social stratification for over two decades (Blau and Duncan 1967; Bowles and Levin 1968; Bowles 1972; Duncan 1972; Hauser et al. 1983): Do they reproduce the preexisting class structure (as represented by the social class backgrounds of their students), or do they introduce a variation in credentials which, while correlated with occupational destinations, is independent of occupational origins (Hope 1984)?

Indirect influences on occupational success were once less important than the direct influences of property, wealth, and position—at least in the United States (Featherman and Hauser 1978, p. 255) and England (Heath 1981, p. 169). Since the 1950s, however, indirect influences have drawn to parity with the direct ones. Blau and Duncan (1967, p. 430) call this trend "heightened universalism" and take note of the strategic part schools play in changing the balance of universalism and particularism in the stratification system of modern society:

> Superior status cannot any more be directly inherited but must be legitimated by actual achievements that are socially acknowledged. Education assumes increasing significance for social status in general and for the transmission of social standing from fathers to sons in particular. Superior family origins increase a son's chances of attaining superior occupational status in the United States in large part because they help him to obtain a better education.

The logic of this system of relationships can be seen in the schematic path diagram in Figure 9.1. A more realistic causal model would contain many more variables (e.g., Hauser et al. 1983), but the key elements are present in this simple diagram. The direct effect of origins on destinations is represented by the arrow labeled *b*. The indirect effect of origins on destinations via education is represented by the two arrows *a* and *c*. If weights are assigned to each of these effects in accord with the algebra of path analysis (Duncan 1966b), then the weight for the total effect (*T*) of origins on destinations is, according to Alwin and Hauser (1975): $T = b + ac$.

Six variables are analyzed here, in the same way as earlier: father's occupation, region, education, first job cohort, first occupation, and current occupation.[19] Four dimensions are identified for each of the occupational variables: prestige, educational qualifications, bureaucratic entry, and personal contact. Men younger than 25 are excluded.[20]

The statistical model is designed as a multinomial logit model with four covariates (Haberman 1979). It is a generalization of the multidimensional intergenerational mobility model. The expected number of men in current occupation *j* who have origin *i*, first job *k*, education *l*, cohort *m*, and region *h* is a log-linear function of the independent variables (origin [*O*], first job [*F*], education [*E*], cohort [*C*], and region [*R*]). The effects of first occupation and origins are constrained to be the sum of a set of linear-by-linear interaction terms that pertain to the four dimensions of interest. Main and diagonal effects are included. In a similar way, the effects of education on each dimension of current occupation are constrained to be the sum of a set of linear-by-linear interaction terms that cross the education category scores (Table 9.5) with each dimension of current occupation. Only main effects are defined for this relationship. Cohort and region are entered as dummy variables. Interaction effects for cohort or regional differences in the effects of occupational origins, first occupation, and education were included in preliminary runs, but these terms were not significant, so they are not reported here. The final model is (for $h = 1, 2; i = 1,\ldots, 16; j = 1,\ldots, 16; k = 1,\ldots, 16; l = 1,\ldots, 6; m = 1, 2, 3; p = 1,\ldots, 4$):

$$\log F_{hijklm} = \log (\alpha_j \beta_j) + \log (\tau_{hiklm}^{ROFEC}) + \Sigma_p \theta_{1p} \mu_l X_{pj} + \Sigma_p \theta_{2p} X_{pi} X_{pj}$$
$$+ \Sigma_p \theta_{3p} X_{pk} X_{pj} + \Sigma_p \delta_{2p} X_{pi} X_{pj} Z_{ij} + \Sigma_p \delta_{3p} X_{pk} X_{pj} Z_{kj}$$
$$+ \Sigma_p \tau_{1p}^R X_{pj} + \Sigma_p \tau_{2p}^C X_{pj} + \Sigma_p \tau_{3p}^C X_{pj} \qquad (9.1)$$

where $\alpha_j \beta_j$ fits the marginal distribution of destinations, τ_{hiklm}^{ROFEC} fits the five-way distribution among the independent variables, *p* indexes the dimensions of occupational mobility, θ_{1p} is the parameter for the general effect of education on current occupation, μ_l is the education score for category *l*,

X_{pj} is the score for current occupation on dimension p, θ_{2p} is the parameter for the general effect of origins on current occupation, X_{pi} is the score for father's occupation on dimension p, θ_{3p} is the parameter for the general effect of first occupation on current occupation, X_{pk} is the score for first occupation on dimension p, δ_{2p} is the parameter for the diagonal effect of origin on destination, Z_{ij} is a dummy variable that equals one if $i = j$ (zero otherwise), δ_{3p} is the parameter for the diagonal effect of first occupation on destination, Z_{kj} is a dummy variable that equals one if $k = j$ (zero otherwise), τ_{1p}^R is the parameter for the effect of region on destination dimension p (coded as the extent to which the mean on dimension p for the Republic exceeds that for Northern Ireland), and τ_{2p}^C and τ_{3p}^C measure the effect of cohort on dimension p (coded as the extent to which the mean on dimension p for cohorts 2 and 3 differs from that for the youngest cohort).[21]

Unfortunately, programming problems and limits to the storage capacity of the computers available for this research preclude estimating this model directly. However, as a linear-by-linear interaction model, equation (9.1) is related to a regression model (Haberman 1979). As a practical solution, ordinary least-squares coefficients from four separate multiple regression equations (one for each dimension p) are taken to be estimates of the θ, δ, and τ parameters of equation (9.1):

$$Y_{pt} = b_0 + b_{1p} X_{1t} + b_{2p} X_{2pt} + b_{3p} X_{3pt} + b_{4p} X_{2p} Z_{2t} + b_{5p} X_{3p} Z_{3t} + b_{6p} X_{4t} + b_{7p} X_{5t} + b_{8p} X_{6t} + e_{pt} \tag{9.2}$$

where Y_{pt} is the score on dimension p for respondent t on his current occupation; the b terms are OLS coefficients: b_{1p} for θ_{1p}, b_{2p} for θ_{2p}, b_{3p} for θ_{3p}, b_{4p} for δ_{2p}, b_{5p} for δ_{3p}, b_{6p} for τ_{1p}^R, b_{7p} for τ_{2p}^C, and b_{8p} for τ_{3p}^C; X_{1t} is the μ score for respondent t; X_{2pt} is the origin score on dimension p for respondent t; X_{3pt} is the first occupation score on dimension p for respondent t; Z_{2t} is a dummy variable equal to one if origin and destination are the same for respondent t (zero otherwise); Z_{3t} is a dummy variable equal to one if first occupation and destination are the same for respondent t (zero otherwise); X_{4t} is a dummy variable equal to one if respondent t lives in the Republic (zero otherwise); X_{5t} is a dummy variable equal to one if respondent t first worked 1945–1958; X_{6t} is a dummy variable equal to one if respondent t first worked 1959–1973; and e_{pt} is an error term. This model has the advantage of being easy to use. It has the disadvantage of statistical inconsistency. A respondent's scores on all four dimensions are fixed by his being in destination j. That information does not enter the model. Despite the disadvantage, coefficients from equation (9.2) are the best estimates currently available of the parameters of equation (9.1).

The parameters of equation (9.1) and the corresponding coefficients in equation (9.2) are estimates of the direct effects of education, origins, (general and diagonal), first occupation (general and diagonal), region, and cohort—the *b* components of Figure 9.1. To compute indirect effects—the *ac* components—additional regressions were run, successively dropping intermediate terms from equation (9.2) (Alwin and Hauser 1975). For example, the indirect effects of education, origins, region, and cohort through first occupation are obtained by taking the difference between the coefficients of equation (9.2) and those of a similar equation that excludes first occupation. The coefficients of such a pared-down equation are the sum of direct and indirect effects. The differences between coefficients from equation (9.2) and those from the pared-down equation are estimates of the *ac* terms. In the same way, the indirect effects of origins, region, and cohort through education are obtained by excluding education from equation (9.2) and taking the differences between total effects and direct effects.

Twelve versions of equation (9.2) were fit, three for each dimension. The first regression in each dimension includes three independent variables: origins, cohort, and region. The second regression adds education as an independent variable; the third adds first occupation as an independent variable. Table 9.13 shows the unstandardized coefficients from these regressions; Table 9.14 shows the decompositions of these coefficients into direct and indirect effects.

Advantaged social origins promote success through positive total effects on each occupational dimension (see the first regression of each set of three in Table 9.13). Men from prestigious origins attain prestige. Men from origins that require a higher level of educational qualifications are more likely to get into those kinds of positions. Having a father who worked in an entry-level position is a disadvantage that increases a man's odds on entry-level work himself. Fathers working in jobs where personal contacts are important provides the needed contact for their sons, promoting intergenerational immobility.

These positive total effects do not constitute evidence of reproduction of social classes in the sense of Bourdieu (1977). The total effects, while obviously greater than zero, are also substantially less than one.[22] Regresssion to the mean on a scale as great as a coefficient of about one-third constitutes far more openness than the deterministic mechanisms of

Table 9.13
Regression of dimensions of current occupation on first occupation, education, father's occupation, region, and first job cohort: men aged 25–65, Ireland, 1973 (N=4379)

Variable	Prestige			Educational qualification			Bureaucratic entry			Personal contact		
	1	2	3	1	2	3	1	2	3	1	2	3
First occupation												
Main	—	—	.444[a]	—	—	.317[a]	—	—	.293[a]	—	—	.194[a]
Diagonal	—	—	-.115[a]	—	—	.035[a]	—	—	.176[a]	—	—	.510[a]
Education[b]	—	.165[a]	.125[a]	—	.316[a]	.227[a]	—	-.023[a]	-.047[a]	—	-.106[a]	-.055[a]
Father's occupation												
Main	.378[a]	.216[a]	.177[a]	.453[a]	.255[a]	.183[a]	.376[a]	.375[a]	.196[a]	.334[a]	.303[a]	.096[a]
Diagonal	.038[a]	.055[a]	.053[a]	-.044[a]	-.034[a]	-.044[a]	.136[a]	.134[a]	.100[a]	.425[a]	.409[a]	.375[a]
Job cohort												
1919–44	—	—	—	—	—	—	—	—	—	—	—	—
1945–58	3.407[a]	.434	.701	6.929[a]	2.049[a]	1.351	-1.188	-.748	-1.138	-.797	.967	.040
1959–73	2.002[a]	-4.799[a]	-3.561[a]	9.684[a]	-2.186[a]	-2.777[a]	2.216[a]	3.198[a]	1.436[a]	2.512[a]	6.574[a]	1.847[a]
Region												
Republic	-1.480[a]	-1.195[a]	-.996[a]	-3.879[a]	-4.487[a]	-3.990[a]	-2.510[a]	-2.569[a]	-1.485[a]	3.779[a]	3.844[a]	1.534[a]
N. Ireland	—	—	—	—	—	—	—	—	—	—	—	—
Constant	24.732	39.814	25.242	29.236	54.203	39.280	23.352	22.144	14.950	9.365	4.862	4.333
R^2	.146	.321	.387	.228	.390	.454	.237	.238	.347	.367	.397	.657
σ_e	12.490	11.137	10.572	22.872	20.332	19.238	17.682	17.664	16.357	17.132	16.719	12.616
σ_y	13.510			26.018			20.226			21.524		
Mean	40.780			50.041			35.061			26.786		

a. Coefficients significant at the .05 level.
b. Education coefficients have been divided by 100 in order to present more significant digits.

Table 9.14
Decomposition of effects of dimensions of origins on
current occupation and first occupation into direct and indirect effects:
men aged 25–65, Ireland, 1973

Dimension	Total effect[a] b	Indirect effects via: Education b	%	Occupation b	%	Direct effect[b] b	%
Prestige							
Main	.378	.162	43	.039	10	.177	47
Diagonal	.038	−.017	−45	.002	5	.053	139
Educational qualifications							
Main	.453	.198	44	.072	16	.183	40
Diagonal	−.044	−.010	23	.010	−23	−.044	100
Bureaucratic entry							
Main	.376	.001	0	.179	48	.196	52
Diagonal	.136	.002	0	.034	25	.100	74
Personal contact							
Main	.334	.031	9	.207	62	.096	29
Diagonal	.425	.016	4	.034	8	.375	88
Education[c] affecting:							
Prestige	.165	—	—	.040	24	.125	76
Qualifications	.316	—	—	.089	28	.227	72
Entry	−.023	—	—	.024	−104	−.047	204
Contact	−.106	—	—	−.051	48	−.055	52
Region[d] affecting:							
Prestige	−1.480	−.285	19	−.199	13	−.996	67
Qualifications	−3.879	.608	−16	−.497	13	−3.990	103
Entry	−2.510	.059	−2	−1.084	43	1.485	59
Contact	3.779	−.065	−2	2.310	61	1.534	41

a. Controlling for cohort and region.
b. Controlling for cohort, region, education, and first occupation.
c. Education coefficients have been divided by 100 to accommodate more significant digits.
d. A positive coefficient indicates that the Republic has a higher value.

reproduction imply. Mobility in Ireland is more constrained than mobility elsewhere, but Irish social structure is not in any sense of the term closed or devoid of opportunity. Social origins affect men's careers without determining them.

Between half and three-fifths of the total effects of the vertical dimensions of origin—prestige and educational qualifications—are mediated by education and first job placement. Slightly over two-fifths of the total effects of these dimensions pass through to current occupations via social inequalities in individual educational attainment and the subsequent effects of education on occupational success. The mediating effect of first job placement does not amount to as much as one-fifth of the total effect.

Indirect effects of origins on destinations ranked by prestige or socioeconomic status in other countries also tend to be in the half-to-three-fifths range (Heath 1981, p. 140). The higher total effect of origins on destinations (within the vertical dimensions) for Ireland appears to be due to the compound effects of a slightly greater social inequality in the access to higher education, a slightly higher return to education, and a slightly stronger direct effect of origins on destinations.

The causal process for nonvertical dimensions of occupational placement operates differently than the vertical system does. Education has direct, negative effects on destinations in nonvertical dimensions, but father's entry-level status has no effect on educational attainment; neither does his access to personal contacts.[23] As a consequence, the educational system does not mediate intergenerational persistence in entry-level employment or personal contact. First job placement is extremely important for intergenerational inequality on these dimensions, accounting for half of the total effect of entry-level origins on entry-level destinations and two-thirds of the general effect of personal contact over the generation.

For three of the four dimensions, diagonal effects are relatively small but significant. The chances of intergenerational immobility increase with prestige and bureaucracy; they decrease with rising educational demands.[24] These effects are not mediated by education or first occupation; they are at least 75 percent direct. In fact, part of the effect of prestige on immobility is masked by education—the net effect in column 2 exceeds the total effect in column 1.

Immobility depends, for the most part, on personal contacts. The diagonal effect of this dimension of social origins actually exceeds its main effect by 27 percent. Education and first job placement do not mediate it. In those segments of the occupational structure where the personal imperative remains an important element of doing business—in self-employment and farming—the formal labor market with its reliance on credentials and career lines does not hold sway. As the composition of the Irish labor force continues to move away from these traditional, small-scale operations, more and more of the overall effect of origins on destinations, pooling all dimensions together, will pass through education. For now, though, immobility fostered by personal contacts remains an important component of social inequality. Ireland is far from unique in the importance of direct immobility for access to self-employment and farming. Throughout Western Europe and the United States about the only way to get into farming is to be born on a farm. This shows up as high net immobility for farmers' sons in these countries (e.g., Erikson and Goldthorpe 1987a). But in most of these countries, farming is a much smaller part of the whole labcr force than it is in Ireland. Because of this compositional difference, immobility in farming contributes less to overall social inequality elsewhere than it does in Ireland.

Education mediates a large proportion of the total effects of the vertical dimensions of origins because it affects prestige and access to occupations that require credentials. The peculiar nature of the μ scores used for education hides some of the strength of the education effect. The μ scores have a range from $-.75$ (primary education only) to $.57$ (complete third-level education or postgraduate degree). Knowing that a one-point change in μ score results in a 16.5-point change in prestige is less informative than it might be, since a one-point change in μ score requires a rather dramatic increase in education. Compare instead the differences between adjacent educational categories in expected prestige. The μ-score gap between primary and nonacademic secondary is $.59$ $[-.75 - (-.16)]$, so the difference between these two educational categories in expected prestige (all else held constant) is 9.74 $[.59 (16.5)]$ points on the Hope-Goldthorpe scale. Roughly ten prestige points separate each of the skill levels among manual occupations; another ten points separate technical and supervisory occupations from skilled occupations. The μ-score gap between complete academic secondary education and complete third-level education (a two-category jump) is $.37$, which translates into an expected prestige difference of 6.11 points—roughly half the difference between service and clerical work or two-thirds the difference between lower and upper salaried professions.

The effect of education on overall social standing combines its effect on prestige with its effect on access to occupations that select men with higher educational credentials. The effect of education on the educational qualifications dimension of current occupation is about twice its effect on prestige, so the returns to education are doubly compounded by this effect. The gap between primary and nonacademic secondary education is 18.6 points on the qualifications scale, an amount somewhat greater than the average difference in the proportion of workers with more than primary education between adjacent skill levels among manual workers. The comparison between complete academic secondary schooling and a university education yields an 11.7-point gap—three times the gap between the educational qualification score for clerical occupations and upper-grade professions.

First job placement mediates a modest amount of these total effects. In all, the direct effect of educational attainment on prestige and educational qualifications exceeds the indirect effect via first occupation by a three-to-one margin.

Men with higher education are less likely to work in entry-level occupations than are other men. When cohort is controlled, more highly educated men have destination positions that require promotion or recruitment. The cohort control is important, because the higher educational attainment of men who first worked since 1959 is somewhat negated by their youth at the time of the survey.

Investment in formal education makes men less dependent on informal contacts than are men who lack credentials. Therefore, it is not surprising that men with high education are less likely to work in occupations that require personal contacts.

Men in the Republic have lower average prestige and educational qualifications than do men in Northern Ireland. They are less likely to enter their occupations through bureaucratic means than are men from the North, and they are more likely to use personal contacts. One-fifth of the lower prestige of men from the Republic is a consequence of their lower educational attainment; one-eighth stems from their lower-prestige first jobs. Education actually masks a portion of the advantage Northern men have in obtaining jobs which require educational credentials; first jobs contribute an eighth to the association between region and current occupations. Two-fifths of the regional difference in bureaucratic entry is indirect via first occupations (education does not mediate this effect). Three-fifths of the higher rate of personal contact in the Republic comes from entering the informal labor market at the time of the first job.

Cohort differences reflect both period and life cycle. The more recent cohorts have higher prestige because of their higher education. Once education is controlled, the life cycle differences appear, showing that young men have less prestige than older men. The pattern of relationships involving educational qualifications is very similar. Education actually masks some of the higher entry-level employment among young men. Their higher exposure to personal contacts is inconsistent with their higher education (thus the increase in the effect of cohort once education is controlled), but about two-thirds of that effect is attributable to their closeness to their first jobs.

The prospects of interaction between region and origins, region and education, cohort and origins, and cohort and education were tested by using product interaction terms. In no instance were any of the effects significant. This result, though surprising, is consistent with the lack of regional and cohort interactions.

Conclusion

Examination of the socioeconomic life cycle from school to first job to employment at midlife reinforces the earlier conclusions about Irish social structure. There are substantial variations in the *strength* of association between earlier and later positions in the social structure, but there are few real differences in the *pattern* of that association. That is, comparison of the δ_{ij} parameters for the association between origins and current occupation with the δ_{ij} parameters for the association between first occupation and occupation at age 25 shows that, for each pair (i,j), the δ_{ij} for intergenerational mobility is greater than the δ_{ij} for intragenerational mobility. This is the difference in the strength of association. When the ratio of the δ_{ij} parameter for one pair of occupations to the $\delta_{i'j'}$ association parameter for some other pair of occupations for one table is compared to $\delta_{ij} / \delta_{i'j'}$ for some other table, the ratios show little table-to-table variation. This is the similarity in the pattern of association.[25]

The intragenerational association between earlier and later social standing is stronger than intergenerational association. Time also attenuates association; the longer the time lapse between earlier and later occupations, the weaker the association. From the comparison of mobility between ages 25 and 35 with mobility between ages 35 and 45, it appears that the overall rate of job shifting declines over the life cycle. This relative inertia among older men means that the association between occupations at one point and at another point ten years later is stronger if the initial point is late rather than early in a worker's career. This conclusion may not be completely reliable in repeated samples, as there is some evidence that differences in association by age are chance fluctuations around a single population value.

Countermobility, or three-step movement from a class of origin to some other class and back again, contributes some degree of articulation to the socioeconomic life cycles of Irishmen. Men who are downwardly mobile from origins to first job are particularly likely to be countermobile. This asymmetry is important because it modifies what the originators of the concept saw as the implications of countermobility for social inequality. Bernard and Renaud (1976; quoted in Goldthorpe 1980), the originators of this concept, expressed concern that a high rate of countermobility could mask substantial social inequality. In particular, they thought of the potentially dire consequences of high countermobility in a stable labor market in which neither the number of desirable positions nor the pool of workers was changing. In conditions of absolute stability, every move upward that returned a man to the desirable class of his origins would necessitate a reciprocal downward move of another man. If those with disadvantaged origins were disproportionately selected for downward mobility, then the same changes that returned worker A to his origins through upward mobility would be returning worker B to his origins through downward mobility. Of course, absolute stability does not occur in real societies. A case in point is the industrial growth of the 1959–1973 period in Ireland. That growth produced thousands of new jobs in manufacturing and services. The newly created positions had a higher average social standing than did the traditional positions. In this way job creation made possible upward mobility for some workers that entailed no reciprocal movement downward. Not only does the distribution of positions change through job creation (and redundancy), but the composition of the labor force also changes continuously. Some men move out of the labor force through death and retirement, while others enter through such moves as school leaving and migration. In age-graded systems such as that in Ireland, age and status are positively correlated. The departure of older men leaves behind high-status vacancies that can be filled from below by advancing men from the next cohort (White 1970). If the advancers were disproportionately drawn from among the workers with advantaged origins, then upward countermobility would be accompanied by an exit from the labor pool rather than by reciprocal downward mobility.

Countermobility in Ireland combines both forms of instability: instability due to job creation and instability due to cohort replacement. The result is a high rate of upward countermobility without much downward countermobility. The upshot is that workers from advantaged origins experience substantial movement over their work lives. They move downward to their first occupations and then upward over the years until they return to their classes of origin. Workers from disadvantaged origins rarely experience the reciprocal pattern of upward mobility that lasts until some son of a well-to-do father comes along to shoulder them back down to the lower class. Historical forces of structural mobility and transhistorical life-cycle factors combine to minimize downward countermobility.

Persistent low status comes about through total immobility, seldom through a pernicious pattern of thwarted upward mobility. Those men over 35 years old from lower-working-class backgrounds whose current occupations involve little in the way of either skills or rewards typically are the workers left behind after most of their cohort has moved onward and upward. Born into that class, they do not move upward in their first job or in subsequent job shifts. The Irish Mobility Study uncovered a kernel of marginal workers from disadvantaged backgrounds whose first and current positions are perhaps best described as "underclass." Of the 30 percent of men of lower manual origins who are immobile at age 35, approximately half are marginally employed in unskilled occupations. They are exposed to substantial risks of unemployment, and they lack the skills needed to advance in the modern sectors of the Irish economies.

As in other countries, educational attainment works for and against social inequality at the same time. Higher education fosters upward mobility for men of disadvantaged backgrounds and secures the higher-status positions of those with advantaged backgrounds. Lack of educational credentials seals the fate of the underclass while diminishing the chances for countermobility on the part of a man from an upper-middle-class background who fails to get an academic education.

The link between educational credentials and occupational success in the more formal, more universalistic, and more modern segments of the Irish economies might be expected to be more direct or stronger than the link between education and occupation in the more traditional segments of the island's economies. Surprisingly, this is not the case. Recent increases in educational attainments in both parts of Ireland have exposed substantial portions of younger cohorts to the prospects of occupational mismatch or the kinds of labor squeeze that reduce the rate of return on human capital investment. However, mismatch and declining rates of return have failed to materialize. Nor has a shrinking outlook for lifetime mobility hampered men of working-class origins, contrary to the expectations of the "counterbalance" thesis.

Finally, the life-cycle mobility in Ireland contradicts notions of class reproduction through the schools. The key variable of cultural capital fails to account for inequalities in educational outcome. Although the schools mediate between origins and destinations, most intergenerational inequality comes about through the direct link between the social standing of origins and destinations or through the effect of origins on the social standing of the first job.

10 The Microdynamics of Industrialization

The lives of the men interviewed in the Irish Mobility Study span the era of most vigorous economic growth in Irish history. The economies of the Republic of Ireland and Northern Ireland expanded at an average of 4 percent per annum. Output grew in manufacturing, services, and agriculture. The patterns of structural mobility in Northern Ireland and the Republic reflect many of these trends.

Industrialization and Mobility

Industrialization has a number of real and supposed effects on occupational mobility. Despite methodological cautions (Duncan 1966a) theory has long treated the relationship between economic development and mobility as fundamental (Smelser and Lipset 1966). The most prevalent hypothesis proposes that economic growth:

Increases overall rates of mobility
Decreases the practice of occupational inheritance
Increases the dissimilarity between the origins of contemporary workers
    and the distribution of available positions
Increases the importance of education as a criterion for sorting individuals
    into occupational roles
Decreases cross-national differences in rates of occupational mobility

Research to date has produced mixed results regarding the thesis of industrialism. On the one hand, cross-national differences in mobility are in some ways consistent with the thesis (Lipset and Bendix 1959; Cutright 1968; Hazelrigg 1974; Erikson et al. 1978, 1982; Tyree et al. 1979; Raftery 1983; Grusky and Hauser 1984; Simkus 1985). Additional evidence has appeared in repeated cross-sections for some countries (e.g., Rogoff 1953a; Featherman and Hauser 1978, pp. 135–138, 199–216; Hout 1984a,b). On the other hand, all such findings are the subject of some debate. Contrary evidence has been found in the same data and in other data—sometimes by the same investigators. Although few researchers continue to press the claims of Lipset and Zetterberg (1956) that mobility rates are constant throughout the industrial world or over long periods of time, many claim that the underlying structures of occupational opportunities, indexed by the association between origins and destinations, are constant (Rogoff 1953b; Duncan 1966; Hauser et al. 1975a,b; Goldthorpe et al. 1978; Goldthorpe 1980); that cross-national variations in mobility rates are likewise attributable to cross-national variations in the difference between origin and destination distributions (Featherman, Jones, and Hauser 1975; Hazelrigg and Garnier 1976; Hardy and Hazelrigg 1978; McClendon 1980; Erikson et al. 1982, 1983; Grusky and Hauser 1984); that there is little correlation between industrialization and patterns of net mobility (Hazelrigg and Garnier 1976; Hardy and Hazelrigg 1978; Grusky and Hauser 1984); or that factors other than industrialization are crucial for temporal or cross-national variation in mobility (Heath 1981, pp. 206–210; Erikson et al. 1983; Grusky and Hauser 1984; Simkus 1984, 1985).

Presumably the contradictions could be resolved in part with some combination of better data and more powerful statistical techniques. But aggregate data, whether in the form of cross-national comparisons or repeated cross-sectional replications, are inherently limited. Even if the questions about cross-national and temporal variation in mobility rates could be resolved, a disjunction between theory and research would remain, because these studies address the question indirectly. Research to date shows how mobility rates may differ for countries at different levels of industrialization and how they may change over time for aggregate labor markets. What is lacking is continuous-time studies that track individuals as industrialization alters the array of occupational opportunities and barriers before them. Most prior research provides repeated snapshots of societies at different stages of economic development. The time series research that does exist analyzes data for postindustrial societies (e.g., Carroll and Mayer 1986). But to understand the effect of industrialization on occupational mobility, we must observe directly the job changes that constitute industrialization.

Continuous time studies are rare largely because the requisite data are lacking. The critical decades of rapid industrialization have passed for the northern and western countries that host most of the research. Although historians' studies of cities and counties have reconstructed some of what went before, these studies are not definitive (e.g., Thernstrom 1964, 1973; Thernstrom and Sennett 1969; Knights 1971; Sewell 1976, 1985; Sharlin 1979; Aminzade 1981). Among the problems in the historical studies are a sample selection bias in favor of the occupationally immobile, a high sample attrition over time, and the lack of a consistent methodology for determining which changes are due to industrialization and which are due to other factors.

In contrast with most available data, the Irish Mobility Study provides first-hand data on the job changes that constitute the industrialization process at the individual level. These data are superior to those in other national studies because they refer to mobility during a period of rapid industrialization and because they include complete work histories for a representative sample of the civilian labor force. This data set also has advantages over the historical time series because the work histories are continuous, a national population is sampled, and selection biases are absent.

The patterns of intragenerational mobility, as well as the timing and destination of each job shift, are analyzed continuously throughout the 1959–1973 period of macroeconomic change. The contribution of these job shifts to *inter*generational mobility is monitored by a technique that distinguishes between moves that lead to greater inequality of opportunity (countermobility) and moves that lead to greater equality (mobility). This analysis requires the development of new statistical estimators. In particular, it entails a synthesis of models of rates in event histories (e.g., Tuma and Hannan 1984) with parametric models of cross-sectional mobility tables. These models view rates of mobility between pairs of occupations as a function of a small number of parameters that relate characteristics of individuals, of occupations, and of historical time to the unobserved rate of mobility. If the industrialization thesis is correct, then historical time will affect mobility rates, independent of changes in the characteristics that individuals bring to the labor market.

Gross Mobility, 1959–1973

The economic takeoff in the Republic of Ireland dates from the economic development plan of 1958, first implemented in 1959. The point of studying microdynamics is to trace individuals as they move through static or, in this case, dynamic social structure. Appendix Tables A.7 and A.8 present the outline of these movements, cross-tabulating men according to their 1959 occupation (if they were at work), their 1973 occupation, and their region in 1973. This cross-tabulation shows how the occupational distributions in both the Republic of Ireland and Northern Ireland changed and how individual moves contributed to those changes. The most striking element of this intertemporal mobility is the clustering of cases on the diagonal. Remarkable individual stasis underlies an era of impressive macrochange. The impression garnered from mobility between 1959 and 1973 is that the vast majority of Irish workers pursued the same occupations throughout the era.

The interaction of career dynamics, cohort succession, and structural change produced the combination of low personal mobility and high net change for the occupational structures of both the Irish Republic and Northern Ireland. Career dynamics prove to be important because the majority of the men at work in 1959 were not in a position to take advantage of the changing economy. Most workers were too committed to careers that were constrained by the grim economic conditions of the 1950s. Many of those workers who were in desperate straits had already gone to England by the time the governments of the Republic and Northern Ireland moved to improve employment prospects. Indeed, these governmental policies were framed less as a means to improve the lot of the underemployed than as an effort to keep the next cohort at home in Ireland.

In that policy context, cohort succession becomes highly important. Evidence of change may well lie not in the comparison of different points in individuals' careers but in the comparison of the overall careers of individuals who began work at different times. The issue of cohort succession shows up on and off the farm. For example, the evidence of diminished farm succession overwhelms the evidence of farm failure. Fewer farmers' sons from recent cohorts entered farming upon leaving school. This is extremely meaningful because of the close link between an agricultural first job and the odds on ever being a farmer. For farmers' sons who began their work lives in agriculture, the odds on becoming a farmer did not vary much from the 1920s to the 1970s. For farmers' sons who began their work lives outside of agriculture, the chances of ever becoming a farmer were virtually zero in every decade. These results apply as well to men of non-farm origins.

The first hints of the importance of cohort succession for understanding the 1959–1973 period are found in Tables A.7 and A.8 in the rows labeled "too young." These rows show the distribution of 1973 occupations for men who took their first jobs after 1959. The readily apparent presence of men in white-collar and skilled occupations (relative to the distribution of occupations for older cohorts) and the offsetting shortfall in the agricultural and unskilled categories speak to important differences between this younger cohort and its predecessors.

Table 10.1 tabulates marginal distributions of intertemporal mobility in percentage form. It shows the 1959 and 1973 occupational distributions for workers who first worked prior to 1959 and the 1973 distribution for the cohort that was "too young," namely, men who took their first job after 1959. In addition to these percentages, Table 10.1 contains the structural mobility coefficients (log α_j; see Sobel et al. 1985).[1]

The differences between 1959 and 1973 occupations for men at work in both years underscore the importance of career dynamics for those men who already had jobs at the onset of macrochange in Ireland. Life-cycle factors actually dominate the period effects. Several hallmarks of the life cycle are present here. First of all, self-employment increased rapidly. Proprietors, self-employed professionals, and farmers make up a larger share of this cohort's work force in 1973 than they did fourteen years earlier. All but one of the log α_j coefficients for categories of self-employment are positive. Second, employment in positions of authority is also up. Management and supervisory employment grows while routine nonmanual employment in clerical, sales, and service jobs declines. Mobility from lower professional and managerial positions to higher ones exceeds the reverse flow by a margin of nearly three-to-one in both the Republic and Northern Ireland; upward mobility from clerical and sales to lower-grade managerial positions exceeds comparable downward mobility by a five-to-one margin; mobility from skilled and semiskilled manual jobs to supervisory positions exceeds downward mobility by better than two-to-one; the same excess of upward over downward mobility holds for moves between unskilled manual and skilled manual positions; and a fair amount of movement occurs from skilled manual jobs to proprietorships (and almost no reverse movement). These points are reiterated by the differences between appropriate pairs of log α_j coefficients. The only exceptions to career advancement patterns are in the balance between upward and downward moves of one skill level within the manual stratum. Both career dynamics and economic growth would be expected to favor more skilled

Table 10.1

Occupation in 1959 and 1973 and structural mobility coefficients (log α_j) for mobility between 1959 and 1973 for men first employed before 1959 and occupation in 1973 for later job cohorts by region: Ireland, 1959–1973

	Republic				Northern Ireland			
	1908–58		log	1959–73	1908–58		log	1959–73
Occupation	1959	1973	α_j	1973	1959	1973	α_j	1973
Professionals & proprietors I[a]	.4%	1.2%	3.4	1.0%	1.0%	1.5%	2.3	.6%
Professionals & managers I	2.8	4.3	1.7	5.8	3.4	5.5	1.9	6.3
Professionals & managers II	4.9	7.2	1.2	10.8	6.1	9.3	1.3	13.1
Clerical & sales workers	5.0	3.2	-.5	9.7	5.8	4.7	.3	8.4
Proprietors with employees[a]	1.8	5.4	2.3	1.9	3.2	6.2	1.8	4.3
Proprietors without employees[a]	3.2	4.2	.4	2.6	2.8	4.8	1.4	2.4
Service workers	4.1	3.2	-.9	4.9	4.6	3.8	-.2	3.5
Unpaid helpers, nonfarm	1.7	.3	-2.1	2.3	1.4	.2	-1.9	.8
Technicians & foremen	4.8	6.0	-.1	8.3	7.6	8.4	.1	7.5
Skilled manual workers	13.6	11.0	-.8	18.3	18.8	15.8	-.5	22.7
Semiskilled manual workers	12.8	13.4	-.6	10.8	18.2	17.9	-.5	16.5
Unskilled manual workers	11.2	8.3	-1.3	7.3	9.8	7.0	-1.0	6.4
Farmers with employees[a]	2.7	5.3	1.5	1.3	1.5	3.3	1.0	1.7
Farmers without employees[a]	12.0	21.6	1.3	3.6	6.2	8.5	-.0	1.5
Unpaid helpers, farm	11.8	1.5	-3.2	7.8	5.7	.9	-3.2	2.9
Farm laborers	7.3	3.6	-2.3	3.7	3.9	2.1	-3.0	1.4
Total	100.0	100.0	—	100.0	100.0	100.0	—	100.0
Valid cases	1531	1455	—	618	1622	1522	—	655
Not at work	69	144	—	73	55	155	—	82

a.   Self–employed workers.

over less skilled positions, so the near parity of upward and downward mobility within the Irish working class is a somewhat surprising exception to a pattern that otherwise shows a strong career dynamics effect.

The existence of temporal effects is difficult to discern in the presence of such strong career dynamics effects. On the one hand, the clear movement of men *into* farming questions the efficacy of economic development effects identified with industrialization and the decline of agriculture. On the other hand, perhaps the observed movement falls short of the potential movement. Farming could grow because of career dynamics effects even in the face of a substantial economic development effect that was distributing agricultural workers into other sectors. If some men employed in paid or unpaid agricultural labor continued to make the transition into self-employed farming at the same time that other men, who might otherwise follow this traditional course, moved out of agriculture, then farming could grow while agriculture as a whole declined. Agricultural labor, paid and unpaid, dropped between 1959 and 1973 in both the Republic and Northern Ireland. If some of the decline were due to economic development luring workers away from agriculture, then it would be evident in the detailed flows of Tables A.7–A.8. The evidence does not favor the economic development argument. Among unpaid family members assisting on farms, an average of 85 percent of job changers stayed in agriculture, mainly by taking over a farm. More movement away from agriculture is evident among paid farm workers, but it is nearly balanced by the counterflow *into* farming by some manual workers. The upshot is that the proportion of the 1908–1958 cohort engaged in agriculture fell only two percentage points between 1959 and 1973. The phenomenal growth of the period probably boosted the standard of living of these workers, but it did not move them out of agriculture. The intragenerational mobility of the 1959–1973 period resulted from structural mobility, but that structural mobility was not dominated by macroeconomic change. The dynamics of the life cycle determined these shifts.

Although intracohort comparisons reveal little change that might be interpreted as evidence of economic development effects, the comparison between the occupational distributions of the pre-1959 and post-1959 cohorts suggests that economic development conditioned the career beginnings of the more recent cohort. Men who began work between 1959 and the interview date were concentrated in professional, technical, and skilled positions. Unskilled, unpaid, and agricultural work was less common for recent entrants to the work force.

Exact comparisons across cohorts are confounded by the same career dynamics effects that disturbed the intracohort comparisons. In an effort to control for career dynamics, Table 10.2 tabulates workers according to first jobs, cohort, and location of first job. Because 4 percent of workers took their first jobs in England and subsequently returned to Ireland, an English column supplements the usual regional breakdown in this table. The first concern is agriculture. Table 10.2 confirms the evidence that the most recent cohort is on a trajectory that will lead it away from farming as a way of life. Farming is a rare first job in all cohorts, but most farmers start out in paid or unpaid agricultural labor. Employment in these typical agricultural first jobs (paid and unpaid) dropped by more than 50 percent in both the Republic and Northern Ireland. The decline clearly began prior to 1959, as the proportion working in agricultural first jobs for members of the 1945–1958 cohort falls between the proportions for the preceding and succeeding cohorts.

Increases that compensate for the decreasing employment in agriculture were spread throughout the wage and salary sector of the work force. Between the first and second cohorts employment in clerical, sales, skilled manual, and semiskilled manual jobs increased significantly in both regions. In the Republic service employment also increased; in Northern Ireland professional, managerial, technical, and supervisory employment increased. Between the second and third cohorts, increases in professional, managerial, clerical, sales, and unskilled manual employment offset the falling agricultural employment in both regions. In the Republic technical and supervisory employment increased; in the North skilled manual employment further increased. Semiskilled manual employment actually decreased in both regions.

These comparisons demonstrate the importance of cohort succession for the relationship between economic development and mobility. To the extent that economic development affected mobility in Ireland, it did so by influencing career beginnings. From there, career dynamics appear to have followed a path that varied little from cohort to cohort. Whereas one perspective on career dynamics emphasizes the lasting effects of first jobs, a different perspective emphasizes the sequence and timing aspects of career. This perspective provides additional opportunities to investigate the prospect that economic development affects mobility in ways that are invisible to the gross mobility analysis.

Table 10.2
First occupation by job cohort and region: men aged 18–65, Ireland, 1973

Occupation	Republic			Northern Ireland			England
	1922–1944	1945–1958	1959–1973	1922–1944	1945–1958	1959–1973	All cohorts
Professionals proprietors I[a]	.1%	.0%	.0%	.0%	.3%	.5%	.6%
Professionals & managers I	1.1	1.6	2.9	.8	2.2	4.1	9.3
Profesionals & managers II	1.7	3.1	5.3	1.6	2.8	6.0	6.8
Clerical & sales workers	3.3	7.6	10.4	4.7	7.7	10.0	9.3
Proprietors with employees[a]	.1	.2	.0	.1	.2	.5	.0
Proprietors without employees[a]	.4	.7	.2	.3	.0	.5	.6
Service workers	3.9	10.2	10.5	8.8	9.9	10.6	9.9
Unpaid helpers, nonfarm	2.0	4.4	3.2	3.1	3.2	.9	.0
Technicians & foremen	2.0	4.4	7.5	3.1	8.4	6.6	6.2
Skilled manual workers	8.9	13.1	14.7	14.0	17.7	24.1	16.8
Semiskilled manual workers	9.5	12.8	9.7	19.7	16.7	14.2	18.0
Unskilled manual workers	7.6	6.7	9.4	10.1	7.4	9.7	14.9
Farmers with employees[a]	.4	.7	.0	.3	.0	.3	.0
Farmers without employees[a]	1.0	.7	.2	.9	.3	.3	.0
Unpaid helpers, farm	38.3	23.8	16.9	18.2	14.2	8.1	1.9
Farm laborers	19.5	10.0	9.1	14.2	9.0	3.6	5.6
Total	100.0	100.0	100.0	100.0	100.0	100.0	100.0
Valid cases	892	609	617	921	598	632	161
Index of dissimilarity between cohorts	—	25.5	33.6	—	16.2	29.5	—

a.   Self–employed workers.

Net Mobility

The focus on gross mobility is typical of the literature on the industrialism thesis. Every study of industrialization and mobility analyzes an intergenerational or intragenerational mobility table as a discrete time process. Discrete time analyses systematically understate the volume of occupational mobility by confining the measurement of mobility to the beginning and ending points of a continuous process. For example, case 246 in the Irish Mobility Study is a man who changed jobs eleven times between 1959 and 1973.[2] His case illustrates the limitations of the discrete time perspective because, despite his considerable mobility, his job on 1 January 1959 and his job on the day he was interviewed in November 1973 were both coded as semiskilled manual (class VIIss), making him one of the "immobile" cases in Table 10.1. Between 1959 and 1973 he had jobs in classes V, VI, and VIIss, but the gross, discrete time perspective puts him on the diagonal.

This case is not unique. Many men changed jobs between 1959 and 1973 but appear to be immobile. To find out how many, consider a new "mobility status" variable:

Men who worked only one job throughout the 1959–1973 period, labeled "Same job"

Men who worked more than one job during the 1959–1973 period but who remained in or returned to their 1959 occupation by the time of interview, labeled "Different job, same occupation"

Men whose 1973 occupation differed from their 1959 occupation, labeled "Different job, different occupation"

Table 10.3 classifies workers according to this new mobility status as well as by 1959 occupation and region. This tabulation shows that the majority of wage and salary workers (except those in class VIIus) who would be classified as "immobile" by the usual procedures actually changed jobs between 1959 and 1973. The self-employed are less mobile. More than half of the self-employed men who appeared to be "immobile" in the discrete time analysis actually were immobile; they worked at the same job throughout the period. Nonetheless, the self-employed are not immune to what might be called "false immobility: between one-fourth and one-third of "immobile" self-employed workers had at least one job change.[3]

One of the hypotheses about how industrialization affects mobility involves overall mobility, namely, job shifts such as those identified in

Table 10.3
Mobility status between 1959 and 1973 by occupation in 1959 and region:
men at work in 1959, Ireland, 1973

| Occupation in 1959 | *Republic* | | | *Northern Ireland* | | |
| | | *Different job* | | | *Different job* | |
	Same job	Same occup.	Different occup.	Same job	Same occup.	Different occup.
Professionals & proprietors I[a]	66.7%	16.7%	16.7%	66.7%	6.7%	26.7%
Professionals & managers I	14.3	52.4	33.3	13.7	56.9	29.4
Professionals & managers II	31.1	39.2	29.7	24.2	38.9	36.8
Clerical & sales	15.8	22.4	61.8	23.1	14.3	62.6
Proprietors with employees[a]	64.0	20.0	16.0	59.6	14.9	25.5
Proprietors without employees[a]	41.9	14.0	44.2	59.5	7.1	33.3
Service workers	10.0	33.3	56.7	19.4	13.4	67.2
Helpers, nonfarm	7.7	.0	92.3	8.7	.0	91.3
Technicians & foremen	27.1	31.4	41.4	18.6	35.6	45.8
Skilled manual	22.1	37.9	40.0	20.4	36.1	43.6
Semiskilled manual	29.4	33.9	36.7	29.0	30.1	40.8
Unskilled manual	34.1	25.2	40.7	18.4	27.2	54.4
Farmers with employees[a]	71.4	11.9	16.7	65.2	17.4	17.4
Farmers without employees[a]	67.6	25.3	7.1	67.4	12.6	20.0
Helpers, farm	6.8	4.0	89.2	13.5	.0	86.5
Farm laborers	22.1	21.1	56.8	28.6	16.1	55.4
All	30.4%	25.9%	43.7%	28.0%	25.7%	46.3%
Valid cases	434	369	624	417	383	689
Not at work in 1959	69	55	144	7	15	33

a.   Self–employed workers.

Table 10.3 that may or may not entail a change of occupation. There are good reasons to believe that wage and salary labor are inherently more mobile than labor that is tied to inheritable property rights. Chief among the reasons for the greater mobility of wage and salary labor is the level of material investment. Even though many employees identify strongly with their firms of employment, few have the material commitment that farmers, shopkeepers, and other self-employed workers have. Professionals, technicians, and skilled workers have investments in their occupations, but not necessarily in particular jobs with particular firms (although "firm-specific human capital" builds up for workers who stay with a specific employer a long time). A corollary is that employees find it easier than self-employed workers to shift jobs. It is simply easier to quit or resign than it is to liquidate material investments. Of course, that does not stop the marketplace from forcing unwanted mobility on some self-employed workers whose farms and businesses fail. This is less of an issue in Ireland than in some parts of the world. Farm failure is virtually unheard of in Ireland. Government subsidies boost prices and keep mortgage interest rates down. Political pressure keeps the number of farm foreclosures very low. Government supports small-scale enterprise as well, ' though the degree of support falls short of the agricultural subsidies in both the Republic and the North.

On this basis it can be said that one of the consequences of industrialization is a redistribution of workers from a less mobile to a more mobile form of labor. The development of industry shifts workers from jobs tied to property—farming and shopkeeping—to wage and salary jobs in manufacturing, commerce, and services. The greater pace of economic activity in the society as a whole augments the higher intrinsic rate of mobility for wage and salary jobs to boost job mobility further. A large portion of that mobility might involve changes of jobs that do not involve changes of occupation. Table 10.3 shows the premise of that line of reasoning to be quite plausible. Wage and salary workers shifted jobs more frequently than self-employed workers did.

Table 10.4 tabulates job shift rates by year, region, and job stratum.[4] Job shift rates are the ratio of the number of job shifts to the number of person years worked in a given year. Person years weight each worker by the fraction of the year he was actually in the labor force. Workers receive one-twelfth of a person year for each month they are at work or looking for work. The men who were at work or looking for work throughout the year in question are weighted 1.0 for that year. As an example, a worker who took his first job in September of a given year and worked through the rest of the year gets a weight of one-twelfth for September, October, November, and December, for a total of .33. Region and stratum refer to 1 January of the year in question, so some errors occur in attributing person years of migrants to their region at the beginning of the year and person years of occupationally mobile men to their stratum at the beginning of the year. Furthermore, sampling error induces some random yearly fluctuations, so five-year moving averages (MA) are also presented for each region.

Table 10.4
Percentage of job spells terminating in each year by region and
stratum of the initial job: job spells, Ireland, 1950–1973

Year	Republic[a] O MA	Northern Ireland[a] O MA	Upper nonmanual	Lower nonmanual	Upper manual	Lower manual	Farm owner	Farm laborer
1950	17% 14%	18% 16%	15%	16%	16%	18%	4%	17%
1951	13 14	15 15	16	13	14	15	2	12
1952	14 14	15 15	6	13	17	17	2	13
1953	14 13	14 14	14	13	14	17	3	13
1954	12 13	15 14	11	12	14	15	3	11
1955	13 13	13 14	11	12	14	15	4	8
1956	13 13	15 14	10	13	15	17	3	12
1957	12 13	14 14	13	12	16	14	2	9
1958	14 14	15 15	12	12	17	16	3	13
1959	12 16	13 15	11	11	15	14	1	11
1960	18 14	16 15	15	17	18	18	6	16
1961	12 14	15 15	10	12	16	15	2	10
1962	12 14	15 16	12	10	17	17	3	11
1963	15 13	16 16	12	15	17	17	2	13
1964	13 14	16 17	11	14	17	17	3	12
1965	15 14	18 17	12	14	19	19	5	15
1966	13 14	18 18	12	14	17	18	4	13
1967	13 14	19 18	13	13	17	20	3	16
1968	14 14	18 19	13	12	18	18	4	13
1969	14 15	19 19	16	14	18	19	3	18
1970	18 15	21 20	17	18	20	22	7	20
1971	15 15	20 20	14	16	21	19	4	17
1972	15 —[b]	20 —	14	14	20	19	6	17
1973	14 —	20 —	—	—	—	—	—	—

a. O = observed; MA = moving average.
b. Cannot be computed.

The largest source of variation in rates seems to be the presence or absence of a zero in the year. The rates for 1950, 1960, and 1970 exceed those for adjacent years by as much as six percentage points. The 1970 rates do not appear to be far from the mark set by the 1969 and 1971 rates, but the high rates for 1950 and 1960 clearly point to some bias in reporting the timing of job shifts that occurred more than five years before the interview. Apparently, many men lacked a clear recollection, so they rounded the date to the nearest year with a zero. Aside from this artifactual variation in rates, there is only a slight increase in net mobility over time. Smoothing the trends with five-year moving averages gives some evidence that rates increased from the early 1950s to the early 1970s by about two percentage points in the Republic and a more substantial six points in Northern Ireland. The increases are not definitive, but they do suggest that some increase in overall mobility took place between 1953 and 1973. Whether the increase is best attributed to industrialization or some other cause requires further investigation.

One way that industrialization can influence mobility rates is by redistributing the work force from jobs that typically involve little mobility (farming and shopkeeping) to jobs that typically involve more mobility (wage and salary work). If a compositional shift out of self-employment is the main force in the modest increases in mobility seen in the first four columns of Table 10.4, then the data should show little change in the rate of job shift out of wage and salary jobs, especially manual jobs, between 1953 and 1973. In fact, when job shifts are broken down according to initial stratum, as in the fifth through tenth columns of Table 10.4, the manual jobs not only show the highest rate of job shift, as expected, they also show the strongest evidence of increasing rates over time. This implies that if industrialization was the source of increasing net mobility between 1953 and 1973, then it not only was affecting composition but also was increasing mobility in specific occupations, especially manual occupations.

The breakdown in Table 10.4 features occupational origins of job shifts. Presumably, the compositional portion of the thesis of industrialism rests not only on the rate of mobility out of certain origins but also on the rate of mobility toward certain destinations. If industrialism is to be regarded as an important impetus to mobility, then the distribution of destinations of job shifts should change over time. Agricultural destinations should become less common, while destinations in manual and nonmanual occupations should increase.

Table 10.5 reports on this aspect of changing job shifts by tabulating the proportion of job shifts that arrived at each occupational destination for eight three-year periods from 1950 to 1973. There are some distinct trends in these data. Most are consistent with the thesis of industrialism, although the changes are rather small and subject to periodic reversals. Upper nonmanual employment increased, as expected. The timing, however, may be somewhat early: half of the increase occurred prior to the macroeconomic changes in the Republic in 1959. Furthermore, the expected increase in shifts to lower nonmanual jobs did not materialize. Nonworking increased rapidly, in part because of a rise in unemployment, but mainly because of retirements. On the one hand, growing retirements

Table 10.5
Destinations of job shifts and first jobs by year:
employed men, Ireland, 1950–1973

Year	Upper nonmanual	Lower nonmanual	Upper manual	Lower manual	Farm owner	Farm laborer	Unemployed	Retired
			Stratum of destination					
Job shifts								
1950–52	7	14	23	30	6	10	11	0
1953–55	8	13	24	30	5	8	11	0
1956–58	10	14	26	29	5	6	9	0
1959–61	10	14	27	29	5	5	10	1
1962–64	10	15	27	28	4	4	9	2
1965–67	12	13	26	27	4	5	12	2
1968–70	13	14	24	25	5	4	12	4
1971–73	12	15	23	23	4	3	15	6
First jobs								
1950–52	3	23	24	22	1	28	—[a]	—[a]
1953–55	5	23	23	20	1	28	—	—
1956–58	5	23	26	21	1	24	—	—
1959–61	7	21	29	24	1	18	—	—
1962–64	7	25	23	21	0	24	—	—
1965–67	7	21	29	21	0	22	—	—
1968–70	13	25	29	21	0	12	—	—
1971–73	22	27	15	23	1	11	—	—

a.   Unemployed and retired are not possible as first jobs.

might well be indicative of prosperity and thus not inconsistent with the thesis of industrialism. On the other hand, the growth might be a consequence more of the age distribution of the sample than of any changes in society in general. Upper manual employment rose during the 1950s (prior to the expected time) and fell from 1964 to 1973. This is a peculiar trend that comes to its peak too soon after the industrial takeoff. The problems for those who wish to interpret the trends in Table 10.5 as support for the thesis of industrialism are compounded by the downward trend in lower manual employment. A trend of this type might be favorable to the thesis of industrialism if there were corresponding increases in upper manual employment. Claims that industrialization can be expected to foster upgrades in the level of skill possessed by and demanded of the working class might lead to declines in unskilled and semiskilled employment. But employment in skilled manual positions does not increase. So we are left with this anomalous decline. Finally, the data show the near demise of the paid farm laborer. Although this category includes unpaid work as well, the vast majority of the job shifts to farm labor involve work for pay.

These weak trends in the destinations of job shifts point to a further lack of support for the industrialization thesis. Four-percent-a-year economic development did surprisingly little to redistribute the labor of Irish men already at work in the late 1950s. But the job shifts in the top panel of Table 10.5, like the gross mobility, miss an important employment transition: the shift from out of the labor force to first job. The destinations of first jobs changed dramatically, as shown in the bottom panel. Nonmanual employment increased dramatically, especially upper nonmanual employment after 1968. The trend for lower nonmanual employment was more uneven but definitely up since 1968. Manual work held steady throughout most of the period, except for an anomalous drop-off of upper manual employment in the last period. Farming, always rare as a first job, is all the more so since 1959. Farm labor, once a very common first job, went into a striking decline after 1964. These changes reiterate the point that cohort succession far outweighed any redistribution of the established work force as the Irish economy modernized in the 1960s.

Event History Analysis of Job Shifts

The most interesting feature of Table 10.4 is the actual rate of job shift itself. There is a rather brisk pace of job shift, even prior to 1959. Each year bore witness to substantial job shifting that varied from one-eighth to one-fifth of active workers. Even more impressive is the rate of job shift among manual workers, which held steady at 20 percent by the early 1970s. This brisk rate of job shift comes as a surprise when mobility in Ireland is compared to mobility elsewhere in Europe. Intergenerational occupational mobility in Ireland lags behind that in the rest of Europe (Erikson and Goldthorpe 1986; Hout and Jackson 1986). On that basis one would expect to find low rates of job shift as well. The brisk rate of job shift in Ireland is therefore a discovery of sorts.

The continuous observation of individuals in an event history analysis offers a richness not available in other forms of data. This richness calls to mind some issues that do not arise in the analysis of more conventional kinds of data. The first such issue is the one known as *censoring*. Cross-sectional analysis and even some more conventional kinds of change data, such as panel data, classify subjects according to their position in some process of interest at the time of interview. Event history analysis does not grant the interview such a privileged status in the analysis. Once attention is focused on the entire dynamic process as it unfolds over continuous time, the interview actually becomes a nuisance, an interruption of the evolution of the process under study. In a work history study such as this one, the interview identifies job shifts that have gone before, and they are of great interest. But in many cases, the *next* job shift—one that occurs after the interview—is the shift of greatest interest. We have individual i who has been working in job j for duration t. We know that this job spell will last for a time greater than the t that has already elapsed, but we do not know how much longer. Some subjects will change jobs shortly after the interview (in a few cases even before all of the other subjects have been interviewed); others will go on in their current position until they die (which may be a long or short time after the interview). Because our knowledge of this job spell is incomplete—we know that no shift occurred prior to duration t but we do not know when the eventual shift will occur— we say that the interview "censored" the mobility process.

Censoring is the aspect of event history analysis that demands new statistical techniques (Cox and Lewis 1966; Cox 1972; Sorensen 1975; Tuma 1976; Tuma and Hannan 1979; Tuma et al. 1979). Note a few new terms. A *job spell* is the interval of time between events; it is the unit of analysis. The *origin state* is the occupational stratum that the worker occupied throughout the job spell. The *destination state* is the occupational stratum to which that worker moved at the end of the spell.[5] *Duration* is the elapsed time between the beginning and the end of a job spell. The *rate*, $r_{hij}(t)$, is the dependent variable in the analysis; it is the unobserved probability that worker h will shift from occupational stratum i to stratum j at any given instant in time.[6] Several related concepts are also used in event history analysis. The *hazard* function is the sum of rates across destinations; the *cumulative hazard* function is the accumulation of hazards over time from the last job shift up to time t; and the *survivor* function is the probability that no shift has occurred prior to time t.[7]

In the most general case, the rate depends on substantive variables of interest, such as education, and on the amount of time elapsed since the last change. In some applications one or the other of these independent variables is not important. The event history analysis, like a conventional multivariate analysis, consists of identifying the independent variables that are important influences on the dependent variable—in this case, the rate of job shift.

Much research gives priority to determining the effect of time (or duration) on the rate. This analysis is no exception. It begins with a discussion of *duration dependence,* the generic name for the effect of time or duration on rates. In the course of that discussion another generic problem is encountered—*heterogeneity*. Some groups have higher intrinsic rates of movement than others do. Skilled workers in the building trades have high rates of movement as a trait of their line of work. Farmers strike the opposite end of the scale; they seldom shift their occupation.[8] In this analysis, heterogeneity is the factor of greater interest, but in order to obtain unbiased estimates of the magnitude of heterogeneity, duration dependence must be controlled.

For most destinations the rate of job shift declines as duration increases. Workers typically have a rate of leaving jobs that they have held a long time which is lower than their rate of leaving jobs that they have only recently entered. This has been shown in a number of studies of American workers (Sorensen 1975; Sorensen and Tuma 1981), German workers (Carroll 1983), and Norwegian workers (Featherman 1986). Figure 10.1 plots the log of the survivorship function (λ_t) against duration (in months) for all job spells in the Irish Mobility Study, broken down by region.[9] The line for the Republic is above the line for Northern Ireland at all points, indicating that mobility is higher in the North than in the South

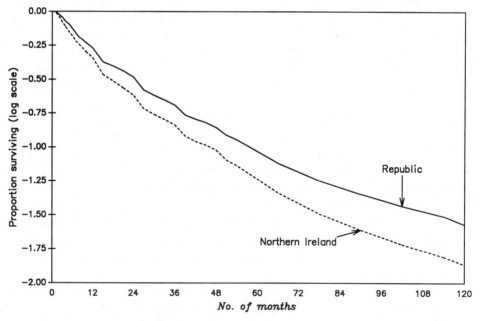

Figure 10.1   Hazard rate, by duration and region: job shifts, Ireland, 1922–1974.

(more survivors mean less mobility). Duration dependence is recognizable as a nonlinear relationship between log λ_t and duration. Both lines in Figure 10.1 are flatter at long durations than at short ones. The slope of this line is the mobility rate, $r_{hk}(t)$, so this figure corroborates the findings for other societies that mobility slows down as duration increases.

As an aid to interpreting Figure 10.1, Table 10.6 presents the probability of remaining in the same job for one, two, five, ten, and twenty years by region and occupational stratum. The brisk pace of job change is evident in these survival probabilities. The probability of surviving the first year in a given job is .76 in the Republic and .71 in Northern Ireland; that is, roughly one-fourth of men change jobs in the first year after taking a new one. After two years the probability of surviving in the same job has fallen to .62 in the Republic and .54 in Northern Ireland. The mobility rate starts to fall off beyond the second year. After ten years an Irish worker has a chance between one-fifth and one-sixth of staying in the same job. The median staying time is three years in the Republic and two years plus two months in Northern Ireland.

Interpreting duration dependence such as that in Figure 10.1 is not as straightforward as it might appear at first. Strictly speaking, we should attribute to time only those effects that are clearly due to the passage of time, such as the accumulation of experience and "firm-specific human capital." While those factors are, in all likelihood, important for the pat-

Table 10.6
Probability of surviving in the same job for one year, two years, five years, ten years, and twenty years by duration, region, and occupational stratum of job: employed men, Ireland, 1935–1973

Category	Duration				
	1	2	5	10	20
Region					
Republic	.76	.62	.36	.21	.10
Northern Ireland	.71	.54	.29	.15	.07
Occupational stratum					
Upper nonmanual	.85	.69	.40	.22	.10
Lower nonmanual, self	.90	.82	.62	.47	.29
Lower nonmanual, employee	.79	.61	.30	.14	.05
Upper manual	.78	.60	.30	.13	.05
Lower manual	.73	.54	.25	.14	.06
Farmer	.95	.90	.79	.65	.53
Farm worker	.76	.66	.42	.25	.09
Unemployed	.37	.22	.10	.06	.04

tern in Figure 10.1, some of the drop-off in the rate might be due to the attrition of workers with high person-specific rates—sometimes called "movers"—leaving behind as survivors those workers with low person-specific rates—sometimes called "stayers" (e.g., Spilerman 1972; Singer and Spilerman 1974, 1976). A general solution to this problem of interpretation is not possible. However, desegregating the job spells and estimating separate survivor functions for different strata within Irish society might give some sense of the importance of person-specific versus duration-specific factors for the apparent duration dependence in Figure 10.1. Specifically, if the relationship between the survivorship (in log form) and duration can be shown to be linear within strata, then selective attrition of subgroups with heterogeneous mobility rates (and not true duration dependence) is probably the source of the curvature in Figure 10.1.

The factor that seems most likely to be important for heterogeneity of rates is occupation itself. Workers who are engaged in different occupations are also very likely to be subject to different risks of moving at any given time. Some occupations involve less mobility than others, with farming the extreme case of immobility and some forms of manual work the extreme case of mobility.

So that we could assess the contribution of occupation to the apparent duration dependence in Figure 10.1, survivorship functions were estimated for each of seven occupational strata plus unemployment, for a total of eight strata. Job spells were classified according to whether the job held during the spell was upper nonmanual (classes Ia, Ib, and II), lower nonmanual—self-employed (classes IVa and IVb), lower nonmanual—employee (classes IIIa, IIIb, and VIIInf), upper manual (classes V and VI), lower manual (classes VIIss and VIIus), farmer (classes IVc and IVd), farm worker (classes VIIf and VIIIf), and unemployed. Figure 10.2 shows the log of the survivor function plotted against duration for each stratum.

Except for unemployment, there is substantially less duration dependence in the panels of Figure 10.2 than was evident in Figure 10.1. This suggests strongly that much of the apparent duration dependence in the work force taken as a whole in fact reflects heterogeneity in the kind of work being done. A constant rate of change (the absence of duration dependence) leads to a straight line in plots like those in Figure 10.2. By that criterion, the nearly straight lines for six of the seven occupations in Figure 10.2 (but not for lower manual workers and the unemployed) indicate that occupation explains much of the duration dependence so evident

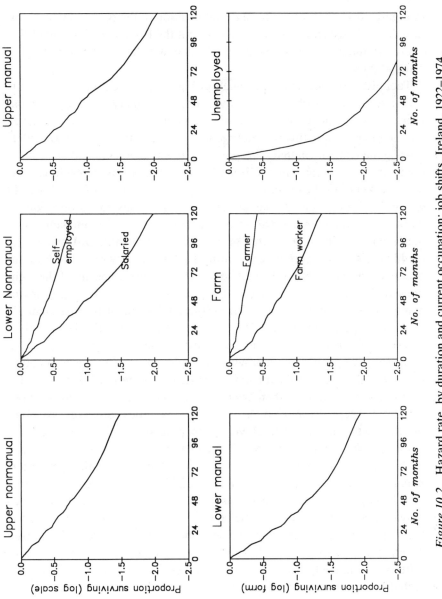

Figure 10.2   Hazard rate, by duration and current occupation: job shifts, Ireland, 1922–1974.

in Figure 10.1. No formula for a decomposition of the proportion of duration dependence explained is available, but the lines in each panel of this figure are much closer to being straight than are the two lines in the preceding figure.

Table 10.6 extracts from the panels of Figure 10.2 the probability of surviving to durations of one, two, five, ten, and twenty years by occupational strata. The extreme variation among these probabilities gives another expression to the heterogeneity present in these data, underscoring the conclusion that *heterogeneity*, not duration dependence, is the dominant force in job shifts in Ireland. Time is important in each occupation; workers exit the occupation over time. But the effect of time is nearly uniform within occupational strata. A nearly constant proportion of workers remaining in a job at time t are removed in the infinitesimal time increment Δt. The point is that to characterize job shifts in Ireland, one could very nearly ignore time in writing a set of mobility rates for different occupations. The t in $r_{hk}(t)$ could be dropped in describing six of the eight lines in Figure 10.2. Job shift rates decrease over time among lower manual workers and the unemployed (these lines are far from straight).

As for heterogeneity of mobility rates, farmers are the least mobile workers, as expected. After one year the probability of continuing to farm in the same way (either with or without employees) is .95. This probability does not fall off rapidly over time. The median time until a job shift for Irish farmers is greater than twenty years. Proprietors and upper nonmanual workers also have high survival probabilities. Survival probabilities for lower nonmanual employees, upper manual worker, lower manual workers, and farm workers are close to one another in a range that is close to the average for the labor force as a whole. Spells of unemployment terminate very quickly. The probability of still being unemployed after one year is only .37; after two years it is just .22. Workers who are still unemployed after two years have little chance of ever working again.[10] This is the most extreme residual duration dependence, and it is probably not true duration dependence. The long-term unemployed can be expected to differ systematically from those unemployed for short spells. This undetected heterogeneity between the long-term and short-term unemployed appears in the figure as if it were residual duration dependence.

The destination of job shifts is of as much concern as is their frequency. Table 10.7 presents the coefficients from a Cox (1975) partial likelihood regression of destination-specific mobility rates on time, region, education, origins, and characteristics of the current occupation.[11] The dependent variables are the rates of mobility into destinations classified as follows:

Upper nonmanual
Lower nonmanual—self-employed
Lower nonmanual—employee
Upper manual
Lower manual
Farm owner
Farm worker
Unemployed

During each job spell the worker is at risk of moving to any of these destinations—the actual destination is not known until the move is made. Once a move closes the spell, it is coded as a completed move to the actual destination and as a censored observation for all of the other destinations.[12] Of course, some spells are interrupted by the interview before any move is observed. As before, these spells ($N = 4,197$) are coded as censored for all destinations.

The main concern in understanding Table 10.7 is with the first panel, the effects of current occupation on job shift rates. As in the case of tabular data, both general linear effects and specific effects of variables like prestige, educational credentials, and labor market conditions are considered. These terms provide a convenient mathematical summary of effects, but the interaction of specific and general effects is not as easy to describe. The problem is the opposite sign for most of the prestige and education coefficients, despite the positive correlation between prestige and education. A post hoc explanation suggests itself. The negative coefficient for prestige arises when immobility and education are controlled. Mobility that is strictly "career" mobility almost always takes the form of moves from subordinate to superordinate positions, that is, from lower to higher prestige. To the extent that the immobility and educational requirements effects capture the proclivity for lateral moves, these prestige coefficients may be seen as indicators of a surplus of upward over downward mobility within the residual left over after adjustment for the main effects of class.

These cross-cutting effects are difficult to comprehend. Figure 10.3 reports the composite statistic:

$$b_{ij} = \Sigma_p \beta_p X_{ip} - \frac{\Sigma_i (\Sigma_p \beta_p X_{ip})}{17} \qquad (10.1)$$

Table 10.7

Effects of selected variables on job shifts by destination (partial likelihood estimates): employed men, Ireland, 1935–1973

				Destination				
Independent variable	Upper nonmanual	Lower nonmanual self–employed	Lower nonmanual employee	Upper manual	Lower manual	Farm owner	Farm worker	Unem- ployed
Current occupation								
Same stratum	1.814[a]	1.358[a]	2.131[a]	1.628[a]	.451	-.451[a]	1.223[a]	—
Prestige/10[b]	-.499[a]	-.402[a]	-.297[a]	-.306[a]	-.332[a]	.089	-.180[a]	.339[a]
Education/10	.283[a]	.237[a]	-.028	-.031	-.087[a]	-.229[a]	-.217[a]	-.151[a]
Bureaucrtic entry/10	-.135[a]	-.062[a]	-.018	-.017	-.006	.081[a]	.016	.556[a]
Personal contact	-.139[a]	-.012	-.152[a]	-.133[a]	-.058[a]	.308[a]	-.085[a]	.254[a]
Education								
Primary	0.	0.	0.	0.	0.	0.	0.	0.
Nonacademic secondary	1.041[a]	.180	.521[a]	.422[a]	-.148[a]	.244	-.620[a]	.016
Some academic secondary	1.318[a]	.027	.628[a]	.356[a]	-.289[a]	.346[a]	-.417[a]	.002
Complete academic	1.593[a]	-.206	.837[a]	.252[a]	-.754[a]	.252	-1.097[a]	.055
Some higher education	1.874[a]	-.088	.873[a]	.220[a]	-.816[a]	1.104[a]	-.621[a]	.009
Higher degree	2.012[a]	-1.661[a]	.486[a]	-.289[a]	-1.061[a]	.722	-1.474[a]	.009
Father's Stratum								
Upper nonmanual	.234[a]	-.076	.279[a]	-.052	-.220[a]	.812	-.234	.219[a]
Lower nonmanual, self	.201[a]	1.019[a]	.400[a]	.081	-.170[a]	.637	-.036	.055
Lower nonmanual, other	.325[a]	.102	.379[a]	.173[a]	-.214[a]	1.117[a]	-.710[a]	.063
Upper manual	.162	.105	.150[a]	.226[a]	-.083[a]	.031	-.442[a]	.008
Lower manual	0.	0.	0.	0.	0.	0.	0.	0.
Farm owner	.036	.271[a]	-.097	-.366[a]	-.395[a]	2.477[a]	.761[a]	-.060
Farm worker	-.119	.198	-.278[a]	-.334[a]	-.177[a]	1.254[a]	.761[a]	-.003

First job cohort								
Before 1945	0.	0.	0.	0.	0.	0.	0.	0.
1945–1958	-.012	.295	-.067	.023	-.077	-.067	.116	-.190[a]
1959–1973	.088	.450	-.002	-.106	.096	-.675[a]	.837[a]	.443[a]
Starting year (/10)	.098	.044	.097[a]	.071[a]	.135[a]	.386[a]	-.236[a]	.242[a]
Starting age								
Linear	-.018	.088[a]	-.094[a]	-.078[a]	-.093[a]	.004	-.059[a]	-.084[a]
Square (/10)	-.001	-.018[a]	.007	.003	.006[a]	.002	.001	.008[a]
Job number								
Linear	.057[a]	.191[a]	.058[a]	.123[a]	.107[a]	.058[a]	.204[a]	.226[a]
Square (/10)	-.016[a]	-.070[a]	-.015[a]	-.021[a]	-.021[a]	-.005	-.032[a]	-.034[a]
Region								
Republic	-.116[a]	-.034	-.007	-.234[a]	-.172[a]	.241[a]	.379[a]	-.340[a]
Northern Ireland	0.	0.	0.	0.	0.	0.	0.	0.
Number of spells								
Complete	1591	633	1780	4317	4994	752	1418	2375
Censored	20466	21424	20277	17740	17063	21305	20639	19682
L^2 (df = 24)	6773[a]	534[a]	3974[a]	4821[a]	4772[a]	1445[a]	3438[a]	3534[a]

a.   Significant at the .05 level.
b.   Variables marked "/10" were divided by 10 in order to show more significant digits.

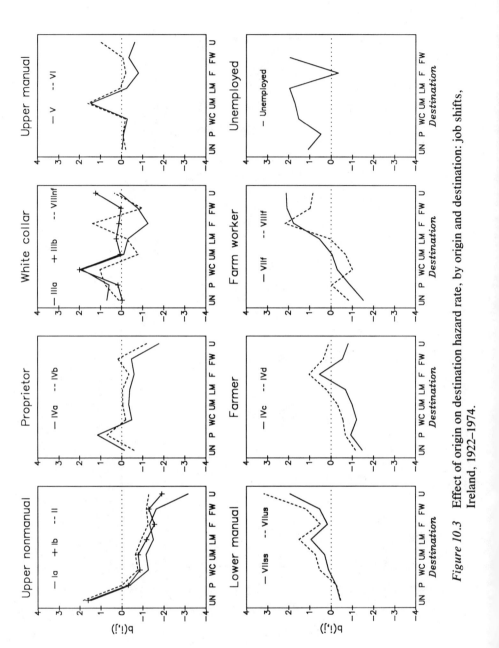

Figure 10.3   Effect of origin on destination hazard rate, by origin and destination: job shifts, Ireland, 1922–1974.

where $i = 1, \ldots, 17$ indexes current occupation in the sixteen categories plus unemployment, $j = 1, \ldots, 8$ indexes destination, $p = 1, \ldots, 5$ indexes the independent variables pertaining to current occupation, X_{ip} is the score for current occupation i on independent variable p, and β_p is the coefficient for variable p in Table 10.7 for each current occupation and each destination. The b_{ij} show the effect of each current occupation on each destination occupation.

The upper nonmanual panel of Figure 10.3 shows the effect on each destination of being a self-employed or salaried professional, a manager, or a large proprietor (classes Ia, Ib, and II). First, the rate of moving from one of these upper nonmanual occupations into another upper nonmanual destination exceeds the rate of moving into any other destination. The rate of moving into proprietorial lower nonmanual occupations is close to the average of the rates for other current occupations. The rate of moving from these upper nonmanual occupations into any of the remaining occupations falls far short of average. The rate of moving from self-employed professional or large proprietor to unemployed is much lower than any other rate on any of the charts. Differences among the three upper nonmanual occupations are, for the most part, trivial. The low rate of movement from self-employed professional or large proprietor to unemployed is the one exception. This rate is appreciably lower than the rates for salaried professionals or managers, regardless of grade. None of the other current occupations has a rate of movement into upper nonmanual occupations that approaches the rate of intrastratum movement.

Proprietors, farmers, technicians, and foremen evidence a similar pattern of high immobility and low mobility to other occupations. The level of intrastratum movement is not quite as great for these occupations as for the upper nonmanual occupations, but it is high relative to their interstratum mobility.

White-collar workers exhibit a great deal of heterogeneity, more than any of the other strata. Clerical, sales, and service workers have high intrastratum movement. The clerical and sales workers also have high rates of mobility into upper nonmanual and proprietorial positions. Service workers do not. Furthermore, service workers have a high rate of mobility into unemployment. Unpaid white-collar workers have a wide range of destinations. Mobility into proprietorships and farming are nearly as likely as intrastratum moves are.

Manual workers—skilled, semiskilled, and unskilled—have high rates of immobility; they also have high rates of movement into unemployment.

Movement into unemployment actually exceeds intrastratum mobility among lower manual workers. Paid farm work is also a relatively common destination for semiskilled and unskilled manual workers.

Paid farm workers have very high rates of mobility into independent farming, farm labor, and unemployment. Rates of movement into these three destinations are nearly indistinguishable. Unpaid farm workers are more likely to move into independent farming than they are to move within the farm work stratum or into unemployment.

Unemployed workers have a unique destination pattern because workers cannot have successive spells of unemployment. Movement to lower nonmanual, upper manual, lower manual, and farm work are all likely. These are the strata that have high rates of mobility into unemployment. This is no coincidence. Nearly three-fourths (72 percent) of unemployed workers return to the stratum they left.

Four generalizations emerge from the details of Figure 10.3. Positions of authority and independence tend to send mobile workers to other positions of authority and independence. Occupations that lack authority and independence are subject to spells of unemployment. Entry-level positions lead to diverse destinations, some of which involve authority and independence. Unemployed workers who used to be in positions of authority and independence have a substantial chance of moving back to jobs similar to their former ones; continuously employed workers from supervised positions have appreciably less chance of a move into authority or independence.

The effect of education on the mobility rate varies widely among destinations. For mobility into upper nonmanual positions, education is extremely important. Each successive level of schooling results in a higher rate of movement into this upper stratum. The negative effect of educational achievement on the rate of movement into lower manual destinations complements this high-status pattern. The destinations of intermediate social status show patterns of mixed (and null) education effects. For mobility into proprietorship, only a university degree matters, and its effect is negative. Men who stopped their schooling after leaving primary school are the ones most likely to move into paid or unpaid farm labor. Education affects mobility into lower nonmanual or upper manual employment in a manner consistent with a positive effect of education on destination status. That is, the curvilinearity in the education coefficients for intermediate-status destinations reflects the concentration of men with intermediate educational credentials in these occupations.

The coefficients for father's stratum reflect some of the patterns of inter-generational persistence, but there are anomalies as well. The first concerns high-status destinations. The men whose fathers worked in clerical, sales, and service occupations are about 30 percent more likely to move into upper nonmanual destinations than are men whose fathers worked in those upper nonmanual occupations. Such a pattern might result from a combination of high mobility from upper nonmanual origins to upper nonmanual first occupations coupled with relatively few job shifts during the career. But more than half of the men from upper nonmanual origins who achieved an upper nonmanual job by the time of interview did so after a period of downward mobility (Table 9.10). In short, most men who eventually worked in the stratum of their origin were countermobile instead of directly immobile, so this suggestion cannot account for the anomaly.

In contrast, mobility into proprietorships displays a perfectly reasonable pattern of very high intergenerational immobility and modest mobility from farm origins to nonagricultural self-employment. The curvilinear distributions of the coefficients that pertain to mobility into white-collar, manual, and agricultural employment likewise stay close to form. The one exception is the mobility into lower manual employment for sons of proprietors; it exceeds the intergenerational immobility of men from lower manual origins.

The coefficients for mobility into farm ownership are not as counterintuitive as they might at first appear. The deleted category has extremely low mobility into farming, as reflected in the very large coefficient for intergenerational immobility (2.477). The coefficient for lower nonmanual employees appears quite large at first because it is not only significant but also greater than 1.0. Taking the lower nonmanual employees as the reference instead preserves the size of the intercategory differences, but it produces the following coefficients:

Upper nonmanual	-0.305
Lower nonmanual, self	-0.480
Lower nonmanual, employee	$0.$
Upper manual	-1.086
Lower manual	-1.117
Farm owner	1.360
Farm worker	0.137

These numbers, though substantively no different from those in Table 10.7, seem to be closer to the expected pattern. The final column of the table contains a completely inexplicable positive coefficient for unemployed men from upper nonmanual origins.

Younger workers are more likely to move into occupations that involve little authority or independence.[13] As workers age, these occupations remain prominent destinations, but workers' rate of movement into self-employment increases.

The year and cohort variables do not succeed in separating these two factors. The positive year coefficients for moves into clerical, sales, service, technical, supervisory, and manual occupations are plausible. In these equations cohort is not significant. In the equations for farm ownership, farm labor, and unemployment, both cohort and period are significant, but the parameter estimates do not make sense. If taken seriously, these coefficients indicate that the trend in farming is upward (positive year coefficient), despite the large decrease in farming for the post-1959 cohort and the lack of an age effect in this equation. Similar contradictions also make the age, period, and cohort effects for the last two equations uninterpretable.

The rate of mobility into each destination increases as the number of previous jobs increases. This term pertains more to the worker than to the job. It is best understood as a proxy for those unmeasured factors that make highly mobile men so prone to move and men with few jobs so stable.

The rate of mobility into professions, management, and blue-collar work is less in the Republic than it is in Northern Ireland. The unemployment rate is also lower in the Republic. However, mobility into agricultural occupations is higher in the Republic than it is in Northern Ireland.

The mobility rate between two occupational strata, $r_{hij}(t)$, depends on the timing of a job shift and on the eventual destination of the shift when it occurs.[14] The timing and the rate of job shifts are two of the three components. The third component is the conditional transition rate between current stratum i and destination stratum j, given that a shift has occurred, $m_{ij}(t)$. These transition rates merit attention on two grounds. First, because both timing and destination affect the mobility rates, $r_{hij}(t)$, it is never clear which constituent part produced an observed change in mobility. For example, did the rate of mobility into upper manual positions increase over time (as indicated by the positive coefficient for year in Table 10.7) because the duration of job spells in categories that send many workers to upper manual destinations decreased or because the transition to upper manual jobs became more likely for men who were moving at constant rates? This issue can be addressed by looking for differences among years in conditional transition rates.

Further justification for considering the $m_{ij}(t)$ comes from the kind of change characterized by the duration index t. Early moves (those occurring while t is close to zero) might contribute more or less to inequality than later moves do.

These two justifications imply different analyses. First, the conditional transition rates for each year must be examined for evidence of change over real time. Second, the conditional transition rates for different durations must be examined for evidence of change over the cycle of employment.

To examine the prospect that the conditional transition rates changed over the time covered by the Irish Mobility Study, a cross-tabulation of job spells according to current occupation (C), next occupation (D), and period (Y) is analyzed using log-linear models.[15] The subject of the analysis is change in the transition rates, not in the association between current and next occupation. For that reason change in the marginal parameters is as important as change in the association parameters. The log-linear analysis begins with simple models. The first model fits the effects [CD][Y].[16] This model allows for the association between current and next occupation but specifies no changes in the distribution of either occupation over time, nor does it specify changes in their association. The model does not fit the data by classical criteria ($L^2 = 2,511.62$; $df = 498$; bic $= -2,460$), but Raftery's bic finds it to be preferable to the saturated model because of the large number of observations. Adding a term for period differences in current occupations, making the model [CD][CY], improves the fit by both classical and Bayesian criteria ($L^2 = 1,387.10$; $df = 466$; bic $= -3,265$). Further improvement is achieved from the addition of a term for changes in the destination distribution, making the model [CD][CY][DY]. Both L^2 and bic go down ($L^2 = 694.51$; $df = 434$; bic $= -3,638$). This evidence establishes that the transition rates changed significantly over the twentieth century. The test statistics do not reveal the size and direction of the changes. Nor do they conclusively rule out change in the association between current and next occupations, even though the evidence on this type of change is more equivocal than the evidence on change in the marginal distributions of current and next occupations. The bic statistic selects [CD][CY][DY] from among the four alternatives considered (including the saturated model as one of the alternatives), but this does not rule out the prospect of change in a more parsimonious model of association. The issue of change in the association between current and next occupation does not need to be pursued, since the evidence of change in the marginal distributions is sufficient to conclude that the transition rates changed.

To assess the size and direction of changes in the marginal components of the conditional transition rates, $m_{ij}(t)$, a more complicated (but by now familiar) model is used in Table 10.8: quasi-symmetry parameterized as in Sobel et al. (1985). The cross-tabulations of current by next occupation for each period can be thought of as three separate mobility tables. Fitting QS to each of them yields estimates of structural mobility (α_j) and size (β_i) effects that will reflect the marginal changes.

In each period structural mobility in job shifts favors upward mobility in the prestige, authority, and autonomy dimensions. The self-employed, professional, managerial, and employer categories all show large positive values for log α_j. Structural mobility diminishes the entry-level positions, especially those that involve agricultural work and work without pay. The

Table 10.8
Structural mobility (α_j) and size effects (β_j) for conditional job transitions by year: employed men, Ireland, 1935–1973

Occupation (j)	log α_j			log β_j		
	1935–1944	1945–1958	1959–1973	1935–1944	1945–1958	1959–1973
Professionals & proprietors I[a]	2.18	1.82	1.17	−2.06	−2.29	−1.24
Professionals & managers I	.13	.51	.72	.15	.29	.29
Professionals & managers II	.53	.28	.41	.08	.39	.58
Clerical & sales workers	−.54	−.12	−.19	.92	.74	.74
Proprietors with employees[a]	.59	.34	.42	−1.68	−1.23	−.93
Proprietors without employees[a]	.37	.49	.72	−.68	−.58	−.67
Service workers	.78	−.68	−.47	1.23	.88	.71
Helpers, nonfarm	−.57	−.86	−.74	−.30	.14	−.43
Technicians & foremen	.18	−.06	−.11	.84	.67	.89
Skilled manual	.05	−.54	−.25	1.58	1.69	1.45
Semiskilled manual	.54	−.37	−.23	1.58	1.26	1.11
Unskilled manual	−.45	−.49	−.38	1.41	1.32	.98
Farmers with employees[a]	.48	1.85	.93	−1.68	−1.72	−1.04
Farmers without employees[a]	1.68	.69	.46	−1.72	−.50	.06
Helpers, farm	−1.42	−1.61	−1.68	1.09	.93	.56
Farm laborers	−1.01	−.81	−.65	1.79	1.06	.49
Unemployed	−.52	−.46	−.14	−2.54	−3.05	−3.56

a.   Self–employed workers.

trends in structural mobility show a dramatic rise in structural mobility into farming with employees between the first two periods, followed by a drop that covers two-thirds of the original increase. The rise is partly offset by the sharp drop in structural mobility into independent farming. In rank order, independent farming falls from having the second highest force of structural mobility in the 1908–1944 period to near the middle of the range in 1959–1974. The upper-grade professions also show countervailing trends. Self-employed professions are less favored by structural mobility in the third period than they were earlier, while salaried professions (and upper-level management) are more favored in the recent period. The only other notable trends in structural mobility involve modest decreases in the rate at which structural mobility is draining the clerical, sales, and farm labor positions.

The size coefficients (log β_i) show the preponderance of job shifts involving manual occupations (at all skill levels). Self-employed and unemployed job statuses are involved in the fewest job shifts. Trends in the log β_i cannot be assessed using the SHD parameterization exactly as it has been used. First, the coefficients must be normed so that they sum to zero in each period. This norming adjusts for the different number of shifts in each period. Using a change of .5 in β_i as the criterion for a meaningful trend produces five trends in Table 10.8. Although professional and employer categories were involved in a relatively small number of the job shifts in each period, they increased their share significantly over time. Farmers without employees, lower-grade professionals, and managers also became more active in the recent job shifts. Service workers and agricultural workers (paid and unpaid) became involved in fewer job shifts over time. Unemployment went from a small to a very small portion of job shifts. Taking a broader definition of trends makes it possible to identify marginal decreases for semiskilled and unskilled manual positions.

The most important implication of this phase of the analysis is the observation that *life cycle* and not *industrialization* dominates the changes in the conditional transition rates. The upward mobility into positions of prestige, authority, and autonomy is affiliated with the socioeconomic life cycle, not with industrialization. Farming increased its share of job shifts for men in the Irish Mobility Study, contrary to the expectations of the thesis of industrialism, because the men became older.

The issue of change in real time leads into the issue of change in conditional transition rates over the duration of a job spell. The analytical question is, Does inequality in job chances emerge immediately upon a job shift, or does it evolve as shifts accumulate? To address this question, consider job shifts that involve transitions to upper nonmanual occupations (transitions to good jobs) and job shifts that involve transitions to lower manual occupations (transitions to jobs in the not-so-good to poor range). The objective is to see whether shifts into upper nonmanual jobs increase relative to shifts into lower manual jobs as duration increases. Nonparametric survivorship functions (Kaplan and Meier 1958) were calculated for durations up to ten years [$\lambda_{ij}(t)$ for $t = 0, \ldots, 120$ months] for the risk of moving into an upper nonmanual ($j = 1$) occupation (shifts to all other destinations were treated as censored observations at the time

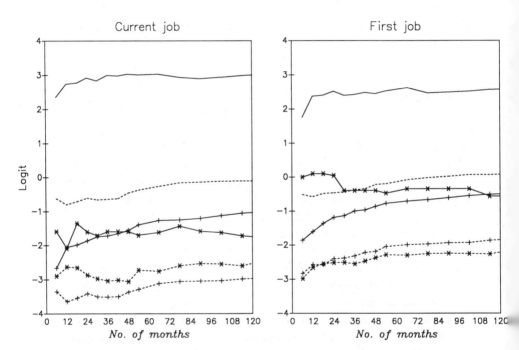

Figure 10.4 Log-odds on a lower professional or managerial next job (relative to unskilled manual), by duration and current occupation (*left*) and by duration and first job (*right*): job shifts, Ireland, 1922–1974. Symbols distinguish among major occupational strata: no symbol for nonmanual, + for manual, and * for farm. Within strata, solid lines indicate higher status; dashed lines indicate lower status.

the job shift occurred) and also for the risk of moving into a lower manual ($j = 5$) occupation (once again shifts to all other destinations were treated as censored observations at the time the job shift occurred) for each current occupation stratum ($i = 1, \ldots, 8$) excluding unemployment and combining self-employed men and employees from the lower nonmanual stratum. The cumulative odds on moving into an upper nonmanual occupation versus moving into a lower manual observation are defined (in log form) as follows:

$$\text{Logit}_i\,(t) \,=\, \log \frac{1 - \lambda_{i1}(t)}{1 - \lambda_{i5}(t)}$$

where $i = 1, \ldots, 8$ and $t = 0, \ldots, 120$. Figure 10.4 plots the results against month. There is a separate line for each of the six origin strata considered. The origin strata are defined as current job in the left panel and as first job in the right panel. The discussion focuses on the data for current job.

The most obvious feature of Figure 10.4 is the most important one: the odds on making a transition to an upper nonmanual occupation depend more on where the transition originates than on the length of the job spell being exited. For men leaving upper nonmanual occupations, the odds are very favorable that the destination will be upper nonmanual rather than lower manual. For men leaving lower nonmanual occupations, the odds are about even that the destination will be upper nonmanual instead of lower manual. For men leaving manual or farming occupations, the odds favor by a sizable margin a lower manual destination over an upper nonmanual one.

This does not imply that duration fails to affect the odds on upper nonmanual destinations. In fact, for most strata the odds on an upper nonmanual destination increase. The key here is not the absence of a duration effect but its uniformity. Because the odds increase over longer durations for nearly every origin group, the differences among origin groups change very little with longer durations. Thus, while the constituent odds change, inequality (as indexed by differences of logits) does not change with longer duration. A notable exception to this generalization is the greater-than-average rise in the odds on a good next job for men in upper manual occupations. Men working in upper manual positions have virtually no advantage over men in lower manual jobs if they leave their current job after a short duration. Between one and five years, a huge gap develops between the chances of men from upper versus men from lower manual current jobs. At three years, the men from upper manual current jobs overtake farmers (who rarely move anyway). Interesting though this exception may be, the overall picture implies little change in inequality for durations up to ten years.[17]

The lack of empirical support for the thesis of industrialism has so far not damaged the thesis sufficiently to warrant its rejection. Apparently, its intuitive appeal renders it immune to attack by data. An implication of this immunity is that failure to support the thesis of industrialism is suspect in some way. In a variation on the medieval practice of killing the bearer of bad tidings, true believers may seek to reject the findings presented here as wide of the mark, arguing that no support was found because the right test was not run. In anticipation of such an assault, yet another approach to finding some evidence of change in mobility rates that conforms to the expectations of the thesis of industrialism was attempted.

Nonparametric survivorship functions (Kaplan and Meier 1958) were estimated for job spells that began in single calendar years from 1955 to 1973. Figure 10.5 plots the log $\lambda(t)$ functions for odd-numbered years. Star, oval, and square symbols show survival at one, two and one-half, and five years. There is some evidence that jobs spells begun more recently terminated more quickly. The probability of surviving one year in the same job was .70 for men who took their jobs in 1955; the comparable probability for men who took their jobs in 1971 was .52. Decreases of lesser magnitude are evident at durations of two and one-half and five years. The probability of surviving two and one-half years fell from .53 for men beginning jobs in 1955 to .33 for men beginning jobs in 1971; the probability of surviving five years fell from .27 for men beginning jobs in 1955 to .20 for men beginning jobs in 1967.

These figures reveal modest change in the rate of mobility. For the most part the changes echo the changes in Table 10.4. These new figures cast those patterns in a different light, but they reflect the same underlying reality. That reality is marked by a modest change in mobility rates, most of which is attributable to the shifting composition of the Irish work force. Overall mobility rose slightly in Ireland between the mid-1950s and the mid-1970s. The principal source of that rise was cohort succession: younger men pursued occupational paths that were heretofore unattainable in Ireland. Those new occupational paths entailed more mobility than the old paths did. In that way overall mobility was boosted upward.

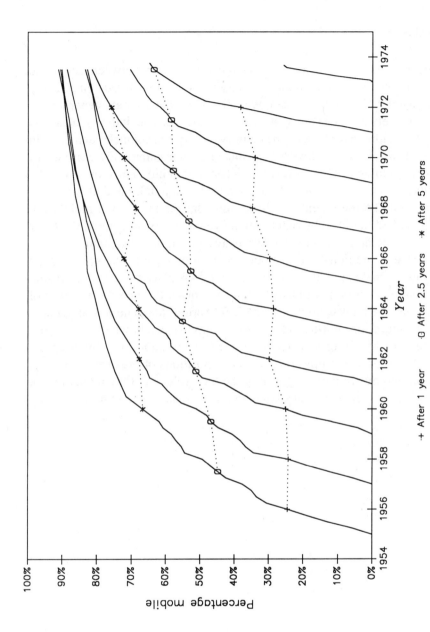

Figure 10.5 Cumulative mobility hazard, by calendar year: job shifts, Ireland, 1955–1974.

Conclusion

Duncan (1966a, p. 51) argued that the relationship between economic development and occupational mobility must be considered "empirically contingent": "There is and can be no fixed and determinate general relationship between measures of economic growth and indexes of social mobility, either over time in one country or between countries at a point in time. A whole set of auxiliary postulates, each empirically contingent, must be adopted before a relation between mobility and growth can be deduced." The microdynamics of industrialization in Ireland illustrate his point well. To the extent to which industrialization affected mobility in Ireland at all, it did so by redistributing young men who entered the labor force for the first time in the 1960s away from traditional, stable pursuits toward less traditional, more mobile occupational paths. Nearly all of the shift in the makeup of the Irish labor force took place through cohort succession. Very little net redistribution took place through the mobility of men employed throughout the 1959–1974 period. Make no mistake: many men changed jobs during this period. Their changes, however, were governed more by career path and life-cycle considerations than by macrosocial change. The net upward mobility to positions of prestige, authority, and autonomy are moves typical of the life cycle, and they reflect few of the macroeconomic changes sweeping Irish society at the time.

11 New Opportunities, Old Inequalities

"Creative destruction" sums up the prevailing image of industrial development. Industrial growth, according to this view, transforms society from top to bottom. The growth of manufacturing establishes a new social order increasingly attuned to achievement, primarily opposed to continuity from one generation to the next.[1] The old order is crushed as new forms of producing goods and exploiting labor advance. The destruction of the old order and the creation of a new one bring with them a historic enlargement of opportunity. Industrial development offers the offspring of the poor more than just the hope of a job at the bottom of the new hierarchy. The school system and other agencies of development offer the promise of substantial rise through a new order that cares about merit more than it cares about the circumstances of birth.

The case study of development and social mobility in Ireland contradicts this image of creative destruction. Even though industrialization swept the Republic of Ireland and economic growth solidified the hold of manufacturing in Northern Ireland during the 1960s, both parts of Ireland continue to carry the marks of the old order. Social class advantages are transported from the countryside to the city. Social mobility per se is not a guarantee of fairness; among mobile men, the stratification process still allocates the better jobs to the men from advantaged social class origins. Notwithstanding economic development and demographic changes, the underlying association between social origins and destinations remains unchanged. The occupational world faced by the current generation of Irish workers differs markedly from that of their fathers, but contrary to popular images of creative destruction, class differences persist.

Class Barriers and Occupational Opportunity

How could the thesis that industrialization remakes society be so wrong —at least in the Irish case? The problem lies in the materials from which the thesis was constructed. This image of creative destruction is the product of inference, not observation. It emerged from analysis of the development of Western industrial democracies during the nineteenth century. The opportunity to observe the first wave of industrialization up close had passed before the social sciences were in a position to record its progress.[2]

The emergence of new industrial societies since 1960 offers a natural experiment against which to test the image based on Western history. That task is well under way, but there are conceptual problems. Most newly industrial societies are non-Western. This creates a problem because Western and non-Western societies differ more profoundly than merely in the timing of industrialization. Studies of industrialization in Asia can hardly be conclusive in their attempts to separate the effects of culture and industrial change. A proponent of the view that industrialization progressively transformed the social order of England cannot be dissuaded just because the effects of industrialization fail to appear in places like Taiwan, Hong Kong, and Korea.

Ireland, as a new industrial society within the Western tradition, therefore takes on crucial importance as a special case in this attempt to evaluate the thesis of industrialization. The preconditions for the natural experiment are met: industrialization occurred recently enough for close observation, and the cultural context is clearly Western. Furthermore, the data themselves—the work histories of living participants in the industrialization process—are of superior quality.

Ireland in the 1950s depended on small-scale, traditional agriculture in an era when richer nations had mechanized agriculture (if they had any agriculture at all). By the winter of 1973–74 Ireland had developed a modern economy with more balance among the agricultural, manufacturing, and service sectors than ever before. This is exactly the kind of rapid change that occupied the early theorists of mobility (especially Sorokin 1927).[3] But in Ireland the sweeping changes so crucial for evaluating the thesis of industrialization occurred during the living memory of contemporary workers. The microdynamics of these changes can be discovered by analysis of detailed reports from the workers who lived through the transformation of Irish society. As a data source, interviews have distinct advantages over the archival sources used earlier. They are more detailed and more accurate.[4]

In addition, the cultural and political climate that contributed to both the lateness and the swiftness of modernization can be studied in its own right. That climate is part of the Western European tradition, but it has its own special features that affect the pattern of mobility. Ireland is strikingly homogeneous. Political divisions along social, economic, and foreign policy issues do not exist to the same extent as they do in other nations of Western Europe. The one deep cleavage—the religious division—goes back centuries and has not changed since modernization began. The combination of conflict and consensus, the ambivalent relationship of the two Irish heritages with British culture, and the ethnic bonds that run out from Ireland to Irish people in the United States, Canada, Australia, and England mark a distinctive national culture—yet not so unique that the observer would fail to learn something about the Western tradition as a whole from the special case of Ireland.

Thus, the lack of change in equality of occupational opportunity in Ireland during the period of rapid industrialization is a telling fact not only about Irish national development but also about industrialization itself. The persistence of class advantage across generations that are separated by a dramatic surge in economic development implies that the thesis of industrialization (with its image of progress through creative destruction) is wrong. In Ireland industrialization affected social mobility, but not in the way supposed (Sorokin 1927; Marshall 1938; Parsons 1940, 1953, 1970; Dahrendorf 1959). Industrialization was expected to lead to a society in which mobility would break down class barriers. Instead, it fostered a kind of mobility that moved people but not class barriers. Economic development created new opportunities for employment in manual and managerial occupations in manufacturing that drew the sons and daughters of agricultural workers off the farm. This kind of mobility, known as structural mobility, is partly a response to new opportunities in manufacturing and services and partly a reflection of the dwindling demand for agricultural labor. In theory, these new positions were to go to talented workers, regardless of their class positions under the old order (or at least with less continuity from generation to generation). But as of 1974, the class barriers were as strong as they had been in the 1950s.

Class Barriers and Education

While the fact that industrialization failed to affect the parameters of social inequality in Ireland is remarkable enough, it is all the more remarkable in view of the wholesale changes in both the Republic and Northern Ireland that accompanied the economic growth of the 1960s. The distribution of occupations, the conditions of work, and the aspirations of the Irish people were all in flux at once. These changes supported correlative changes in the systems of education in both parts of Ireland.

Secondary and higher education expanded rapidly in the 1960s. This expansion led to huge gains in Irish human capital. In both the Republic and Northern Ireland working-class students found their chances of advanced education greatly improved relative to their counterparts in prior generations. Despite a surprising lack of change in the effect of origins on educational transitions, there was a decline in overall inequality of educational opportunity (see Halsey et al. 1980 for similar results in Great Britain). The educational reforms of the late 1940s in Northern Ireland (and the rest of the UK) and of the late 1950s and 1960s in the Republic benefited the working class more than the middle class in two ways. First, the expansion occurred in parts of the educational system that already had middle-class representation. The new positions went to young people from working-class origins (from both urban and rural working classes) in part because they were a much bigger pool of untapped talent. But this factor was not as important as might be supposed. There was enormous room for improvement in education, even for youth from middle-class homes.

Far more important for the educational gains of the Irish working class was the pattern of class-based selection in Irish schools. In Ireland (as elsewhere), students get to higher education by passing a succession of hurdles: from primary to lower secondary school, from lower secondary to upper secondary, from upper secondary to college or university. The students who fail to make the earliest transitions are almost all from lower-class and working-class families. Further on, the students who stop are more evenly distributed across the social classes. In more technical terms, the educational system is very sensitive to social class at the transition from primary to secondary school and is less sensitive to class at each transition after that. By delaying the age of school leaving for all, the educational reforms removed the point of greatest class difference from the system. Many students still leave school at the minimum age, but now that the minimum age is higher, early school leavers are not exclusively lower and working class. Free secondary education and mandatory attendance to age 14 cause students from lower- and working-class families to bypass the point in the educational system where class selection is the greatest. The overall effect of raising the minimum school leaving age was to reduce class differences in educational attainment by removing one educational hurdle without altering the class balance of selection at any other particular point in the educational system.

This increase in educational opportunity for youth from lower- and working-class origins put them in a position to take advantage of the occupational opportunities that opened up as they were taking their leaving certification exams. Schooling fostered mobility by preparing more working-class students for middle-class careers. When professional and managerial opportunities exceeded the supply of middle-class school leavers, employers could find working-class youth with credentials who could fill the newly created jobs.

Mobility and Inequality

Aside from the growing equality of educational opportunity, Irish social stratification did not change from the 1950s to the 1970s. Ireland has the same array of occupations that is found in other modern societies. But its distribution of the work force across those occupations is distinct. Despite the changes of the 1960s, the Irish economy, North and South, can still be described as "proprietorial" in scale and in social organization.

Irish workers are among the most autonomous in Europe. Self-employment exceeds that in other European nations for which comparable data exist (see Table 11.1).[5] Among employees, few work for large corporations or for the state in either Northern Ireland or the Republic (Wickham 1986). Many firms are family run, so formal strictures, such as bureaucratic hiring practices, have less to do with the on-the-job experiences of Irish workers than they do for workers in more bureaucratized societies of Western or Eastern Europe.

Likewise, few Irish workers spend their time managing other workers. Given the small scale of Irish enterprise, even owners contribute to production in most cases. This makes for "career ladders" of few rungs and little built-in mobility. The mean number of jobs for workers in the Irish Mobility Study was 5.6. Even among workers over 40 years old, the incidence of 10 or more jobs was rare, and it indicated unstable employment

Table 11.1
Distribution of employed men by occupation: selected European countries

| | | | | | *Country* | | | | |
Occupation	Irish Republic	Northern Ireland	England	Scotland	France	West Germany	Sweden	Hungary	Poland
Professionals & managers	14%	18%	25%	21%	20%	28%	24%	15%	18%
Routine white collar	9	9	9	9	10	5	8	7	2
Proprietors	8	10	8	6	9	7	8	2	2
Skilled	20	26	33	33	24	37	30	31	31
Semiskilled & unskilled	21	24	22	25	21	18	22	30	19
Farmers	22	10	2	3	11	4	5	1	25
Farm laborers	7	3	2	3	3	3	2	14	3
Total	100	100	100	100	100	100	100	100	100

Source: Erikson and Goldthorpe (1987a).

more often than a busy career (American men average 17 jobs by the time they reach 45 years of age; Featherman 1983).

Within a proprietorial economy, there are important class distinctions. Inequalities of status are no less important in an informal economy than under bureaucratic formalism. Inequalities of opportunity abound. Upper-middle-class origins carry enormous advantages over working-class origins and some advantages over agricultural origins. The extent of those advantages does not differ in Northern Ireland and the Republic.

For illustrative purposes, compare the relative chances of working in a lower-level professional or managerial occupation (e.g., schoolteacher, supervisor of clerical workers, journalist, laboratory technician) and of working in an unskilled manual occupation (e.g., day laborer, porter, office cleaner, messenger). Clearly the odds compared here are those on a "good" job relative to a "poor" one; on the Hope-Goldthorpe prestige scale, these jobs differ by 42 points. The extent of unequal opportunity is gauged by the ratio of sons with "good" (lower professional) jobs to sons with "poor" (unskilled) jobs for different origins. The relative chances of different social classes (the odds ratios) are the same in both 1959 and 1973. Among sons of semiskilled workers, the ratio of lower professionals to unskilled workers is one to three; among sons of proprietors without employees, the ratio is five to four; among sons of upper professionals, the ratio is eight to one. The advantage of upper-middle-class origins is clear. In numerical terms, upper professionals' sons have a chance of landing a good job that is *six* times higher than the chance of proprietors' sons and *twenty-four* times higher than the chance of semiskilled workers' sons.

As might be expected in the proprietorial economy, nonvertical aspects of mobility are also very important. Labor market factors, especially the extent of formalization in occupational recruitment, play an important part in mobility that is discernible even within prestige levels. The emerging formal economy is in many ways distinct from the more traditional economy. Men whose fathers work (or worked) in the bureaucratic sector tend to stay in that sector, even if they are mobile in prestige terms. Similarly, personal contacts are more important in the traditional sector than in occupations that recruit more formally.

Mobility and Family

Irish inequality from generation to generation depends on two key factors: strong family values and a political culture that is not based on social class. In principle, religion and emigration might be expected to play significant roles in Irish stratification as well (e.g., Thernstrom 1973); in fact, they are less crucial.

Family values are important because they make legitimate certain employment practices that might otherwise be disapproved or even banned. Favoritism in hiring and special favors on the job are opposed in many societies, but they are taken for granted (and approved) in Ireland. Special treatment for family members aids in the maintenance of privilege (and poverty) from one generation to the next.

Not only does the word *clan* come to English from the Irish language, but personal honor and the precedence of familiar connections have deep roots in Irish culture and in Irish social structure (Greeley 1972). The data on Irish mobility have verified this connection several times. Family affects both vertical and nonvertical aspects of occupational mobility in Ireland.

Universalism is the opposite of special favors. It is the practice of hiring on merit, without regard to family ties, social class, gender, religious belief, or other factors unrelated to job performance. According to classical sociological theory, universalism ought to be expanding in contemporary Ireland (Sorokin 1927; Blau and Duncan 1967). Supposedly, the expansion of secondary and higher education dilutes the influence of family ties and class as grounds for hiring, firing, and promotion. In Ireland, however, the secondary schools and universities have expanded without bringing universalism to the labor market.

Once again, a theory fails to predict the course of development in Ireland. A clue to why education failed to override the influence of the family in Ireland is found in this passage from Sorokin (1927, p. 185): "Other conditions being equal, in a society where the family is sacred and durable; intermarriages between different social strata are few; the training and education of the children go on principally within the family; the number of testing and selective agencies is small; and they receive the young generation for training only at a relatively late age; in such a society, the family, as a testing, selecting, and distributing agency, plays an exclusively important role." According to the theory, universalism will expand when these conditions are reversed. Modernization of the economy, the spread of formal schooling, and the professionalization of employment are supposed to transfer the responsibility for socializing children from the family to the society at large. That shift will end the hold of the family and its special favors, supplanting it with the code of universalism. In Ireland the preconditions of this proposition have been fulfilled. Modernization proceeds; training has shifted from the family to the schools; the schools receive their charges at a young age. Despite these trends, the family continues to exert "an exclusively important role."

The theory of universalism seems reasonable enough. Why then did the shift in responsibility for socialization from family to school in Ireland fail to erode the influence of the Irish family over social stratification? The theory is based on an unwarranted assumption. Central to it is the assumption that society and family are in opposition. The theory implicitly assumes that family and external testing and selecting agencies are at odds with one another. That assumption does not appear to be true in Ireland. And the reason is this: if a society is homogeneous, the criteria for selection in public institutions can be expected to mirror those in private institutions. Ireland is certainly as homogeneous a society as one is likely to encounter. Suffice it to say that the contradiction between family values and institutional values assumed by Sorokin does not hold in Ireland, and that the expected decline in family influence over social stratification did not emerge.

Ireland is more stratified than are other European nations (Whelan and Whelan 1984; Breen and Whelan 1987; Erikson and Goldthorpe 1987a,b). Furthermore, its high level of association persisted over a period of significant macroeconomic change. A multidimensional model of that association demonstrates the importance of personal (mostly family) contacts in the Irish labor market. Together, these findings demonstrate the persistent importance of the family in Irish stratification.[6]

Mobility and Religion

Class, not religion, is the principal determinant of socioeconomic fortunes in Northern Ireland. This is an astounding conclusion to those who see a facile analogy between the denial of civil rights to blacks in the United States and discrimination against Catholics in the North. But once you have compared the squalor of Protestant slums in the Shank Hill section of Belfast with the squalor of Catholic slums in the Falls Road, the role of class becomes clear. The *social* distance from the suburbs that skirt the edge of Belfast to the slums is as great, whether they are the Protestant slums in Shank Hill or the Catholic slums in Falls Road.

The basis for this conclusion is firmer than simple observations of physical conditions in working areas inhabited by Catholics and Protestants.

The work histories show that Catholics from middle-class origins have advantages in the pursuit of professional employment over most Protestants from working-class backgrounds. Holding constant the workers' class of origin, Protestants have an advantage over Catholics, but that "main effect" of religion is not sufficient to overcome the "main effect" of class. Furthermore, the effect of origin status on destination status is as strong for Catholics as it is for Protestants.

This pattern of parallel class effects has been interpreted by the Equal Employment Commission in Northern Ireland in a most sanguine light. Miller (1984, 1986) uses data from the Irish Mobility Study to absolve Northern society of all charges of employment favoritism. Yet the current state of affairs is hardly just. Equal class disadvantages in both Protestant and Catholic slums do not equal justice. The middle class of Belfast lives as well as the middle class anywhere (the same cannot be said of the middle class elsewhere in Ireland); the conditions of the poor are absolutely wretched. With the working classes and the poor of both groups shut out of a game with such high stakes, the equal sharing of disadvantage deserves censure even if religion does not compound the injustice. Indeed, without the religious war, class barriers this strong would never be called fair.

Mobility and Emigration

The economic expansion of the 1960s and the ensuing structural mobility of the Irish labor force shut off 120 years of emigration. Population on the island fell from 8.3 million in 1841 to a low of 4.2 million in 1961 (Jackson 1963, p. 25). During that time births exceeded deaths by a wide margin— even during the famine of the 1840s—but emigration outstripped natural increase. Emigration fluctuated around a very high average, peaking in the 1880s and again in the 1950s (Kennedy 1973, p. 213). This emigration led to declines in the total population of Ireland between each of the censuses from 1841 to 1966, save for the censuses of 1946 to 1951 (when population in the Republic increased by 6,000). Net emigration averaged 15,000 persons a year in the 1950s (Kennedy 1973, p. 213). If we consider that the combined adult population of all of Ireland was just under 3 million in 1951, the figure of more than 200,000 emigrants for the decade is staggering.[7]

Population has grown since 1966, despite a falling rate of natural increase (Central Statistics Office of Ireland 1986a, table A). Net migration was actually positive in the 1970s, when an average of 13,600 more persons entered the Republic than left it (Central Statistics Office of Ireland 1986a, table J). Given the opportunity to stay, the youth of Ireland sought and found work in their homeland. That opportunity is eroding in the 1980s.

Mobility and Public Policy

This study of development and mobility in Ireland is not the first to strike a blow against the industrialization thesis. The idea that economic advance weakens the association between socioeconomic origins and destinations has received little support in comparative work and even less in studies of trends in single countries.[8] Moreover, evidence is mounting that public policy directed at equalizing socioeconomic opportunities can effectively shrink class barriers.[9] The evidence on this point includes studies comparing Sweden with England and France (Erikson, Goldthorpe, and Portocarero 1979, 1982; Hauser 1984), Hungary before Communism with Hungary afterward (Simkus 1984), Sweden and Hungary with several European and non-European countries (Erikson and Goldthorpe 1987a,b), and the United States in 1962 with the United States since then (Featherman and Hauser 1978; Hout 1988), as well as less detailed studies of larger samples of countries (Grusky and Hauser 1984).

Sweden is more open than other European societies in the specific sense that the association between origins and destinations is significantly weaker in Sweden than it is in other countries for which data are available. Class boundaries are weaker in Sweden than in England or France (Erikson, Goldthorpe, and Portocarero 1979, 1982). This finding has been replicated using a variety of methods (Hauser 1984) and a broader sample of countries (Erikson and Goldthorpe 1987a,b). Sweden's openness is attributed to the long-running hegemony of the Social Democratic philosophy. Successive governments have aggressively pursued educational and employment policies that have been designed to equalize the chances of all Swedes to achieve their socioeconomic potential without the impediment of social class origins (Korpi 1983). Hungary broke down class barriers during the same period by consciously favoring individuals of working-class background in the recruitment of people for state-controlled professional and managerial positions (Simkus 1984). American governments have not espoused the same political philosophies as Sweden or Hungary, yet the association between origins and destinations in the United States has fallen 50 percent since 1962 (Hout 1988). The key to weaker class barriers in the United States is the system of higher education. And the trend in inequality of occupational opportunity is clearly tied to the trend in educational attainment. American public policy, through support for public colleges and universities and periodic direct aid and loans to students (contingent on financial need), has indirectly accomplished the same improvements in equality of opportunity as Sweden and Hungary have.

The cases of public policy and mobility in Sweden, Hungary, and the United States are more suggestive than conclusive. Supporting evidence comes from studies of broader samples of countries (but cruder data). In their analysis of sixteen countries Grusky and Hauser (1984; see also Hauser and Grusky 1988) find an effect of "political commitment to equality" on the association parameters. That finding was replicated, using an even larger data base by Ganzeboom, Treiman, and Luijkx (1988).

This study of mobility in Ireland can be counted as left-handed corroboration of the thesis that public policy is decisive for change in openness or equality of opportunity. Irish politics does not conform to the class-based model prevalent in much of Europe (Brown 1984). The largest parties trace their roots to the civil war over the partition of Ireland. Both recruit their support from all social classes. While some welfare state provisions are made in Ireland, no large working-class movement has emerged to push the case for the reform of Irish social inequality. Thus the case for believing that public policy must be a factor in breaking down class barriers has to be a left-handed one. In Ireland class barriers to achievement were never on the political agenda, and those barriers remained intact despite substantial economic development.

The Irish staked their hopes for economic equity on the old adage that "a rising tide lifts all boats." To some extent Irish workers have been well served by this tack. Most Irish families were better off in the mid-1970s than their counterparts had been in the mid-1950s. But it is clear that after a period of very impressive economic growth, Ireland was no more open in the mid-1970s than it had been in the mid-1950s. To reduce class barriers in the Republic and Northern Ireland, government policy directed at the class barriers themselves will be necessary.

A variety of programs that have succeeded in other countries might distribute opportunity in Ireland more equitably. The scale of economic enterprise in Ireland is too small, however, for the broad guarantees of equal access found in Sweden to be effective. Employment decision making is too diffuse and family prerogatives are too deeply ingrained to permit the kind of regulation that would be necessary to bring Irish employers into line with the practices of their Swedish counterparts. Nor would the radical working-class favoritism of the Hungarian Communist Party garner much support in Dublin or Belfast.

Public policy on equality of occupational opportunity must be in line with local conditions. The American policy of indirectly fostering equal opportunity through the schools seems to be a plausible model for Ireland. Slots in Irish universities are already fairly distributed among students with leaving certificates. More outreach is needed to guarantee that working-class youths stay in school long enough to take the leaving certificate exams. Later selection of students for academic and nonacademic education would also diminish the influence of social class origins on educational outcomes. Origins correlate more highly with early performance in the classroom and on tests than with later performance in both France (Garnier and Hout 1982) and the United States (Jencks 1972). It seems reasonable to assume that a similar relationship holds in Ireland. Selection of students for academic careers based on early performance exaggerates the importance of origins. If academic selection were held off until later, the late bloomers (who are disproportionately working class in origin) would be less likely to be overlooked.

One recommendation is to focus educational resources on working-class students of *average* ability (Coleman and Kilgore 1987). These are the students who are most susceptible to school effects. Bright students succeed regardless of how well or how poorly they are treated. Likewise, dull students cannot advance beyond a certain level no matter what is done for them. Ironically, a disproportionate share of school programs are directed at these extremes. The forgotten students in the middle of the academic stream are, in fact, the ones who sink or swim depending on how they are treated. The Republic, Northern Ireland, and other countries would do well to bolster the success rates of students in the middle of the academic ability spectrum.

Successful programs will deliver to the labor market an array of school leavers that is as clearly certified as today's entering cohorts are. The difference will be the extent to which those credentials of certification reflect differences of social origin. There is now a substantial correlation between origins and education—an association that contributes to the overall correlation between origins and destinations. If the link between origins and education could be broken, great strides in the direction of fairness in employment would follow.

A precondition for the success of any of these reform measures is economic growth. Structural mobility must be maintained, or fairness programs will be attacked by those whose interests are threatened. Redistributive equity achieved by taking from A to give to B is almost never politically feasible. Improvements in fairness must come in a context of growth. Growth hides redistribution, because the battleground is the apportionment of new positions rather than the redistribution of existing positions. Vigorous growth seems a long way off during this time of retrenchment in Ireland, but growth of some sort must be rekindled before equity can become feasible.

Where is the growth to come from? Contemporary models—Reaganomics, Thatcherism, and supply-side voodoo economics—will not work for Ireland. Those policies are predicated on giveaway tax cuts for the rich. The economic elite in Ireland is quite simply too small. It lacks the capital (before or after taxes) to haul the island out of its current fiscal bog.

Nor does the current austerity offer much hope for success. Belt tightening will depress foreign and domestic investment, exacerbate the current brain drain, and return the Irish economy to the stagnant state of the 1950s. That was an era of lost opportunities brought on by a fear of deficits (Kennedy and Dowling 1975). The new middle class of service sector professionals and managers have had their ranks thinned by Thatcher, Fitzgerald, and Haughey. The current consensus in both North and South considers cuts in health, education, and social services inevitable, as political leaders appeal to this year's bottom line. But the accountants do not factor into the equation the cost of losing the best and the brightest of the current generation. Make no mistake: that cost is great. The doctors, teachers, researchers, and engineers who have been made redundant by the cuts see no alternative but to quit the country that paid for their training. Every day more Irish leave for London, New York, and points beyond.[10] Neither the Republic nor Northern Ireland can afford the loss.

To stop the backsliding, out-of-vogue Keynesian pump priming with an up-to-date high tech twist offers much more in the way of hope for Ireland. Straight old-fashioned Keynesian policies are not needed. The physical plant does not need any more public spending. The industrial parks built in the 1960s and 1970s still offer excess capacity. Instead, the service sector needs to be stimulated by reversing the current round of cuts in universities, hospitals, and research. High tech services like telecommunications need to be expanded. After all, it is easier to phone California from Dublin than it is to phone Dingle from Cork. Public expenditures to improve services will provide employment for the young professionals, managers, and engineers who are most likely to emigrate.

Human capital is Ireland's greatest asset with enormous unrealized potential. Current policies are leading to the export of that talent. Past borrowing against a brighter future might well have contributed to the current tight money situation because the bright future failed to materialize on the schedule set by the lenders. Be that as it may, unless new investment presents itself soon, the rent money must be wagered once again. In the final analysis, more debt is a gamble worth taking because, unless something is tried soon, another generation will be lost to Ireland. This generation is all the more precious and irreplaceable because society has so much invested in it.

Conclusion

This study has been first and foremost an effort to measure the extent of inequality of opportunity in Irish society. The data and methods of modern quantitative sociology are uniquely well suited to this task. The work histories collected in the Irish Mobility Study provide a rich data source about a very important period in Irish history.

In the end, in qualitative terms, we see that there is some opportunity in Ireland, but not enough. What opportunity there is ought to be shared more equitably. To some extent, the inequalities reflect the weaknesses in the economies of the Republic and Northern Ireland. But not totally. Inequalities are ingrained in Irish education as it is structured in both the Republic and Northern Ireland. The inequalities also are rooted in the traditional prerogatives of the Irish family. Deep-rooted though they may be, the inequalities in Irish social structure are not immutable. A number of changes have been suggested for reducing class barriers in Ireland. They are feasible changes that have produced positive results elsewhere. I can only hope that the next Irish Mobility Study will find greater equality of opportunity.

Appendix Tables   Supporting Data

Table A.1

Occupational origin by current occupation: men aged 18–65, Republic of Ireland, 1973

Origin	Code	Ia	Ib	II	IIIa	IVa	IVb	IIIb	V	VI	VIIss	VIIus	IVc	IVd	VIIf	Total
									Current occupation							
Professionals & proprietors[a]	Ia	7[b]	8	1	1	0	1	1	0	0	0	0	0	0	0	19
Professionals & managers	Ib	0	8	10	2	0	0	3	2	1	1	0	0	0	0	26
Professionals & managers	II	4	15	23	11	5	3	3	8	8	7	3	1	2	0	93
Clerical & sales workers	IIIa	2	12	12	13	2	2	2	8	6	7	2	0	2	0	70
Proprietors with employees[a]	IVa	1	13	17	8	5	8	9	9	6	10	3	0	1	1	111
Proprietors no employees[a]	IVb	1	6	10	2	8	16	4	8	11	20	10	2	3	4	105
Service workers	IIIb	0	1	1	5	1	1	4	3	7	7	2	1	0	2	35
Technicians & foremen	V	1	1	8	6	4	3	1	12	23	10	5	0	2	0	76
Skilled manual workers	VI	1	11	23	12	6	0	10	18	86	43	24	1	0	1	236
Semiskilled manual workers	VIIss	2	5	20	13	7	6	13	19	46	50	26	0	5	8	220
Unskilled manual workers	VIIus	0	2	6	12	4	7	12	15	52	52	52	0	5	22	241
Farmers with employees[a]	IVc	1	6	14	1	8	5	3	5	5	10	8	55	47	7	175
Farmers no employees[a]	IVd	3	10	28	16	14	21	13	26	31	46	44	25	262	16	557
Agricultural workers	VIIf	0	3	1	5	3	13	6	9	16	27	33	2	10	37	165
Total		23	100	175	107	87	86	84	143	298	290	212	87	339	98	2130

a.   Self–employed workers.
b.   Frequencies are weighted counts rounded to nearest integer. Row and column totals were rounded independently, so some totals may differ slightly from the sum of the numbers in the table.

Table A.2

Occupational origin by current occupation: men aged 18–65, Northern Ireland, 1973

Origin	Code	Current occupation														Total
		Ia	Ib	II	IIIa	IVa	IVb	IIIb	V	VI	VIIss	VIIus	IVc	IVd	VIIf	
Professionals & proprietors[a]	Ia	4[b]	5	3	0	3	0	0	0	2	1	0	1	1	0	20
Professionals & managers	Ib	5	17	12	5	1	0	0	2	3	4	1	0	0	0	50
Professionals & managers	II	5	20	39	13	1	2	5	9	10	10	4	0	1	3	122
Clerical & sales workers	IIIa	1	7	16	16	6	2	7	4	13	8	3	0	0	0	82
Proprietors with employees[a]	IVa	2	17	16	10	28	8	2	8	16	17	2	1	4	2	133
Proprietors no employees[a]	IVb	1	4	8	8	10	14	4	7	15	14	7	0	0	0	92
Service workers	IIIb	0	3	9	6	4	2	6	5	13	9	1	1	1	0	60
Technicians & foremen	V	1	8	13	7	10	6	5	16	26	11	8	1	1	0	113
Skilled manual workers	VI	3	17	35	16	18	12	20	38	109	70	31	0	0	5	374
Semiskilled manual workers	VIIss	2	15	31	13	8	15	18	41	90	106	52	1	0	8	400
Unskilled manual workers	VIIus	1	4	11	16	5	5	8	25	50	77	33	1	1	0	238
Farmers with employees[a]	IVc	2	8	19	7	16	10	5	3	6	17	5	41	24	5	168
Farmers no employees[a]	IVd	1	3	14	12	14	17	5	12	40	47	24	13	107	11	320
Agricultural workers	VIIf	0	2	7	2	1	5	5	11	23	30	16	0	3	14	119
Total		28	130	233	132	125	98	90	181	416	421	187	60	143	48	2292

a. Self-employed workers.
b. Frequencies are weighted counts rounded to nearest integer. Row and column totals were rounded independently, so some totals may differ slightly from the sum of the numbers in the table.

Table A.3

Occupational origin by first occupation: men aged 18–65, Republic of Ireland, 1973

Origin	Code	Ia	Ib	II	IIIa	IVa	IVb	IIIb	VIIInf	V	VI	VIIss	VIIus	IVc	IVd	VIIf	VIIIf	Total
Professionals & proprietors[a]	Ia	2[b]	7	1	5	0	1	1	1	3	0	1	0	0	0	0	0	22
Professionals & managers	Ib	0	3	4	7	0	0	2	0	1	5	1	0	0	0	1	2	26
Professionals & managers	II	0	6	13	21	0	0	9	3	6	8	10	6	0	1	2	5	90
Clerical & sales workers	IIIa	0	5	8	23	0	0	9	1	3	6	7	3	0	0	1	1	67
Proprietors with employees[a]	IVa	0	8	4	11	0	1	11	30	4	27	7	5	1	0	3	5	116
Proprietors no employees[a]	IVb	0	1	2	6	0	3	13	12	3	25	14	10	1	0	3	11	104
Service workers	IIIb	0	0	0	3	1	0	6	0	3	6	5	4	0	0	0	3	31
Unpaid workers, nonfarm	VIIInf	0	0	0	1	0	0	1	1	0	1	1	0	0	0	0	0	5
Technicians & foremen	V	0	2	4	7	0	1	4	1	10	13	10	11	0	3	3	9	75
Skilled manual workers	VI	0	2	5	13	0	0	22	4	11	67	49	32	0	2	3	10	220
Semiskilled manual workers	VIIss	0	2	5	16	0	0	28	0	17	33	47	39	0	0	8	18	213
Unskilled manual workers	VIIus	0	1	4	10	1	0	19	1	10	39	48	31	0	0	12	58	234
Farmers with employees[a]	IVc	0	3	7	4	0	0	7	4	4	7	2	3	7	4	127	15	194
Farmers no employees[a]	IVd	0	5	14	11	0	4	24	3	15	23	13	23	1	7	407	57	607
Agricultural workers	VIIf	0	0	0	1	0	0	0	0	0	0	0	0	0	0	3	0	4
Unpaid workers, farm	VIIIf	0	0	1	3	0	0	8	0	7	14	14	12	0	0	12	93	164
Total		2	45	72	142	2	9	164	61	97	274	229	179	10	14	585	287	2172

a.   Self–employed workers.

b.   Frequencies are weighted counts rounded to nearest integer. Row and column totals were rounded independently, so some totals may differ slightly from the sum of the numbers in the table.

Table A.4

Occupational origin by first occupation: men aged 18–65, Northern Ireland, 1973

Origin	Code	First occupation																Total
		Ia	Ib	II	IIIa	IVa	IVb	IIIb	VIIInf	V	VI	VIIss	VIIus	IVc	IVd	VIIf	VIIIf	
Professionals & proprietors[a]	Ia	0[b]	6	2	1	1	0	2	4	1	3	1	0	0	0	0	0	21
Professionals & managers	Ib	0	12	4	8	0	0	3	2	3	6	9	0	0	0	1	0	48
Professionals & managers	II	2	4	13	26	0	0	15	3	11	14	21	9	0	0	3	4	125
Clerical & sales workers	IIIa	0	3	7	16	0	0	10	0	7	18	8	4	0	0	0	1	74
Proprietors with employees[a]	IVa	1	7	7	13	2	1	12	32	4	23	8	6	0	0	5	8	135
Proprietors no employees[a]	IVb	0	1	3	5	0	0	10	4	6	17	14	12	0	0	6	3	84
Service workers	IIIb	0	0	2	6	0	0	10	2	5	14	14	5	0	0	0	1	59
Unpaid workers, nonfarm	VIIInf	0	0	1	1	0	0	1	0	2	1	2	0	0	0	0	0	8
Technicians & foremen	V	0	1	8	12	0	0	11	0	13	34	15	11	0	0	1	3	109
Skilled manual workers	VI	0	7	7	28	0	1	35	2	22	110	85	38	0	0	2	21	358
Semiskilled manual workers	VIIss	1	5	8	26	0	1	43	2	16	88	119	51	0	0	3	27	390
Unskilled manual workers	VIIus	0	1	1	8	1	0	27	1	10	43	56	42	0	0	4	32	226
Farmers with employees[a]	IVc	1	3	5	9	1	0	12	6	7	7	4	2	5	3	95	12	172
Farmers no employees[a]	IVd	0	5	7	4	0	1	13	1	10	24	15	14	0	9	186	48	337
Agricultural workers	VIIf	0	0	0	0	0	0	0	0	0	1	0	0	0	0	5	0	6
Unpaid workers, farm	VIIIf	0	0	2	0	0	0	13	0	7	15	12	8	0	0	1	55	113
Total		5	55	77	163	5	7	217	59	124	418	389	202	5	12	312	215	2265

a. Self–employed workers.

b. Frequencies are weighted counts rounded to nearest integer. Row and column totals were rounded independently, so some totals may differ slightly from the sum of the numbers in the table.

Table A.5

First occupation by current occupation: men aged 18–65, Republic of Ireland, 1973

First occupation	Code							Current occupation										Total
		Ia	Ib	II	IIIa	IVa	IVb	IIIb	VIIInf	V	VI	VIIss	VIIus	IVc	IVd	VIIf	VIIIf	
Professionals & proprietors[a]	Ia	2[b]	0	0	0	0	0	0	0	0	0	0	0	0	0	0	0	2
Professionals & managers	Ib	9	31	2	1	1	1	0	0	0	0	0	0	0	0	0	0	45
Professionals & managers	II	2	10	49	5	1	1	1	0	1	0	2	0	0	0	0	0	72
Clerical & sales workers	IIIa	5	23	33	45	6	2	4	2	9	4	6	3	0	0	0	0	142
Proprietors with employees[a]	IVa	0	0	0	0	0	1	0	0	0	0	0	0	0	0	0	0	2
Proprietors no employees[a]	IVb	0	1	0	0	1	0	0	0	0	1	0	1	0	2	0	0	9
Service workers	IIIb	0	6	19	12	11	8	35	2	7	20	26	6	4	2	2	4	162
Unpaid workers, nonfarm	VIIInf	1	2	7	4	12	4	1	8	2	6	10	1	0	3	0	0	61
Technicians & foremen	V	1	0	7	4	7	3	0	0	45	7	11	3	2	2	1	3	96
Skilled manual workers	VI	1	11	17	3	20	16	2	4	19	133	24	14	1	6	0	1	272
Semiskilled manual workers	VIIss	2	9	10	9	11	4	13	2	16	38	72	36	0	3	0	5	230
Unskilled manual workers	VIIus	0	1	4	8	4	6	8	0	11	31	43	40	4	9	0	4	173
Farmers with employees[a]	IVc	0	0	0	0	1	0	0	0	0	0	0	0	7	0	0	0	9
Farmers no employees[a]	IVd	0	0	0	0	0	0	0	0	0	0	0	2	0	12	0	0	14
Agricultural workers	VIIf	0	1	18	7	12	17	7	2	14	19	37	35	57	268	77	13	579
Unpaid workers, farm	VIIIf	0	2	5	2	3	15	9	0	13	21	45	58	10	30	2	69	284
Total		23	97	166	100	90	82	80	20	137	280	276	199	85	338	80	99	2152

a.   Self-employed workers.

b.   Frequencies are weighted counts rounded to nearest integer. Row and column totals were rounded independently, so some totals may differ slightly from the sum of the numbers in the table.

Table A.6

First occupation by current occupation: men aged 18–65, Northern Ireland, 1973

First occupation	Code	Ia	Ib	II	IIIa	IVa	IVb	IIIb	VIIInf	V	VI	VIIss	VIIus	IVc	IVd	VIIf	VIIIf	Total
										Current occupation								
Professionals & proprietors[a]	Ia	4[b]	0	0	0	0	0	0	0	0	1	0	0	0	0	0	0	5
Professionals & managers	Ib	6	39	6	1	1	0	0	0	0	0	2	0	0	0	0	0	55
Professionals & managers	II	0	9	54	2	3	2	2	0	2	2	2	1	0	0	0	0	77
Clerical & sales workers	IIIa	2	26	40	50	9	2	4	0	11	7	9	2	0	0	0	0	162
Proprietors with employees[a]	IVa	0	0	0	0	4	0	0	0	0	0	1	0	0	0	0	0	5
Proprietors no employees[a]	IVb	0	0	0	0	0	4	0	0	0	0	1	1	0	0	0	0	7
Service workers	IIIb	2	10	33	25	16	8	29	1	8	27	41	10	1	3	1	1	216
Unpaid workers, nonfarm	VIIInf	3	3	5	3	19	7	0	1	3	1	7	2	2	3	0	0	59
Technicians & foremen	V	1	4	9	4	10	12	6	0	51	12	9	5	0	1	0	1	125
Skilled manual workers	VI	7	17	32	7	26	22	4	2	32	178	64	25	1	3	0	2	422
Semiskilled manual workers	VIIss	3	10	26	16	17	7	20	3	27	74	128	47	2	1	4	3	388
Unskilled manual workers	VIIus	0	2	11	2	7	6	13	0	25	50	55	29	0	2	0	2	204
Farmers with employees[a]	IVc	0	0	1	1	0	0	0	0	0	0	0	1	2	0	0	0	5
Farmers no employees[a]	IVd	0	0	1	0	0	0	0	0	0	0	0	0	1	10	0	0	12
Agricultural workers	VIIf	0	2	8	9	11	17	6	0	3	20	34	12	48	107	27	9	313
Unpaid workers, farm	VIIIf	0	4	6	2	5	6	5	0	17	32	48	45	3	13	0	26	212
Total		28	126	232	122	128	93	89	7	179	402	401	180	60	143	31	46	2267

a.   Self–employed workers.

b.   Frequencies are weighted counts rounded to nearest integer. Row and column totals were rounded independently, so some totals may differ slightly from the sum of the numbers in the table.

Table A.7

Occupation in 1959 by occupation in 1973: men aged 18–65, Republic of Ireland, 1973

1959 occupation	Code	Ia	Ib	II	IIIa	IVa	IVb	IIIb	VIInf	V	VI	VIIss	VIIus	IVc	IVd	VIIf	VIIIf	Out of work	Total
Professionals & proprietors[a]	Ia	5[b]	0	1	0	0	0	0	0	0	0	0	0	0	0	0	0	0	6
Professionals & managers	Ib	6	28	5	0	0	0	0	0	0	2	0	0	0	1	0	0	1	43
Professionals & managers	II	2	13	53	3	2	1	0	0	0	2	0	0	0	0	0	0	1	79
Clerical & sales workers	IIIa	2	7	17	30	11	2	2	0	2	1	4	0	2	0	0	0	0	81
Proprietors with employees[a]	IVa	1	0	2	0	21	1	0	0	0	0	0	0	0	0	0	0	2	27
Proprietors no employees[a]	IVb	0	0	0	0	6	24	2	1	4	1	4	0	0	5	1	0	6	49
Service workers	IIIb	0	1	7	6	2	2	28	0	3	3	7	4	5	0	0	0	4	68
Unpaid workers, nonfarm	VIInf	1	0	1	2	9	2	0	2	1	4	0	0	1	1	1	1	0	26
Technicians & foremen	V	1	3	6	1	5	13	0	0	43	4	5	1	0	2	2	1	4	79
Skilled manual workers	VI	1	8	6	1	10	4	1	1	15	117	15	2	1	3	0	0	14	211
Semiskilled manual workers	VIIss	0	3	5	6	8	6	1	1	12	11	115	7	0	4	4	0	17	203
Unskilled manual workers	VIIus	0	0	3	1	1	6	0	0	6	10	19	81	0	6	1	1	36	175
Farmers with employees[a]	IVc	0	0	1	0	0	0	0	0	0	0	0	0	35	6	0	0	0	42
Farmers no employees[a]	IVd	0	0	0	0	0	0	0	0	0	0	0	0	8	169	1	0	2	184
Agricultural workers	VIIf	0	0	0	1	2	3	0	0	7	7	7	19	3	13	40	0	18	114
Unpaid workers, farm	VIIIf	0	0	0	0	3	2	2	0	9	2	9	2	29	105	1	20	4	183
Too young		4	35	63	55	9	15	26	14	48	107	63	41	7	21	23	47	72	650
Out of work		0	0	2	1	3	2	0	0	3	4	6	8	0	0	0	2	36	67
Total		23	98	172	107	91	77	77	19	139	273	256	158	85	336	73	70	217	2287

a.   Self–employed workers.

b.   Frequencies are weighted counts rounded to nearest integer. Row and column totals were rounded independently, so some totals may differ slightly from the sum of the numbers in the table.

Table A.8

Occupation in 1959 by occupation in 1973: men aged 18–65, Northern Ireland, 1973

1959 occupation	Code	Ia	Ib	II	IIIa	IVa	IVb	IIIb	VIIInf	V	VI	VIIss	VIIus	IVc	IVd	VIIf	VIIIf	Out of work	Total
Professionals & proprietors[a]	Ia	11[b]	2	1	1	0	0	0	1	0	0	0	0	0	0	0	0	1	16
Professionals & managers	Ib	7	37	5	1	0	0	0	0	0	2	1	0	0	0	0	0	4	57
Professionals & managers	II	0	14	61	6	3	3	7	0	1	2	2	0	0	1	0	0	4	102
Clerical & sales workers	IIIa	3	11	30	36	6	1	1	0	2	1	5	1	0	0	0	0	4	101
Proprietors with employees[a]	IVa	0	1	1	3	36	2	0	0	1	2	1	1	0	0	0	0	5	53
Proprietors no employees[a]	IVb	0	0	1	1	8	27	1	0	0	1	1	0	0	0	0	0	5	46
Service workers	IIIb	0	1	12	8	7	3	22	0	3	3	10	3	0	0	0	0	8	80
Unpaid workers, nonfarm	VIIInf	0	1	2	2	10	3	0	2	0	0	1	0	0	2	0	0	0	23
Technicians & foremen	V	0	7	6	8	6	6	3	0	65	11	9	1	0	0	0	0	5	127
Skilled manual workers	VI	2	7	17	3	14	15	4	0	24	165	35	6	0	1	1	0	25	319
Semiskilled manual workers	VIIss	0	4	6	5	5	7	12	0	20	33	166	20	1	0	3	1	23	306
Unskilled manual workers	VIIus	0	0	2	4	0	5	4	0	9	22	26	57	0	0	0	0	33	163
Farmers with employees[a]	IVc	0	0	1	0	2	0	0	0	0	0	0	0	19	2	0	0	1	25
Farmers no employees[a]	IVd	0	0	0	0	0	1	0	0	2	1	4	2	8	76	1	0	5	100
Agricultural workers	VIIf	0	0	0	0	2	2	0	0	2	2	11	5	1	6	25	0	8	64
Unpaid workers, farm	VIIIf	0	0	0	0	0	1	0	0	0	3	7	4	21	43	3	13	4	99
Too young		3	38	79	49	24	13	23	5	45	135	96	40	10	8	8	18	79	673
Out of work		1	2	3	0	0	0	2	0	3	8	5	9	1	1	0	0	23	58
Total		26	123	224	126	123	89	78	8	174	381	376	140	60	139	41	32	237	2413

a. Self-employed workers.
b. Frequencies are weighted counts rounded to nearest integer. Row and column totals were rounded independently, so some totals may differ slightly from the sum of the numbers in the table.

Table A.9

Occupational origin by current occupation: Catholic men aged 18–65, Northern Ireland, 1973

Origin	Code	Current occupation																Total
		Ia	Ib	II	IIIa	IVa	IVb	IIIb	VIIInf	V	VI	VIIss	VIIus	IVc	IVd	VIIf	VIIIf	
Professionals & proprietors[a]	Ia	1[b]	0	0	0	1	0	0	0	0	0	0	0	0	0	0	0	2
Professionals & managers	Ib	0	1	2	0	0	0	0	0	1	0	1	0	0	0	0	0	5
Professionals & managers	II	2	6	13	3	0	1	4	0	2	2	4	2	0	0	0	0	39
Clerical & sales workers	IIIa	0	0	3	3	2	0	3	0	2	4	6	2	0	0	0	0	25
Proprietors with employees[a]	IVa	1	2	8	2	0	4	1	1	3	5	6	3	0	2	0	1	49
Proprietors no employees[a]	IVb	0	1	5	3	6	6	0	1	3	8	5	4	0	0	0	0	42
Service workers	IIIb	0	0	4	1	3	1	2	0	3	7	1	0	0	0	0	0	22
Unpaid workers, nonfarm	VIIInf	0	0	0	0	0	0	0	0	0	2	0	0	0	0	0	0	2
Technicians & foremen	V	1	0	2	2	3	1	2	0	5	10	3	3	0	0	0	0	32
Skilled manual workers	VI	0	1	7	4	5	7	9	0	10	34	25	13	0	0	2	2	117
Semiskilled manual workers	VIIss	0	2	5	4	4	5	12	1	11	25	44	25	0	0	0	4	144
Unskilled manual workers	VIIus	1	0	3	7	2	1	6	0	13	21	29	17	1	1	0	0	102
Farmers with employees[a]	IVc	1	2	2	0	5	5	2	0	1	1	6	2	3	8	2	1	41
Farmers no employees[a]	IVd	0	0	4	7	9	7	2	0	7	23	23	17	4	46	4	7	160
Agricultural workers	VIIf	0	0	0	0	0	0	0	0	0	0	1	1	0	1	1	0	4
Unpaid workers, farm	VIIIf	0	0	0	0	2	2	2	0	5	8	13	7	0	0	0	5	46
Total		7	15	60	37	51	40	45	3	66	150	167	96	8	58	9	20	832

a.   Self-employed workers.
b.   Frequencies are weighted counts rounded to nearest integer. Row and column totals were rounded independently, so some totals may differ slightly from the sum of the numbers in the table.

Table A.10

Occupational origin by current occupation: Protestant men aged 18–65, Northern Ireland, 1973

Origin	Code	Ia	Ib	II	IIIa	IVa	IVb	IIIb	VIIInf	V	VI	VIIss	VIIus	IVc	IVd	VIIf	VIIIf	Total
																	Current occupation	
Professionals & proprietors[a]	Ia	3[b]	5	2	0	2	0	0	0	0	2	1	0	1	1	0	0	17
Professionals & managers	Ib	5	15	9	5	1	0	0	0	1	2	2	1	0	0	0	0	41
Professionals & managers	II	3	13	24	10	1	1	1	1	5	8	5	2	0	1	0	3	78
Clerical & sales workers	IIIa	1	7	11	12	4	2	4	0	2	9	2	0	0	1	0	0	54
Proprietors with employees[a]	IVa	1	13	8	8	18	5	1	2	6	11	11	0	1	2	0	0	88
Proprietors no employees[a]	IVb	1	3	3	5	5	4	4	0	3	4	9	2	0	0	0	1	43
Service workers	IIIb	0	3	5	5	2	1	4	0	2	6	8	1	1	1	0	0	39
Unpaid workers, nonfarm	VIIInf	1	0	1	0	1	0	0	0	1	1	0	0	0	0	0	0	5
Technicians & foremen	V	0	8	11	5	6	5	3	0	11	16	8	5	1	1	0	0	80
Skilled manual workers	VI	3	16	27	13	3	5	11	1	27	74	44	17	0	0	0	3	254
Semiskilled manual workers	VIIss	1	13	25	8	4	10	6	0	29	64	61	28	1	0	0	4	254
Unskilled manual workers	VIIus	0	3	8	9	3	4	2	1	11	29	45	15	0	0	1	0	131
Farmers with employees[a]	IVc	1	6	17	7	11	5	3	0	2	5	11	2	38	16	5	4	133
Farmers no employees[a]	IVd	1	3	10	4	6	9	3	0	5	17	24	5	8	60	17	4	176
Agricultural workers	VIIf	0	0	0	0	0	0	0	0	0	1	0	1	0	0	0	1	3
Unpaid workers, farm	VIIIf	0	2	5	1	0	3	3	0	6	15	17	9	0	3	0	9	73
Total		21	110	166	92	77	54	45	5	111	264	248	88	51	85	23	29	1469

a. Self–employed workers.

b. Frequencies are weighted counts rounded to nearest integer. Row and column totals were rounded independently, so some totals may differ slightly from the sum of the numbers in the table.

Table A.11

Occupational origin by first occupation: Catholic men aged 18–65, Northern Ireland, 1973

Origin	Code	First occupation																Total
		Ia	Ib	II	IIIa	IVa	IVb	IIIb	VIIInf	V	VI	VIIss	VIIus	IVc	IVd	VIIf	VIIIf	
Professionals & proprietors[a]	Ia	0[b]	1	0	1	0	0	0	0	0	0	0	0	0	0	0	0	2
Professionals & managers	Ib	0	0	1	1	0	0	0	0	0	0	2	0	0	0	1	0	5
Professionals & managers	II	1	2	4	3	0	0	6	1	2	5	5	6	0	0	2	0	37
Clerical & sales workers	IIIa	0	0	1	3	0	0	5	0	2	5	4	1	0	0	0	0	21
Proprietors with employees[a]	IVa	1	1	5	3	1	3	4	15	2	4	6	3	0	0	2	1	46
Proprietors no employees[a]	IVb	0	0	2	1	0	0	5	1	2	12	5	8	0	0	2	0	41
Service workers	IIIb	0	0	0	1	0	0	4	0	2	7	3	3	0	0	0	0	21
Unpaid workers, nonfarm	VIIInf	0	0	0	0	0	0	1	0	0	0	1	0	0	0	0	0	2
Technicians & foremen	V	0	0	1	1	0	0	4	0	5	11	7	1	0	0	0	0	30
Skilled manual workers	VI	0	0	1	9	0	1	14	0	6	30	25	16	0	0	0	6	108
Semiskilled manual workers	VIIss	1	1	2	5	0	0	19	0	2	19	48	27	0	0	2	9	135
Unskilled manual workers	VIIus	0	0	1	5	0	0	13	1	4	16	25	11	0	0	3	14	93
Farmers with employees[a]	IVc	1	1	3	2	0	0	1	1	1	3	1	2	0	0	19	4	39
Farmers no employees[a]	IVd	0	1	2	2	0	0	4	0	4	14	5	9	0	3	91	24	159
Agricultural workers	VIIf	0	0	0	0	0	0	0	0	0	0	0	0	0	0	3	0	3
Unpaid workers, farm	VIIIf	0	0	0	0	0	0	5	0	4	6	2	2	0	0	1	21	41
Total		4	7	24	37	1	4	85	19	34	132	139	89	0	3	126	79	783

a. Self–employed workers.

b. Frequencies are weighted counts rounded to nearest integer. Row and column totals were rounded independently, so some totals may differ slightly from the sum of the numbers in the table.

Table A.12

Occupational origin by first occupation: Protestant men aged 18–65, Northern Ireland, 1973

Origin	Code	Ia	Ib	II	IIIa	IVa	IVb	IIIb	VIIInf	V	VI	VIIss	VIIus	IVc	IVd	VIIf	VIIIf	Total
									First occupation									
Professionals & proprietors[a]	Ia	0[b]	5	2	0	1	0	2	3	1	3	1	0	0	0	0	0	18
Professionals & managers	Ib	0	12	2	7	0	0	2	2	3	6	6	0	0	0	0	0	40
Professionals & managers	II	1	2	8	22	0	0	8	2	8	9	14	3	0	0	1	4	82
Clerical & sales workers	IIIa	0	2	6	13	0	0	5	0	4	13	4	2	0	0	0	1	50
Proprietors with employees[a]	IVa	0	6	1	10	1	1	8	17	4	18	8	3	0	0	3	6	86
Proprietors no employees[a]	IVb	0	1	1	4	0	0	5	3	4	5	9	4	0	0	4	3	43
Service workers	IIIb	0	0	1	5	0	0	6	2	3	7	11	2	0	0	0	1	38
Unpaid workers, nonfarm	VIIInf	0	0	0	1	0	0	0	0	2	1	1	0	0	0	0	0	5
Technicians & foremen	V	0	1	6	11	0	0	7	0	8	23	8	10	0	0	1	3	78
Skilled manual workers	VI	0	7	5	19	0	0	21	2	16	79	59	22	0	0	2	15	247
Semiskilled manual workers	VIIss	0	4	6	20	1	1	22	2	14	66	71	24	0	0	1	18	249
Unskilled manual workers	VIIus	0	0	0	3	1	0	13	0	5	25	30	31	0	0	1	18	127
Farmers with employees[a]	IVc	0	2	2	7	1	0	11	5	6	4	3	0	5	3	76	7	132
Farmers no employees[a]	IVd	0	4	5	2	0	1	9	1	6	10	10	5	0	5	94	23	175
Agricultural workers	VIIf	0	0	0	0	0	0	0	0	1	1	0	0	0	0	2	0	3
Unpaid workers, farm	VIIIf	0	0	0	0	0	0	8	0	3	9	10	6	0	0	0	34	72
Total		1	46	47	124	4	3	127	39	87	279	245	112	5	8	185	133	1445

a. Self-employed workers.

b. Frequencies are weighted counts rounded to nearest integer. Row and column totals were rounded independently, so some totals may differ slightly from the sum of the numbers in the table.

Table A.13

First occupation by current occupation: Catholic men aged 18–65, Northern Ireland, 1973

First occupation	Code	Ia	Ib	II	IIIa	IVa	IVb	IIIb	VIIInf	V	VI	VIIss	VIIus	IVc	IVd	VIIf	VIIIf	Total
																		Current occupation
Professionals & proprietors[a]	Ia	3[b]	0	0	0	0	0	0	0	0	1	0	0	0	0	0	0	4
Professionals & managers	Ib	1	4	2	0	0	0	0	0	0	0	0	0	0	0	0	0	7
Professionals & managers	II	0	0	20	1	1	0	1	0	0	1	0	0	0	0	0	0	24
Clerical & sales workers	IIIa	0	4	8	10	4	1	4	0	1	1	2	1	0	0	0	1	37
Proprietors with employees[a]	IVa	0	0	0	0	0	0	0	0	1	0	0	0	0	0	0	0	1
Proprietors no employees[a]	IVb	0	0	0	0	0	0	0	0	0	1	0	2	0	0	0	1	4
Service workers	IIIb	1	3	8	10	6	3	14	1	3	11	19	4	0	1	0	1	85
Unpaid workers, nonfarm	VIIInf	1	1	1	1	7	1	0	0	2	0	1	2	1	1	0	0	19
Technicians & foremen	V	0	2	5	0	1	4	1	0	17	3	1	0	0	0	0	0	34
Skilled manual workers	VI	1	1	5	1	1	9	2	0	10	63	17	20	0	0	1	2	133
Semiskilled manual workers	VIIss	0	0	6	5	7	10	10	0	9	18	50	25	0	2	0	1	138
Unskilled manual workers	VIIus	0	0	5	1	6	4	4	0	11	20	23	12	0	2	0	1	87
Farmers with employees[a]	IVc	0	0	0	0	0	0	0	0	0	0	0	0	0	0	0	0	0
Farmers no employees[a]	IVd	0	0	0	0	0	0	0	0	0	0	0	0	0	3	0	0	3
Agricultural workers	VIIf	0	0	1	4	4	4	0	0	2	11	17	9	7	49	6	1	126
Unpaid workers, farm	VIIIf	0	0	2	1	3	2	2	0	8	16	21	12	0	2	0	10	80
Total		7	15	60	34	51	39	42	3	63	139	149	85	8	58	8	18	782

a. Self-employed workers.

b. Frequencies are weighted counts rounded to nearest integer. Row and column totals were rounded independently, so some totals may differ slightly from the sum of the numbers in the table.

Table A.14

First occupation by current occupation: Protestant men aged 18–65, Northern Ireland, 1973

First Occupation	Code	Ia	Ib	II	IIIa	IVa	IVb	IIIb	VIIInf	V	VI	VIIss	VIIus	IVc	IVd	VIIf	VIIIf	Total
Professionals & proprietors[a]	Ia	1[b]	0	0	0	0	0	0	0	0	0	0	0	0	0	0	0	1
Professionals & managers	Ib	5	34	3	1	1	0	0	0	0	0	2	0	0	0	0	0	46
Professionals & managers	II	0	8	30	1	1	2	1	0	2	0	1	1	0	0	0	0	47
Clerical & sales workers	IIIa	1	22	32	40	5	1	0	0	10	6	6	0	0	0	0	0	124
Proprietors with employees[a]	IVa	0	0	0	0	3	0	0	0	0	0	1	0	0	0	0	0	4
Proprietors no employees[a]	IVb	0	0	0	0	0	2	0	0	0	0	0	1	0	0	0	0	3
Service workers	IIIb	1	6	23	15	5	5	15	0	5	15	22	5	1	2	0	1	127
Unpaid workers, nonfarm	VIIInf	2	2	3	2	12	6	0	1	1	1	5	1	1	2	0	0	39
Technicians & foremen	V	1	2	7	3	9	8	5	0	32	9	8	2	0	1	1	1	88
Skilled manual workers	VI	6	16	27	5	15	13	2	0	20	114	44	17	1	2	0	0	283
Semiskilled manual workers	VIIss	3	10	20	11	10	3	10	3	17	56	77	20	2	1	2	2	248
Unskilled manual workers	VIIus	0	2	6	1	1	4	9	0	13	30	32	16	0	1	0	0	115
Farmers with employees[a]	IVc	0	0	1	1	0	0	0	0	0	0	0	1	2	0	0	0	5
Farmers no employees[a]	IVd	0	0	1	0	0	0	0	0	0	0	0	0	1	6	0	0	8
Agricultural workers	VIIf	2	2	7	5	6	7	2	0	1	9	17	3	40	58	21	8	186
Unpaid workers, farm	VIIIf	0	4	4	1	2	3	3	0	9	20	32	22	3	11	0	16	132
Total		20	108	164	86	75	54	47	4	110	260	247	89	51	84	23	28	1456

a. Self–employed workers.

b. Frequencies are weighted counts rounded to nearest integer. Row and column totals were rounded independently, so some totals may differ slightly from the sum of the numbers in the table.

Table A.15
Occupational origin by educational attainment
and region: men aged 25–65, Republic of Ireland, 1973

		Educational attainment				
Origin	Primary	Non–academic secondary	Incompete academic secondary	Complete academic secondary	Some higher education	Higher degree
Ia	0[a]	0	5	4	4	11
Ib	5	5	1	5	4	7
II	10	11	21	24	15	16
IIIa	9	7	18	23	9	7
IVa	29	20	24	27	9	12
IVb	53	22	17	7	4	3
IIIb	14	8	7	0	0	5
V	23	26	12	9	6	3
VI	93	79	32	18	10	6
VIIss	117	56	22	10	12	5
VIIus	176	44	14	10	3	1
IVc	98	26	45	12	6	11
IVd	426	92	41	28	16	14
VIIf	138	21	9	4	1	0
Total	1191	417	268	181	99	101

a.   Frequencies are weighted counts rounded to the nearest integer. See Table A.1 for a key to the category labels.

Table A.16
Occupational origin by educational attainment and region:
men aged 25–65, Northern Ireland, 1973

Origin	Primary	Non–academic secondary	Incompete academic secondary	Complete academic secondary	Some higher education	Higher degree
			Educational attainment			
Ia	3[a]	3	1	1	7	8
Ib	6	5	11	12	6	15
II	22	27	17	23	19	26
IIIa	15	30	9	10	10	11
IVa	53	29	13	22	11	16
IVb	51	23	3	3	5	3
IIIb	21	25	4	6	3	2
V	36	48	10	10	7	3
VI	190	134	14	18	13	7
VIIss	205	137	15	21	18	12
VIIus	136	89	5	3	6	2
IVc	91	35	20	10	12	10
IVd	233	77	14	7	8	5
VIIf	87	29	1	4	2	0
Total	1149	691	137	150	127	120

a. Frequencies are weighted counts rounded to the nearest integer. See Table A.1 for a key to the category labels.

Table A.17
Occupation at first job by educational attainment and region:
men aged 25–65, Republic of Ireland, 1973

First full-time occupation	Primary	Non–academic secondary	Incompete academic secondary	Complete academic secondary	Some higher education	Higher degree
			Educational attainment			
Ia	0[a]	0	0	0	0	2
Ib	0	0	1	4	11	31
II	3	5	8	19	8	35
IIIa	6	20	32	54	19	13
IVa	2	0	0	0	0	0
IVb	3	3	2	1	0	1
IIIb	70	41	29	21	6	4
VIIInf	19	11	13	13	5	1
V	21	46	13	9	11	0
VI	98	115	42	8	14	4
VIIss	151	41	20	16	7	3
VIIus	111	40	18	9	3	2
IVc	4	0	3	0	2	0
IVd	11	1	2	1	0	0
VIIIf	438	61	67	14	6	1
VIIf	247	25	14	4	3	2
Total	1184	409	264	173	95	99

a.   Frequencies are weighted counts rounded to the nearest integer. See Table A.1 for a key to the category labels.

Table A.18
Occupation at first job by educational attainment and region:
men aged 25–65, Northern Ireland, 1973

First full–time occupation	Primary	Non–academic secondary	Incompete academic secondary	Complete academic secondary	Some higher education	Higher degree
			Educational attainment			
Ia	0^a	1	0	0	1	3
Ib	1	2	1	8	10	31
II	4	10	7	10	4	36
IIIa	16	52	20	41	22	11
IVa	1	2	1	1	0	0
IVb	5	2	0	0	0	0
IIIb	89	78	16	14	11	6
VIIInf	31	13	6	5	0	3
V	37	58	8	7	12	1
VI	157	189	16	21	21	12
VIIss	227	119	13	16	9	3
VIIus	125	55	9	6	7	3
IVc	2	0	2	0	0	1
IVd	8	1	0	0	2	0
VIIIf	233	50	21	5	2	1
VIIf	174	29	2	4	5	0
Total	1110	661	122	138	106	111

a. Frequencies are weighted counts rounded to the nearest integer. See Table A.1 for a key to the category labels.

Table A.19
Occupation at first full–time job by educational attainment:
first job prior to 1945, Ireland, 1973

First full–time occupation	Primary	Non–academic secondary	Incompete academic secondary	Complete academic secondary	Some higher education	Higher degree
			Educational attainment			
Ia	0[a]	0	0	0	0	1
Ib	1	0	2	2	5	13
II	4	6	1	2	3	17
IIIa	18	14	16	15	10	7
IVa	2	0	0	0	0	0
IVb	6	1	0	1	0	1
IIIb	83	18	13	8	1	1
VIIInf	32	5	5	4	0	1
V	30	14	3	4	1	1
VI	143	58	13	7	8	8
VIIss	230	36	9	4	1	0
VIIus	149	14	5	1	1	0
IVc	5	0	0	0	1	1
IVd	15	0	1	1	0	0
VIIIf	439	27	35	7	4	1
VIIf	292	10	5	1	1	0

a. Frequencies are weighted counts rounded to the nearest integer. See Table A.1 for a key to the category labels.

Table A.20
Occupation at first full–time job by educational attainment:
first job 1945–1958, Ireland, 1973

First full–time occupation	Primary	Non– academic secondary	Incompete academic secondary	Complete academic secondary	Some higher education	Higher degree
			Educational attainment			
Ia	0[a]	0	0	0	0	2
Ib	0	0	0	4	4	19
II	1	1	5	15	4	12
IIIa	4	24	12	37	9	7
IVa	1	1	0	0	0	0
IVb	1	1	2	0	0	0
IIIb	51	43	17	10	1	1
VIIInf	16	10	8	7	3	2
V	24	35	10	4	6	0
VI	74	67	30	12	12	7
VIIss	113	45	9	9	6	4
VIIus	60	23	7	1	0	0
IVc	1	0	3	0	1	0
IVd	3	1	1	0	1	0
VIIIf	178	24	25	3	0	0
VIIf	94	15	4	3	2	0

a.   Frequencies are weighted counts rounded to the nearest integer. See Table A.1 for a key to the category labels.

Table A.21
Occupation at first full-time job by educational attainment:
first job 1959–1973, Ireland, 1973

First full–time occupation	Primary	Non– academic secondary	Incompete academic secondary	Complete academic secondary	Some higher education	Higher degree
			Educational attainment			
Ia	0[a]	1	0	0	1	2
Ib	0	2	0	6	12	30
II	2	8	9	12	5	42
IIIa	0	34	24	43	22	10
IVa	0	1	1	1	0	0
IVb	1	3	0	0	0	0
IIIb	25	58	15	17	15	8
VIIInf	2	9	6	7	2	1
V	4	55	8	8	16	0
VI	38	179	15	10	15	1
VIIss	35	79	15	19	9	2
VIIus	27	58	15	13	9	5
IVc	0	0	2	0	0	0
IVd	1	1	0	0	1	0
VIIIf	54	60	28	9	4	1
VIIf	35	29	7	4	5	2

a.   Frequencies are weighted counts rounded to the nearest integer. See Table A.1 for a key to the category labels.

Table A.22
Design matrix for multilevel model of Erikson and Goldthorpe

Origin	Destination	Hierarchy		Inheritance			Sector	Affinity			N
		1	2	1	2	3	1	1	2	X	
I+II	I+II	0	0	1	1	0	0	0	0	0	0
	III	1	0	0	0	0	0	0	1	0	0
	IVa+b	1	0	0	0	0	0	0	1	0	0
	IVc	1	0	0	0	0	1	0	0	0	0
	V+VI	1	0	0	0	0	0	0	0	0	0
	VIIa	1	1	0	0	0	0	0	0	0	0
	VIIb	1	1	0	0	1	1	1	0	0	0
III	I+II	1	0	0	0	0	0	0	1	0	0
	III	0	0	1	0	0	0	0	0	0	0
	IVa+b	0	0	0	0	0	0	0	0	0	0
	IVc	0	0	0	0	0	1	0	0	0	0
	V+VI	0	0	0	0	0	0	0	0	0	0
	VIIa	1	0	0	0	0	0	0	0	0	0
	VIIb	1	0	0	0	0	1	0	0	0	0
IVa+b	I+II	1	0	0	0	0	0	0	1	0	0
	III	0	0	0	0	0	0	0	0	0	0
	IVa+b	0	0	1	1	0	0	0	0	0	0
	IVc	0	0	0	0	0	1	0	1	0	1
	V+VI	0	0	0	0	0	0	0	0	0	0
	VIIa	1	0	0	0	0	0	0	0	0	0
	VIIb	1	0	0	0	0	1	0	0	0	0
IVc	I+II	1	1	0	0	0	1	0	0	0	0
	III	1	0	0	0	0	1	0	0	0	0
	IVa+b	1	0	0	0	0	1	0	1	0	1
	IVc	1	0	1	1	1	0	0	0	0	0
	V+VI	1	0	0	0	0	1	0	0	0	0
	VIIa	0	0	0	0	0	1	0	1	0	0
	VIIb	0	0	0	0	0	0	0	0	1	0
V+VI	I+II	1	0	0	0	0	0	0	0	0	0
	III	0	0	0	0	0	0	0	0	0	0
	IVa+b	0	0	0	0	0	0	0	0	0	0
	IVc	0	0	0	0	0	1	0	0	0	0
	V+VI	0	0	1	0	0	0	0	0	0	0
	VIIa	1	0	0	0	0	0	0	1	0	0
	VIIb	1	0	0	0	0	1	0	0	0	0
VIIa	I+II	1	1	0	0	0	0	0	0	0	0
	III	1	0	0	0	0	0	0	0	0	0
	IVa+b	1	0	0	0	0	0	0	0	0	0
	IVc	1	0	0	0	0	1	0	0	0	0
	V+VI	1	0	0	0	0	0	0	1	0	0
	VIIa	0	0	1	0	0	0	0	0	0	0
	VIIb	0	0	0	0	0	1	0	0	1	0
VIIb	I+II	1	1	0	0	0	1	1	0	0	0
	III	1	0	0	0	0	1	0	0	0	0
	IVa+b	1	0	0	0	0	1	0	0	0	0
	IVc	1	0	0	0	0	0	0	0	1	0
	V+VI	1	0	0	0	1	0	0	0	0	0
	VIIa	0	0	0	0	0	1	0	1	1	0
	VIIb	0	0	1	0	0	0	0	0	0	0

Table A.23

First occupation by occupation at age 25: men aged 25–65, Ireland, 1973

First occupation	Code	Ia	Ib	II	IIIa	IVa	IVb	IIIb	VIIInf	V	VI	VIIss	VIIus	IVc	IVd	VIIf	VIIIf	Total
Professionals & proprietors[a]	Ia	3[b]	0	0	0	0	0	0	0	0	0	0	0	0	0	0	0	3
Professionals & managers	Ib	1	63	4	0	0	0	0	2	0	2	0	0	0	0	0	0	72
Professionals & managers	II	2	5	81	7	1	2	2	0	2	2	2	0	0	0	0	0	106
Clerical & sales workers	IIIa	0	16	30	125	6	3	8	4	8	16	21	5	0	0	0	0	242
Proprietors with employees[a]	IVa	0	0	0	0	5	0	0	0	0	1	0	0	0	0	0	0	6
Proprietors no employees[a]	IVb	0	1	0	0	1	10	0	1	0	1	0	0	0	0	1	0	15
Service workers	IIIb	1	4	22	22	8	5	82	6	19	46	58	16	0	1	4	5	299
Unpaid workers, nonfarm	VIIInf	3	2	7	8	6	5	3	39	1	13	12	4	1	1	0	1	106
Technicians & foremen	V	0	6	8	6	2	7	5	0	85	23	19	4	1	1	2	1	170
Skilled manual workers	VI	0	8	32	5	15	19	9	5	34	308	54	31	2	3	6	2	533
Semiskilled manual workers	VIIss	0	10	20	23	8	7	20	6	27	133	174	78	0	0	7	5	518
Unskilled manual workers	VIIus	0	0	8	4	1	8	8	2	18	64	89	79	0	4	9	1	295
Farmers with employees[a]	IVc	0	0	1	0	0	0	0	0	0	0	1	0	10	0	0	1	13
Farmers no employees[a]	IVd	0	0	1	0	0	0	0	0	0	0	0	0	0	22	0	0	23
Agricultural workers	VIIf	0	2	5	3	0	16	8	1	14	50	61	79	2	17	184	8	450
Unpaid workers, farm	VIIIf	0	3	21	10	9	18	11	3	8	40	43	51	22	82	26	452	799
Total		10	120	240	213	62	100	156	69	216	699	534	347	38	131	239	476	3650

a. Self-employed workers.
b. Frequencies are weighted counts rounded to nearest integer. Row and column totals were rounded independently, so some totals may differ slightly from the sum of the numbers in the table.

Table A.24

Occupation at age 25 by occupation at age 35: men aged 35–65, Ireland, 1973

Occupation at age 25	Code	Ia	Ib	II	IIIa	IVa	IVb	IIIb	VIIInf	V	VI	VIIss	VIIus	IVc	IVd	VIIf	VIIIf	Total
Professionals & proprietors[a]	Ia	7[b]	0	0	0	0	0	0	0	0	0	0	0	0	0	0	0	7
Professionals & managers	Ib	9	52	5	2	1	1	0	0	1	4	0	1	0	1	0	0	77
Professionals & managers	II	0	16	98	2	0	1	0	0	1	2	3	1	1	0	0	0	126
Clerical & sales workers	IIIa	1	12	27	77	9	9	1	0	3	3	4	1	2	0	0	1	150
Proprietors with employees[a]	IVa	0	0	0	0	33	2	1	0	0	3	1	2	0	0	0	0	40
Proprietors no employees[a]	IVb	0	1	1	0	7	39	0	0	1	4	1	1	0	5	0	0	64
Service workers	IIIb	0	3	10	9	9	6	50	1	2	4	12	3	1	3	2	0	115
Unpaid workers, nonfarm	VIIInf	0	2	5	4	10	4	2	20	0	5	2	1	0	2	0	1	58
Technicians & foremen	V	0	4	7	2	8	7	3	1	72	11	7	6	2	1	1	0	132
Skilled manual workers	VI	3	7	12	13	20	22	4	3	31	296	43	21	0	1	5	0	481
Semiskilled manual workers	VIIss	0	1	7	8	6	9	8	1	29	30	249	24	1	9	5	1	388
Unskilled manual workers	VIIus	0	2	0	3	1	7	7	0	10	21	49	137	1	10	10	3	261
Farmers with employees[a]	IVc	0	0	1	2	0	0	0	0	0	1	0	0	19	0	0	0	23
Farmers no employees[a]	IVd	0	0	0	0	0	1	0	0	0	0	1	0	0	57	0	0	59
Agricultural workers	VIIf	0	0	0	2	1	3	1	0	3	7	27	35	6	16	104	4	209
Unpaid workers, farm	VIIIf	0	0	2	3	1	4	0	0	3	5	13	10	36	132	11	183	403
Total		20	100	175	127	106	110	79	26	157	394	415	243	69	241	138	193	2593

Occupation at age 35

a. Self-employed workers.
b. Frequencies are weighted counts rounded to nearest integer. Row and column totals were rounded independently, so some totals may differ slightly from the sum of the numbers in the table.

Table A.25
Occupation at age 35 by occupation at age 45: men aged 45–65, Ireland, 1973

Occupation at age 35	Code	Occupation at age 45																Total
		Ia	Ib	II	IIIa	IVa	IVb	IIIb	VIIInf	V	VI	VIIss	VIIus	IVc	IVd	VIIf	VIIIf	
Professionals & proprietors[a]	Ia	15[b]	1	1	0	0	0	0	0	0	0	0	0	0	0	0	0	17
Professionals & managers	Ib	6	50	3	0	0	0	0	0	1	1	0	0	0	0	0	0	61
Professionals & managers	II	0	14	81	3	3	1	4	0	0	0	0	0	0	0	0	0	106
Clerical & sales workers	IIIa	0	5	10	58	2	1	0	0	2	0	5	0	1	0	0	0	84
Proprietors with employees[a]	IVa	1	0	4	0	53	1	0	0	0	0	2	0	2	0	0	0	61
Proprietors no employees[a]	IVb	0	1	0	0	6	50	0	0	1	4	2	1	0	2	1	0	68
Service workers	IIIb	0	0	3	5	2	1	38	0	2	2	2	0	0	0	0	0	55
Unpaid workers, nonfarm	VIIInf	0	0	0	0	7	2	0	7	0	1	2	0	0	0	0	0	19
Technicians & foremen	V	0	2	4	4	4	1	0	0	64	5	5	0	0	0	0	0	89
Skilled manual workers	VI	1	5	3	2	9	6	2	0	14	179	22	9	1	4	0	0	257
Semiskilled manual workers	VIIss	0	2	2	3	1	6	6	0	14	12	218	11	0	3	4	0	282
Unskilled manual workers	VIIus	0	0	2	1	0	1	6	0	7	14	13	135	0	9	4	1	193
Farmers with employees[a]	IVc	0	0	0	0	0	0	0	0	0	0	0	0	40	1	1	0	42
Farmers no employees[a]	IVd	0	0	1	0	0	1	0	0	1	2	4	1	5	174	2	0	191
Agricultural workers	VIIf	0	0	0	0	0	3	1	1	1	0	5	21	1	8	65	0	106
Unpaid workers, farm	VIIIf	0	0	0	1	1	4	0	0	0	0	2	6	14	67	4	60	158
Total		23	80	114	76	88	78	57	8	107	220	280	184	64	268	81	61	1789

a. Self-employed workers.
b. Frequencies are weighted counts rounded to nearest integer. Row and column totals were rounded independently, so some totals may differ slightly from the sum of the numbers in the table.

Notes

Introduction

1. This view finds theoretical expression in Sorokin (1927) and Schumpeter (1955, quoted in Lipset and Bendix 1959, p. 75) but is most closely associated with empirical work that distinguishes between the structural mobility that is tied to the disparity between the marginal distributions of origins and destinations in the labor force and the exchange mobility that stems from the imperfect association between origins and destinations in a mobility table (e.g., Rogoff 1953; Featherman, Jones, and Hauser 1975; Sobel, Hout, and Duncan 1985).

2. This view is the classic perspective on occupation and class found in Marx and Weber. It has found a variety of expressions in Collins (1974), Goldthorpe (1980), Brieger (1982), and Wright (1985). There is even some hint of it in Blau and Duncan (1967, pp. 67–75).

3. Interactionalists would be more likely to ask, Did the channels of mobility that opened up due to change in the functional division of labor restructure class relations? Did new channels of mobility forge new class alliances while weakening other, more traditional ones?

1. The Context of Social Change in Ireland

1. From de Valera's radio address to the nation on 17 March 1943. I first heard this passage while watching a Radio Telefis Eireann (RTE) special on the life of de Valera in 1983. The term "frugal comfort" struck me as an apt characterization of the lifestyle in the Jeffersonian democracy that de Valera (and quite probably the Irish people) sought in the period from Fianna Fail's ascendancy in 1932 through the end of the Second World War. The term expresses my sense of where Ireland came from, and it serves as a point of departure in describing the changes that form the context of the Irish Mobility Study. The quote appears in the epigraph to Benedict Kiely's novel *Nothing Happens in Carmincross* (Boston: David R. Godine, 1985). Kiely attributes the quote as "an euphoric or idiotic statement by a well-known twentieth-century Irishman of Spanish and Irish origins." The speech is well known in Ireland, frequently quoted in books on de Valera. See also Brown 1985, p. 113.

2. From an internal Department of Finance document dated 12 December 1957 (Whitaker 1958, p. 104), released by the government shortly after the beginning of 1958. Although the report received little attention from the popular press, its influence within government cannot be underestimated (Brown 1985, p. 164). See also Lyons 1972, p. 599; Walsh 1979, p. 29; Brown 1985, p. 164.

3. In addition to the inherent popularity of economic nationalism in an age of nationalism, the program achieved some economic success. While the rest of Europe and America were mired in depression, industrial employment rose 50 percent between 1931 and 1938 and industrial output rose 40 percent between 1931 and 1936 (Cullen 1972, p. 178).

4. Arthur Griffith, the father of Sinn Fein, advocated economic nationalism in the *New Ireland Review* and elsewhere long before he united the strands of nationalism under the banner of Sinn Fein in 1907–1908 (Lyons 1973, p. 230). Griffith opposed the emphasis on landownership as the principal resource of the Irish people. He favored rapid industrialization on a scale that Fianna Fail failed to achieve prior to the mid-1960s (Lyons 1973, pp. 252–257).

5. Many tariffs were held in abeyance during the war years, but most were returned to their prewar levels by 1950 (Kennedy 1971, pp. 29–30).

6. Irish leaders were intent on showing the world that Ireland (then in the form of the Saorstat Eireann) was a viable nation in all respects. An important element of such claims was the maintenance of parity between the Irish currency (punts) and the British currency (pounds sterling). Borrowing could threaten Irish independence by devaluing the punt. In international trade, governments protect the integrity of their currency by maintaining foreign reserves. When imports exceed exports, these external reserves can pay off the balance due. If external reserves are insufficient, then the government must borrow money to equalize the balance of payments. The borrowed money creates unwanted domestic currency in international markets, decreasing the value of the currency already in circulation while causing inflation at home. So foreign reserves are a cushion against the inflationary pressures that arise when imports exceed exports. For that reason the Irish government maintained large external reserves of cash. It was in the noble interest of protecting national integrity (and probably national sovereignty) that the borrowing phobia developed.

7. All profits derived from export of goods manufactured under the auspices of the Shannon Free Airport Development Company (a semistate body) were tax exempt through 1983. All goods entering the duty free zone "and intended for re-export enter and leave the area without imposition of customs or excise duties and with minimal customs inspection. Exports from Shannon, which were negligible in 1960, amounted to £35 million in 1968, while imports amounted to £20 million" (Kennedy and Dowling 1975, p. 114).

8. Net capital flow is the difference between balance of payments and external reserves.

9. Agricultural output increased despite fewer workers, indicating an appreciable boost to farm productivity, although the growth was less than immediately after World War II (Kennedy and Dowling 1975, p. 186). The sequence of cause and effect is not clear from the data. The increasing emigration of labor may have

made investment in farm machinery necessary, or machine power may have spurred emigration.

10. The policy of even-handed treatment of the superpowers demonstrates the moral certitude of Irish neutrality, because Ireland has stuck to this course despite slights against it by the Soviet Union, especially when the USSR blocked admission of the Republic of Ireland into the United Nations in successive sessions from 1946 until 1955.

11. Although the war years were an exception for shipbuilding in most of the rest of the world, German bombing crippled shipbuilding in Northern Ireland for much of the war.

12. This wrangling over social services and welfare put the unionist politicians in a compromising position. As allies of the Conservatives in Westminster, they opposed most of the legislation that established the British welfare state. As advocates on behalf of their Northern Ireland constituents, they pursued guarantees that all legislation, once passed over their objections, applied to all parts of the UK equally. Among other things, this stance meant that MPs who voted against welfare legislation in Westminster voted for it in Stormont because, under the home rule charter, Northern Ireland could not participate in the welfare state without the approval of the (unionist-controlled) Stormont home rule parliament.

13. Protestants outnumber Catholics four-to-one east of the Bann; the two groups are of equal size west of the Bann (O'Leary 1979, p. 160).

14. The figure of 200,000 assumes that the rate of emigration in Northern Ireland is the same as the rate in the Republic. This assumption implies an annual average of 5,000 emigrants from Northern Ireland, which is added to the 15,000 emigrants a year from the Republic and multiplied by 10.

15. The percentages change slightly to 29 percent and 13 percent if region at age 14 is used instead of current region.

16. I cannot compete with the eloquence of Lyons (1973, p. 15): "The tired old witticism that every time the English came within sight of solving the Irish question, the Irish changed the question, contains, like most jokes about Ireland, a small grain of truth submerged in a vast sea of misconception. The Irish did not change the question between the Famine and the War of Independence any more than they had changed it between the Union and the Famine. The 'national demand,' as it used to be called, remained in essence what Wolfe Tone had declared it to be as long ago as 1791, 'to break the connection with England, the never-failing source of all our political evils.' It is true, of course, that men differed in the nineteenth century, as they have continued to differ in the twentieth, about how complete the break should be, or more precisely, perhaps, about how far the full separatist ideal was practicable. But whether they took their stand on the rock of the Republic, or were prepared to settle for repeal of the Union and some form of Home Rule based upon a reanimated Irish parliament, they were emphatic that the first step toward real independence was to recover for Irishmen the right to control their own affairs."

17. Prior to 1885, nationalist MPs voted as a bloc on acts of Parliament relevant to Ireland, but each nationalist MP was free to affiliate with either the Liberal Party or the Conservative Party on other legislation. Since the aim of the

nationalist organization was to win the support of the major British parties for social reform legislation favorable to Ireland, this inability to deliver the nationalist vote as a bloc weakened the negotiating position of the nationalist leaders in their dealings with the leadership of the Liberal and Conservative parties. If the nationalists always voted as a bloc, it was reasoned, they could influence the selection of the prime minister by promising always to vote with one party or the other. This would greatly enhance the ability of the Irish nationalist leader to extract promises from the leaders of the major parties in Britain. With the formation of the National League, the nationalist leader, at that time Parnell, was able to secure a pledge, in writing, from each nationalist candidate promising that he would vote with the nationalist bloc or resign his seat. This device greatly enhanced the bargaining position of the Irish nationalist leader.

18. The Home Rule Bill of 1886 went down to defeat when 93 Liberals joined the Conservatives in voting against it. The defection led to a vote of no confidence in the Liberal leadership and the formation of a new government by the Conservative Party leadership.

19. A second Home Rule Bill was passed by Commons in 1893, during Gladstone's last ministry. It was defeated in the House of Lords, and the issue was allowed to die. In this instance hope of passage was low from the start, and failure did not result in the fall of the government. In 1906 the Liberals put forth an Irish Councils Bill that fell far short of home rule. The Irish nationalists rejected this bill before it came to a vote in Parliament.

20. Under the new Parliament Act, a bill could become law without the consent of the Lords if it passed Commons in three consecutive years.

21. Protestant militias throughout Ulster gave some credence to these claims, although Liberal prime minister Henry Herbert Asquith seemed to discount the unionists claims until the separate bands were united as the Ulster Volunteer Force in January 1913 (Lyons 1973, p. 306). Even at that point Redmond dismissed the prospect of an Ulster rebellion.

22. Support was not unanimous. Sinn Fein, the Irish Volunteers, and the Irish Republican Brotherhood were all small factions that gained support at this time, in part in response to the militancy of Ulster unionists but also because of what many nationalists saw as the lack of progress in parliamentary nationalism.

23. Carson opposed partition, but he figured that if his amendment passed, the nationalists would withdraw support from the bill, thereby killing home rule (Beckett 1981, p. 429).

24. The men in jail were not held in connection with the Easter Rising. They were held on suspicion of conspiring with the Germans. Although the Germans showed some interest in supporting the IRA, the government produced no concrete evidence against any Irish leaders at the time. No evidence since then has implicated the Irish Republican Brotherhood or Sinn Fein (Lyons 1973, p. 396).

25. The depth of the conflict in Ulster can be gauged in many ways. One telling way is that even the name of the city on the River Foyle is an object of dispute. At the time of these riots, it was known as Londonderry. Recently the Borough Council reinstated the traditional name of Derry. Many, including the BBC and the *New York Times,* still use Londonderry.

26. The 124 Sinn Fein members took seats in the second Dail Eireann. The four non–Sinn Fein members held one meeting as the home rule parliament and adjourned permanently a month after the election.

2. *The Irish Mobility Study*

1. In addition to the survey, the project included a study of Census data (Boyle, 1977), a postal questionnaire limited to Northern Ireland, and an occupational ranking study. The project received funding from the Social Science Research Council (SSRC), London, UK, under grant number HR 1430/1. Neither the original investigators nor the SSRC or its successor, the Economic and Social Research Council, bears any responsibility for the opinions and conclusions expressed in this report.

2. This is the practice used in the American mobility studies (Featherman and Hauser 1978, p. 22) but not in the British mobility study (Goldthorpe 1980, p. 44).

3. Respondents with educational attainment scores of less than two are excluded from analysis of this transition since they did not survive far enough in the educational system to be "at risk" of making such a transition.

4. Respondents with educational attainment scores of less than four are excluded from analysis of this transition since they did not survive far enough in the educational system to be "at risk" of making such a transition.

5. Respondents with educational attainment scores of less than five are excluded from analysis of this transition since they did not survive far enough in the educational system to be "at risk" of making such a transition.

6. This necessitates separating the seventh employment status code in the original Hope-Goldthorpe scheme into paid and unpaid employees. The number of unpaid workers in England is so small that Hope and Goldthorpe merged them with wage earners in their protocol.

7. This figure drops as low as 40 percent when a simple nonmanual-manual-farm trichotomy is used to construct a 3×3 mobility table.

8. A low estimate of 41 percent is obtained from the 3×3 nonmanual-manual-farm table.

9. These models are more generally known as the models of statistical independence and quasi-independence (Goodman, 1968), and they are labeled as such in the tables.

10. The other kind of zero is a "fixed zero," one that arises because a particular combination of variables is impossible or because the researcher wishes to treat it as such for statistical reasons. Observing no Jewish farmers in a cross-classification of occupation by religion is an example of a sampling zero (there are Jewish farmers, but none fell into the survey), or observing no male obstetrical patients in a cross-classification of reason for being in the hospital by gender for a sample of hospital patients is an example of a structural zero (the probability of being an obstetrical patient is really zero for males; Fienberg 1980, pp. 140–159).

11. If QS fails to hold, SHD argue that it is not reasonable to equate the α_j parameters (or, for that matter, any set of parameters pertaining just to rows or

columns) with the concept of structural mobility. When QS does not hold, marginal heterogeneity is due not only to the kind of across-the-board changes usually thought to underlie structural mobility but also to interaction effects not usually considered. SHD give the name "unreciprocated mobility" to the combination of marginal and interaction effects that produce total marginal heterogeneity when QS fails to hold. In sum, when QS fails to hold, the concepts of exchange and structural mobility do not suffice to describe the flows in a mobility table.

12. Dudley Duncan invented this method of comparing the index of dissimilarity with the α_j (Hout, Duncan, and Sobel 1987).

13. SHD conclude (p. 367): "The Brazilian case is an instance of massive structural mobility moving men through a very rigid class structure."

14. An equivalent procedure is to "block out" diagonal cells by specifying a zero expected frequency as the starting value for diagonal cells (Duncan 1979; Goodman 1979a). The trouble with the term "occupational inheritance" has to do with the level of aggregation and the mechanism by which workers' destinations come to resemble their origins. While legal inheritance may apply to some workers, especially farmers, for most workers who have destinations in their category of origin the source of similarity is either an aggregation bias that classifies different occupations into the same category (e.g., the son of a judge who becomes a chemistry professor in a university) or a pattern of advantages (and corresponding disadvantages) that might get the son of an electrician into an electrician's apprenticeship program, which results in an identity between origins and destinations that has nothing to do with legal inheritance.

15. The first dimension is invariably correlated with occupational status or prestige (e.g., Klatsky and Hodge 1972).

16. Other applications of the mover-stayer concept have the same problem of heterogeneity and implausible estimates (e.g., Spilerman 1972; Singer and Spilerman 1974, 1976).

17. At the time of this survey, the Irish currency was tied to English pounds sterling.

18. Job changes, and therefore events, include the obvious changes of occupation that probably come to mind most readily. The definition of events used here includes other kinds of changes as well. For example, changes of employer are counted as events, even if the subject remains in the same occupation. Changes of employment status (e.g., from apprentice to regular employee, from self-employed without employees to self-employed with employees, from unemployed to employee, and from part-time to full-time) are also counted.

19. Note that K extends into the future, beyond the time of the interview to the last job this individual will eventually take. This approach is not standard, but it has some advantages with respect to censoring.

20. Note the distinction between K, which is the index for the final job in the individual's career, and k, which is the index for any job from 1 to K (including 1 and K). Both k and K must be integers.

21. At any time after T_k, $t_k = T_k + t_{k'}$.

22. For most spells $T < \omega$, but for every h there is one spell for which $T = \omega$.

23. Of course, many workers experience multiple events, suggesting that

the cumulative density might exceed one. But a separate integral refers to each event k. None of the individual integrals exceeds one, although their sum (across $k = 1, \ldots, K$) might do so.

3. Exchange, Structure, and Mobility

1. For basic data in this chapter, see the Appendix. Tables A.1 and A.2 cross-classify Irish workers by father's occupation, current occupation, and region. Most of the analyses in this chapter exclude unpaid workers (i.e., leave out the last two rows and columns of Table A.1). The counts in Tables A.1–A.2 are the weighted counts rounded to the nearest integer. In the log-linear analyses in this chapter, the counts have been transformed to eliminate sampling zeros.

2. The index of dissimilarity understates structural mobility because it fails to take account of the strength of association between origins and destinations in the mobility table. The difference between the Republic and Northern Ireland of 2.7 percent in the index of dissimilarity may also overstate or understate the relative degrees of structural mobility in the two parts of Ireland; the direction of the bias depends on whether the dependence of destinations on origins is greater in the North or in the Republic.

3. Because combining destination categories reduces the number of zero cells considerably, the tests in Table 3.2 are based on the weighted counts without adjustment.

4. The use of the term *immobile* does not imply that a respondent has had only one job in his life. Some immobile men have had several jobs, all in the same occupation. Others have had several jobs in several occupations. All that is meant by *immobile* in the present context is that the respondent reports that when he was 14 years old (or 16 in some cases), his father was working at an occupation that falls into the same category of the PREF scheme as does the respondent's current occupation.

5. The correlation between the two columns of Table 3.1 is $r = .70$.

6. The model of no three-way interaction—$[OR][OM][RM]$—is preferred over the saturated model for these data. The likelihood ratio chi-square has a probability of .11, and bic is negative. This model is also preferred over simpler models. The only simpler model for which a plausible case could be made is the model of no effect of region on mobility-immobility—$[OR][OM]$. The test for the difference between these two models is significant ($\Delta L^2 = 30.67 - 19.40 = 11.27$; $df = 1$; $p < .01$; bic $= 3$). By the bic criterion, the effect of region on mobility-immobility is of borderline significance; by classical criteria, it is clearly significant.

7. Immobility in the proprietorial occupations would be even higher if unpaid workers were excluded from this analysis, as they are from many of the other tables in this chapter.

8. This hypothesis cannot be tested directly without access to data on career mobility within firms. The Irish Mobility Study has excellent data on career mobility, but unfortunately it lacks the requisite data on the firms, so direct tests of this hypothesis are not presented in this book.

9. Raftery's bic is negative for QI in both the Republic and Northern Ireland. However, as subsequent modeling shows, even better fits, namely bics that are farther from zero, are obtained for models that structure off-diagonal mobility.

10. The percentages in each row sum to 100 percent minus the percent immobile reported in Table 3.1. For example, the sum of the percentages in the first row for the Republic of Ireland is 65 percent. (Table 3.1 shows that the other 35 percent were immobile).

11. An argument could be made that service workers (class IIIb) are better classified as part of the urban working class composed of classes V, VI, VIIss, and VIIus. In fact, the American occupational coding scheme treats many technicians from class V as white collar and most service workers as manual.

12. Readers familiar with the conditions of farming in other countries but unfamiliar with Irish agriculture might wonder that mobility from farm manager (an occupation in class IVc) to farm owner without employees (the principal occupation of class IVd) could be called "downward" mobility. After all, the owner without employees nonetheless farms his own land. In Ireland a manager is hired only for the largest, most prosperous commercial farms. For that reason most farm managers have higher socioeconomic status and prestige than farm owners without employees, most of whom work farms of less than 50 acres.

13. Table 3.5 also includes the structural mobility multipliers from the SHD (1985) parameterization of QS. Departures of the α_j coefficients from unity indicate that structural mobility contributes to the dissimilarity between supply and recruitment. For particular coefficients, $\alpha_j > 1$ indicates that occupational class j is favored by structural mobility; $\alpha_j < 1$ indicates that occupational class j is diminished by structural mobility.

14. The model of "conditional quasi-symmetry" (CQS) hypothesizes that QS fits in each region, but it allows the parameters of QS to differ between regions. For the $14 \times 14 \times 2$ table, there are 28 β_i parameters, 26 α_j parameters, and 182 δ_{ij} parameters, leaving 156 degrees of freedom.

15. Sobel (1988) names this model "conditional quasi-symmetry with homogeneous association" (CQSHA). The "conditional" in the name refers to the fact that the model fits exactly the marginal distributions of the two subtables (the one for the Republic and the one for the North, in this case).

16. This statistic has not appeared in the literature, but it is a plausible extension of the index of dissimilarity between origins and destinations to specific occupations.

17. The c_j have been normed so that their product is one, the same as the product of the α_j.

18. The log-ratio is calculated from the expected frequencies [$\log (F_{ji} / F_{ij})$] under the CQSHA model. This value is not the same as the log-ratio of the observed frequencies [$\log (f_{ji} / f_{ij})$] in Tables A.1–A.2 (in fact, $f_{21} = 0$ for the Republic).

19. First, bic is negative. Second, the portion of the L_{cqsha}^2 due to differences between symmetric association in the Republic and in Northern Ireland is greater than the portion due to asymmetry; the difference between L_{cqsha}^2 and L_{cqs}^2 is 110.27, while the difference between L_{cqsha}^2 and L_{ha}^2 is just 33.32.

20. It is not obvious why flows must be equal under exchange mobility. See SHD (1985) for the derivation of this constraint.

21. This is the concept of exchange found in Berger and Snell (1957), Hutchinson (1958), and Persson (1977). The more common definition of exchange as the mobility that exceeds what is required by structural mobility lacks substance (e.g., Yasuda 1964; McClendon 1980; Hope 1982). In its lack of specificity, it tells nothing. Furthermore, as Sobel (1983) points out, residual definitions of this type lead the researcher into logical inconsistencies.

22. The δ_{ij} parameters are less than or equal to .15 for all farm-nonfarm pairs except the associations between farm labor and service (class IIIb), small shop (class IVb), and semiskilled and unskilled labor (classes VIIss and VIIus).

23. The analysis was carried out for each region separately, despite the preference for a homogeneous association model (CQSHA), because the multidimensional models have far fewer association parameters than CQSHA. The smaller number of parameters makes the multidimensional models more powerful as a tool for detecting regional differences in association (Duncan 1979, p. 801).

24. The test of the difference between two coefficients is a t-test of the form: $t = (b_1 - b_2) / \sqrt{(\sigma_1^2 + \sigma_2^2)}$, with $n_1 + n_2 - 2$ degrees of freedom, where b_1 and b_2 are the coefficients being compared and σ_1 and σ_2 are their standard errors.

25. This refers both to the finding that the association between origins and destinations is homogeneous across region (i.e., that the CQSHA model fits the data) and to the finding of only a single significant regional difference among the effects of the four dimensions. The pair of occupational categories being compared does not differ much on the one dimension (personal contacts) for which there is a significant regional interaction.

26. The logit of -1.02 for men from the Republic with origins in class VIIss translates to an odds of ($e^{-1.02}$ =) .36 (i.e., just slightly better than one-in-three).

27. When growth fails to accommodate the rural exodus, emigration takes up the slack. For that reason an Irish Mobility Study of the 1930s would most likely have detected much less structural mobility than the present one finds, not because rural pressures were less in the past but because urban opportunities were lacking. The "structurally mobile" Irish men and women of the 1930s contribute to the dissimilarity between origins and destinations in their new homelands—Britain, Australia, and America—not in Ireland.

4. The Gap between Working Class and Middle Class

1. There are some problems with the comparability of the nonmanual-manual distinction that may invalidate even this crude set of comparisons (Hazelrigg and Garnier 1974).

2. However, Erikson and Goldthorpe (1985) and Kerkhoff, Campbell, and Winfield-Laird (1985) show a common pattern of fluidity in the two countries.

3. In the class scheme used by Goldthorpe, all elements of class VII are combined, so no distinction is made among classes VIIss, VIIus, and VIIf.

4. The closure thesis argues that elite positions recruit from a narrow range of origins, thereby maintaining homogeneity and hegemony over business, culture, and the military. Neither the English nor the Irish data support this thesis.

5. Featherman and Hauser (1978, p. 179) say this about their similar finding for the United States: "First, there is great immobility at the top and at the bottom of the occupational hierarchy, here represented by upper nonmanual and by farm occupations, respectively. This immobility is far more extreme than has heretofore been supposed by most students of the mobility process; it may even be consistent with the beliefs of the more extreme critics of rigidity in the American class structure." Whelan and Whelan (1984, pp. 92–96) also find high immobility among Dublin men from upper nonmanual origins. The comparable data for the whole of the Republic of Ireland and for Northern Ireland are similar.

6. The pattern of structural mobility in Britain cannot be discerned from Goldthorpe's results because the levels of his model are not symmetrical around the diagonal of the mobility table.

7. As shown in Table 2.9, class V (prestige = 47; education = 64) ranks above classes IIIa (prestige = 42; education = 89) and IIIb (prestige = 31; education = 52) in prestige, and above classes IIIb and IVb (prestige = 48; education = 38) in education; class VI (prestige = 38; education = 55) ranks above class IIIb in prestige and classes IIIb and IVb in education. The criteria employed by Wright (1985) also put class V over classes IIIa and IIIb.

5. The Occupational Mobility of Farmers' Sons

1. The original intent was to include "farm manager" as a separate category in this analysis, but there are too few cases to do so. The six cases of fathers from class IVc who were managers rather than self-employed are excluded from this chapter. The four sons of self-employed farmers who manage farms that they do not own are included here as farmers in accord with the practices of the Hope-Goldthorpe classification scheme used throughout the analysis (and also that of the Irish Census).

2. It would be interesting to know how many of the last two forms of entry into farming—purchase and nonfamilial succession—involve transactions within the extended family. It is conceivable, for example, that nephews take over for their bachelor uncles.

3. Because of small numbers of cases, the nonfarm categories are combined into aggregate categories in Table 5.2 and in several other tables in this chapter. The new categories (with categories from the preferred classification in parentheses) are farm (IVc, IVd), farm helper (VIIIf), farm laborer (VIIf), self-employed (Ia, IVa, IVb), white collar (Ib, II, IIIa, IIIb, VIIInf), blue collar (V, VI, VIIss, VIIus), and unemployed.

4. The pooling entails some loss of information. The preceding results show how farmers' sons in the Republic are more likely to go into farming than are farmers' sons in Northern Ireland. Furthermore, farm succession progresses faster in Northern Ireland than in the Republic. The cohort results presented here are therefore biased to an unknown extent by the failure to control region. How-

ever, the alternative is to conduct the cohort analysis separately for each region, leaving such small numbers of cases as to vitiate any conclusions one might want to draw.

5. Table 5.4 is an "inflow" table, while Table 5.5 is an "outflow" table (Hout 1983, pp. 11–13). That is, Table 5.4 takes as a basis the number of farmers and tabulates the proportional distribution of farmers' origins, given that they moved into farming at some time. Table 5.5 takes as a basis the number of men working in an origin occupation and tabulates the probability of moving from that origin to farming over a five-year period.

6. For illustrative purposes, consider the usual test of the null hypothesis of independence between education and first occupation. The likelihood ratio test (L^2) for independence between the five-category education scale used in this analysis and the six-category occupational classification (with 20 degrees of freedom) is 118.89 in Northern Ireland and 185.50 in the Republic. Combining categories (2) with (3) and categories (4) with (5) reduces L^2 (with 12 degrees of freedom) to 108.40 in Northern Ireland and to 177.31 in the Republic.

7. Education is coded to five levels: (1) incomplete primary, (2) complete primary, (3) incomplete secondary, (4) complete secondary, and (5) postsecondary.

8. The bic criterion leads to an even simpler model that includes only the effect of education on first occupation. The parameter estimates show clearly that the effects of region and siblings, though significant by traditional statistical criteria, are, with one exception, of little substantive import.

9. While deletion of $[EJ]$, $[RJ]$, or $[SJ]$ would increase L^2 significantly (implying that the effects of education, region, and siblings on occupation at first job are all significant), individual contrasts, (e.g., between having no siblings and one sibling) might not be significant. For this reason it might be useful to have standard errors for the coefficients in Table 5.8. Unfortunately, the coefficients reported there are composites of parameter estimates for the log-linear model in which log F_{ijkl} is the dependent variable, so the standard errors of the coefficients are unknown, even though the standard errors of the constituent parameter estimates are known.

10. The logit corresponding to a probability of .10 is log $(.1/.9) = -2.197$. The effect of postsecondary education is to raise that odds by 4.90 to 2.703. The probability that corresponds to a log-odds of 2.703 is the antilog of 2.703 divided by one plus the antilog of 2.703, which turns out to be 14.924/15.294, or .94.

11. Compulsory education makes it virtually inconceivable that any farmers' sons from contemporary cohorts could stop their schooling before completing at least the primary cycle.

6. *Scales, Levels, and Dimensions of Mobility*

1. See also Smelser and Lipset (1966, p. 19).

2. This statement does not imply that nonhierarchical distinctions are absent from the discussion. On the contrary, most of it also includes at least some mention of deviations from simple order.

3. The terminology *vertical* and *nonvertical* refers to the presence or absence of assumptions about order among the occupational categories. Vertical models make assumptions about order; nonvertical models do not. This terminology appears to derive from Hope (1982).

4. They collapse categories I and II, IVa and IVb, and V and VI. Their table is actually $7 \times 7 \times 11$, as they use the model for cross-national comparisons.

5. Their reason for the asymmetrical treatment of farmers is the increased average size of farms within most countries in their data set. The plus signs in the notation here designate categories that Erikson and Goldthorpe combine for their analysis; the commas separate categories that are grouped into the same hierarchical level. So, for example, (IIIa + b, IVa + b, V + VI) indicates that the second hierarchical level scores six of the categories used in this analysis at the same hierarchical level, but the scoring concerns only three categories in the Erikson and Goldthorpe tables.

6. For the Republic of Ireland, Hout and Jackson (1986) found that both scales and levels contribute to understanding mobility barriers. The levels considered in that research are the levels of the Erikson et al. (1982) "common social fluidity" model.

7. The multidimensional models are more parsimonious not only because they have more degrees of freedom but also because they contain terms with clear substantive reference. Although this substantive parsimony has no statistical analog, it must be an important consideration in any assessment of the relative efficacy of approaches to data analysis that are based on levels versus approaches based on scales.

8. Recall that AF1 is the term for long-distance mobility between agricultural labor (class VIIf) and the service class (I + II)—an effect that may be considered to be an extreme hierarchy effect.

7. Religion and Mobility in Northern Ireland

1. Some of the material in this chapter is taken from Hout (1986).

2. For example, the United Kingdom Census of 1911 enumerated 314,031 Catholics and 508,809 non-Catholics in the six counties that were to become the province of Northern Ireland (quoted in Buckland 1981, p. 3).

3. Symbolic differences abound. In the summer of 1986, residents of Falls Road displayed the Irish tricolor (it used to be illegal) and pictures of Pope John Paul II, while residents of Shankhill countered with the Union Jack and pictures of the Queen and royal couples: Charles and Diana or Andrew and Sarah. The graffiti tell the tale. "IRA," "The Spirit of Freedom," the names of imprisoned IRA men, and paintings of birds with machine guns mark the walls of Falls Road. There is less graffiti in the Protestant areas, but banners abound announcing "Ulster Says No" (a reference to the Anglo-Irish agreement of December 1985).

4. Although each of these authors expects a replication of the pattern prevalent among blacks in the United States in the data on Catholics in Northern Ireland, none actually observes it.

5. Note the X^2 values at the bottom of each column.

6. The American definition used to define the category of "service workers" in Table 7.2 encompasses a set of occupations that differs substantially from the composition of class IIIb in Table 7.1.

7. The linen industry also provides many of Northern Ireland's manufacturing exports, but textiles employ more women than men, and the degree of inequality of access to textile jobs for Catholic women is lower (OPCS 1974, table 8).

8. These nonprotective service positions are considered lower manual in studies based on the U.S. Census major groups (Blau and Duncan 1967, pp. 27ff).

9. What constitutes "few" observations depends on the size of the percentage difference in the population. Even 2,000 observations are insufficient to detect a difference of one percentage point (at the conventional 95 percent confidence level). However, about 80 cases will suffice to infer that a 20 percent difference is significant if the ratio of Protestants to Catholics is not far from two-to-one and the percentages compared are 20–80 percent.

10. A positive difference indicates that structural mobility favors Catholics; a negative number means that structural mobility favors Protestants.

11. Miller (1982, 1984) misses this crucial point in part because he uses broader occupational categories and in part because he uses a much less sensitive log-linear model.

12. The term $H(t) = -\log \lambda(t)$. Since $\lambda(t)$ is a probability, $\log \lambda(t)$ will always be negative. Since $\lambda(t)$ is inversely related to mobility (it is the probability that a job shift occurs after t), a low probability (high mobility) will result in a large negative logarithm. Multiplying by -1 produces a large positive $H(t)$ when mobility is high.

13. The mobility rate is $1 - \lambda(t)$, so the mobility rate is $1 - \exp(-H(t))$.

14. Mobility to a destination other than the one in question is treated as a censored spell (logically equivalent to the interview).

15. I am not denying the weight that religion carries in Northern Ireland. My argument for class over religion does not stray beyond the occupational sphere. Within that ambit, class rules the domain of class relations.

16. Hout (1986) details a number of important differences between Protestants and Catholics within major occupational groups.

8. *Expanding Schools, Persistent Inequality*

1. Portions of this chapter were written in collaboration with Adrian E. Raftery. See also Raftery and Hout (1985).

2. Leaving school before age 16 is no longer legal, but the minimum school-leaving age has been increased by national and local governments several times in this century. Leaving at age 14 (or younger) was acceptable for most of the period covered by the Irish Mobility Study.

3. Since 1963, second-level students in the Republic sit an exam for the Intermediate Certificate at the end of the second year in their curriculum, whether it is a two-year or a four-year curriculum. For most men in the Irish Mobility Study, creation of this exam came after they left school.

4. Classical inference theory implies a preference for model 10 over model 9.

5. To obtain this result, first convert the percentage into a logit: logit (20 percent) = log (20/(100 − 20)) = − 1.39. Then add the .51 to obtain an expected logit for class II of − .88. The percentage for class II is then: percent (− .88) = [exp (− .88)/(1 + exp (− .88))] × 100 = 29. This calculation assumes that the educational dimension of origin is held constant—an impossibility given the design.

6. Because of the constant effect of prestige at all levels, social origins significantly affect the transition to third level, despite the insignificance of the effect of the educational dimension of origins.

7. The expectation of transition roles is based on model 9.

8. Six students died or emigrated before completing junior cycle.

9. Father's occupation is scored according to the Hope-Goldthorpe prestige scale (Goldthorpe and Hope 1974). Preliminary analyses used a 14-category class scheme. However, replacing the prestige score with the 13 dummy variables that capture all the deviance due to father's occupation does not improve fit significantly, so the more parsimonious version is used.

10. More formally, let p_{ij} be the probability that student i makes transition j ($i = 1,\ldots, 468; j = 1,\ldots 5$) conditional on his or her attaining the level of education immediately below transition j. For example, if $j = 3$, the focus is on the transition from junior cycle to senior cycle. Thus p_{i3} is the probability that student i enters senior cycle; this probability is relevant for students who have completed junior cycle but not for students who dropped out prior to that point. The model is Raftery and Hout (1985): logit $(p_{ij}) = \log (p_{ij}/(1-p_{ij})) = \beta_{0j} + \Sigma_k \beta_{kj} X_{ki}$, where the β_{kj} ($k = 0,\ldots, m; j = 1,\ldots, 5$) are unknown parameters and the X_{ki} are the observed values on the independent variable k for student i ($k = 1,\ldots, m$; $i = 1,\ldots, 468$). The values of the index k are as follows: 1, father's occupation; 2, academic ability; 3, type of school; and 4, gender. The parameter β_{0j} is similar to the intercept of the standard linear regression model. The other β_{kj} parameters ($k > 0$) quantify the effect of variable X_{ki} on transition j. Parameter estimation was carried out by the maximum likelihood method using GLIM (Baker and Nelder 1978). Constraints of the form $\beta_{kj} = \beta_{kj'}$ were implemented using techniques described by Fienberg and Mason (1979; see also Mare 1980).

11. No satisfactory overall goodness-of-fit test has yet been developed for the logistic linear regression model used here. This is not a limitation, however, because the focus is on the extent to which the introduction of any one explanatory variable improves the fit of the model to the data. The most widely used measure of fit for logistic linear regression models is the deviance, which is denoted L^2. The deviance is equal to minus twice the log-likelihood of the model, given the data (under the assumption of binomial sampling). It generalizes the residual sum of squares used for the standard normal linear model (Nelder and Wedderburn 1972). The smaller the deviance, the better the model fits the data. The difference between the deviance for one model that includes m independent variables and another that includes the same m variables plus m' others is a measure of the contribution of the additional variables to the fit of the model (Raftery and Hout 1985).

12. In a first pass of the data, the effects of class and ability differed little for transitions within the second level, so constraints were placed on the coefficients: $\beta_{21} = \beta_{31} = \beta_{41}$ and $\beta_{22} = \beta_{32} = \beta_{42}$.

13. Occupations receiving a score of 18 include building-site laborers, factory laborers, messengers, and street vendors.

14. Occupations receiving a score of 75 include dentists in private practice, architects who are partners in their firms, and veterinary surgeons.

15. Whelan and Whelan (1984, pp. 159–175) also reanalyze the Drumcondra data. Their basic conclusion accords well with the conclusion that Greaney and Kellaghan have seriously understated the effects of social class on educational attainments in the Republic. However, they also conclude that the effect of father's occupation on the probability of remaining in school increases as students advance in the system. This conclusion is contradicted by the reanalysis here, and it does not accord with findings of studies of other European countries (Greaney and Kellaghan 1984, p. 252). The problem with the Whelan and Whelan reanalysis is apparently the measure of social class that they use. Since they must rely on published tabulations, they use Greaney and Kellaghan's simplistic categorization of class, the limitations of which are most evident to them.

16. The model is logit $(p_{ia}) = \beta_{0a} + \beta_{1a}X_{1i} + \beta_{2a}X_{2i} + \beta_{3a}X_{3i}$, where p_{ia} is the probability that student i attends an academic rather than a nonacademic second-level school (given the transition to second-level education), the β_{ka} ($k = 0, \ldots, 3$) are unknown parameters, and the X_{ki} are the observed scores on class ($k = 1$), ability ($k = 2$), and gender ($k = 3$)—a dummy variable equal to one for girls and zero for boys. The estimate of β_{0a} (not presented here) is -6.602 with an approximate standard error of .956. The sample size is only 441 because students who did not enroll in a second-level school are excluded.

17. The coefficient of gender is not significant in the second row of the fourth panel of Table 8.9.

18. It is just a coincidence that both indirect effects work out to be .119.

19. Note the contradiction between counterbalance and overtraining on this point.

9. The Socioeconomic Life Cycle

1. The L^2 values in Table 9.2 show these to be significant differences.

2. The means are as follows:

Occupation	Status		Prestige	
	Republic	North	Republic	North
Origins	34.38	39.22	39.20	39.35
First	32.56	37.43	34.15	34.83
Current	40.95	46.44	39.99	41.28

3. The regional differences in the relationship are significant; the L^2 for the null hypothesis of no three-way interaction is 117.01 ($df = 81$; $p < .01$).

4. These models are analogous to regression models for continuous data. The hypothesis is that the odds on a high-scoring first occupation relative to another

first occupation with a lower score increase as the score for education increases. Counts such as those in Tables A.17 and A.18 can be used to estimate the scores and the slope of the relationship, subject to some normalizing constraints.

5. This model is also known as the model of conditional independence (Goodman 1970; Fienberg 1982).

6. Homogeneous overall association parameters for the Republic and Northern Ireland would be a reasonable constraint to place on this model, considering the other evidence of homogeneous association. However, computer software to implement such a constraint was not available at the time this analysis was performed.

7. The simple correlations between the μ parameters and each of the scales is .94 for SES, .91 for primary education, and .84 for prestige.

8. The term *mean occupational standing* is intentionally vague. Any "vertical" ranking of occupations might be filled in for the actual test. Occupational scores (μ parameters) from the homogeneous RC model of the association between education and first occupation are used here. Socioeconomic status scores or prestige scores could be used instead.

9. These are the same cohorts that were used in Chapter 7.

10. These numbers are weighted means produced by multiplying the μ_j ($j = 1, \ldots 16$) for each occupation by the number of men with the specific combination of education (i) and first occupation (j) and dividing by the total number of men with that amount of education: mean $\mu_i = (\Sigma_j \mu_j f_{ij}) / (\Sigma_j f_{ij})$, where f_{ij} is the observed count of men with education i and first occupation j.

11. These two models differ only in their specification of the change in the rate of return to education: homogeneous UA allows no change, while heterogeneous UA permits change in ϕ. The failure of heterogeneous UA to improve over the fit of homogeneous UA suggests that changes in ϕ are insignificant.

12. The large number of zeros in Appendix Tables A.3 and A.4 caused problems in fitting models, so the technique of adjusting cell counts described in Chapter 2 was applied here.

13. Because of the symmetry of δ_{ij} parameters, $\delta_{57} > 1$ also means that those very few men whose fathers were unpaid nonfarm workers are more likely to start their work life as proprietors than to find employment as unpaid nonfarm workers. This unlikely result comes from the strong tendency mentioned in the text and a lack of observations on unpaid fathers. The observed frequencies on which the estimate of δ_{57} are based are in four cells: in the Republic the four counts that contribute to δ_{57} are $f_{55} = 0, f_{57} = 30, f_{75} = 0$, and $f_{77} = 1$; in Northern Ireland they are $f_{55} = 2, f_{57} = 32, f_{75} = 0$, and $f_{77} = 0$.

14. A $\delta_{ij} = 1.00$ indicates even odds (the chance of moving equals the chance of staying within the origin class).

15. The standard error for log δ_{ij} is the square root of $(1/F_{ij} + 1/F_{ji} + 1/F_{ii} + 1/F_{jj})$. If an odds ratio and its standard error are known, then the formula in Fienberg (1980, p. 37) for the difference between two odds ratios can be used to test the difference between log δ_{ij} for origins to first occupations and log δ_{ij} for origins to current occupations.

16. A log-linear analysis of the frequencies that were used to calculate the proportions in Table 9.10 produced the following results, where O is origin, R is region, and T is mobility type:

Model	df	L^2	p	bic
[OT][OR]	38	86.45	<.01	−219
[OT][OR][RT]	30	62.19	<.01	−179

While classical inference concludes from this analysis that the three-way interaction among origin, region, and mobility type is significant, bic indicates that the only reliable regional difference is the origin distribution. The apparent regional difference in mobility type is, according to bic, attributable to the regional difference in the distribution of origins and the association between origins and mobility type.

17. Standard errors can be computed for ratios of structural mobility multipliers, i.e., for $\alpha_j/\alpha_{j'}$ ($j \neq j'$), but not for normalized α_j (Sobel et al. 1985). In an application like Table 9.11 in which all of the α_j are changing, the ratios of structural mobility multipliers are very difficult to interpret, so none are reported.

18. Treating the three mobility tables—mobility from first occupation to occupation at age 25, ages 25–35, and ages 35–45—as the components of a 14 × 14 × 3 table, the model of conditional independence yields $L^2 = 16,087.86$ ($df = 507$). Deleting the diagonal cells of that table, the model of conditional quasi-independence yields $L^2 = 2,519.93$ ($df = 465$). The latter figure is only 15.6 percent as large as the L^2 for conditional independence.

19. Preliminary analyses also included father's educational level and number of siblings, but these variables did not affect any of the dimensions of current occupational attainment, so they were dropped from the analysis (see Whelan and Whelan 1984, chap. 6, for corroborating evidence for Dublin men).

20. Men 18–24 years old were excluded because the most highly educated members of their cohorts were still in school at the time of the survey. Excluding the best-educated members of a cohort could bias the estimates of the effect of education on first and current occupation, so all members of the affected cohorts are left out of this part of the analysis.

21. The values of p are (1) prestige, (2) educational qualifications, (3) bureaucratic entry, and (4) personal contacts.

22. Evidence supporting this claim must be deduced from the data in Table 9.13 since the standard errors needed for a definitive statement are not included in the table. Reporting the standard error for each coefficient would complicate the table too much. However, a footnote indicates that a coefficient is significantly greater than zero (at the .05 level). The confidence intervals of regression coefficients are symmetrical, and all coefficients for origins are less than .5. If the confidence interval of a coefficient that is less than half does not overlap the limit of zero, it cannot overlap the limit of one.

23. According to Table 2.9, lower manual occupations are highest on bureaucratic entry; upper manual and routine nonmanual occupations also score relatively high on this dimension; and low scores go to self-employed and unpaid

workers. Scores on personal contacts are extremely high for unpaid workers, moderate for farmers and agricultural workers, and low for professionals, technicians, and clerical workers.

24. For prestige and bureaucratic entry, these diagonal effects are in line with the results in Table 3.9. For educational qualifications, the diagonal effect in Table 3.9 is not significant.

25. For example, if the δ_{ij} association parameter for $i = 7$ (class IIIb, service workers) and $j = 11$ (class VIIss, semiskilled labor) is greater than the $\delta_{i'j'}$ association parameter for $i' = 4$ (class IIIa, clerical and sales workers) and $j' = 12$ (class VIIus, unskilled labor) in one table, then $\delta_{7,11}$ will be greater than $\delta_{4,12}$ in all others as well.

10. The Microdynamics of Industrialization

1. The α_j are from the SHD parameterization of the model of quasi-symmetry. Fitting the model to a table with as many zero cells as Appendix Tables A.7 and A.8 requires some adjustments (see Fienberg 1980, pp. 140–142). The exact results depend on how the adjustments are made, so three adjustments were used here to see how sensitive the inferences to be drawn were to the adjustment procedure. The first is described by Fienberg (1980, p. 141): if $f_{ij} = f_{ji} = 0$, then $F_{ij} = F_{ji} = 0$. Unfortunately, while this solution yields the best test of the model, it does not yield estimates of the α_j coefficients. Two other solutions involve adding a constant to each observed frequency (Goodman 1972a,b; Haberman 1979). Adding a constant biases L^2 and X^2 toward zero, but it yields estimates of α_j. In one version of this solution, each cell gets $\frac{1}{2}$. This approach is recommended by Haberman and Goodman for small tables. When the number of cells in the table gets large, this solution can substantially inflate the sample size. For a 16×16 table, adding $\frac{1}{2}$ to each cell increases sample size by 128. The third alternative is to add a smaller amount (e.g., $\frac{1}{16}$) to each cell and then readjust the marginal totals to the observed marginal totals using iterative proportional fitting (as in previous chapters). Following are the fit statistics obtained by using each of these solutions. For both regions quasi-symmetry provides an acceptable fit to the data, especially as judged by the likelihood ratio chi square:

Type of adjustment	df	L^2	X^2	bic
Republic				
$F_{ij} = 0$	72	91.01	95.39	-434
Add $\frac{1}{2}$	105	92.99	110.95	-681
Add $\frac{1}{16}$, adjust	105	82.69	122.74	-682
Northern Ireland				
$F_{ij} = 0$	65	117.29	221.37	-362
Add $\frac{1}{2}$	105	120.16	147.20	-663
Add $\frac{1}{16}$, adjust	105	108.42	189.66	-666

The log λ_j in Table 10.1 were obtained using the third type of adjustment.

2. The case was not chosen at random. This man is the first in the data file with more than ten jobs and more than two occupations between 1959 and 1973, who nonetheless is coded into the same occupational category in 1959 and 1973.

3. Further analysis might seek to separate the men in the "same occupation, different job" group who worked in only one occupation throughout the period from those who worked for a time in a different occupation but subsequently returned to the occupation they were pursuing in 1959. Although such a distinction is not crucial to the point of this section, much of the analysis in the rest of this chapter takes such a distinction into account.

4. Statistical tests are conspicuously lacking in this section. A proper model for testing the claims and inferences made follows later in this chapter. The results in this section, conjectural though they are, offer a heuristic sense of the size of changes that are tested later on.

5. The destination state may be the same occupational stratum as the origin state. This will be the case whenever a worker changes jobs without changing occupation. It will also be true when a worker changes jobs and occupation but moves to a similar occupation (e.g., if a firefighter shifts to a job as a police officer, he changes job and occupation but not occupational stratum).

6. Formally the rate is the limit (as Δt approaches zero) of the probability that worker h is in state j at time $t + \Delta t$, given that he was in state i at time t divided by Δt: prob$[Y(t + \Delta t) = j \mid Y(t) = i] / \Delta t$.

7. Exact expressions of these functions are given in Chapter 2.

8. This analysis will detect some job shifts among farmers because the coding scheme distinguishes employers from other self-employed workers. Therefore, a job shift is recorded whenever a farmer takes on a first employee or lays off the last one.

9. These are Kaplan and Meier (1958) estimates of the survivor function obtained from SPSS^X.

10. In fact, the long-term stability of unemployment after two years' duration suggests the possibility that some disabled or retired workers were incorrectly coded as unemployed.

11. Time is not actually included as a regressor; it is factored out as a nuisance factor (Cox 1975; Carroll 1983; Tuma and Hannan 1984). The BMDP program P2L was used (Dixon et al. 1985).

12. The logic of this procedure is spelled out in Chapter 2. The number of completed spells and censored spells is shown in the bottom panel of Table 10.7.

13. The usual identification problem associated with age, period, and cohort effects is not an issue in these results because the linear terms for two (but not three) of the dimensions solve the identification problem.

14. Precisely, $r_{hij}(t) = h_{hi}(t)m_{ij}(t)$, where $h_{hi}(t)$ is the origin-specific hazard rate for individual h and $m_{ij}(t)$ is the probability of moving from occupational stratum i to occupational stratum j, given that a move has occurred (Carroll 1983). Note that $m_{ij}(t)$ does not vary across individuals.

15. Current occupation is the occupation held throughout the job spell; destination or next occupation is the occupation shifted to. Current and next occupations

are classified into the 17 categories shown in Table 10.8. Period is divided into 1908–1944, 1945–1958, and 1959–1974. There are 21,646 job shifts.

16. The notation is that of Goodman (1970). For example, [CD][Y] means that C affects D, but Y does not affect C or D. The cells for unemployment in the current and destination occupations in each period are treated as structural zeros in this analysis because the combination of unemployment with unemployment cannot occur.

17. Longer durations were considered in preliminary analyses. The more extreme durations, too, failed to produce any evidence of change.

11. New Opportunities, Old Inequalities

1. Treiman (1970) reviews this extensive literature.

2. I suppose an argument could be made—and probably has been—that the social sciences themselves are creatures of the industrial revolution.

3. Much subsequent empirical and theoretical work has been devoted to this topic (e.g., Lipset and Bendix 1959; Featherman, Jones, and Hauser 1975; Grusky and Hauser 1984).

4. The sampling frame employed and the questions asked also make these interview data more comparable with other contemporary national mobility studies (e.g., Erikson and Goldthorpe 1987a).

5. Poland has a comparable number of farmers, but they are not all self-employed.

6. To be equally certain that the correspondence between family values and institutional values in Ireland is the source of this persistent strength of association would require more research.

7. The 200,000 assumes that the rate of emigration in Northern Ireland is the same as the rate in the Republic. This implies an annual average of 5,000 emigrants from Northern Ireland every year. Added to the 15,000-a-year figure for the Republic and multiplied by 10, we get the 200,000 estimated in the text.

8. See Chapter 10 (also Grusky and Hauser 1984) for a review of the negative evidence.

9. Reasons why this might be so are enumerated by Parkin (1971).

10. To cite a personal example, my Dublin landlord—an engineer—lived in Abu Dhabi in 1984. He moved from there to Japan; he now lives in Norway.

References

Allison, Paul D. 1985. *Event History Analysis*. Beverly Hills, Calif.: Sage.

Alwin, Duane F., and Robert M. Hauser. 1975. "The Decomposition of Effects in Path Analysis." *American Sociological Review* 40 (February): 37–47.

Aminzade, Ronald. 1981. *Class, Politics, and Early Industrial Capitalism*. Albany, N.Y.: SUNY Press.

Arensberg, Conrad. 1937. *The Irish Countryman*. Garden City, N.J.: Natural History Press.

Arensberg, Conrad, and Solon T. Kimball. 1940. *Family and Community in Ireland*. Cambridge, Mass.: Harvard University Press.

Beckett, J. C. 1981. *The Making of Modern Ireland: 1603–1923*, 2nd ed. London: Faber and Faber.

Berg, Ivar. 1970. *Education and Jobs: The Great Training Robbery*. New York: Praeger.

Bernard, P., and J. Renaud. 1976. "Contre-mobilité et effets différés." *Sociologie et Sociétés* 8 (October): 81–97.

Bernstein, Basil. 1977. "Class and Pedagogies: Visible and Invisible." In Jerome Karabel and Anthony H. Halsey, eds., *Power and Ideology in Education*, pp. 511–534. New York: Oxford University Press.

Bertaux, Daniel. 1974. "Mobilité sociale bibliographique: une critique de l'approche transversale." *Revue Française de Sociologie* 15 (July–September): 329–362.

Bielby, William T. 1981. "Models of Status Attainment." In Donald J. Treiman and Robert V. Robinson, eds., *Research in Social Stratification and Mobility*, vol. 1, pp. 3–26. Greenwich, Conn.: JAI.

Bielby, William T., and James N. Baron. 1986. "Sex, Segregation, and Statistical Discrimination." *American Journal of Sociology* 91 (January): 759–799.

Bishop, Yvonne, Stephen E. Fienberg, and Paul M. Holland. 1975. *Discrete Multivariate Analysis: Theory and Practice*. Cambridge, Mass.: MIT Press.

Blalock, Hubert M., Jr. 1967. "Path Coefficients versus Regression Coefficients." *American Journal of Sociology* 72 (May): 675–676.

Blau, Peter M. 1965. "The Flow of Occupational Supply and Recruitment." *American Sociological Review* 30 (August): 475–490.

Blau, Peter M., and Otis Dudley Duncan, with Andrea Tyree. 1967. *The American Occupational Structure*. New York: Wiley.

Bottomore, Tom. 1965. *Classes in Modern Society*. London: Allyn and Unwin.

Bourdieu, Pierre. 1977. "Cultural Reproduction and Social Reproduction." In Jerome Karabel and Anthony H. Halsey, eds., *Power and Ideology in Education,* pp. 487–511. New York: Oxford University Press.

Bourdieu, Pierre, and J. C. Passeron. 1977. *Reproduction: In Education, Society, and Culture*. Beverly Hills, Calif.: Sage.

Boyle, James. 1977. "Educational Attainment, Occupational Achievement, and Religion in Northern Ireland." *Economic and Social Review* 8 (January): 79–100.

Breen, Richard. 1985. *Education and the Labour Market: Work and Unemployment among Recent Cohorts of Irish School Leavers*. Dublin: Economic and Social Research Institute.

Breen, Richard, and Christopher T. Whelan. 1987. "Vertical Mobility in the British Isles." *British Journal of Sociology* 36 (May): 175–192.

Breiger, Ronald L. 1981. "The Social Class Structure of Occupational Mobility." *American Journal of Sociology* 87 (September): 578–611.

Brint, Stephen, and Jerome Karabel. 1989. *Diverted Dreams: The Junior College Movement in the United States*. New York: Oxford University Press.

Brown, Terence. 1984. *Ireland: A Social and Cultural History, 1922 to the Present*. Ithaca, N.Y.: Cornell University Press.

Carroll, Glenn R. 1983. "Dynamic Analysis of Discrete Dependent Variables: A Didactic Essay." *Quality and Quantity* 17 (October): 425–460.

Carroll, Glenn R., and Karl Ulrich Mayer. 1986. "Job Shift Patterns in the Federal Republic of Germany: The Effects of Social Class, Industrial Sector, and Organizational Size." *American Sociological Review* 51 (June): 323–341.

Census of Northern Ireland. 1974. Vol. 7, *Occupation*. London: Her Majesty's Stationery Office.

Central Statistics Office of Ireland. 1971. "Characteristics of the Population: Occupation." Dublin: Stationery Office.

—— 1986. *Census of Population of Ireland: Occupations*. Dublin: Stationery Office.

Clancy, Patrick. 1982. *Participation in Higher Education*. Dublin: Higher Education Authority.

—— 1985. "Symposium on *Equality of Opportunity in Irish Schools:* Editorial Introduction." *Economic and Social Review* 16 (January): 77–82.

—— 1986. "Socialization, Selection, and Reproduction in Education." In Patrick Clancy, Sheelagh Drudy, Kathleen Lynch, and Liam O'Dowd, eds., *Ireland: A Sociological Profile,* pp. 116–136. Dublin: Institute of Public Administration.

Clogg, Clifford C. 1979. *Measuring Underemployment: Demographic Indicators for the United States*. New York: Academic Press.

———— 1981. "Latent Structure Models of Mobility." *American Journal of Sociology* 86 (January): 836–868.

———— 1982a. "The Analysis of Association: Models for Social Data." *Journal of the American Statistical Association* 77 (December): 803–815.

———— 1982b. "Analysis of Association: Sociological Examples." *American Journal of Sociology* 88 (July): 114–134.

Clogg, Clifford C., and James W. Shockey. 1984. "Mismatch between Occupation and Schooling: A Prevalence Measure, Recent Trends, and Demographic Analysis." *Demography* 21 (May): 235–257.

Clogg, Clifford C., and Teresa A. Sullivan. 1983. "Labor Force Composition and Underemployment Trends, 1969–1980." *Social Indicators Research* 12 (February): 117–152.

Coleman, James S. 1981. *Longitudinal Data Analysis*. New York: Basic Books.

Collins, Randall. 1974. *Conflict Sociology*. New York: Academic Press.

Commins, H., and Carmel Kelleher. 1973. *Farm Inheritance and Succession*. Dublin: Macra na Feirme.

Commins, Patrick. 1986. "Rural Social Change." In Patrick Clancy, Sheelagh Drudy, Kathleen Lynch, and Liam O'Dowd, eds., *Ireland: A Sociological Profile*, pp. 47–69. Dublin: Institute of Public Administration.

Cox, D. R. 1972. "Regression Models and Life Tables (with discussion)." *Journal of the Royal Statistical Society*, ser. B, 34: 187–220.

———— 1975. "Partial Likelihood." *Biometrika* 62: 269–276.

Cox, D. R., and P. A. W. Lewis. 1966. *The Statistical Analysis of Series of Events*. London: Methuen.

Cullen, L. M. 1972. *An Economic History of Ireland since 1660*. London: B. T. Batsford.

Cutright, Phillips. 1968. "Occupational Inheritance: A Cross-National Analysis." *American Journal of Sociology* 73 (January): 400–416.

Dahrendorf, Ralf. 1959. *Class and Class Conflict in Industrial Society*. Stanford: Stanford University Press.

Davis, James A., and Tom Smith. 1985. *General Social Survey: Cumulative Codebook, 1972–1985*. Storrs, Conn.: Roper Center.

Dixon, W. J. 1985. *BMDP Statistical Software*. Berkeley: University of California Press.

Duncan, Beverly. 1965. *Family Factors and School Dropout: 1920–1960*. Ann Arbor: University of Michigan Cooperative Research Project no. 2258, U.S. Office of Education.

———— 1968. "Trends in the Output and Distribution of Schooling." In Eleanor B. Sheldon and Wilbert E. Moore, eds., *Indicators of Social Change*, pp. 601–672. New York: Russell Sage Foundation.

Duncan, Beverly, and Otis Dudley Duncan. 1979. *Indicators of Sex Typing*. New York: Academic Press.

Duncan, Otis Dudley. 1961. "A Socioeconomic Index for All Occupations." In Albert J. Reiss, Jr., ed., *Occupations and Social Status,* pp. 109–138. Glencoe, Ill.: Free Press.

—— 1966a. "Methodological Issues in the Analysis of Social Mobility." In Neil J. Smelser and Seymour Martin Lipset, eds., *Social Structure and Mobility in Economic Development,* pp. 51–97. Chicago: Aldine.

—— 1966b. "Path Analysis: Sociological Examples." *American Journal of Sociology* 72: 1–16.

—— 1968. "Social Stratification and Mobility Problems in the Measurement of Trend." In Eleanor B. Sheldon and Wilbert E. Moore, eds., *Indicators of Social Change,* pp. 675–719. New York: Russell Sage Foundation.

—— 1979. "How Destination Depends on Origin in the Occupational Mobility Table." *American Journal of Sociology* 84 (January): 793–804.

Duncan, Otis Dudley, and Robert W. Hodge. 1963. "Education and Occupational Mobility." *American Journal of Sociology* 68 (May): 629–644.

Duncan, Otis Dudley, David L. Featherman, and Beverly Duncan 1972. *Socio-economic Background and Achievement*. New York: Seminar Press.

Edlefsen, Lee E., and Samuel D. Jones. 1985. *Reference Guide to GAUSS*™. Kent, Wash.: Applied Technical Systems.

Efron, Bradley. 1977. "The Efficiency of Cox's Likelihood Function for Censored Data." *Journal of the American Statistical Association* 72: 557–565.

Erikson, Robert, and John H. Goldthorpe. 1985. "Are American Rates of Social Mobility Exceptionally High? New Evidence on an Old Question." *European Sociological Review* 1 (May): 1–22.

—— 1987a. "Commonality and Variation in Social Fluidity in Industrial Nations. Part I: A Model for Evaluating the FJH Hypothesis." *European Sociological Review* 3 (May): 54–77.

—— 1987b. "Commonality and Variation in Social Fluidity in Industrial Nations: Part II: The Model of Core Social Fluidity Applied." *European Sociological Review* 3 (September): 145–166.

Erikson, Robert, John H. Goldthorpe, and Lucianne Portocarero. 1979. "Intergenerational Class Mobility in Three Western European Societies: England, France, and Sweden." *British Journal of Sociology* 30 (December): 415–430.

—— 1982. "Social Fluidity in Industrial Nations: England, France, and Sweden." *British Journal of Sociology* 33 (March): 1–34.

—— 1983. "Intergenerational Class Mobility and the Convergence Thesis: England, France, and Sweden." *British Journal of Sociology* 34 (September): 303–343.

Eurostat. 1985. *Basic Statistics of the European Economic Community,* 23rd ed. Luxembourg: Office for Official Publications of the European Communities.

Featherman, David L. 1983. "Biography, Society, and History: Individual Development as a Population Process." Madison, Wis.: Center for Demography and Ecology, Working Paper 83–29.

Featherman, David L., and Robert M. Hauser. 1978. *Opportunity and Change.* New York: Academic Press.

Featherman, David L., Frank Lancaster Jones, and Robert M. Hauser. 1975. "Assumptions of Mobility Research in the United States: The Case of Occupational Status." *Social Science Research* 4 (December): 329–360.

Fienberg, Stephen E. 1980. *The Analysis of Cross-Classified Categorical Data,* 2nd ed. Cambridge, Mass.: MIT Press.

Fitzgerald, Garrett. 1972. *Towards a New Ireland.* Dublin: Gill and Macmillan.

Freeman, Richard. 1976. *The Overeducated American.* New York: Academic Press.

—— 1977. "The Decline in Economic Rewards to College Education." *Review of Economics and Statistics* 59 (February): 18–29.

Ganzeboom, Harry B., Donald J. Treiman, and Ruud Luijkx. 1988. "International Comparisons of Intergenerational Occupational Mobility Tables." Revision of a paper presented at the meeting of the International Sociological Association Research Committee on Stratification and Mobility, Berkeley, California, 12–15 August 1987.

Garnier, Maurice A., and Michael Hout. 1976. "Inequality of Educational Opportunity in France and the United States." *Social Science Research* 5 (September): 225–246.

—— 1982. "Schooling Processes and Educational Outcomes in France." *Quality and Quantity* 15 (March): 151–177.

Geertz, Clifford. 1973. "After the Revolution: The Fate of Nationalism in the New States." In Clifford Geertz, *The Interpretation of Cultures,* pp. 234–254. New York: Harper & Row.

Giddens, Anthony. 1973. *The Class Structure of Advanced Societies.* New York: Harper & Row.

Girod, Roger. 1971. *Mobilité sociale: faits établis et problèmes ouverts.* Geneva: Droz.

Glass, David V. 1954. *Social Mobility in Britain.* London: Routledge and Kegan Paul.

Goldstrom, J. M. 1981. "Irish Agriculture and the Great Famine." In J. M. Goldstrom and L. A. Clarkson, eds., *Irish Population, Economy, and Society: Essays in Honour of the Late K. H. Connell,* pp. 155–172. Oxford: Clarendon Press.

Goldthorpe, John H., with Catriona Llewellyn and Clive Payne. 1980. *Social Mobility and Class Structure in Modern Britain.* Oxford: Clarendon Press.

Goldthorpe, John H., and Keith Hope. 1972. "Occupational Grading and Occupational Prestige." In Keith Hope, ed., *The Analysis of Social Mobility: Methods and Approaches,* pp. 1–64. Oxford: Clarendon Press.

—— 1974. *The Social Grading of Occupations.* Oxford: Clarendon Press.

Goldthorpe, John H., and Catriona Llewellyn. 1977a. "Class Mobility in Modern Britain: Three Theses Examined." *Sociology* 11 (May): 257–287.

—— 1977b. "Class Mobility: Intergenerational and Work Life Patterns." *British Journal of Sociology* 28 (September): 269–302.

Goldthorpe, John H., Clive Payne, and Catriona Llewellyn. 1978. "Trends in Class Mobility." *Sociology* 12(3): 441–468.

Goodman, Leo A. 1961. "Statistical Methods for the Mover-Stayer Model." *Journal of the American Statistical Association* 56 (December): 841–868.

—— 1962. "Structured Methods for Analyzing Processes of Change." *American Journal of Sociology* 68 (July): 57–78.

—— 1965. "On the Statistical Analysis of Mobility Tables." *American Journal of Sociology* 70 (March): 564–585.

—— 1968. "The Analysis of Cross-Classified Data: Independence, Quasi-Independence, and Interaction in Contingency Tables with or without Missing Entries." *Journal of the American Statistical Association* 63 (December): 1091–1131.

—— 1969a. "How to Ransack Social Mobility Tables and Other Kinds of Cross-Classification Tables." *American Journal of Sociology* 75 (July): 1–39.

—— 1969b. "On the Measurement of Social Mobility: An Index of Status Persistence." *American Sociological Review* 34 (December): 831–850.

—— 1970. "The Multivariate Analysis of Qualitative Data: Interactions among Multiple Classifications." *Journal of the American Statistical Association* 65 (March): 226–256.

—— 1972a. "Some Multiplicative Models for the Analysis of Cross-Classified Data." In Lucien LeCam et al. eds., *Sixth Berkeley Symposium on Mathematical Statistics*, pp. 649–696. Berkeley: University of California Press.

—— 1972b. "A General Model for the Analysis of Surveys." *American Journal of Sociology* 77 (May): 1035–86.

—— 1978. *The Log-Linear Analysis of Cross-Classified Data*. Boston: Abt Press.

—— 1979a. "Simple Models for the Analysis of Association in Cross-Classifications Having Ordered Categories." *Journal of the American Statistical Association* 74 (September): 537–552.

—— 1979b. "Multiplicative Models of the Analysis of Mobility Tables and Other Kinds of Cross-Classification Tables." *American Journal of Sociology* 84 (January): 804–819.

—— 1981a. "Criteria for Determining Whether Certain Categories in a Cross-Classification Table Should Be Combined." *American Journal of Sociology* 87 (September): 612–650.

—— 1981b. "Three Elementary Views of Log-Linear Models for the Analysis of Cross-Classifications Having Ordered Categories." In Samuel Leinhardt, ed., *Sociological Methodology, 1981*, pp. 193–239. San Francisco: Jossey-Bass.

—— 1984. *The Analysis of Cross-Classified Data Having Ordered Categories*. Cambridge, Mass.: Harvard University Press.

—— 1985. "The Analysis of Cross-Classified Data Having Ordered and/or Unordered Categories: Association Models, Correlation Models, and Asymmetry Models for Contingency Tables with or without Missing Entries." *Annals of Statistics* 13 (March): 10–69.

Granovetter, Mark. 1974. *Getting a Job*. Cambridge, Mass.: Harvard University Press.

Greaney, Vincent, and Thomas Kellaghan. 1984. *Equality of Opportunity in Irish Schools*. Dublin: Educational Company.

—— 1985. "Factors Related to Level of Educational Attainment in Ireland." *Economic and Social Review* 16 (January): 141–156.

Greeley, Andrew M. 1972. *That Most Distressful Nation: The Taming of the American Irish*. Chicago: Quadrangle Books.

Grusky, David B., and Robert M. Hauser. 1984. "Comparative Social Mobility Revisited: Models of Convergence and Divergence in Sixteen Countries." *American Sociological Review* 49 (February): 19–38.

Haberman, Shelby J. 1974. "Log-Linear Models for Frequency Tables with Ordered Classifications." *Biometrics* 30 (December): 589–600.

—— 1977. "Log-Linear Models and Frequency Tables with Small Expected Cell Counts." *Annals of Statistics* 5 (November): 1148–69.

—— 1979. *The Analysis of Qualitative Data*, 2 vols. New York: Academic Press.

Haller, Max, and Robert W. Hodge. 1981. "Class and Status as Dimensions of Career Mobility: Some Insights from the Austrian Case." *Zeitschrift für Soziologie* 10 (April): 133–150.

Halsey, Anthony H., Anthony F. Heath, and J. M. Ridge. 1980. *Origins and Destinations: Family, Class, and Education in Modern Britain*. Oxford: Clarendon Press.

Hannan, Damian F. 1982. "Peasant Models and the Understanding of Social and Cultural Change in Rural Ireland." In P. J. Drudy, ed., *Ireland: Land, Politics, and People*, pp. 141–165. Cambridge: Cambridge University Press.

Hardy, Melissa A., and Lawrence E. Hazelrigg. 1978. "Industrialization and the Circulatory Rate of Mobility: Further Tests of Some Cross-Sectional Hypotheses." *Sociological Focus* 11 (March): 1–10.

Hauser, Robert M. 1978. "A Structural Model for the Mobility Table." *Social Forces* 56 (March): 919–953.

—— 1979. "Some Exploratory Methods for Modeling Mobility Tables and Other Cross-Classified Data." In David R. Heise, ed., *Sociological Methodology, 1980*, pp. 141–158. San Francisco: Jossey-Bass.

—— 1981. "Hope for the Mobility Ratio." *Social Forces* 60 (September): 572–584.

—— 1984. "Vertical Class Mobility in England, France, and Sweden." Part I: *Acta Sociologica* 27 (2): 87–110. Part II: *Acta Sociologica* 27 (4): 387–390.

Hauser, Robert M., Shu-Ling Tsai, and William H. Sewell. 1983. "A Model of

Stratification with Response Error in Social and Psychological Variables." *Sociology of Education* 56 (January): 20–46.

Hazelrigg, Lawrence E. 1974. "Cross-National Comparisons of Father-to-Son Occupational Mobility." In Joseph Lopreato and Lionel S. Lewis, eds., *Social Stratification,* pp. 469–493. New York: Harper & Row.

Hazelrigg, Lawrence E., and Maurice A. Garnier. 1976. "Occupational Mobility in Industrial Societies: A Comparative Analysis of Differential Access to Occupational Ranks in Seventeen Countries." *American Sociological Review* 41 (June): 498–511.

Heath, Anthony. 1981. *Social Mobility.* London: Fontana.

Hechter, Michael, 1975. *Internal Colonialism: The Celtic Fringe in British National Development, 1536–1966.* Berkeley: University of California Press.

Hodge, Robert W. 1973. "Toward a Theory of Racial Discrimination in Employment." *Social Forces* 52 (September): 16–31.

—— 1981. "The Measurement of Occupational Status." *Social Science Research* 10 (November): 396–415.

Hogan, Dennis P., and David L. Featherman. 1977. "Racial Stratification and Socioeconomic Change in the American North and South." *American Journal of Sociology* 83 (July): 100–126.

Hope, Keith. 1972. "Quantifying Constraints on Social Mobility: The Latent Hierarchies of a Contingency Table." In Keith Hope, ed., *The Analysis of Social Mobility: Methods and Approaches,* pp. 121–190. Oxford: Clarendon Press.

—— 1982. "Vertical and Non-Vertical Class Mobility in Three Countries." *American Sociological Review* 47 (April): 99–113.

—— 1983. "Are High Schools Really Heteronomous?" *Sociology of Education* 56 (July): 111–125.

—— 1986. *As Others See Us: Educational and Occupational Mobility in Scotland.* Cambridge: Cambridge University Press.

Horan, Pat. 1974. "The Structure of Occupational Mobility." *Social Forces* 53 (September): 33–45.

Hout, Michael. 1983. *Mobility Tables.* Beverly Hills, Calif.: Sage.

—— 1984a. "Status, Autonomy, and Training in Occupational Mobility." *American Journal of Sociology* 89 (May): 1379–1409.

—— 1984b. "Occupational Mobility of Black Men: 1962–1973." *American Sociological Review* 49 (June): 308–322.

—— 1986. "Opportunity and the Minority Middle Class: A Comparison of Blacks in the United States and Catholics in Northern Ireland." *American Sociological Review* 51 (April): 214–223.

—— 1988. "Expanding Universalism, Less Structural Mobility: The American Occupational Structure in the 1980s." *American Journal of Sociology* 93 (May): 1358–1400.

Hout, Michael, and Maurice A. Garnier. 1979. "Educational Stratification and Curriculum Placement in France." *Sociology of Education* 52 (July):146–156.

Hout, Michael, and John A. Jackson. 1986. "Dimensions of Occupational Mobility in the Republic of Ireland." *European Sociological Review* 2 (September): 114–137.

Hout, Michael, Otis Dudley Duncan, and Michael E. Sobel. 1987. "Association and Heterogeneity: Structural Models of Similarities and Differences." In Clifford C. Clogg, ed., *Sociological Methodology, 1987,* pp. 145–184. Washington, D.C.: American Sociological Association.

Hughes, J. G., and Brendan M. Walsh. 1980. *Internal Migration Flows in Ireland and Their Determinants.* Dublin: Economic and Social Research Institute.

Hutchinson, Bertram. 1969. *Social Status and Intergenerational Mobility.* Dublin: Economic and Social Research Institute.

——— 1973. *Social Status in Dublin: Marriage, Mobility, and First Employment.* Dublin: Economic and Social Research Institute.

Irish Ministry of Education. 1966. *Investment in Education.* Dublin: Stationery Office.

Jackson, John A. 1963. *The Irish in Britain.* London: Routledge and Kegan Paul.

Jackson, John A., and Robert Miller. 1983. "Who Gets the Farm?" Paper presented at the annual meeting of the International Sociological Association research committee on stratification and mobility, Amsterdam, 12 October.

Jencks, Christopher S., with M. Smith, et al. 1972. *Inequality: A Reassessment of the Effect of Family and Schooling in America.* New York: Basic Books.

Kahl, Joseph A. 1964. *The American Class Structure.* New York: Holt, Rinehart, and Winston.

Kaplan, E. L., and P. Meier. 1958. "Nonparametric Estimation from Incomplete Observations." *Journal of the American Statistical Association* 53 (June): 457–481.

Kennedy, Kieran A. 1971. *Productivity and Industrial Growth: The Irish Experience.* Oxford: Clarendon Press.

Kennedy, Kieran A., and Brendan R. Dowling. 1975. *Economic Growth in Ireland: The Experience since 1947.* Dublin: Gill and Macmillan.

Kennedy, Robert E. 1973. *The Irish.* Berkeley: University of California Press.

Kerckhoff, Alan C., Richard T. Campbell, and J. M. Trott. 1982. "Dimensions of Educational and Occupational Attainment in Great Britain." *American Sociological Review* 47 (June): 347–364.

Kerckhoff, Alan C., Richard T. Campbell, and Ivie Winfield-Laird. 1985. "Social Mobility in Great Britain and the United States." *American Journal of Sociology* 91 (September): 281–308.

Klatzky, Sheila, and Robert W. Hodge. 1971. "A Canonical Correlation Analysis of Occupational Mobility." *Journal of the American Statistical Association* 66 (March): 16–22.

Knights, Peter R. 1971. *The Plain People of Boston, 1830–1860: A Study of City Growth.* New York: Oxford University Press.

Kohn, Melvin. 1969. *Class and Conformity.* Homewood, Ill.: Dorsey Press.

Korpi, Walter. 1983. *Democratic Class Struggle*. London: Routledge and Kegan Paul.

Lee, J. J. 1979. "Continuity and Change in Ireland, 1945–1970." In J. J. Lee, ed., *Ireland: 1945–1970*, pp. 166–177. Dublin: Gill and Macmillan.

Lees, Lynn Hollen. 1979. *Erin's Exiles: Irish Migrants in Victorian London*. Ithaca, N.Y.: Manchester University Press.

Lenski, Gerhardt. 1959. *The Religious Factor*. New York: Anchor.

Lieberson, Stanley. 1978. "Selective Black Migration from the South: A Historical View." In Frank D. Bean and W. Parker Frisbie, eds., *Demography of Racial and Ethnic Groups*, pp. 119–141. New York: Academic Press.

—— 1980. *A Piece of the Pie: Blacks and White Immigrants since 1880*. Berkeley: University of California Press.

Lipset, Seymour Martin, and Reinhard Bendix. 1959. *Social Mobility in Industrial Society*. Berkeley: University of California Press.

Lipset, Seymour Martin, and Hans Zetterberg. 1956. "A Theory of Social Mobility." *Transactions of the Third World Congress of Sociology* 5: 155–177.

Lockwood, David. 1958. *The Blackcoated Worker: A Study in Class Consciousness*. London: Allen and Unwin.

Logan, John A. 1983. "A Multivariate Model for the Mobility Table." *American Journal of Sociology* 89 (September): 324–349.

Lynch, Kathleen. 1985. "An Analysis of Some Presuppositions Underlying the Concepts of Meritocracy and Ability as Presented in Greaney and Kellaghan's Study." *Economic and Social Review* 16 (January): 83–102.

Lyons, F. S. L. 1973, *Ireland since the Famine*, rev. ed. London: Fontana.

Mare, Robert D. 1980. "Social Background and Educational Continuation Decisions." *Journal of the American Statistical Association* 75 (June): 295–305.

Marshall, T. H. 1938. *Class Conflict and Social Stratification*. Ledbury: LePlay House. Reprinted in Reinhard Bendix and Seymour Martin Lipset, eds., *Class, Status, and Power*, pp. 81–87. Glencoe, Ill.: Free Press, 1953.

Mayer, Karl Ulrich, and Glenn R. Carroll. 1987. "Jobs and Classes: Structural Constraints on Mobility." *European Sociological Review* 3 (May): 14–38.

McAleese, Dermot. 1981. "Political Independence, Economic Growth, and the Role of Economic Policy." In P. J. Drudy, ed., *Ireland: Land, Politics, and People*, pp. 271–295. Cambridge: Cambridge University Press.

McClendon, McKee J. 1980a. "Occupational Mobility and Economic Development: A Cross-National Analysis." *Sociological Focus* 13: 331–342.

—— 1980b. "Structural and Exchange Components of Occupational Mobility: A Cross-National Analysis." *Sociological Quarterly* 21 (4): 493–509.

McCullagh, Michael. 1986. "The Social Construction of Unemployment in Northern Ireland." In Patrick Clancy, Sheelagh Drudy, Kathleen Lynch, and Liam O'Dowd, eds., *Ireland: A Sociological Profile*, pp. 307–325. Dublin: Institute of Public Administration.

Meenan, James. 1970. *The Irish Economy since 1922*. Liverpool: Liverpool University Press.

Miller, Donald, and Guy E. Swanson. 1958. *The Changing American Parent*. New York: Wiley.

Miller, Robert. 1984. "Occupational Mobility in Northern Ireland: A Comparison of Protestants and Catholics." In R. J. Cormack and R. D. Osborne, eds., *Religion, Education, and Employment: Aspects of Equal Opportunity in Northern Ireland*, pp. 64–77. Salem, N.H.: Salem House.

—— 1986. "Stratification and Social Mobility." In Patrick Clancy, Sheelagh Drudy, Kathleen Lynch, and Liam O'Dowd, eds., *Ireland: A Sociological Profile*, pp. 221–243. Dublin: Institute of Public Administration.

Miller, S. M. 1961. "Comparative Social Mobility." *Current Sociology* 9 (1): 1–89.

Mills, C. Wright. 1961. *The Sociological Imagination*. New York: Oxford University Press.

Murray, Dominic. 1986. "Educational Segregation: Rite or Wrong?" In Patrick Clancy, Sheelagh Drudy, Kathleen Lynch, and Liam O'Dowd, eds., *Ireland: A Sociological Profile*, pp. 244–264. Dublin: Institute of Public Administration.

Nelder, J. A., and R. W. M. Wedderburn. 1972. "Generalized Linear Models." *Journal of the Royal Statistical Society*, ser. A, 135: 370–384.

New Ireland Forum. 1984. *Final Report*. Dublin: Stationery Office.

O'Clery, Conor. 1986. *Phrases Make History Here*. Dublin: O'Brien Press.

O'Dowd, Liam. 1986. "Beyond Industrial Society." In Patrick Clancy, Sheelagh Drudy, Kathleen Lynch, and Liam O'Dowd, eds., *Ireland: A Sociological Profile*, pp. 198–220. Dublin: Institute of Public Administration.

Office of Population Censuses and Surveys. 1970. *Classification of Occupations*. London: Her Majesty's Stationery Office.

O'Leary, C. 1979. "Northern Ireland, 1945–1972." In J. J. Lee, ed., *Ireland: 1945–1970*, pp. 152–165. Dublin: Gill and Macmillan.

O'Muircheartaigh, Colm A. and R. D. Wiggins. 1977. "Sample Design and Evaluation for an Occupational Mobility Study." *Economic and Social Review* 8 (January): 101–115.

Parkin, Frank. 1971. *Class Inequality and Political Order*. New York: Praeger.

Parsons, Talcott. 1940. "An Analytical Approach to the Theory of Social Stratification." *American Journal of Sociology* 45 (May): 841–862.

—— 1953. "A Revised Analytical Approach to the Theory of Social Stratification." In Reinhard Bendix and Seymour Martin Lipset, eds., *Class, Status, and Power*, pp. 92–128. Glencoe, Ill.: Free Press.

—— 1970. "Equality and Inequality in Modern Society, or Social Stratification Revisited." In Edward O. Laumann, ed., *Social Stratification: Research and Theory for the 1970s*, pp. 13–72. Indianapolis: Bobbs-Merrill.

Peillon, Michel. 1982. *Contemporary Irish Society*. Dublin: Gill and Macmillan.

Pöntinen, Seppo. 1982. "Models and Social Mobility Research: A Comparison of Some Log-Linear Models of a Social Mobility Matrix." *Quality and Quantity* 16 (September): 406–421.

————— 1984. *A Comparison of Social Mobility in Scandinavian Countries.* Helsinki: Sociological Institute.

Pullum, Thomas. 1970. "Statistical Models of Stratification." In Edward O. Laumann, ed., *Social Stratification: Research and Theory for the 1970s,* pp. 258–280. Indianapolis: Bobbs-Merrill.

————— 1975. *Measuring Occupational Inheritance.* New York: Elsevier.

Raftery, Adrian E. 1983. "Comment on 'Gaps and Glissandos'." *American Sociological Review* 48 (August): 581–582.

————— 1985a. "Social Mobility Measures for Cross-National Comparisons." *Quality and Quantity* 19 (March): 167–182.

————— 1985b. "A Model for High-Order Markov Chains." *Journal of the Royal Statistical Society,* ser. B, 47: 528–539.

————— 1985c. "A New Model for Discrete-Valued Time Series: Autocorrelations and Extensions." *Rassegna di Metodi Statistici ed Applicationi* 3–4: 149–162.

————— 1986a. "Choosing Models for Cross-Classifications." *American Sociological Review* 51 (February): 145–146.

————— 1986b. "A Note on Bayes Factors for Log-Linear Contingency Table Models with Vague Prior Information." *Journal of the Royal Statistical Society,* ser. B, 48: 249–250.

Raftery, Adrian E., and Michael Hout. 1985. "Does Irish Education Approach the Meritocratic Ideal?" *Economic and Social Review* 16 (3): 115–140.

Robinson, Robert V., and Maurice A. Garnier. 1985. "Class Reproduction among Men and Women in France: Reproduction Theory on Its Home Ground." *American Journal of Sociology* 91 (September): 250–281.

Rogoff, Natalie. 1953a. *Recent Trends in Occupational Mobility.* New York: Free Press.

————— 1953b. "Recent Trends in Urban Occupational Mobility." In Reinhard Bendix and Seymour Martin Lipset, eds., *Class, Status, and Power,* pp. 442–454. Glencoe, Ill.: Free Press.

Rottmann, David B., and P. J. O'Connell. 1982. *The Changing Social Structure of Unequal Achievement.* Dublin: Institute of Public Administration.

Rottman, David B., Damian F. Hannan, Niamh Hardiman, and Miriam Wiley. 1982. *The Distribution of Income in the Republic of Ireland.* Dublin: Economic and Social Research Institute.

Scheper-Hughes, Nancy. 1979. *Saints, Scholars, and Schizophrenics: Mental Illness in Rural Ireland.* Berkeley: University of California Press.

Schumpeter, Josef A. 1955. *Imperialism and Social Classes.* New York: Meridian Books. Originally published in German in 1926.

Sewell, William H., Jr. 1976. "Social Mobility in a Nineteenth Century European City: Some Findings and Implications." *Journal of Interdisciplinary History* 7 (May): 217–233.

————— 1985. *Structure and Mobility: The Men and Women of Marseille, 1820–1870.* New York: Cambridge University Press.

Share, Bernard. 1978. *The Emergency: Neutral Ireland, 1939–1945*. Dublin: Gill and Macmillan.

Sharlin, Allen N. 1979. "From the Study of Social Mobility to the Study of Society." *American Journal of Sociology* 85 (September): 338–360.

Simkus, Albert. 1984. "Structural Transformation and Social Mobility: Hungary, 1938–1973." *American Sociological Review* 49 (June): 291–307.

——— 1985. "Social Mobility in Eastern Europe: How Has State Socialism Made a Difference?" Paper presented at the annual meeting of the American Sociological Association, Washington, D.C., 29 August.

Simkus, Albert, and Rudolf Andorka. 1982. "Inequalities in Educational Attainment in Hungary, 1923–1973." *American Sociological Review* 47 (June): 740–751.

Singer, Burton, and Seymour Spilerman. 1974. "Social Mobility Models for Heterogeneous Populations." In Herbert L. Costner, ed., *Sociological Methodology, 1973–74*, pp. 356–401. San Francisco: Jossey-Bass.

——— 1976a. "The Representation of Social Processes by Markov Models." *American Journal of Sociology* 82 (July): 1–54.

——— 1976b. "Some Methodological Issues in the Analysis of Longitudinal Surveys." *Annals of Economic and Social Measurement* 5 (Fall): 447–474.

Smelser, Neil J., and Seymour Martin Lipset. 1966. "Social Structure, Mobility, and Development." In Neil J. Smelser and Seymour Martin Lipset, eds., *Social Structure and Mobility in Economic Development*, pp. 1–50. Chicago: Aldine.

Smith, Herbert. 1986. "Overeducation and Underemployment: An Agnostic Review." *Sociology of Education* 59 (April): 85–99.

Sobel, Michael E. 1983. "Structural Mobility, Circulation Mobility, and the Study of Occupational Mobility." *American Sociological Review* 48 (October): 721–727.

——— 1988. "Models of Partial and Complete Symmetry and Quasi-symmetry for Three-way Tables Having Identically Coded Rows and Columns." In Clifford C. Clogg, ed., *Sociological Methodology, 1988*, pp. 165–192. Washington, D.C.: American Sociological Association.

Sobel, Michael E., Michael Hout, and Otis Dudley Duncan. 1985. "Exchange, Structure, and Symmetry in Occupational Mobility." *American Journal of Sociology* 91 (September): 359–372.

——— 1986. "Saving the Bath Water." *Sociological Methods and Research* 14 (February): 281–289.

Sorensen, Aage B. 1975. "The Structure of Intragenerational Mobility." *American Sociological Review* 40 (August): 456–471.

Sorensen, Aage B., and Nancy B. Tuma. 1981. "Labor Market Structures and Job Mobility." *Research in Social Stratification and Mobility* 1: 67–94.

Spilerman, Seymour. 1972. "Extensions of the Mover-Stayer Model." *American Journal of Sociology* 78 (November): 599–626.

Sullivan, Teresa A. 1978. *Marginal Workers, Marginal Jobs.* Austin:University of Texas Press.

Thernstrom, Stephan. 1964. *Poverty and Progress: Social Mobility in a Nineteenth Century City.* Cambridge, Mass.: Harvard University Press.

———— 1973. *The Other Bostonians: Poverty and Progress in the American Metropolis, 1880–1970.* Cambridge, Mass.: Harvard University Press.

Thernstrom, Stephan, and Richard B. Sennett. 1969. *Studies in the New Urban History.* New Haven: Yale University Press.

Thurow, Lester C. 1975. *Generating Inequality.* New York: Basic Books.

Treiman, Donald T. 1970. "Industrialization and Social Stratification." In Edward O. Laumann, ed., *Social Stratification: Research and Theory for the 1970s,* pp. 207–234. Indianapolis: Bobbs-Merrill.

———— 1977. *Occupational Prestige in Comparative Perspective.* New York: Academic Press.

Tuma, Nancy Brandon. 1976. "Rewards, Resources, and the Rate of Mobility: A Non-Stationary Multivariate Stochastic Model." *American Sociological Review* 41 (April): 338–360.

Tuma, Nancy Brandon, and Michael T. Hannan. 1979. "Dynamic Analysis of Event Histories." *American Journal of Sociology* 84 (November): 820–854.

———— 1984. *Social Dynamics: Models and Methods.* New York: Academic Press.

Tuma, Nancy Brandon, Michael T. Hannan, and Lyle P. Groenveld. 1979. "Approaches to the Censoring Problem in the Analysis of Event Histories." In Karl Schuessler, ed., *Sociological Methodology, 1979,* pp. 209–240. San Francisco: Jossey-Bass.

Tyree, Andrea, Moshe Semyonov, and Robert W. Hodge. 1979. "Gaps and Glissandos: Inequality, Economic Development, and Social Mobility in 24 Countries." *American Sociological Review* 44 (June): 410–424.

Vannemann, Reeve. 1977. "The Occupational Composition of American Classes." *American Journal of Sociology* 82 (January): 783–807.

Walsh, Brendan M. 1979. "Economic Growth and Development, 1945–1970." In J. J. Lee, ed., *Ireland: 1945–1970,* pp. 27–37. Dublin: Gill and Macmillan.

Welch, Finis T. 1979. "Effects of Cohort Size on Earnings: The Baby-Boom Babies' Financial Bust." *Journal of Political Economy* 87 (Supplement): S65–97.

Whelan, Christopher T. 1980. *Employment Conditions and Job Satisfaction: The Distribution, Perception, and Evaluation of Job Rewards.* Dublin: Economic and Social Research Institute.

Whelan, Christopher T., and Richard Breen. 1985. "Vertical Mobility in Dublin." Dublin: Economic and Social Research Institute, manuscript.

Whelan, Christopher T., and Brendan J. Whelan. 1984. *Social Mobility in the Republic of Ireland: A Comparative Perspective.* Dublin: Economic and Social Research Institute.

———— 1985. *"Equality of Opportunity in Irish Schools:* A Reassessment." *Economic and Social Review* 16 (January): 103–114.

Whitaker, T. K. 1953. "The Finance Attitude." In Basil Chubb and Patrick Lynch, eds., *Economic Development and Planning: Readings in Irish Public Administration,* vol. 1, pp. 39–48. Dublin: An Foras Riarachain. Originally published in *Administration* 2 (1953).

———— 1956. "Capital Formation, Saving, and Economic Progress." In Basil Chubb and Patrick Lynch, eds., *Economic Development and Planning: Readings in Irish Public Administration,* vol. 1, pp. 48–76. Dublin: An Foras Riarachain. Originally published in *Administration* 4 (1956).

———— 1958. "Economic Development." In Basil Chubb and Patrick Lynch, eds., *Economic Development and Planning: Readings in Irish Public Administration,* vol. 1, pp. 100–113. Dublin: An Foras Riarachain. Originally published in a Department of Finance Bulletin (1958).

White, Harrison C. 1970. *Chains of Opportunity.* Cambridge, Mass.: Harvard University Press.

Whyte, J. H. 1971. *Church and State in Modern Ireland, 1923–1970.* Dublin: Gill and Macmillan.

Wickham, James. 1986. "Industrialisation, Work, and Unemployment." In Patrick Clancy, Sheelagh Drudy, Kathleen Lynch, and Liam O'Dowd, eds., *Ireland: A Sociological Profile,* pp. 70–96. Dublin: Institute of Public Administration.

Wright, Erik Olin. 1986. *Classes.* London: New Left Books.

Yamaguchi, Kazuo. 1982. "The Structure of Intergenerational Occupational Mobility: Generality and Specificity in Resources, Channels, and Barriers." *American Journal of Sociology* 88 (January): 718–745.

Yasuda, S. 1964. "A Methodological Inquiry into Social Mobility." *American Sociological Review* 29 (February): 16–23.

Zunz, Olivier. 1983. *The Face of Inequality: Detroit in the Late Nineteenth and Early Twentieth Centuries.* Chicago: University of Chicago Press.

Index